GREAT GOLF STORIES

GREAT GOLF STORIES

EDITED BY
ROBERT TRENT JONES

Hurtig Publishers
Edmonton

A Giniger Book

Hurtig Publishers Ltd.
10560-105 Street
Edmonton, Alberta

Published in association with The K. S. Giniger
Company, Inc., 235 Park Avenue South, New
York, New York, 10003, U.S.A.

Canadian Cataloguing in Publication Data

Main entry under title:
Great golf stories

   ISBN 0-88830-221-5

   1. Golf—Addresses, essays, lectures.
I. Jones, Robert Trent, 1906–
GV965.G73   796.352   C82-091199-2

Printed and bound in Canada by
T. H. Best Printing Company Limited, Don Mills, Ontario

For Ione
my own
forever
> *Bob*

Contents

Introduction

BOB JONES CALLED golf "The Greatest Game" and there was no one who knew golf better or appreciated it more than he. There are few, if any, who ever achieved the heights of the "Immortal Bobby," but millions regard the game in the same reverent manner.

I am one of them, and I have been more fortunate than most.

Golf has been my game and, I might add, my life ever since I scuffed my way up a dusty entrance road to the Country Club of Rochester and, cap in hand, awaited my first caddie assignment. Little did I know at the time that I was being introduced to a game and a way of life which would take me to every state in the United States, the far corners of the globe and hundreds of island way-stations in between. It also would serve as an entrée to presidents, premiers, potentates and princes of business, industry and commerce.

Golf has also afforded me an opportunity permitted few men: to create on one of the broadest canvasses known to man and, in doing so, to complement and, sometimes, to improve on the work of the greatest Creator of all. Golf courses are built by men, but God provides the venues.

Golf course architecture is the most fascinating endeavour ever conceived for man's pleasure, not only for those of us who are fortunate enough to practise it, but also for those who are the beneficiaries of the end product.

During a career which now is extending into its second half-century, I have been fortunate in knowing, and in one instance being a partner with, some of the giants of this unique form of creativity.

Donald Ross of Pinehurst was the first. It was a chance meeting with him that aroused my initial interest in golf course architecture. I was only a teenager at the time Ross was building the Oak Hill Country Club in Rochester, New York, a course which, coincidentally, I subsequently would remodel in preparation for the 1956 United States Open.

Ross was kind and indulgent enough to take the time to explain, briefly, the purpose of the project, the need for the independence of design for each hole despite its being only one of eighteen constituting a golf course, and the paramount consideration of shot values incumbent in the development of a fair and true test of golf. "The Wizard of Dornoch," as he was known because of his birthplace in northern Scotland, would be responsible for an estimated six hundred golf courses in his prolific career, but none would be appreciated by me more than Oak Hill.

That is because, although at the time I was a golfer of some merit with a couple of course records to my credit and, later, the distinction of being low amateur in the 1927 Canadian Open, I knew little or nothing about what a golf course was other than an area for playing the game.

Ross opened my eyes. In doing so, he unintentionally directed me toward a lifetime endeavour which has exceeded my greatest expectations. My brief encounter with Ross, plus an unexpected ulcer flare-up which curtailed any competitive golf aspirations, focused my sights on golf architecture as a way to be part of the game without further jeopardizing my health. It was to this end that I enrolled in Cornell University where, with the precedent-shattering approval of the Dean of Admissions, I was permitted to enroll in several of its units — agriculture, landscape architecture, engineering, chemistry and liberal arts — to specifically prepare for "golf course work." The designation of golf course architecture as a profession was some years away from inclusion in the golf lexicon.

It was also in my home town of Rochester where I met Stanley W. Thompson, shortly after completing my course of studies at Cornell. Thompson was a Canadian from Toronto, and he and I were competing for a contract to design a course for the Midvale Golf Club. I received the job despite the fact I was an absolute neophyte, while Thompson had been in the business nearly a quarter of a century. My local residence was the reason, I guess, but the award was given with the provision that Thompson oversee my work as an adviser.

Unfortunately, the backers of Midvale went broke before the job was completed, but from this disaster emerged the firm of Thompson and Jones, Golf Course Designers. Stanley and I had realized a mutual affection and admiration for our respective works, although my portfolio at the time was little more than a page while his was a volume.

Thompson was a pioneer developer of courses of strategic design which might be described as "thinking man's golf courses." They leave up to the individual player the decision of how best to play a hole as he stands on a tee and is confronted, generally, with a direct route to the hole and alternatives by which — depending on the hazards which lie in between and the capabilities of his shotmaking — he may achieve his objective. The strategic differs from the penal style of architecture in that the latter requires a golfer to follow absolutely the design dictates of the architect. Such courses are the ultimate in target golf in that every shot must be pin-pointed to avoid an unrelenting progression of hazards such as ankle-deep grass, weeds, trees, a preponderance of bunkers or mounds, and often unseen water.

It goes without saying that I subscribed to Thompson's strategic principles as opposed to those of the penal approach, in that the ultimate result is a course which affords pleasure instead of punishment and fun instead of frustration. Regrettably, there has been a trend in recent years among some golf architects to return to the penal style of architecture as a way of thwarting the inroads being made on par by professional tournament players. I am not one of those architects.

Thompson's style of architecture is best typified by courses he did in the Canadian Rockies at the Banff Springs Hotel and Jasper National Park and at the Capilano Golf and Country Club in Vancouver. Although the three were brought into being more than a half-century ago, all remain evergreen. Each today stands as a monu-

ment to the genius of Stanley Thompson, Canada's greatest golf architect.

Albert W. Tillinghast, whom I met during the playing of the 1934 U. S. Open at Merion, was another architect with whom I shared a similar philosophical approach to our profession. "Tilly," termed "golf's forgotten genius" by Frank Hannigan of the United States Golf Association, was remarkable for the variety and beauty of his courses which grace landscapes across the United States from Winged Foot in Mamaroneck, New York, to California's San Francisco Golf Club.

He was also responsible for the Baltusrol Golf Club in Springfield, New Jersey, which, in 1980, played host to a record sixth United States Open. It might be said that the present Lower Course there was a joint effort by Tillinghast and me. He was responsible for the original course, which came into being in 1922, and thirty years later I was commissioned to remodel and modernize it to bring its challenges in line with the great advances in scoring and shotmaking techniques which had been made in the interim by the greatest players in the game.

Typical of the Baltusrol changes were those made to the "Famous Fourth" hole, which has been selected on every list of the "Best Eighteen" ever published. Tillinghast was responsible for the original gem, a beautiful par-three over water with a green partially encircled by trees and flanked by sand. The gem lost no sparkle when it was updated with an additional fifty yards carry to reach a green which had been enlarged by a third and terraced with a backdrop of reverse-slope bunkers between the putting surface and the stately trees beyond.

It was the product of this protracted collaboration between Tillinghast and Jones that twice helped inspire Jack Nicklaus to his most memorable Open victories. He won in 1967 with a record score of 275 and then, thirteen years later, again shattered the scoring mark for the championship with a 270 total.

Ross, Thompson and Tillinghast notwithstanding, the most esteemed personage with whom I ever shared ideas was my namesake, Robert Tyre Jones, the achiever of the unique "Grand Slam" and the greatest amateur golfer who ever lived. As the founder and perpetual president of the Augusta National Golf Club, he was the inspiration and major influence in the design of the renowned course which annually hosts the Masters.

The course was the work of Dr. Alister Mackenzie, a Scottish physician turned golf architect, whose other most notable effort in the United States is the Cypress Point Club on California's Monterey Peninsula. With considerable input by Bob Jones, especially in the design and contour of the greens, the Augusta course emerged as the ultimate in strategic design. With its extremely broad tree-lined fairways, a minimal number of bunkers — thirty originally, now about forty-four — and almost no rough on the 235 acres it occupies, Augusta National presents no intimidating problems off the tee. It does, however, require precise placement of a drive to set up the second — or third — shot to its greens which, because of their deployment, are limited in their accessibility to approach shots. Also, because of extreme slope, bold contour and rapid pace, the greens require a meticulous "touch" and an infallible ability to "read" the line if a golfer is to negotiate them in two putts or less. This is particularly true during the playing of the Masters, when the course is stretched to its full 7,000 yards and the greens are brought to a speed and firmness with which only the most skilled can cope.

Despite its almost immediate acceptance as one of the finest golf courses ever designed, Augusta National, since coming into being in the early thirties, has undergone numerous changes by half a dozen or so golf architects. I was one of the first.

Shortly after World War II, Bob Jones approached me regarding changes he deemed necessary to the short 16th hole. The result was an entirely new hole which involved relocating the green and the teeing area, and the imposition of a major hazard — a pond, the entire length of which had to be carried to reach the green on the 190-yard hole. The water hazard was Bob Jones's suggestion. That scenic feature, along with the configuration of its terraced green which wraps around the far side of the pond, plus the white splashes of sand which embrace it in the form of

three bunkers, has made it one of the most beautiful par-3 holes in all of golf. It also is one of the best known, thanks to the millions who have viewed it during the annual telecasts of the Masters.

Bob Jones was also responsible for my appreciably changing the drive-and-pitch 11th hole into one of the strongest and most unusual par-4 holes ever to confront a player. It was remodelled into a 455-yard test requiring a second shot to a sunken green partially encircled by water on two sides. It is the first of three consecutive water holes in an area where the course reverses directions. Tony Lema most appropriately dubbed the turnaround "Amen Corner."

Incidentally, I should explain that it was because of my work with Bob Jones that I elected to adopt the use of my middle name, Trent. This was done to avoid the obvious confusion which ensued as a result of two men intimately involved in golf having the same name.

Bob Jones and Trent Jones also were involved in the development of the Peachtree Golf Club in Atlanta, which has as its modest clubhouse a colonial brick building that served as headquarters for General William T. Sherman, when he commanded the Union Army which burned the city to the ground during its march to the sea.

Peachtree was a milestone in my career in that it afforded me, with considerable assistance from Bob Jones, a free hand to put into practice many theories regarding golf course architecture with which I since have been identified.

These included extended teeing areas, fifty to seventy-five yards in length, the strategic positioning of fairway bunkers, and greens of such size and contour as to assure easy entrance for member play but of limited access when set up for championship competition. The greens at Peachtree average more than ten thousand square feet in area and incorporate four to six distinct sectors for placement of the cups to reflect the calibre of play which might be expected on a given day. Bob Jones and I worked hand-in-hand in the development of the course. After my primary design was approved, his aid was invaluable in plotting the problems to be built into the greens. He was a firm believer that there should be hazards to putting, a theory which is manifest on the greens of the Augusta National Golf Club. The locations of the bunkers at Peachtree, in fact, were dictated by him in that he drove hundreds of balls and hit a like number of approach shots to best determine the positioning of these hazards.

It is a little known fact that his shotmaking efforts at Peachtree were his last. Shortly thereafter, the effects of a creeping paralysis which afflicted him—syringomyelia—made subsequent activity impossible.

The result of our collaboration was a golf course of unlimited flexibility, a course which epitomizes the strategic concept. Peachtree can be played from 6,354 to 7,219 yards depending on the placement of the tee markers. Its fairway bunkers are limited in number, but each is significant. And, because of the size and contour of the greens, there is a need for thought in approaching them, regardless of distance. Otherwise, a ball can come to rest on the wrong side of the hole with the resultant putting problems built into the design of the greens.

Bob Jones was the finest man I have ever known, a true gentleman of charm and grace. He was a champion in every facet of his being. I cherish the time spent with him and the once-in-a-lifetime opportunity of working with him.

The theories put into practical application at Peachtree, which previously had been manifest at Augusta National, have had a major influence on golf course architecture ever since. To have been partially responsible for this continuing trend has been most gratifying.

I lay no claim to the strides which have been made in the playing of the game in the last fifty years, during which I have been a more than interested observer. In that time, par has been transformed from a standard to be achieved into a foundation to be ruthlessly undermined. Equipment improvements and innovations, better playing conditions, and the natural evolution of more effective means of striking a golf ball all have contributed to playing performances which today consistently border on the fantastic.

I have seen steel—and, to a lesser degree, graphite and titanium—replace the wooden shaft, the golf ball become a sphere of quality-controlled consistency and velocity, and the introduction of the wedge, which makes a mockery of trouble shots, especially from sand. Grasses, which guarantee good fairways and carpet-smooth greens have been developed for every climate and growing condition. Special mowers have been devised, sophisticated irrigation systems have emerged, and all sorts of chemical applications have been formulated to assure the proper maintenance, feeding and protection of those grasses.

The players have not been content just to accept the benefits of better equipment and better conditions. Since the first shepherd hit the first stone at a distant mole hole, better ways have been sought for performing such an act. It has been an unending quest, one which will continue as long as the game is played. No better proof is needed than to leaf through the statistics of the professional golf tour, a cauldron of competition where annually one will find a half-dozen or so new scoring marks. Any technique improvement can mean money in the bank for a pro and unbridled satisfaction for an amateur. No wonder the search persists!

By luck and longevity, it has been my good fortune to have been almost everywhere the civilized game of golf is played, and some places where it wasn't until I arrived. My profession has provided entrée to the palaces of the Aga Khan, ex-King Leopold of Belgium, King Hassan II of Morocco, and the chambers of the Mayor of Moscow, and introductions to the men who occupy them. I also have played golf with U.S. Presidents Dwight D. Eisenhower and Gerald R. Ford and numerous American senators and congressmen. I have been on a first-name speaking basis with hundreds of golfers, professional and amateur, and the men and women who direct the game as officials in the United States and half a dozen other countries. Such associations have been part of the business in which I am engaged.

My greatest pleasure has been derived from golf tournaments. I would estimate that I have been witness to at least one hundred majors. What a pleasure it is to welcome spring at the Masters; to view every June the rough and the rigours imposed on a course which hosts the United States Open; to return each July to a links for the Open in Great Britain; and to be at the August wind-up of the Big Four when the PGA is contested. Add the Inveraray Classic, The World Series of Golf and The World Cup at some distant venue, and you have a tournament schedule which defies comparison. It takes some doing, but for anyone who travels nearly a quarter-million miles a year, as I do, it is not that difficult.

Attendance at tournaments is mandatory for me. Such spectacles serve to keep me abreast of the current crop of players, to meet and greet old friends, to exchange ideas with other golf architects and to learn of golf course projects under consideration and, in many instances, to contact the men responsible for such undertakings. But most important, the tournaments are where the golf writers are.

Since 1457, when an ill-advised King James III of England had parliament enact a law banning the game, there have been writers who have chronicled every aspect of golf. The sport is unusually rich in the accounts of its beginnings, its development and its emergence as one of the most universal pastimes enjoyed by man. Its great courses, champions and competitions have not lacked for identification or documentation because there always has been someone with quill and parchment, or pad and pencil, or microphone and tape recorder on hand to report the accomplishments of the moment or to transcribe for posterity the ever-increasing history of golf.

What once was only a handful of such scriveners now has grown into an army of hundreds who annually compose thousands of articles for millions of readers. And this reportage no longer is confined to just the printed media. Radio and then television have become integral means of "covering" golf, particularly tournaments.

During my long involvement with golf, it has been my good fortune to have met almost every golf writer of consequence since Bob Jones reigned supreme in 1930. I have walked miles of fairways with many of them, been a welcomed visitor in their press rooms, press tents and, more recently, media headquarters. I also have been a source of technical information, particularly in regard to golf course architecture, and

the subject of innumerable personal interviews. The writers are my friends and, through their generally kind treatment, have contributed much to my public identity and to my success.

To me, good golf writing is one of the real treasures of the game. It is something I have read with abiding interest since I was a teenager. And, because it is the source of some of my most enjoyable quiet moments in an otherwise hectic life, I have made a point of compiling an extensive library of books, periodicals, pamphlets and papers relating to the game. Many are timeworn and dog-eared from constant reference and the pleasure afforded me.

Consequently, when I was approached concerning the possibility of collecting an anthology, I welcomed the opportunity to share a select distillation of my treasure trove. The assembling of articles for this book has been a labour of love in that it has, in many instances, recalled memorable moments and associations with the writers of the pieces that are included.

Many no longer are with us: Bernard Darwin, Henry Longhurst, Red Smith, Grantland Rice, Ring Lardner, John Kieran and Fred Corcoran. Others more renowned for writing of national issues, like Alistair Cooke, Art Buchwald and James Reston also are a part of this collection. Pat Ward-Thomas has retired, but still contributes to periodicals and books.

Among the outstanding articles which grace this collection are those written by Charles Price, Bob Sommers, Ben Wright, George Plimpton, Dan Jenkins, Barry McDermott, Dwayne Netland, Al Barkow, Peter Dobereiner, Cal Brown and Furman Bisher. Also represented are those writers—William Barry Furlong, Al Stumpf and Bud Harvey—who have given voice to some of our greatest golfers.

There also are numerous selections from Herbert Warren Wind, with whom I collaborated in writing on golf course architecture for *The Complete Golfer*. Will Grimsley, who provided a similar exposure of my ideas in *Golf: Its History, People and Events*, also is included, along with many, many others.

It is my sincere hope you will find in this book as much interest, amusement and insight into golf as I did in compiling this collection.

GREAT GOLF STORIES

The Lure of Golf
Herbert Warren Wind

To anyone who knows him or who is familiar with his work, it's obvious that Herbert Warren Wind has been in love with golf since he first dug a divot as a teenager at the Thorny Lea Golf Club in Brockton, Massachusetts. Fortunately, it has been a public love affair which everyone has been able to appreciate.

Few people write about golf as thoroughly, intelligently and beautifully as this master of American letters. And his output has been tremendous. Herb has dealt with every aspect of the game in his numerous books including a monumental history of the game, The Story of American Golf, in countless articles in almost every magazine devoted to the sport, and in his incomparable "Profiles" in The New Yorker. He also has been the collaborator in autobiographies of two of our greatest champions, Gene Sarazen and Jack Nicklaus, and the author of the text for The Modern Fundamentals of Golf by Ben Hogan.

His knowledge of golf is encyclopedic. No better example is needed than to point out that he was the first non-member to receive the coveted Donald Ross Award from the American Society of Golf Course Architects in recognition of his having "helped to create an awareness of golf course architecture in the overall enjoyment of the game."

Herb and I have been staunch friends since he selected me as the subject of his first New Yorker "Profile" in June, 1951. It was an article which did much to further my career. He also was kind enough to credit me as the source for his chapter on golf course architecture and for having designed eight of the world's best golf courses which were included in his The Complete Golfer, published in 1954.

There are a million explanations for the lure of golf. No one is better able to enumerate them with the respect and appreciation they richly deserve than Herbert Warren Wind.

ONE OF SPORT'S oldest stories concerns the golfer who threw his clubs into the sea after a painfully bad round and almost drowned trying to rescue them. That particular golfer happened to be a Scotsman, which adds a certain amount of relish to the story, but it is also irrelevant. Of all the games man has devised, supposedly for his enjoyment, golf is in a class by itself in the anguish it inflicts. For each good reason a golfer can cite (after a fine round) why it is the most satisfying of games, he knows there are at least two equally good reasons for giving it up for good. Few ever do it. Golf has been played for about eight centuries now. In its modern form — that is, since the feather-stuffed ball was replaced by the gutta-percha — it is just about 120 years old. Over that period, golfers have continuously counseled their nongolfing friends that the game is a pernicious, habit-forming drug and that a man is better off not to touch the stuff. The result has been that golf's popularity has kept on expanding and the game is now played by 20,000,000 in every corner of the globe. You might as well tell a fellow not to have anything to do with pretty girls.

As if life in mid-century United States were not sufficiently conducive to strain and frustration, 10,000,000 of the world's 20,000,000 golfers are Americans. This represents an astounding growth considering that in 1888 there were less than a dozen golfers in the country — most of them the charter members of the St. Andrews Golf Club of Yonkers, N.Y., the first permanent golf club organized in the United States. As late as 1913 there were only 350,000 American golfers; at the turn of the twenties scarcely 1,000,000. Then the rush began and it has been continuing ever since. Today, to take care of the horde, there are approximately 10,000 golf courses. (About a thousand of this number are par-3 layouts.) These courses are spread over the entire country. For the most part, however, they are congregated where the population is thickest, and one of the most fantastic and yet characteristic aerial views of America is the multiplicity of courses, each with its clearly defined fairways and its kidney-shaped traps around the greens, that the traveler sees as his plane approaches any sizable city.

It is customarily recognized, I think — even among men who are devoted to sailing, tennis, huntin'-shootin'-fishin', or other participant sports — that the most dedicated follower of these diversions never becomes quite as intensely and hopelessly embroiled as does the man whom golf takes up. When you ask most golfers why this is so, they are of very little help. They fall back on the fifty-year-old cliché about being "bitten by the golf bug" and then each rattles on about how bad his particular case is, like kids proudly comparing the size of mosquito bites.

There are a few contemplative golfers who have attempted to analyze why the golf virus hits a man so hard. The game's singular fascination, in their concensus, rests on the fact that while you play against par, against your opponent, against the topography, and against the elements, in golf, as in no other sport, *your principal opponent is yourself*. No one touches the golfer's ball but the golfer himself. If you slice your approach with your 5-iron into a luxurious patch of brier, you cannot slink out of the responsibility for a rotten shot by turning to your adversary, as you can in tennis, and exclaiming, "Beautiful forehand, Reg! Nor can you alibi out in the other direction with the muffled insinuation that something your partner did accounts for your seemingly poor showing. Nobody else sliced that ball into the rough. Furthermore, since you get no second serve, no third strike, no fourth down, you're stuck with it. On the other hand, when you recover neatly from the brier patch and hole your slippery 20-foot putt for a par, nobody else had a hand in it either. All the glory of the accomplishment rests squarely on the shoulders of the guy who best appreciates your colossal skill.

While man's battle against himself is undoubtedly at the heart of golf's abiding appeal, there are a number of subsidiary reasons for the game's acceptance by its wide and variegated following. The setting in which it is played is, for most golfers, one of the most wonderful things about it. Were it not for the good greensward of the golf course, many hard-pressed American males, their lives increasingly tethered by the rites of city living, might never get any farther back to nature than growing chives in the window box of their apartment. Golfers never really lose their awareness of the natural beauties of a golf course — the freshness of the air in the morning when the dew is heavy on the striped greens, the pungent quietness in the evenings when the crickets start up and the setting sun makes the fairways ahead seem lusher than velvet. Veteran golfers breathe in these sensuous charms, but they don't talk much about them. They view them as part of the obvious bounty of golf. They are annoyed rather than diverted when some golfer-come-lately begins to rhapsodize on the scene like some self-elected Tennyson. "This is golf, man!" the veteran golfer is apt to snarl on these trying occasions. "What did you expect to find out here? A bowling alley?"

Very few golfers ever get to that stage of nature-loving where they can identify any flora other than grass, dandelions, and occasionally poison ivy. This is understandable. Trying to hit their shots correctly is too absorbing an occupation to admit any avocations. You will find, with few exceptions, that any seasoned golfer who suddenly exhibits an intimate knowledge of agronomy is deep in the throes of some concealed discomfiture. At the course where I grew up, our leading expert on the various grass strains was not the greenkeeper but an aging boy wonder whose game had long gone sour and who could no longer break 85 except when he played by himself. He persisted, however, in regarding himself as a 74 golfer, and this made a knowledge of grasses a must. "I don't see how you fellows can putt on this Merion blue grass," he would groan in exasperation, his hands on his hips, his eyes fixed captiously on the green, after he had jabbed a 3-foot putt a foot off line. "Creeping bent, that's the only grass a man with a delicate touch can putt on," he would continue. "The whole course has gone to pot. You know that spoon shot of mine that looked smothered? I hit it perfectly, really, but you can't get a ball up in the air from these fescue and redtop fairways. I ask you: How are you expected to play golf on a lousy pasture?"

Every enthusiast of the game, though, is a golf course architect as well as a golfer. He knows exactly where each hole falls short of championship quality: the green on the first is located in the wrong spot; the trap to the right of the second green improperly penalizes a well-played shot; the third hole should not be a dogleg; the fourth (a straightaway par 5) should be a dogleg par 4; and so on, with infinitely more detail and passion. If he were chairman of the Green Committee with a free hand and the necessary funds, he'd know what had to be added and what had to come out to change his course into a testing but fair examination in golf — "which, after all, Harry, is the idea of this game, in case you've forgotten."

What this golfer-architect would end up by doing, should he ever come to power as head of the Green Committee, would be to remodel the course so that it compensated as perfectly as possible for his own peculiar and habitual shortcomings as a player. This is no wild assumption. Chairmen of the Green Committee — the men elected or appointed to watch over the golf course — have historically watched over themselves. For example, when the chairman happens to be a short hitter, all those traps out by the 200-yard marker are suddenly condemned as unfit for human habitation, filled in, and turfed over. Show me, as the old saying goes, the Green Committee chairman who hasn't chopped at least five strokes off his score, and I'll show you a very angry man.

This purposeful myopia among amateur course designers goes back to an old pro at the business, Charles Blair Macdonald, who flourished just before the turn of the century as our first official National Amateur champion and as the designer of the nation's first eighteen-hole course, at the Chicago Golf Club in Wheaton, Illinois. Macdonald laid out the course so that the holes marched clockwise around the perimeter of the club's plot. The golfer who hooked on any hole ended up in heavy rough, and if he hooked quite badly, his ball shot off the course and out of bounds and he was penalized loss of stroke and distance. Old Charley, of course, never hooked. He had a fine grooved slicy swing, and when he sliced, there was always ample room out there on the right to take good care of his ball. The old boy was unbeatable on his home course for years!

Golf is unique among the "active sports" in

that a man can be lacking in youth, brawn, speed of foot, suppleness of muscle, clearness of eye, and the other athletic virtues and still be a pretty fair golfer. This is certainly one of golf's attractions, this fact that it is a game which a man, or a woman, can carry through life. In Gene Sarazen's opinion, a golfer with good health and a sound swing should be able to play with his competence little diminished until he is sixty-five.

There is no debating, though, that the younger a person is when he takes up golf, the easier it is for him to develop a correct and rhythmic swing. The golf swing is not a facile natural movement (like batting a baseball) so much as it is a disciplined exercise in coordination — what Ben Hogan calls "muscle memory." Nonetheless, a man can take up the game with some expectation of attaining a reasonable proficiency at an age when it is no longer safe to indulge in contact or team sports. The same sanguine prospect applies for a man who was never conspicuously good at games and has no athletic prime to be past. The classic example is Walter Travis who decided to become a golfer when he was thirty-five, and four years later — in 1900 — captured the first of his three National Amateur Championships.

A Travis comes along once a century, and most men who start golf after thirty, or who begin to concentrate on the game around that age, are not fools enough to think they can duplicate Travis' miracle. It is the rare golfer, nevertheless, be he novice or old-timer, who can resign himself to the unflattering reality that he is no better than his usual score. In golf, the score is the prime consideration, whatever a man may profess to the contrary. Golfers periodically sound off about how they really don't care about their scores; all they want to do is hit the ball well, they'll settle for that. In translation this means that the speaker has been chipping and putting poorly, or is in the throes of some such score-defeating malaise, and hasn't much confidence of getting his touch back for a while.

That Ol' Debbil Score, for some abstruse reason, makes double-talk experts out of men who ordinarily have their feet on the ground, and

it hatches not only more liars per capita than any other sport (not excluding fishing) but also the most implausible liars in the world. The fish that got away is one thing, but there is no rational accounting for the otherwise solid citizen who, frankly in front of your gaze, plays nine shots to get his ball into the hole and, when asked what his score was, says, "Six, dammit." The game, in some mysterious way, must have a direct pipeline to man's pride.

It can be truthfully stated, I think, that outscoring his opponent does wonders for a golfer's morale, but what really sets him up on a cloud is outscoring himself. To illustrate — once or twice a year a golfer who regularly shoots between 95 and 100 will come onto one of those days when he can do no wrong and will score an 88, no putts conceded other than the usual "gimmes" under a foot and a half. As far as that golfer is concerned, he is an 88 shooter. Those rounds between 95 and 100 to which he immediately returns are all "off-rounds," he is not shooting his game, his game is 88. A player can have his hot streaks in football or basketball or any other sport, but after the inevitable letdown sets in, most men are not too stubborn about admitting that they were playing over their heads. Golfers are a race apart. They are all convinced that they habitually play "under their heads."

There is something about the nature of the game, too, that eternally deludes the golfer into believing that he is on the verge of "coming into his own" and that if he corrects one tiny movement — the way he bends his left knee or the position of his right thumb — then his swing will overnight become a vision of beauty and even-par rounds will be no trouble at all. He begins to dream about how he will phrase his acceptance speech after winning the National Open. This is what makes golf such a humbling game. It looks to be the easiest of sports but it is in fact the hardest to play consistently well. Quite frequently, the very moment a golfer thinks he has mastered *the* critical technique is the precise moment when he discovers he cannot hit *any* shot. He wobbles off the course buried beneath such a mountain of powerlessness that he seriously doubts if he will be able to drive his automobile home and negotiate the difficult coordinative feat of climbing the front stairs.

In their pursuit of lower scores and higher self-esteem, American golfers invest prodigally in foolproof accessories, the latest models in clubs, "stroke-saving" home-practice equipment — more aids to success than for all other sports rolled together. There is nothing wrong in this, as any good pro with a well-stocked shop will tell them. In the view of many responsible critics, however, American golfers, in their obsession with lower scores at any price, have gone too far and done themselves and the game a considerable disservice over the last twenty years. They have successfully pressured Green Committees to soften up our courses to that lamentable degree where a golfer is often no worse off after a mis-hit shot than after a superb one. Greens are overwatered so that a half-topped niblick will stick. Overhanging lips have been removed from traps so that a man can scramble out with a putter. Roughs, above all, have been domesticated to where they are often indistinguishable from the fairways.

This mollycoddling of the heart of the game has produced lower scores, all right, and also a new breed of golfers who have forgotten that much of the game's satisfaction results from dealing resourcefully with the hazards. And with the weather, too, it might be added. On a recent trip to Britain, a young friend of mine, who had grown up with the idea that only a cloudless, windless day was fit for golf, walked onto the first tee at Sandwich on such a day and was staggered when his English host declared that it was disappointingly poor weather for golf. "The course will be dull today," the Englishman added apologetically. "There's hardly any wind for us to contend with."

The outstanding difference in the attitudes of Britain and America, the world's two great golfing communities, is, very probably, the Britisher's zest for subduing the authentic hazards and battling the elements. He is a more accomplished bad-weather golfer than his American counterpart, not simply because his native island provides him with such a fine supply of bad weather, but also because the top-heavy percentage of British courses, including those not on the seaside, have the general characteristics of links. The typical fairways in Britain are not tree-lined, as are ours, and the wind rampages unopposed across the exposed holes and becomes the major hazard. In the opinion of Henry Longhurst, the celebrated "golf correspondent" of the *London Sunday Times*, the American pro's minutely detailed, synchromeshed type of swing could have evolved only in a country where golf is a warm-weather game and not the all-weather sport it is in Britain, where there is no "south" to head for in winter. Bundled up in two sweaters, a strong wind making perfect balance impossible, even the most talented British pro, in the cold months, must forgo the niceties of what Mr. Longhurst calls "the shirt-sleeve swing."

(Incidentally, it might be mentioned that Mr. Longhurst — along with such other British golf writers as the incomparable Bernard Darwin and Sam McKinlay, plus our own late writers, Grantland Rice and O. B. Keeler — has given golf a vitality in print that is probably superior to that enjoyed by any other popular game.)

British golfers play their rounds at a much faster pace than we do, a distinction that is also true of other European golfers, South American golfers, African golfers, Asiatic golfers, and aged Australian golfers with blisters. It is undeniable: the American, Speed's own child, is a tortoise on the golf course. Where it was once possible to play eighteen holes on a Saturday afternoon or Sunday morning in three and a half hours, now you are doing handsomely if you get around in under five. Our courses are clogged by new players who are polite as all get-out but are never ready to play when it is their shot and by veterans who grew up in the era when caddies were plentiful and have never learned how to watch and mark a shot themselves, which they must when a caddie cart is carrying their bag. Above all, traffic on our courses bogs down because our golfers (of all degrees of skill) have taken to overstudying their shots in imitation of our professional stars who, before playing each stroke, do everything but telephone the American Geographic Society for a report on the green ahead.

Golf is certainly not the only participation sport which offers release and relaxation, but golfers are convinced that golf does it best. In what other game, they ask, are the pleasures of sociability interwoven so naturally with the pleasures of an athletic contest? The rhythm of golf *is* unique. After a man gets into it—and always assuming that he is playing well enough so that golf acts as a counterirritant to the pressures of the outside world and not as a positive irritation in itself—it becomes second nature for him to slide effortlessly from a conversation with the members of his foursome into the concentration necessary to play his stroke and then to resume the conversation as if there had been no interruption at all. "Hit your shot—I'll finish the story afterwards" is a remark that occurs with such usualness, as a friendly foursome makes its way around the course, that a golfer is hardly conscious of hearing it or saying it. Contrast this camaraderie with the grim silence that overtakes competitors in other sports which are played in a purportedly affable atmosphere. Conversational exchanges on a tennis court, for instance, often begin and end with one word: "Shot!" This is an abbreviated form of "Good shot!" If a player uses the entire expression, he is classified as gabby. Besides, he is wantonly expending his wind.

Golfers talk a lot, and they talk very well as a rule. Out in the privacy of the course, invigorated by the sweet air and the spring of the turf, a man opens up. He speaks his mind candidly on almost any subject. Things strike him humorously, including himself. With so little premium placed on formal politeness, he becomes—if not precisely "a boy again," as some golfers like to think of themselves—at least a pretty outward-going fellow. As long as a golfer doesn't misuse the privilege of self-expression in the company of his golfing cronies, he is free, after making some stupid error, to vent his infuriation by cursing, sulking, criticizing the condition of the course, and slamming his clubs into the ground or throwing them at any handy tree. In the outside world, this spontaneous petulance would be held against a man. Not so among his golfing friends. They have been in the same position; they understand.

True companionship flourishes on a golf course as it does in few other climes, and because it does, it is only to be expected that this boon should be abused. The most skillful offenders—well enough known to have been accepted as a permanent part of American folklore—are the country-club businessmen, the salesmen who have discovered that they can nail their man much more easily out on the golf course, where his guard is down, than in his office. If the salesman possesses a tournament-quality golf game, it helps immeasurably. Every golfer admires a well-hit shot—the fluid swing, the crispness with which the clubhead makes contact with the ball, the ever-delightful sensation of watching the ball streak for the pin, brake itself neatly on the green, and then bobble toward the hole "as if it had eyes." If you're going to have to buy from someone, you might as well give your business to a guy who can treat you to a succession of first-class golf shots. A seasoned golfing salesman knows when to win, when to come out all even, and when to fall apart at the seams and absorb a valuable thrashing. For many a golfer's money, one of the unsung classics of American art is the cartoon, executed in the twenties, depicting the "star salesman" out on the practice green practicing missing his short putts.

The fine fabric of golf is also frequently tugged to the ripping point by golfers who are not above deliberately "using" the social relationships the game affords as their chief tactic for winning their matches. A sprinkling of these "natural competitors" can be found at almost every golf club. Most of them have long since stopped trying to improve their own games, for they discover early that a surer road to victory is helping the other fellow to lose. It is easy in golf. Your opponent is always within conversational range.

At a club in my home town there was a golfer of this victory-first disposition who, whenever his opponent or opponents happened to be playing well, would pretend complete lack of interest in the outcome of the match. "How can anyone concentrate on a simply gorgeous day like this?" he would babble in a dreamy cadence. "I just can't take the game seriously when I'm out with you fellows—you're too much fun to be with," he would sigh with affecting wistfulness, or, sometimes, it would be something on the order of "What a fool I am not to play more of these lazy rounds when no one gives a damn if he wins or loses." This fellow would hack away at you with sweet talk until he made you feel like an out-and-out boor for wanting to play your best game. Then, having lulled you into a deep torpor, he would be all business, concede not even an 8-inch putt, become extremely technical about the rules, and relax not for a second until he had the match safely tucked away. Walter Hagen, the granddaddy of all tactical golfers, used to resort to a variation of this technique when he found himself trailing a hopeful young rival in a tournament. "My, you're hitting the ball beautifully!" Walter would purr, all admiration. "After you win this title, kid, you and I will go on an exhibition tour together." The young man's head would start to spin with dreams of fame and glory, his concentration would weaken, Hagen would pull the match out, and then, of course, there was no more talk of that exhibition tour together.

The ways by which victory-bent golfers attempt to throw their opponents off their games are as innumerable as the facets of human nature. Learning how to combat or ignore them is an essential part of learning to play the game, as basic as keeping your head down. A few years ago when Stephen Potter, an Englishman, published his book *Gamesmanship*, subtitled "The Art of Winning Games Without Actually Cheating," golfers' reactions to Mr. Potter's elaboration of "ploys," "gambits," and other devices for conquering a superior opponent were drastically different from the reaction of nongolfing readers. This latter group looked upon Mr. Potter as a creative man with the gift of humorous invention. Golfers, however, were inclined to view him as a reporter who had submitted a survey on a field of old and common knowledge, and they checked his findings in the same let's-see-how-well-he's-done-it spirit with which a Vermonter would read a treatise on how to make maple sugar.

The recognition of gamesmanship, by any name, is as old as golf, and books on the subject are almost as old. Around the turn of the century Horace Hutchinson, an early British Amateur champion, published *Hints on the Game of Golf*. Here are a few typical passages from the section called "Hints to Golfers of Riper Years."

> If your adversary is badly bunkered, there is no rule against your standing over him and counting his strokes aloud, with increasing gusto as their number mounts up; but it will be a wise precaution to arm yourself with a niblick before doing so, so as to meet him on equal terms.
>
> If your adversary is a hole or two down, there is no serious cause for alarm in his complaining of a severely sprained wrist, or an acute pain resembling lumbago which checks his swing. Should he happen to win the next hole, these symptoms in all probability will become less troublesome.

And gamiest of all:

> If you find yourself being outplayed by the excellent iron approaches of your adversary, it is sometimes a good plan to say to him, in a tone of friendly interest, "Really you are playing your iron wonderfully well today — better than I ever saw you play it before. Can you account for it in any way?" This is likely to promote a slight nervousness when he next takes his iron in his hand; and this nervousness is likely, if the match is at all a close one, to be of considerable service to you. There is no rule to prevent your doing this; only after a time will people stop playing with you.

The most difficult rounds in golf, it follows, are those you play with strangers. If you do not open yourself to their personalities, you deny yourself half the flavor of golfing. And if you do expose yourself, you render yourself vulnerable to the artifices of a possible "natural competitor." The sharpest illustration that comes to mind is the story of two middle-aged golfers I know, a doctor and a laundryman, who fled the winter in Massachusetts and drove to Pinehurst. On the first tee of the Number Two course they were informed by the starter that only foursomes were being sent out onto the crowded course and were subsequently introduced to two men from Ohio who were in the same boat. The four jovially but warily went about the business of arranging "a little match—to make things more interesting." Since each of the four described his usual game as being between 90 and 95, a four-ball match for "dollar Nassaus" was agreed on, the two Ohioans to oppose the two Massachusetts men on even terms. The doctor won the first hole with a par. Shooting way over his head, he won the second with a birdie, the third with a par, and the fourth with another birdie. He had never been so "hot" before and kept apologizing to his opponents and assuring them his streak couldn't last. En route to the fifty tee, the two New Englanders overheard one of the Ohioans growl in grim disgust to his partner, "A 95 golfer and he's two under par! Why, I'll bet that lying shyster isn't even a doctor!"

When the charms of golf are listed, a priority consideration must be given to the game's uniqueness in not being played on a field or court of specified dimensions with set regulation appointments. Each golf course possesses its own distinct and recognizable character. On a first-rate course, every hole—or almost every hole—has its own especial character. When a golfer speaks of the third at Augusta, the fifteenth at North Berwick, the sixteenth at Oakland Hills, the eighth at Pebble Beach, the fifth at Mildenhall, or the thirteenth at Myrtle Beach, in his mind's eye is an image every bit as individual and defined as the face of a friend. The traveling golfer is always bumping into new faces or renewing old acquaintances, and both experiences can be tremendously enjoyable.

The more a golfer travels, the clearer it becomes that, though each golf course has a separate personality, there is an inescapable sameness to practically all nineteenth holes. Antigolf men have the nineteenth hole in mind when they call golf "the hoof-and-mouth disease," their point being that after a golfer hoofs his eighteen holes, he comes in and tells you about his round at length and boringly. This charge is not entirely true. At the nineteenth hole, men talk at length and boringly on a wide variety of subjects.

Another golfing hazard to be avoided as sedulously as the bar is the country club dance. Whether it is a good thing or a bad thing, it is a fact that golf in the United States always has had overly strong social connotations. A man may own a Cadillac and send his son to the right prep school, his wife may be active in the right charity drives, and he may have all the other hallmarks of success, but he really hasn't made the grade unless he belongs to the right country club. Once he has "made" it, there are times when he wonders if it was worth all the huffing and puffing, and the club dance is one of the times he is most conscious of the Marquandary he is in. It is understood at most club dances that anything goes—you confide in people how much you have always liked them, you carefully explain to other people why you had previously thought they were uppish, you discuss in a very frank way what's wrong with the social setup in the community and at the club, and, furthermore, to make these points stick, you show these people how democratic and carefree and uninhibited you can be. Life can be pretty exhausting when the proper thing is to be conventionally improper.

The more a golfer travels, the clearer it also becomes to him that the breadth of golf's popularity arises from the wondrous flexibility of the game. A man can play golf any way he wants to. Or, to put it the other way round, the matrix of golf is so all-encompassing that people of the most utterly different personalities are convinced that golf is *the* game which best gives them what they hope to find in a game.

Every club has not only its gamesmen but also its suprasportsmen who are addicted to golf because of the incomparable opportunities it presents for demonstrating how self-controlled and gallant they can be under circumstances which would shatter the poise of weaker men, such as D'Artagnan and the Scarlet Pimpernel. . . . It has its technical watchdogs who are devoted to golf because no other game can fulfill quite so well their fondness for protocol or offer them as many rules to be wrangled over . . . its loners, introverts given to brooding and endless practice, who gravitate to golf because it is one game a man can play and enjoy without an opponent or a partner . . . its Hemingway types who still burn with the old desire to best their buddies at physical prowess and who, when they edge into the thirties, find the golf course one of the last safe fields of combat left to them...its intellectuals who are crazy about golf since no other sport affords them the opportunity for deep-purple theorizing as does this game in which a stationary ball is hit from a stationary stance...its gamblers who find the game ideal for arranging twenty-seven or so different bets that can be decided simultaneously...its dressers who see in golf the chance they have always wanted to express their colorful personalities, which they do by wearing chartreuse-and-borsch-colored slacks, plaid berets, and sports shirts depicting a Pacific island volcano in the process of eruption...its lovers of power who need not be reminded when they bash out a 200-yard drive, a commonplace achievement in golf, that they hit that ball farther than Babe Ruth's mightiest home run...its misogynists who revere the locker room as one of the last strongholds of all-male companionship...and its chasers who like their drinks with a woman on the side and can usually find a very pretty one on the veranda.

The wonder is that only 10,000,000 Americans are golfers.

The Birth of the Linksland Courses
Guy Campbell

Nature was the first golf course architect and needed only a few embellishments to complete its job, as this article by Sir Guy Campbell clearly establishes. Some of the greatest, most enduring courses in the world trace their origin to Linksland, and Sir Guy details the evolution which made them possible.

Except for the British Isles, there are not too many areas of the world which are able to offer the majestic qualities of Linksland — treeless, rolling dunes; firm turf; and an abundance of greensites. I have been privileged in being one of the few golf architects who has had the opportunity to adapt what nature provided into a Linksland golf course.

The first such opportunity was on a peninsula in Portugal called Troia, which emerged from the sea where the River Sado empties into the Atlantic Ocean. It was a one-in-a-million site of billowing sand dunes that begged for refinement into a golf course. From this naturally-endowed site emerged the Troia Golf Club, which still retains its wild, unkempt look save for the ribbons of grass which mark the route a golfer must follow.

Even more impressive was the site of a second course which I authored at Ballybunion in Ireland where, following the dictates of nature, fairways meander through grass-covered dunes nearly fifty feet in height and where pockets near their bases provide an unlimited number of greensites. Although Troia and Ballybunion are courses which have only recently been brought into being, both have the appearance of having been in place since the sand which supports them first was pushed up from the sea to form the Linksland.

Besides his detailed description of how Linksland came about, Sir Guy also traces the development of St. Andrews and the many changes which have been effected to the "Old" course, in addition to relating how the "New," the "Eden," and the "Jubilee" came about.

BRITISH GOLF WAS first played over links or "green fields." The earliest of them were sited at points up and down the eastern seaboard of Scotland, of which Dornoch, Montrose, Barry, Scotscraig, St. Andrews, Elie, Leven, Musselburgh, North Berwick, and Dunbar were, and Dornoch, Barry (Carnoustie), and North Berwick are typical. Nature was their architect, and beast and man her contractors.

In the formation and over-all stabilization of our island coastlines, the sea at intervals of time and distance gradually receded from the higher ground of cliff, bluff and escarpment to and from which the tides once flowed and ebbed. And as during the ages, by stages, the sea withdrew, it left a series of sandy wastes in bold ridge and significant furrow, broken and divided by numerous channels up and down which the tides advanced and retired, and down certain of which the burns, streams and rivers found their way to sea.

As time went on, these channels, other than those down which the burns, streams and rivers ran, dried out and by the action of the winds were formed into dunes, ridges, and knolls, and denes, gullies and hollows, of varying height, width and depth.

In the course of nature these channel-threaded wastes became the resting, nesting and breeding places for birds. This meant bird droppings and so guano or manure, which, with the silt brought down by the burns, streams and rivers, formed tilth in which the seeds blown from inland and regurgitated from the crops of the birds germinated and established vegetation. Thus eventually the whole of these areas became grass-covered, from the coarse marram on the exposed dunes, ridges and hillocks, and the finer bents and fescues in the sheltered dunes, gullies and hollows, to the meadow grasses round and about the river estuaries and the mouths of the streams and burns. Out of the spreading and intermingling of all these grasses which followed, was established the thick, close-growing, hard-wearing sward that is such a feature of true links turf wherever it is found.

On these areas in due course and where the soil was suitable, heather, whins, broom and trees took root and flourished in drifts, clumps, and coverts; terrain essentially adapted to attract and sustain animal life.

Nature saw to this. First came the rabbits or "cunninggis" as an ancient St. Andrews charter describes them; and after the "cunninggis" as naturally came the beasts of prey, followed inevitably by man.

This sequence had a definite effect on these wastes or warrens. In them the rabbits bred and multiplied. They linked up by runs their burrows in the dunes and ridges with their feeding and frolicking grounds in the straths and sheltered oases flanked and backed by whins and broom. The runs were then gradually worn into tracks by foxes, and man the hunter in his turn widened the tracks into paths and rides. Generations later when man the sportsman, having adopted golf as a pastime, went in search of ground suitable for its pursuit, he found it waiting for him, in these warrens, almost ready to hand. In form it was certainly primitive but it supplied lavishly what today are regarded as the fundamental and traditional characteristics of golfing terrain.

The rides leading from one assembly place to another made the basis of each fairway; the wild and broken country over which the rides threaded their way provided the rough and hazards — rough and hazards that would now bring a blanch to the faces of the most accurate and phlegmatic of our "Professors," and the sheltered *enclaves* used by the "cunninggis" for their feeding halls and dancing floors presented the obvious sites for greens.

Shortly the original layout of nature, interpreted and completed by beast and man, not only hallmarked golf as a point-to-point game, but from then on became the blueprint and sealed pattern for every links and course constructed by intention; indeed it remains today the ideal of all quality design.

As a complete and concentrated example of these "combined operations," the alliance between nature, beast and man (the foundation of our first links with a governing influence on their descendants here and all over the world), the area known as St. Andrews links is outstanding. Its coastline back in the dim ages started from the cliffs guarding the Scores, then ran inland and below what is now known as the Station Hill, and continued along under the high ground of the Strathtyrum estate policies to where the River Eden makes its break for the sea at Guard Bridge—a perimeter extending from east through south, southwest, west to northwest. As the sea retreated from it the process of natural reclamation progressed until today the links area is bounded by a long belt of fertile farmland, an expanse of saltings, the Eden estuary and St. Andrews Bay.

What is now the Old Course was primitively in existence when the University was founded in 1414. As today, it then "pointed" generally north by west and south by east in the shape of a hill-hook. Then, however, it occupied the narrowest of strips between the arable land on the west and a dense mass of whins that spread east to the high ridge of dunes flanking the sands. So narrow a strip that until towards the middle of the nineteenth century there was room only for single greens; at first eleven and later nine. Accordingly in the full round, eventually of eighteen holes, golfers had to play to the same holes both going out and coming home, with priority in approaching to, and putting on them, at the call of those homeward bound. The nine holes all had names which were used both going and coming home, i.e., "The Heather Hole out," "The High Hole home," a custom that still continues.

With the advent of the gutta ball the game became so popular that the old method, as it were, of flow and return along the same pipe, became impossible. Consequently six of the nine greens were extended laterally so as to allow two holes to be cut upon them, thus establishing the double greens for which the Old Course has so long been famous. A new site for the seventeenth green was established due north of the Road hole and just west of the Swilken Burn.

The three single-hole greens were and are the first, the ninth or End, and the eighteenth or Home. When the eighteen separate holes were first played the original nine holes were used on the outward half, and the six holes on the extended greens and the newly sited seventeenth green on the return journey. This caused two "crosses" in play, one between the first and Home holes, and the other between the seventh or High hole out and the short eleventh or High hole home. Before long the course was sampled in the reverse order, or "right-handed" going out and coming home. Leaving only one "cross," between the seventh and eleventh holes, was found so satisfactory that this layout—the right-hand course—came to be accepted as the "official" presentation for all major events, although up to the First World War the right-hand and left-hand courses were used alternatively a week at a time, except during the high season.

In this connection and as a fact historically interesting, the Amateur Championship of 1886, won by Horace Hutchinson, was played at St. Andrews over the left-hand course. It happened by chance. The week for the great event coincided with the turn of the left-hand course, the Old Course was so prepared, and play in the tournament was begun over it, before authority was aware what had occurred. Accordingly, the Amateur was continued and completed over the left-hand course for the first and only time. This has been recorded by Jack Tait—Freddy Tait's eldest brother—who was himself a competitor, and for the occasion acted as the special correspondent of the *Times*.

Incidentally this "alteration" of course presentation was due chiefly to the representations of Old Tom Morris, the curator of the links, who declared the "switch" was necessary to prevent constant wear and tear in defined areas—the Old Tom who said to a golfer deploring the taboo on Sunday golf, "Weel, sir, the links want a rest on the Sabbath, even if you don't."

This "spreading" of the Old Course (for the width of the fairways was also extended sufficiently to provide a distinct route for both the outward and homeward journeys) was not the only change that time and the increasing popularity of the game brought to St. Andrews links. In 1894 the New Course running parallel to and east of the Old Course was constructed out of the mass of whins already mentioned, but leaving a belt—now steadily and regrettably disappearing—to separate it from its ancient neighbor. Three years later a number of additional holes were made east of the New Course and close to the dunes or sandhills, which became the exercising ground of children and beginners under the name of the Jubilee Course.

Golf continued to gain fresh adherents year by year in such numbers that in 1912 the Town Council of St. Andrews had a fourth course constructed on each side of the railway line, west of the Old Course and between it and the farmland, and the Eden estuary. This was named the Eden Course and is today a representative expression of modern golf architecture.

And year by year while all this was happening, the sea continued its retreat. Up till the First World War this was so gradual as to rouse little if any attention. But in the interval between the first and second cataclysms, the pace quickened at such a rate that by 1939 an entirely fresh tract of golfing ground had formed between the sandhills and high-water mark. A case for St. Andrews links of *ein Drang nach Osten*. On this freshly surrendered expanse the Town Council prepared another full eighteen-hole course, during the Second World War, incorporating the holes of the former Jubilee Course under which name this latest extension is now known. Thus, thanks to nature, the cooperation of beast and man, and finally of man alone, nine-tenths of St. Andrews links as today existing is devoted to golf, and supports four full-sized eighteen-hole courses — two of them used in championships — and three putting courses of eighteen holes and generous dimensions.

This may seem a somewhat lengthy description accorded to one place, but it is justified because it crystallizes the story of the origin, evolution and development of all similar areas in our islands: such as Carnoustie and Machrihanish in Scotland; Westward Ho! and Prince's in England; Harlech and Aberdovey in Wales; Portrush and Portmarnock in Ireland, and many other happy hunting grounds that will quicken the minds of the faithful golfers to and by whom they are known and held in esteem. And it is on such a foundation stone, historical in its laying, that the edifice of British links and courses has been built.

What Makes It Great?
Robert Trent Jones

To have included in this collection an article I have written would seem to be blatantly self-serving. Nothing could be farther from the truth as it was done with the purpose of establishing the relative positions and interdependence of the golf course architect and the golf player.

Despite the fact that golf course architecture has been an integral part of the game since the days of the "feathery," when Allan Robertson remodelled the "Old Course" at St. Andrews in 1842, no steps ever were taken to formalize the practice as a profession until 1947, when the American Society of Golf Course Architects was organized at Pinehurst with thirteen charter members. I was one of them. Since then, the ASGCA membership has grown to over one hundred whose influence and contribution to the game have been monumental.

There still is, however, a certain mystery about a profession which, in effect, converts what can be termed a "sow's ear" of terrain features into a "silk purse" of landscape beauty. The mystery, of course, is how this is accomplished. The simplest explanation I can give is: ingenuity, earth-moving and irrigation, plus the understanding and indulgence of a client and the cooperation of the weather.

It is purely a subjective question how one determines the merits of a particular eighteen holes: is it a good golf course, is it a bad golf course, or does it rate somewhere in between?

The article that follows attempts to define those factors that go into the creation of a more than acceptable golf course, both from the standpoint of the architect and of those who will play it, and to show the interdependence of each in what can only be termed an adversary relationship.

I'VE LIVED WITH this question for many years, both professionally and personally. Professionally, I have wandered over countless acres of virgin land — fording streams, climbing hills, wandering through woods — in all seasons of the year, everywhere. I have watched all the masters from Jones to Watson in the world's greatest tournaments, everywhere. Personally, I have hit thrilling shots over beautiful ponds close to well-placed pins. I have dumped bad shots into nasty little ponds and watched them sink to a watery grave, everywhere. In seeing and contributing to many of the world's great courses, I have spent a lifetime in observing, analyzing, dissecting, and playing. I think I know what makes a great golf hole.

There is the legitimate "mother" of golf courses — St. Andrews. It is nature's created "monster." Down through the ages its contours have been created by receding seas and swirling winds which have left in their wake plateaus for greens, pockets for traps and undulating fairways. The result is a grandeur, a rhythm of flowing line unique to itself in all the world. The first time Bob Jones at a very youthful age played St. Andrews in a tournament, he blew up in despair. Later, his game and emotions under control, he came to love it.

The Old Course has probably had more effect on golf architecture than any other single course. It requires thought and in turn rewards the thinking golfer. Conversely it penalizes to distraction the player who does not think.

No course, however, should overpenalize. All golfers cannot be great players. The target area for an average golfer must be larger to offset somewhat his lack of skill. Where the direct route confronts him with a formidable hazard — trap or water — beyond his repertoire of shots he should be offered an alternate route less risky, less demanding, less toll-taking, but not limp in character or it becomes boring. Keeping the tingle of excitement, the exhilaration of the game, for all classes of players both male and female, is the test of a great golf course. To sum up, each hole must be a demanding par and a comfortable bogey.

It was about the turn of the century that the game, bursting with converts, required more and more courses to meet the popular demand. This required the services of specialists, creating the profession of golf course architecture. As the game moved inland the architects' model was the "linksland" — courses nature had nurtured. The mimicry was both good and bad, but the models were there. The beautiful rhythm of line made by the dunes along the sea, the natural hewn plateaus, were unlikely to be copied exactly. For a fertile imagination, with golf knowledge to match, the guidelines were there to adapt and create holes of outstanding character.

For architects and players alike had noted that some holes stood out as being superior — in interest, strategy or play and beauty — to be categorized in golf's honor list of great holes. Fortunately, what the earth's surface offers rarely repeats itself, except in dead flat land, so opportunities are unlimited for creative manipulation, be it on meadowland, on mountain valleys, or on the desert, each course can have distinctive features all its own.

I believe that the vitality of the game of golf is that it offers man his own personal challenge for combat. He attacks the course and par. The architect creates fair pitfalls to defend its easy conquest. In a true sense, the game is a form of attack and counterattack. New and improved instruments are created which, together with practice and skill may bring the course to its knees. The architect calls on his ingenuity to create a hole that will reward only for achievement.

The modern professional with his precision-made equipment, carpetlike and weed-free turf, low unpunishing rough, on many courses makes a mockery of par. The shattering of par without the proper challenge is a fraud; a diamond is valued only by its texture, cut and polish, so should be the standard of a round in par.

My name has been taken in vain many times on courses we have designed and/or remodeled for play in championships after some great players have been frustrated playing the courses. This was particularly true when we opened Spyglass Hill, on the fabulous Monterey Peninsula at Pebble Beach, California. The scores were high and the wails of anguish loud. Many have told me since it was the condition not the course that bothered them, and while tough, it was a fair and great course. Bing Crosby himself shortly thereafter shot a 77, and proclaimed it to be one of the world's great courses.

But emotions are part of the game, sometimes a very large part of the game. There's certainly exhilaration that comes with great performance. And just as certainly there's terrible dismay with a poor round. Golf, however, offers much more than perpetual battle between man and setting. Just to be out there, to walk and enjoy natural surroundings is *almost* enough by itself.

Aside from the battle, though, there is a tranquilizing effect of golf. Many courses are truly beautiful. Wandering through woods, observing a tormented sea, relaxing near a reflective pool, observing the majesty of a mountain range—all are part of the game. The seaside vistas of Dorado Beach, Maura Kea, Spyglass Hill, Kanaapali, Mid-Ocean are all inspiring in their sheer beauty; the mountains of Jackson Hole, Colorado Springs, Hot Springs, Jasper and Gleneagles are exhilarating and eye-filling in their beauty; Augusta National is an arboretum of placid beauty.

There are thousands of courses throughout the world with ribbons of trees lining fairways that are soul-satisfying to the golfers who play them. The greenness of the fairways, the menacing texture of the rough, the fearful aspect of the water, the carpetlike appearance of the greens— all become elements which, blended properly, make a great golf course.

However, while a great golf course should have beauty, it should above all else have great playing values. To me, the two are inextricably linked. Yet, holes should be fair. As the player stands on the tee, he should be able to weigh risk against benefit. If he decides to bite off a slice of pond on a par 5, for example, so that he has a chance of being on in two, he assumes the responsibility of perhaps a 230 yard carry dead straight, and a terrible penalty if he doesn't make it. The position of trapping tilt or contour of fairways as well as width or narrowness are factors to be considered as you stand on the tee.

As an example of what I mean, there is the 13th hole, a par 5, severe dogleg left on the East Course at Dorado Beach in Puerto Rico. It is one of my favorites. The player may hit straight out to a relatively wide fairway. But to the left there is a pond of considerable width. Question: does the player attempt to traverse the short route, thereby placing himself in good position for a try at the green? Suppose he does, and makes it, is he going to be home safe in two? Here again, he is faced with a decision. The green is elevated, and protected in front by another pond about 75 yards wide. Behind the green, about 30 yards away is the Atlantic Ocean. And the green is well surrounded by traps as well. The courageous and capable golfer can reach it. But he will have made two thoroughly superb shots.

On the other hand, the hole may be played conservatively as well. If he doesn't try to carry the first pond, but hits straightaway, he has an excellent chance of making par. In this case, however, he has no opportunity to try to make the green in two. His second shot must be played to the left which is the only approach by land to the green. The hole is fair to all, demanding to all to be sure, but it demonstrates clearly the rewards and penalties that should be innate to all great golf holes.

Just a word about the ultimate target: the green. To me, there's simply nothing more enjoyable than to play a shot to a well-placed, beautifully designed green where the guardian traps and contours are in harmony with a subtle pin position. Variety in green design is infinite— elevated, terraced, tilted, mounded contours, flank trapping on the sides, direct trapping or water in the front. Varied green designs contribute to the joy of playing a great golf course as they contribute to the misery of failure to respond to its demands.

What makes a great golf course? Like the human beings who play them, they vary widely in style and character, but possess character all their own. One thing to remember: great ones may be beaten, but never defeated.

The Rise and Fall of Penal Architecture
Red Hoffman

Relative to my explanation of "What Makes It Great?" another recurrent question often asked me is, "How was golf in the good old days?" In a word, frustrating. It still is, but not so absolutely.

I speak from experience. My introduction to golf was back in the twenties, as a caddie, when the penal style of golf course architecture flourished. Except for the true experts, it had a tendency to reduce most golfers to the status of "hackers." Because their style was generally weighted heavily in favour of the golf courses, architects were not averse to making the courses as difficult as possible. Fortunately, this was a style that did not persist, as it was replaced subsequently by the strategic design, which is considerably more forgiving and infinitely more conducive to the enjoyment of the game. The latter style, with few exceptions, has since remained constant. Millions of golfers can be thankful that it has.

By way of enlightening them as to the reason I suggest their appreciation, I have included "The Rise and Fall of Penal Architecture." It graphically details what that form of designed punishment was all about and why it made the game so frustrating. In reading it, today's golfer, who may never have been exposed to the pitfalls of the penal, should be able to realize why the game played by his forebears was anything but fair. It was not intended to be.

This highly descriptive piece was written by Red Hoffman, who also was exposed to the diminishing vestiges of the penal as a caddie. Red was, for many years, golf editor of the Newark News. *In addition to his regular writings about golf, he took it upon himself to make a thorough study of golf course architecture. As one who can appreciate his efforts to the fullest, I can say that Red is a lay expert on the subject.*

TURN BACK THE CLOCK a half century and visualize the trials of a golfer affluent enough to belong to a country club. As a neophyte in the game his play is more noteworthy for inconsistency than it is for competence. Despite the growing popularity of golf as an American pastime, the British influence still is very much in evidence, particularly the scene of his pleasure.

Our golfer is dressed in a Burberry suit — knickerbockers and a Norfolk jacket with an ingenious pivot sleeve — a shirt with collar and cuffs and a four-in-hand tie, heavy brogues with steel nubs, and the inevitable argyle stockings. Accompanying him is a caddie bearing a stovepipe bag containing woods by Cuthbert Butchart, irons by Stewart, Nichols or Forgan, and a Mills Putter — all with wooden shafts and leather grips as slick and as smooth as a polished floor. Our sportsman breaks out a new Silver King from its paper wrapping, and reaching into a nearby bucket he grabs a handful of sand which he wets in another bucket and then molds into a pedestal. This is his tee. (The peg had been patented in 1899, but its use was not yet widespread.)

Rearing back with a palms-opposed grip, the golfer sends off the mesh-marked sphere on a low trajectory, and it eventually drives into a hay field that waves menacingly between the small rectangular teeing ground and the dun-brown, unwatered fairway some 150 yards away.

The caddie, fortunately, is able to locate the ball. The golfer is up to his knees in grass and he selects a mashie niblick to further his progress. He slashes his way out, propelling the ball some 100 yards despite a sheaf of wild grass clinging to the clubhead. Regretfully, he watches the flight of the ball terminate in a shallow cross bunker. His next shot, picked cleanly from the sand with a mid-mashie slices toward the right rough, but it evokes a shout of glee when it bounds off the side of a chocolate drop and threads its way past a nest of pot bunkers which indiscriminately punctuate the right side of the fairway, 50 yards short of the green. A short pitch is left if he is to reach a green that stands like a giant mushroom surrounded by a moat of sand. Naturally the pitch is short and the ball buries in the sand.

Now the golfer must contend with a cone-shaped dragon-tooth mound which contorts his stance. He needs a shot with his Cardinal niblick — the clubhead the size and shape of a dinner plate — to extricate the ball and another to cut it from a more favorable lie to the ultimate target. The three putts he expends to traverse a six-inch-high terrace over a crusty, bristly green is not unexpected. This goes on for the remaining 17 holes, and because of national prohibition, there is no 19th hole to soothe our man's shattered soul.

Our tale may seem exaggerated, but it is only slightly so. Our golfer was playing a course which was penal in concept, a style of architecture which offered more in the way of punishment than of pleasure. It was a style which dominated the design of British courses, flourished briefly in this country, and which even today remains as a subordinate characteristic of innumerable courses and particular holes that can be found wherever golf is played.

That any vestige of penal architecture survived is a miracle, because play on a penal course had to be one of life's most frustrating experiences. Those courses demanded disciplined shotmaking. You might say that this type of design precluded individual enterprise, minimized strategy, and reduced the game to an almost mechanical performance. Basically, there was only one route to follow on each hole; the golfer was not required to think very much, only to obey. As Bob Jones once commented: "I have found that most of our courses in America may be played correctly the same way round after round."

Off-fairway areas were almost jungles; the safe route along the fairways was hemmed with bunkers and mounds and the greens were small, exacting targets guarded by steep-faced craters of sand. The bunkers often were reinforced with logs or pilings, occasionally terraced and frequently pitted by grotesque islands of disheveled sod. Viewed from any angle these tortuous tracks bore a striking resemblance to bomb-pocketed battlefields, even to the extent of including walls, revetments and roads, potholed and rutted. In truth, they were a constant scene of conflict with the golfer, armed with a disreputable collection of weapons, attempting to storm the ramparts of nature and to by-pass the sadistic sentries of the architect's creation. Following a line of play on each hole was an exacting, demanding assignment; every shot had to be controlled and placed precisely so that it would avoid a multiplicity of hazards. Accuracy was paramount; any error was costly. The inexpert golfer suffered penalties. His mis-hit or mis-directed shots were ensnared by deep grass, encircled by trees, buried in sand and swallowed by water. There was no escape; there was no alternate way to circumvent the dictates of the architect. Truly, everyone played the same course. There is no better description of penal golf than that uttered by an anonymous Scot: "It's a humbling game."

The penal-style course proliferated in this country shortly after World War I. The popularity of this architectural concept stemmed, in part, from the success of Pine Valley Golf Club in Clementon, N. J. Even today it enjoys a reputation as the world's toughest golf course. Pine Valley was the creation of Philadelphia hotelman George Crump, who borrowed strategic concepts from the British. Harry S. Colt, the English architect, worked with Crump on the design, and after Crump's death, Hugh Wilson, the architect of Merion Golf Club in Ardmore, Pa., helped complete the course. Pine Valley has been described as one vast bunker with islands of grass that serve as tees, fairways and greens. Nevertheless, it is one of the world's great golf courses. It is unquestionably penal in nature with its severity modified to the extent that a competent golfer finds its fairways and its greens reasonably expansive, with one or two exceptions. Make no mistake, Pine Valley offers unremitting punishment for those unable to conform to its island-hopping requirements.

Oakmont Country Club, near Pittsburgh, site of the 1973 United States Open, also is penal in concept, particularly as it was originally. Built in 1903, some 15 years before Pine Valley, Oakmont is rife with bunkers — 350 originally, 187 at present count. Its original notoriety, in the main, stemmed from its treatment of those hazards in which the heavy, dark-brown sand was furrowed to a depth of four inches. This was in keeping with the concept of its creator, Henry C. Fownes: "A poorly played shot should result in a shot irrevocably lost."

Fownes coupled this punishment with greens regarded universally as the fastest ever sown by man. Tommy Armour won the 1927 at Oakmont, and when it was over he had this to say about putting: "You had to manipulate the ball into the hole, not putt it."

Oakmont's terrors have been tempered somewhat. The infamous furrows, trenches the depth of a golf ball, have been eliminated, and the rough, coarse river-bottom sand has been replaced by lighter, more manageable white sand. Despite this, Oakmont still remains one of the most formidable tests in all of golf. It derives much of its strength from the penalties it can inflict.

Though not always as evident, courses selected by the USGA to host the Open Championships always include more than a suggestion of the penal: narrowed fairways bordered by graduated rough, aprons surrounded by two-inch grass and greens shaved to 3/16 inch or less.

Open sites notwithstanding, it was inevitable that the penal style of architecture give way to less-demanding, more pleasurable golfing challenges. Also the high cost of maintenance and the general dissatisfaction of the average golfer were major factors contributing to its demise. The intervening 50 years since the heyday of the penal concept has seen the emergence of the "heroic" and the "strategic" styles of golf course construction. The heroic, to some extent, derives some of its character from the penal, in that it imposes demands for a monumental shot to reach its objective, but at the same time it offers an easier, less hazardous approach to playing a hole. Merion is one of the finest examples of the heroic. The last five holes present one of the strongest finishes in golf, in that each demands either a tee shot or an approach of heroic character if a golfer is to achieve par, or if he is to have a chance for a birdie. On the other hand, the heroic course may be played in such a way that the hazards are by-passed. By avoiding the risk, though, the golfer invariably must settle for a lesser achievement.

Golf became a thinking man's game with the

emergence of the strategic style of architecture. This concept offers more than one way to play a hole and imposes on the individual the responsibility for making the choice. Credit for this revolutionary premise must go to Dr. Alister Mackenzie, a Scottish physician who gave up medicine to build courses in the late 1920s, and who collaborated with Bob Jones to create the Augusta National Golf Club. Jones had some theories of his own which modified some of Mackenzie's extremes. Jones believed that a course had to require thought as well as sheer technical skill to test a player's true ability. Further, it was his conviction that a really great course must be a source of pleasure to the greatest number of players, giving the average player a fair chance and at the same time demanding the utmost from the expert to break par. Augusta National is a classic manifestation of this concept — a concept which has been a dominant consideration in great golf course design ever since.

Although modern golf course architecture incorporates all three architectural concepts, the absolute penal, particularly in this country, is a thing of the past. It was too difficult, too demanding and too deflating to a golfer's ego. The American golfer thinks only in terms of par. He considers a bogey a failure.

Nature's Masterpiece
Dwayne Netland

As a golf course architect, I can only admire the inspired work of Jack Neville and Douglas Grant in creating the Pebble Beach Golf Links. I also cannot but envy their having been given the most desirable site of the Del Monte Properties to effect their masterpiece; today's developers probably would have relegated them to an area deep in the forest and erected condominiums on the cliffs of the golf course site.

Pebble Beach, of course, is not just another resort for numerous reasons, most of all because it is the annual site of the Bing Crosby National Pro-Amateur, the granddaddy of all such events. In it, the pros partner with amateurs of far lesser skills, usually amateurs from the glamour and glitter of the entertainment world. Television was quick to capitalize on this combination, and the Crosby, for more than twenty years, has been viewed by more non-golfers than any other tournament. And for good reason: some of the "shots" of the course are of such beauty as to leave the viewer breathless, even if he doesn't know the difference between Sam Snead and Sam Spade.

Dwayne Netland, a Senior Editor of Golf Digest, *traced the history of the tournament in his book* The Crosby: The Greatest Show in Golf, *and he did a bang-up job in conveying the fun, the festivities and the flavour of the tournament which the great pop singer originated in 1937 and which his wife, Kathy, and his son, Nathaniel, have perpetuated.*

Netland, who plays an inspired game of golf as a left-hander, knows and appreciates the Pebble Beach course. His chapter devoted to it, "Nature's Masterpiece," gives every evidence of that, and provides an interesting mix of some of the incidents and anecdotes that have become legend during the playing of the Crosby over the years.

ALTHOUGH IT IS frequented by the rich and often associated with a *Social Register* clientele, Pebble Beach is a public golf course. It is surely the most prominent public course in America, having fashioned its international reputation partially with its artful severity and partially with its natural beauty.

Catering primarily to the guests of Del Monte Lodge, Pebble Beach is open to the general public at $20 per round on week days and $30 on weekends, plus a $10 golf car fee. Over 36,000 rounds are played there annually.

Pebble Beach is, above all, a working course. It held the U.S. Amateur in 1929, when it was won by Harrison R. (Jimmy) Johnston of Minneapolis with a shot off the receding waters of the beach along the 18th fairway; in 1947, when Skee Riegel outshot a strong field and again in 1961, when Jack Nicklaus won his second and last Amateur championship. In 1972 the U.S. Open finally came to Pebble Beach. It was a memorable tournament, won by Nicklaus with a score of 290, two strokes over par. Pebble has, in addition, held the California Amateur annually since 1919.

Ever since Crosby moved his tournament to the Monterey Peninsula in 1947, Pebble has been the anchor course. The final round is traditionally played there, and the network telecasts have made the closing holes as familiar to most American golf fans as those at their own courses. Pat Ward-Thomas of the *Manchester Guardian* in England has written:

The quality of the dramatic is the lasting impression of Pebble, and this is emphasized by its peaceful beginning which gives the stranger no hint of what is to come. There are many great finishing holes in golf, but none in my view can compare with the last at Pebble, that noble curve along the iron-bound shore. One can imagine the joy, and, too, the hint of malice there must have been in the hearts of Jack Neville and Douglas Grant when they saw what nature had presented them for their fashioning of a masterpiece.

A golfer from Edinburgh once came over to visit his good friend Peter Hay, the Scottish-born pro at Pebble Beach for many years until his death. The Scot told Hay that he, the Scot, could not play the course. "It's too dommed beautiful," he burred. "I can't keep my mind on the game."

Hay understood. He is gone now, but his name is perpetuated by the lovely little par-3 course, named for him, at the entrance to Del Monte Lodge.

"Playing Pebble Beach is like fighting Rocky Marciano," Jack Burke observed twenty years ago. "Every time you step onto the course, you're a cinch to take a beating."

Time hasn't changed a thing. Today Burke could allude to Muhammed Ali instead of Marciano. Billy Farrell would agree. Farrell took 55 strokes on the first nine in the 1967 Crosby, before the round was washed out by a storm.

The course measures 6,343 yards from the regular tees and 6,815 yards from the championship tees, with ratings of 72 and 75. The competitive course record is 64 — 8 under par — by Rod Funseth in the 1972 Crosby.

"I doubt if many people realize what a fantastic score that was," says Art Bell, the Pebble Beach pro. Bell, a native of the Hawaiian Islands, is sixty-five, and he has seen just about every quality course in the United States. "Pebble is No. 1," Bell says. "It has every characteristic required of a great course."

The basic design Neville incorporated is roughly a figure 8. Beginning at the Del Monte Lodge, which overlooks Carmel Bay, the course moves inland for the first three holes, all rather modest in severity. The next seven holes, with the exception of the par-3 5th, move along the cliffs. From 11 through 16 the holes loop inland and then back to the water, finishing with the ocean very much in play at 17 and 18.

The course really begins on the 6th hole, an uphill par-5 that Byron Nelson considers the toughest of the eighteen. The next four holes are perched high atop a craggy spit that overhangs the ocean. The 7th is a tiny 110-yard downhill pitch, a soft wedge shot on calm days for the pros but a long iron into the gale. The 8th is one of the great two-shotters anywhere. After a blind drive to a plateau the approach must carry 180 to 190 yards, across the chasm that resembles a shark's maw, to a green surrounded by bunkers.

The 9th, 450 yards, and the 10th, 436 yards, stretch hard along the ocean. These are brutally difficult holes, under any conditions. Nicklaus nearly threw away his 1972 Open championship on the 10th, slicing a drive over the cliff down onto the beach below and taking a double bogey. Dale Douglass took a 19 on the hole in the 1963 Crosby.

In 1965 Tony Lema, the defending champion in the Crosby, was paired with Father John Durkin, a fine player who always showed up with a formidable handicap. As they stood on the 8th tee, Lema turned to the priest and said, "Partner, you will have to get bogeys on these next three holes, and with your strokes we'll get out alive. There is no way I can par them all."

The remaining holes are scarcely easier. In the final round of the 1967 Crosby, Arnold Palmer was one stroke behind Nicklaus when he came to the 14th, a 555-yard par-5. Attempting to reach the green with his second, Palmer hit a mighty 3-wood that ticked the branches of a tree on the right and caromed out of bounds. Arnold hit the tree with his next shot, and that one also landed OB. He took 9 on the hole and finished third, behind Nicklaus and Billy Casper.

That night a storm struck Pebble Beach, and when the grounds crew went out the next morning to survey the damage, they discovered the tree had been uprooted and blown to the ground.

Johnny Miller led Nicklaus by a stroke on the final round of the 1972 Crosby as they walked together down the 16th fairway. "I can't say that I've played very well, Jack," Miller said. "It's taken me 69 holes to figure my problem out. But I've got it corrected now." On his next shot, a 7-iron, Miller shanked the ball. He wound up in a tie with Nicklaus, and lost to Jack's birdie on the first play-off hole.

Jack Burke and George Coleman appeared to have the pro-am wrapped up in 1971 until Coleman 4-putted the 17th green, enabling Lou Graham and Father Durkin to win. The priest had a momentary twinge of conscience over his handicap, then 17. "I'm expecting a wire from the Vatican any day," he said, "asking for a review of my handicap."

No golfer has ever been more vividly associated with disaster on any one hole than Palmer on the 17th at Pebble Beach. It wiped him out two years in succession.

A rugged, 218-yard hole requiring anything from a long iron to a driver, the 17th runs toward the ocean to a green flanked by rocks and the Pacific. In the third round of the 1963 Crosby, Palmer's 2-iron shot sailed over the green and disappeared, apparently into the water.

Invoking the lost-ball rule, Arnold hit another from the tee. His first ball was found lying in the rocks on the beach, however, and so he played that onto the green. Following the completion of the tournament the next day, PGA officials, in a review of the situation, decided that Palmer had struck an unauthorized provisional ball — that he, in effect, had abandoned his first ball by hitting the second. He was disqualified, even though he had played the fourth round, and his string of 47 consecutive tournaments in the money was over.

The next year, the 17th at Pebble, served as the scene for the famous "Palmer on the Rocks" incident, resulting in a 9 for Arnold and seventeen minutes of memorable footage for the television cameras. It occurred, again, on the third round.

Palmer hit his tee shot over the cliff behind the green, into shallow water in front of the 18th tee. The bay and its beaches were then played as "part of the course," meaning that a golfer could not take a lateral water penalty stroke (the local rule was later abolished and the beaches are now regarded as a water hazard).

Palmer stood there, with a stray dog watching him curiously, and flailed away at the ball. Jimmy Demaret was working the tournament as a roving television commentator. Observing Palmer's predicament, Demaret pointed out the options under the unplayable ball rule. He reported that Palmer could lift and drop, keeping the line behind the position of the ball. "In that case," remarked Demaret, "his nearest drop would be Honolulu." Palmer continued to play it off the rocks.

Jim Murray of the Lost Angeles *Times*, staring wryly at the scene from the vantage point of his living-room television set, described it in this manner:

Palmer...was so far out on a moor in the ocean he looked like Robinson Crusoe. His only companions were a dog and a sand wedge. I thought for a minute we had switched channels and Walt Disney was bringing us another of those heart-warming stories of a boy and his dog, but a companion, peering closely had a better idea: 'Shouldn't that dog have a cask around his neck?'

In contrast to Palmer's woes on the 17th is the historic shot struck on the 18th in 1952 by an amateur, Billy Hoelle, then employed as a salesman for Bing Crosby's Minute Maid orange juice firm.

Hoelle and his partner, Art Bell, trailed the pro-am leaders, Bob Toski and Dr. Bob Knudson, by 4 shots on the 17th tee. Bell dropped a long birdie putt on 17, then on 18 Hoelle chopped an 8-iron shot out of a wet sand trap into the cup for a net 2, a double eagle. The 2-2 finish earned Bell and Hoelle a share of the pro-am championship with Toski and Knudson.

"It was a million-to-one shot," groaned Crosby, whose Calcutta money had been on the Toski team.

The incident which best symbolizes the capricious qualities of Pebble Beach occurred in 1965. A San Francisco amateur, Matt Palacio, hit his drive on the 18th in the general direction of China and muttered, "Only God can save that one." The waves suddenly receded, the ball struck a bare rock, and it caromed back onto a favorable spot on the fairway. Palacio gazed up at the heavens and mumbled, "Thank you, God."

It remained for Mason Rudolph, the touring philosopher from Clarksville, Tennessee, to analyze Pebble Beach. After a particularly rugged round in the 1972 Open, Mason smiled weakly and said, "This course is built right around my game. Unfortunately, it touches no part of it."

Pine Valley: Monumental Challenge to Accuracy
Cal Brown

Pine Valley has been described as "one vast sand trap with island way stations for playing golf." A truly inspired creation of George A. Crump, with help from English golf course architect Harry S. Colt and from Hugh Wilson, who designed Merion, it has achieved a world-wide reputation for difficulty despite the fact that it is located in a remote, rural area of southern New Jersey. As a long-time member, I know it can enact a frightful toll of strokes for any golfer unable to comply with its exacting standards. Bernard Darwin described it best when he called it "an examination in golf."

Pine Valley is the ultimate penal golf course. It has had a significant impact on the design of hundreds of others since it came into being shortly before World War I. Frankly, it even has influenced my work, although I have long been regarded as an active advocate of the strategic style of golf course architecture.

Given situations approximating those of Pine Valley, I have not been averse to deviating in the direction of the penal. At the sites for the Spyglass Hill Golf Club on California's Monterey Peninsula and for the Troia Golf Club, thirty miles below Lisbon in Portugal, the natural features — soil and terrain — were such that any thought of not using them for the penal concept was foolhardy. As a result, the first five holes along the beach at Spyglass Hill and the entire eighteen in the dunes at Troia each have strong Pine Valley overtones.

Cal Brown, in this article from Golf Digest, graphically details what Pine Valley is all about. Cal was particularly well-qualified for the assignment as, prior to leaving the magazine, for many years he was head of a panel that makes a biennial selection of "America's 100 greatest golf courses." I should add that Pine Valley, since the list was first compiled twenty-five years ago, always has been rated among the top ten.

TUCKED AWAY FROM public view down an anonymous country road near the small town of Clementon in southwestern New Jersey is Pine Valley Golf Club.

This magnificent—some say fiendish—creation, hewn from the pine-covered sand hills that eons ago formed the ocean floor, is as good an argument as you will find that backbreaking length is not essential to a great test of golf.

Pine Valley's full length of 6,765 yards (6,442 from the regular tees) does not strike fear into anyone's breast—not until one steps to the first tee. There one catches a glimpse of the two principal design features that give Pine Valley its stern, intimidating character—vast, sandy wilderness and thick forest. There is no "rough" at Pine Valley. Instead, desert-like scrub surrounds every fairway and most of the greens, which are immaculately conditioned and appear, in contrast, as islands of green velvet.

One must play to these "islands" from start to finish. Tee shots must carry expanses of up to 175 yards of unkempt dune on every hole to reach safe ground. The careless, wild or indifferent shot is dealt with severely. Since rakes are forbidden on the course, the sandy soil expanses are pocked with footprints, mounds, holes of burrowing animals, roots and ragged clumps of scrub, heather, Scotch broom and Poverty grass. If you can find your ball in this or in the woods (which Pine Valley caddies are devilishly adept at doing) you play it as it lies, for there is out-of-bounds on only one hole.

The all-male club is strictly private. Its president for the past 40 years, John Arthur Brown, has assiduously guarded its sanctity and the comfort of its members owing to the fact that Pine Valley is widely discussed wherever genuine golfing spirits gather and has more requests for visits than can possibly be accommodated. It is widely regarded as the toughest golf course in the world. This is certainly not true for the fine player who can strike the ball consistently and truly. It may well be the most testing for the average player of, say, seven handicap or more, whose shotmaking is less reliable. Handicap records of Pine Valley members tend to bear this out. For the low handicapper, three or under, there is no difference between his handicap at

Pine Valley and other courses he plays. As handicaps increase, however, the player's handicap at Pine Valley tends to be two or three shots greater than his handicap at another course; in some cases the difference is four or five strokes.

One or two mistakes is all it takes to hike your score dramatically at Pine Valley. There is a story about one gentleman who needed a bogey 5 on the 18th hole for an 84 to win a substantial bet that he could break 90. He finished with 97. The late British golf writer Bernard Darwin is said to have played the first seven holes in even par. Following a good drive, he proceeded to take 16 strokes on the short eighth hole and returned to the clubhouse. It was this kind of thing that could lead Darwin to remark later, "It is all very well to punish a bad stroke, but the right of eternal punishment should be reserved for a higher tribunal than a Greens Committee." On another occasion, Bob Hope stepped to the 130-yard 10th flushed with relief after a 43 on the front side; he finally holed out with an 11.

It may be adventures like these that inspire poets and writers to describe Pine Valley with adjectives like heroic, majestic, monstrous, sublime, deadly, beautiful and one or two uncomplimentary terms of Anglo-Saxon origin. One would be hard put to soften any of these epithets. It also has been called a penal golf course which is true only in the sense that it so ruthlessly penalizes poorly struck shots.

The truth is that Pine Valley is eminently fair. The landing areas for tee shots are very wide. Alternate routes to the greens are provided on at least nine of the fourteen long holes, although a safe routing will not get you to the green in regulation figures. There is little margin for the player who chooses to risk everything, a feature upholding the principle that a risk is not worthy of the name if one can get away with an error, however slight. The course demands that if you accept challenge you must be prepared to execute.

It is no secret that a number of professional players, particularly long hitters, do not rate Pine Valley among the great challenges in golf. One suspects the reason for this is that Pine Valley is not the place for raw power. It is a place where subtlety and a well-positioned tee shot will pay rewards, where brute strength is tolerated only if accompanied by great control and nerve. The professionals, who are accustomed to letting it fly to get all the advantages of length without severe penalty, do not like the idea of laying up with an iron or 4-wood. Yet, there is ample room for power at Pine Valley, with sufficient tests of strength for even the heaviest hitters on six holes.

"It is only penal if you are not playing well," says George Fazio, the former touring pro who now is designing courses himself, and who was once the professional at Pine Valley. "I think it has been proved over the years in competition, both amateur and professional, that the best player will win at Pine Valley. You must play the course, not necessarily your own game. The player who does not possess all the shots would not thrive there." It is, in short, a golf course for the man who relishes the game above his own individual prowess.

What sets Pine Valley apart from all but a handful of courses is not only its unusual terrain, but also the number of absolutely first-rate holes it throws at you. It probably has more classic holes than any other course in America.

There are but two par-5s and both are superb. The 15th is surely one of the greatest in the world. Some of the best (and longest) players in golf have surveyed its 603-yard length — Nicklaus, Snead, Harney, Souchak, Bayer, Thomson — and none has ever reached it in two, not even from the middle tees which cut its distance to 584 yards. It is that rare, totally honest hole that hides nothing and yet will succumb to nothing short of perfection. The tee shot must carry over a lovely lake to a wide landing area which slopes lazily uphill and around a gentle bend to the right to a tiny green, perched like a sentinel in the distance. The closer one approaches to the green, the tighter the fairway becomes as woods and sand converge on a narrow neck that is not more than green's width across. The fairway tilts to the right near the green to send any half-hearted approach careening to disaster. The hole yields par with three adequate shots, but even with a drive of 300-plus yards one would have to hit a career second shot absolutely straight, all carry, to get home in two.

The 585-yard seventh hole boasts Hell's Half Acre, considered the largest sand trap in the world, an acre and a half of the most unholy-looking territory this side of the Badlands. It stretches across the entire fairway from about 270 to 370 yards out, and men have been known to disappear here for hours. Once across, the golfer must contend with an approach to a peninsula of putting surface that juts out into a huge estuary of sand.

Pine Valley's four par-3s, collectively, are unmatched for variety and pure splendor. Any one would be the showcase of most courses. Except for No. 5, they provide no safe tee shots except onto the green. The long-iron third hole is surrounded by a sea of sand. The 10th, a 9-iron pitch, features Satanic bunkering. The 14th, a middle-iron shot, nestles between forest and lake.

The fifth hole is one of the most dramatic one-shot holes anywhere. One aims over a narrow lake to an open green 226 yards away. The terrain slopes sharply down to the water about 100 yards from the tee, and then the far slope rises to fearsome bunkers 50 yards in front of the green. Forest closes in on all sides. Standing on the tee with a 1-iron or 3-wood can be the loneliest experience imaginable. The hole has no tricks, and even allows a generous margin of error to be short. But don't hit it off line.

One of the popular refrains at Pine Valley is that at the fifth, "only God can make three." The Almighty has company, to be sure, but all of Pine Valley's par-3s have brought good men to their knees. Gene Littler, in a televised match with Byron Nelson, caught one just a little off line at the fifth, watched his ball tumble down the steep ridge at the right of the green, and eventually scrambled for a 7. The 14th was the scene of the most catastrophic shotmaking in Pine Valley's 56-year history. It was there that John Brooks, a low-handicap player, took 44 blows to negotiate its mountainous, jungle-bestrewn, lake-guarded 185 yards, a score that stands as the single-hole record, if you go for that sort of thing.

Pine Valley is not really the demon it is made out to be in these yarns, however. A great course, believes Pinehurst's respected president, Richard Tufts, should yield to a great round of golf.

Scores would indicate that Pine Valley is such a course. The record in competition is 67, by club member George Rowbotham, while the four-round mark is 286 (71 – 69 – 71 – 75) set by Craig Wood. Nicklaus and Ted Turner, the club's professional before Fazio, have posted 66 in informal rounds when tee and pin positions were at less than maximum severity. But the record shows that no one has ever given Pine Valley's par 70 a battering.

There have been some sensational starts, the most recent made in 1968 by Major Tom Fotheringham, then captain of Great Britain's Royal and Ancient Golfing Society. Forced to start at the short 10th because the course was crowded, the Major put his first shot at Pine Valley straight in the hole. "Of course, you will keep the ball as a memento of this historic ace," a friend suggested afterwards. "Oh dear, no," the Major replied. "I put it in the water at 16."

The best round by a first-timer was 67, scored by a British naval officer who was warming up for the club's annual Crump Memorial Tournament, named after the late George Crump who created Pine Valley. In the competition next day, he was unable to break 90. The most popular piece of local folklore has J. Wood Platt, a gifted amateur of the Bobby Jones era, opening his round with 3, 2, 1, 3 — two birdies and two eagles — and then repairing to the bar. He failed to emerge to finish the round.

One must play Pine Valley the same way a porcupine courts its mate — very carefully. In a professional tournament, Ed Dudley shot 68 in the first round and followed with 77 and 85. One player, who scored 79 his first time around, came back the next day with 98. "I was fine until I found out where all the trouble is," he wailed. Bill Campbell, the former National Amateur champion and Walker star, tells of his first experience in the Crump tournament. "In one match, I scored seven 3s in 10 holes and closed out my match on 13. I thought I really had Pine Valley's number. The next day, Bill Hyndman beat me 7 and 5. We walked in from the same place I had won the day before, but if I had finished the round I would have scored in the mid-80s. Pine Valley tests the mind as well as the stroke. You must think well, and you can never make the mistake of trying to steer the long shot."

This demand for mental exercise is not the only reason Pine Valley is celebrated. Its quality and character stand as a bastion against the "mischievous tendencies" of modern course design that tradition-minded architects warned about years ago. The notion that length and huge greens make for testing golf has spawned a rather dreary assemblage of courses of little distinction, monotonous replicas of one another. If it is true that life rebels at conformity, it is not hard to see why we react with interest and excitement to a golf course that is imaginative, thought-provoking, appealing to the eye and challenging. A truly testing course should demand consideration, not merely muscle, on every shot, and will offer the opportunity of testing every club in the bag and every type of shot.

From beginning to end, Pine Valley can hardly be faulted on any of these counts. Its greens are large and true, and not so fast as to discourage bold putting. Yet they present varying degrees of slope that demand correct reading and stroking. Visually the course stirs the blood; there is scarcely a hole that does not present a memorable image.

The first hole is a splendid opener, a 427-yard dogleg that allows absolutely no wayward flighting of the approach shot. It is a shade tougher than one might prefer, but it properly sets the tone for what is to follow. The 424-yard 18th is a solid finishing hole that looks from a high plateau across the barrens to the fairway below, guarded by water and sand on the right and thick woods on the left. The approach must clear water and a series of bunkers gouged in front of the huge, raised putting surface where three-putts are as regular as the sunrise.

A great test of golf should be a little like an honest judge: no bribes accepted. Pine Valley is like that. For all of its lurking danger and uncompromising retribution, it is a course one plays with relish, where pars are collected gratefully and where birdies are small treasures to be hoarded against one's next visit.

Workers, Arise! Shout Fore
Alistair Cooke

Millions of television viewers of "Masterpiece Theatre" will confirm that Alistair Cooke is a master of the spoken word. So will I. A slightly lesser known fact is that he is equally as talented sitting before a typewriter as he is sitting before an audience. His printed efforts incorporate the same enthralling wit and charm as does his urbane presence before the camera. And well they should. As a former long-time correspondent for the Manchester Guardian and the BBC, and the author of half a dozen books, Cooke is a proven master of the written word.

He also is a golfer and a golf follower who, his schedule permitting, makes the annual pilgrimage to Augusta, Georgia, for the playing of the Masters every April. He has contributed to the game as a spokesman for the United States Golf Association in pointing out — on television, naturally — some of the courtesies a golfer extends to his playing companions.

I have selected "Workers, Arise! Shout Fore" from one of Cooke's books, The Americans, for obvious reasons. The article concerns a golf course my son Bobby and I were commissioned to build in Russia. The project elicited world-wide interest as it was to have been the first golf course ever to be built in that country. Unfortunately, it is still on the drawing board.

Regardless, the words and wit of Alistair Cooke were never more in evidence than in his most amusing treatment of the possibilities of such an undertaking. The article, which was broadcast to England on December 27, 1974, was one of fifty talks of life and times which make up the contents of The Americans.

THERE IS SOMETHING I ought to talk about and something I must talk about. What I ought to talk about is the end of the annual General Assembly of the United Nations, a leaden piece of Christmas cake I have obediently chewed on for the past thirty-odd years. What I must tell you about is an encounter I recently had with the Russians that is altogether cockeyed and hilarious, but it is not without deep significance of a ritual kind. Let us skip the cake and come to the icing.

A few weeks ago I was staying in San Francisco, and I had a call one morning asking me to lunch with the Russian Consul General and his deputy. The invitation came from an unlikely host, a friend, a lawyer, an affable and fastidious gent, a Republican, and a first-rate golfer to whom the great game is not only a major exercise in military strategy and tactics but also a minor rehearsal of the Ten Commandments. He is, indeed, the chairman of the championship committee — and will without doubt soon become the president — of the United States Golf Association. His pairing with the Russian Consul General seemed improbable in the extreme. Where, I asked, shall we meet? "At the golf club, of course," was his mad reply. But why, why? "It is very important," he said, "I should surmise that the Consul General is coming under orders, and the whole point of the lunch is to talk golf." This was like being invited by a rabbi to lunch with the Pope to discuss stud poker. I accepted instantly.

The co-host was a young American, a boyish type, who is associated with his famous father in the most successful golf-architecture firm on earth. Golf architecture is the art and science of designing and building golf courses, and it involves much knowledge of landscape, soils, grasses, water drainage, engineering, meteorology, and sometimes — I feel — black magic. Let us call the young man Mr. Jones, for that happily is his name.

It seems he had recently got back from Moscow, where he and his father had responded to what must have sounded like a joke more unlikely than the reason for our lunch: a call from the Mayor of Moscow to consider building the first Russian golf course. The impulse, apparently, had come from a Soviet diplomat who had been exposed to the decadent West and had become one maniacal golfer. This in itself should give us pause. I should have guessed that any Russian who had yielded to such a capitalist diversionary activity as golf would have been, on his first homecoming, bundled off to Siberia, where he'd have been condemned to play golf with a red ball and a snow sled. But he was a close friend of the Mayor of Moscow. When he returned from a foreign, Western, post, he came into the airport carrying a golf bag. The customs men — as also, I imagine, the military and the narcotics squad — examined the weaponry, but reluctantly gave him the benefit of his diplomatic passport. Somehow the man sold the Mayor of Moscow on the idea of a city — public, of course — golf course. I don't suppose things rested there. The matter went up to the Kremlin. And, from all I could gather, Mr. Brezhnev gave the nod.

Well, we sat down to lunch, and the Consul General — a stocky man in the regulation Sears Roebuck suit — turned out to have a puckish humor. When we asked him if the Russians would take to golf, he said: "I think, because, you see, the Russian people like quick games." Somebody said, "Like chess." He came back on the hop: "Yes, we like a quick win." He plainly and admittedly knew nothing. But he asked everything. And to help him with the rudiments — of building rather than playing — young Mr. Jones put on a lantern lecture, with color slides showing rice paddies in Bangkok being transformed — slide by slide — into a bulldozed mess, then into terraced ground, then into ground being planted with gravel and soil and seed, and eventually emerging as a pastoral golf hole. Through a series of other slides we went to Hawaii and Florida and Scandinavia and, in the end, to the five sites around Moscow from which they will choose the one on which to build the course.

After that, the Consul General was given a lesson in weaponry. ("Golf," said Winston Churchill, "is a game whose aim is to hit a very small ball into an even smaller hole, with weapons singularly ill-designed for the purpose.") We went off in electric carts, like a little motorized battalion, to the eleventh tee on the noble San Francisco Golf Club course, a swaying landscape of lush green meadows flanked with towering cypresses and pine and occasional stands of eucalyptus.

The eleventh hole is a par three: that is to say, you are required to hit the green with your first shot and then sink the ball with two putts.

Our lawyer host, Mr. Frank (Sandy) Tatum, straightened his waistcoat (all *ex officio* members of the United States Golf Association board are very sensitive to the ancient amenities and insist on playing in ties and waistcoats, like the respectable Scots in the old prints). Offhand, I would bet that this Tatum, on that hole, would hit the green ninety-nine times in every hundred. He hit about six inches behind the ball, which rose in an unsteady arc and landed about 150 yards away, well short of a cavernous bunker. "Dear me," he said with splendid restraint.

"So," said the deputy consul (a pretty fresh type, I thought), "the first pancake is never any good." Ignoring this gem of Russian folk wisdom, Mr. Tatum set up another ball, and this time was comfortably on the green. Now, with many open-handed gestures and facetious bows, the Consul General was motioned to "have a go." He took off his jacket, looked down at the ball, gripped the club with all ten fingers (the so-called baseball grip, which about one professional in a thousand uses). His two hands were far apart. He missed the ball at the first swipe, but at the second it fell just a little short of Tatum's first effort. There was general applause. "A natural talent," purred the gallant Mr. Tatum. "Please!" said the Consul General.

Then the deputy had a go, and he slithered the ball about thirty yards along the ground. "That deputy," one of our group whispered, "he sure knows what he's doing." Well, then we all departed for the clubhouse, had our pictures taken, and the Consul General was presented, by young Mr. Jones, with a copy of an article I had once written on the origins of golf. Mysterious, this. "Why?" I asked young Jones. He looked for a second over his shoulder. "Don't you see," he hissed, "it supports the main argu-

ment?" And what would that be? "What we kicked around at lunch."

I realized then why I had been seated at lunch next to the Consul General. He had dropped several uncomfortable hints that he knew golf was a rich man's hobby, and I sensed that Moscow has asked him to check on this repulsive legend. I hastened to disabuse him with — young Jones later assured me — deeply moving eloquence. "No, no," I said, "that used to be so long ago, even then only in England and America, never in Scotland." I painted a picture, all the more poignant for being true, of poor little boys going off with their sticks and paying a few pennies to play some of the most hallowed courses on earth. "In Scotland," I said, "the people learn to play golf as simply as they learn to drink tea. And St. Andrews, which is the Vatican — pardon me, the Kremlin — of golf is a public course. On Sundays they close it so that little old ladies and dogs and babies can frolic — can walk around — for it is a public park *absolutely for the people*." "No?" said the Consul General. "Yes," I said.

"What," he asked, "will our people do, will they succeed at this sport?" No question, I said, "ten years from now" — we were well along with the vodka martinis — "I swear to you the British or American Open champion" — ("Open? What means this open?") — "the golf champion of Britain or America will be a Russian. After all, not so many years ago you sent a Russian basketball team, and Americans shook with laughter. Until you wiped the floor with both the Americans and the Canadians."

"Wiped?"

"Beat, trounced, massacred, defeated!"

"It is so," said the Consul, looking gloomily into his vodka.

"Very well, then," I went on, "maybe the big switcheroo will come sooner then ten years. Maybe four, five years from now, there will be a match between the best player in the world, Jack Nicklaus, and Nicholas the Third."

"There was never any Nicholas the Third," said the knowing Deputy.

"But there will be," I cried, "and he will win!"

"Iss possible?"

"Is certain."

I went back to town feeling I had done creditably on my first assignment as ambassador without portfolio. There were, of course, certain little nuisances: of having to learn to play the game (from whom?), to find courses to learn it on, pros willing to spend a couple of years teaching the first Russian golfer how, for God's sake, to hit a golf ball straight. I thought of Nicklaus, at the age of eight, going on the practice tee every day for a year to have his head gripped for an hour on end by the hand of an assistant pro so he could learn to keep his head still. Perhaps I should have stretched the apprenticeship period to ten or twenty years.

Still, if they get around to building the Jones course, I like to imagine Mr. Brezhnev or his successor, or *his* successor, standing on the first tee and approaching a ribbon with a mighty pair of shears. He will carry in his hand a note or two from our San Francisco Summit, and he will proclaim to a vast assembly of the peoples of all the Russias: "So! I have the extremely great honor to say to the citizens of our Soviet Socialist Republics—let us begin to play Goalf! The pipple's sport!"

The Masters Is Made in Japan
Richard W. Johnston

"The Masters Is Made in Japan" is included in this collection not because of its several references to me and the role I played in helping to stage the initial Taiheiyo — Pacific — Masters in October, 1972. It is included because it is a brilliant account of the first big-money tournament ever played in Japan and the remarkable impact it had on golf in that country. It was a tournament which proved that, given the right incentives, established American tour players would make the long hop across the Pacific to play in Japan. Their participation triggered a series of rich tournaments, which now constitute a late-season schedule that is attracting more and more competitors.

The editors of Sports Illustrated must have recognized the potential of the Taiheiyo Masters when they went to considerable expense to dispatch Richard W. Johnston from his home in Hawaii to cover the event. Johnston, a former managing editor of the magazine, had retired from that post to less-demanding assignments as a Special Correspondent. He did a masterful job of putting everything relating to the tournament into its proper perspective, despite the obvious language barrier and a rule which barred him from entering the clubhouse. Another American writer, hearing of Johnston's plight, rescued him from the confinement of the press tent where his only company was about two hundred Japanese golf writers and cameramen who spoke a language which Johnston did not understand.

Despite these difficulties, Johnston was able to get his story. It is one of the best I ever have read. Besides serving as a clear insight into the "anatomy of a tournament," it includes every aspect of the competition from the caddies to the condition of the course and the weather. It even includes a prediction which time since has fulfilled, proving that Dick Johnston was as able a forecaster as he was a writer.

EVER SINCE 1945 the Japanese, denied the privilege (and the expense) of preparing for World War III, have worked indefatigably at winning World War II. First came the transistors. Then Nikon. Then stereo. Then Sony. Then Toyota, Datsun and Subaru. Now, abetted as usual by U.S. interests, they have decided to capture golf, partly by seduction and partly by taking another foreign product and doing it better than its inventors. Their chosen instrument is a soon-to-be-refined replica of the Masters championship at Augusta, and they already can boast not one but two Bob Joneses—Robert Trent Jones, that is, and his son Bob Jr., both golf course architects. In fact, the tournament was Bob Jr.'s idea.

The campaigning began last week at the Sohbu Country Club, a Jones-polished, 45-hole spa an hour southeast of Tokyo, in Chiba prefecture. The event was the first Taiheiyo (Pacific) Club Masters championship, and for openers the sponsors put up $300,000 in prize money. This did not make it the first $300,000 tournament—Dow Jones in 1970 was, and everyone knows what happened to the U.S. economy after that—but it offered several things Dow Jones did not: top first-place money of $65,000, no cut after 36 holes, $1,000 for every entrant who finished the 72 holes, $2,000 each day for low score and a $10,000 bonus to anyone who made a hole in one on the 16th. Nor was that all. U.S. pros were promised free transportation from San Francisco to Japan and back for themselves and their wives. Similar offers went to other countries, Australia and England among them. Oh, yes—are you ready for this, golfers? Free hotel, free ground transportation, free meals and free booze also were included. No pearls—but this was only the first year.

Well, Jack Nicklaus wasn't ready for it and neither were Arnold Palmer, Doug Sanders, Bobby Nichols, Bob Charles, Sam Snead, Tommy Aaron, Julius Boros or Frank Beard. No matter. Really. None of these players actually had promised to come, and it is understandable that Taiheiyo, in its enthusiasm, mistook signs of interest for assurances. Anyway, all of these no-shows—even Arnie—are now more famous in Japan than they were before because each had

his picture (in color yet) along with a brief biography in the Taiheiyo Masters program. Palmer got even more. The club reproduced his letter of regret, also in color, and slipped it into each program.

If Taiheiyo was dismayed by these postprinting defections, the club was not deterred. Its leaders had one firm promise—Supermex was coming. "Jack Nicklaus is a samurai," one of them told Bob Jr., "but Lee Trevino is a samurai, too." They also had reason to believe that a whole galaxy of slightly lesser U.S. samurais would be on hand.

And they were right, although a good many of the guests were somewhat mystified as to the identity of their host. In Honolulu Bob Rosburg, pausing en route for a couple of practice rounds, said, "I don't quite know what Taiheiyo is. But when the trip is free and everybody who finishes gets $1,000 regardless of his score, this seems like one tournament you can't lose, even if you don't win." One of the mysteries, at least to the Americans, was the fact that the Taiheiyo Club Masters was going to be played at the Sohbu Country Club. Why not at Taiheiyo's own course? Simple: it doesn't have one.

The Taiheiyo Club is in reality one of the many financial arms of the Heiwa Soga Bank. It was organized early this year to develop leisure facilities, not only in Japan but in such distant places as Jakarta, Bangkok and Alaska. Although it still has no golf club of its own in Tokyo, it is building an 18-hole course and marina in Guam and a 36-hole course and marina in Korea. It is also investigating possible investment in existing facilities in San Francisco and Los Angeles. The Joneses, *père et fils*, got into the act last March when Taiheiyo consulted them on recommendation of another consortium for whom they had designed Golf 72 at a mountain resort east of Tokyo. As Bob Jr. remembers it, he said, in effect, "Why don't you start off your program with a bang by staging the biggest and richest golf tournament ever held?"

The Heiwa Soga Bank gave this a lot of thought—three days' worth, to be precise—and then said yes. Almost before they knew it Bob and Bob Jr. were at work selecting the best 18 of 27 holes that lie on one side of Sohbu's elaborate complex in Chiba. Getting Sohbu was no problem. The bank owns it, too. Sohbu's 2,400 golf-crazy members, whose memberships are currently valued at five million yen (about $16,500) apiece, were more than willing to sacrifice some of their playing time for the glory of it all. In June the Joneses came back to polish the chosen 18 holes. Meanwhile, Taiheiyo emissaries had infiltrated the U.S., notebooks and invitations in hand — even visiting, by God, the Masters itself. If Japan has a national motto, it might well be: first do it their way, and then do it right.

Possibly to avoid boring their prospective guests, the Taiheiyo people didn't get into the intricacies of Japanese expansion in their sales talks. They simply stated the Taiheiyo Masters' aims: "To promote international goodwill through the golf tournament, to help promote the golf world, to contribute to improving the art of golf, to work for bringing up the sound rising generation and to resolve a part of income resulting from the golf tournament into the social public." Who could knock that? Taiheiyo also mentioned that His Imperial Highness, Prince Takamatsu, was the club's honorary governor. Has Apawamis got a prince? Has Westchester? Baltusrol? Even Augusta? The Japanese also, naturally enough, mentioned the prizes and the perquisites.

And so it came to pass that on Oct. 1 and 2 Japan Air Lines planes began crossing the Pacific with an array of U.S. pros — Gay Brewer, Bert Yancey, Tom Shaw, Dan Sikes, Billy Casper, Phil Rodgers, Bob Murphy, Orville Moody, Gene Littler, Dave Marr, Homero Blancas, George Archer, Charles Coody, Al Geiberger, Bob Goalby and Ray Floyd, to name a few of the 38. Not to mention some Aussies: Bruce Crampton, Bruce Devlin and a PGA rookie named David Graham, who had won the 1972 Cleveland Open. And wives. And at least one child, Crampton's 3-1/2-year-old tow-haired son Jay. But no Trevino.

They landed at Haneda Airport in Tokyo to be greeted by the world's most sulphurous smog, although buses provided by Taiheiyo quickly carried them beyond it to Chiba city. (Except for a very few days of the year residents of the capital of the Land of the Rising Sun have to drive outside Tokyo to make sure the sun is still rising.)

Whatever misgivings the players may have had on the subsequent drive from Chiba to the Sohbu Country Club, a 45-minute ride past seemingly endless construction, interspersed with stores and houses dismally clad in corrugated metal, with only an occasional dusty pagoda roof to remind one that this was indeed Japan, were dissipated by the course itself. The clubhouse is a long, handsome building with a beamed dining room overlooking a fountain and four putting greens. Beyond it lie fairways so carefully nurtured and delicately manicured that they resemble greens on some U.S. courses. Almost without exception the rolling fairways are lined with graceful groves of cedar and pine, and the greens look as velvety as pool tables. Also awaiting the visitors, of course, were Japan's celebrated girl caddies, their heads swathed in the voluminous white scarves that make them look like golfing nuns. After his first practice round Jerry McGee — asked if he minded having a girl transport his clubs — exclaimed, "Mind! Is there a two-stroke penalty for falling in love with your caddie?" An amused onlooker said, "Tomorrow you will see a 50-kilo girl carrying a 17-kilo golf bag for a 100-kilo golfer." (Not so — the girls were allowed to use two-wheeled carts during competition.)

On Tuesday night the Taiheiyo Masters tournament suddenly developed a kind of soap-opera quality — Mexican soap opera, at that. Trevino, poised to leave San Francisco, had been called home to El Paso by the illness of his wife and child. Would he come to Japan? Would he not? There was consternation among the sponsors. Without samurai Supermex, would anybody come to the tournament? As one functionary wistfully remarked, "I am sure Gibby Gilbert is a fine golfer, but he is not exactly a household word in Japan."

Wednesday, a sunlit day with a light breeze, the psychological clouds rolled back, too. Supermex was coming. And early on Thursday, a damp, dark, muggy morning, he was there, his skin a sort of gray-brown from sleeplessness and fatigue, but his red shirt festive and his sudden smile infectious as ever. He attracted most of what gallery there was—perhaps 2,000—as he teed off, attended by red-jacketed officials, green-coated marshals and the girl caddies, flowering now in military-looking, olive-drab uniforms, their scarves replaced by green and white kepis, their hands demurely encased in white gloves. For a man who had never even seen the course, let alone played it, Trevino did well. After a two-over-par 37 on the first nine, he came home in 34—two under—to match the club's 71 par.

Others, however, did better. Phil Rodgers, in with a 66, was asked if the greens were bumpy (there had been a few complaints). "Man," Rodgers said, "I never think they're bumpy when my putts keep rollin' in." Gardner Dickinson, who had a 75, said later, "It's a real good course, but walking from the greens to the next tee is like playing nine extra holes." (Bob Jones conceded that it sometimes was a long trip, the result of choosing the best 18 of 27 and phasing out intervening holes.) Mostly, however, there was praise. Bruce Crampton said, "I wish we could roll these fairways up and take them along with us."

The oppressive Thursday heat presaged a natural phenomenon: on Friday everybody learned that Typhoon No. 22 had hit the tip of the Chiba Peninsula (the Japanese are pragmatic about typhoons—they give them numbers instead of girls' names). Sohbu was only on the fringe of it, but even so the weather was formidable. The winds blew erratically, up to 30 mph, and they brought continuous cold and slashing rain. (A few old Japan hands wondered if Amaterasu-Ohmikami, the sun goddess, had sent a *kamikaze* to repel this latest invasion. Once before this divine wind, which Shinto legend says saved Japan from Mongolian conquest in the 13th century, was delivered at the wrong time, possibly because of bad intelligence. It hit Okinawa on Oct. 2, 1945, and it would have sunk the entire U.S. invasion fleet if the atomic bomb had not intervened.)

Whatever the source of the weather, it sent many scores skyrocketing. Trevino himself had to settle for another par, but a few golfers seemed to thrive on adversity—notably that little-known Aussie, David Graham. Graham had shot a 67 on the first day, but it went almost unnoticed. Now, in the wind and rain, he did it again to card a 134 and lead at the halfway mark. Gay Brewer, also obscured but hardly awed by the Trevino melodrama, came in with a 138—an opening-day 67 plus a par 71. Afterward Graham, who is still understandably annoyed that he had to spend two years clearing the PGA school to play in the U.S. despite his status as an Australian-Asian and World Cup star, said, "Remember one thing. It is the players who make these tournaments possible, not the sponsors."

As though to prove that the Pacific Masters can provide any and every kind of weather, Saturday dawned opalescently clear—even in Tokyo. Typhoon No. 22 had blown the smog away and Sohbu glistened under a bowl of Maxfield Parrish blue. But about all the good weather proved was that both Graham and Brewer are men for all seasons. Brewer finished at 205, eight under par, and Graham was right behind him at 206. Another Aussie, Graham Marsh, was next at 209. Gene Littler, making a grand recovery from cancer, was tied for fourth at 211.

On Sunday the tournament came down to a battle between the husky, amiable Brewer, who played with implacable solemnity, and the slight, wiry and volatile Graham. The day was sweet and clear as sake as they moved around Sohbu's stately course: even, exchanging the lead, then even again. Coming into 18 they were both eight under, but Brewer had a chance at a $65,000, 10-foot birdie putt. The ball halted two inches from the cup.

The playoff had been advertised as sudden death, but it was death by torture instead, a three-hole playoff over the 16th, 17th and 18th holes. In real sudden death Brewer would have won on 17 when Graham got a bogey, but there was still the 18th, and Brewer once again found himself with a 10-footer for par and the money. For the second time the ball trembled to a halt at the cup's edge. Bogey—and back to 16, this time for the real thing.

The 16th—a 214-yard par 3—requires a carry across a ravine bottomed on the left by a lily pond. Both Brewer and Graham missed the green, but it took Graham three more shots to get down. Brewer chipped stiff to the pin for a par 3—and had his biggest pot, plus $2,000 extra won Saturday for low score of the day. Brewer's victory in the 1967 Augusta Masters undoubtedly is still his No. 1 thrill in sports, but Sunday's $67,000 win may seem more memorable to the Internal Revenue Service. No other golfer has ever won as much money in four days. Not many have withstood as much pressure.

Thus ended the first Pacific Masters and thus began—maybe—a new era. The Taiheiyo Club, which had spent more than $1 million on prizes, preparation of the course and transport, care and feeding of players, was happy. So were about 27,000 Japanese fans who had paid 130 million yen ($433,000) to see the tournament. Taiheiyo saw the deficit as well worthwhile to publicize and establish its local and overseas leisure expansion plans and to bring Japan into the forefront of international golf.

The tournament did one more thing by providing the format from which a genuine international Japanese superstar could emerge. His name is Masashi Ozaki, and he is called Jumbo, not only because he is big and strong and hits the ball like Jack Nicklaus but because he is a superlative golfer from tee to green. "Jumbo can play anywhere—he and Nicklaus would be a hell of a match," Trevino said before leaving. How good is Ozaki really? Well, good enough to beat everybody in the tournament except Brewer, Graham and Charlie Coody.

Unless the Komiyama family, which controls the Heiwa Soga Bank and its many subsidiaries, has an enormous change of heart, the Pacific Masters is here to stay. After all, they can hardly disappoint the honorary chairman, Prince Takamatsu, can they? Will the foreign players return? Trevino, who finished 12th, told all Japan by radio and on TV that he would come back "to show you why I'm supposed to be one of the world's best players." And as for Gay Brewer, you better believe it.

Is it possible then for the Taiheiyo Masters to become an annual event with the stature of the U.S. Masters? Don't bet against it. Remember Nikon and Sony and Toyota—and perhaps even Wankel, which powers Mazda in Japan and is moving in and up, and giving Detroit new headaches.

Watch out, Augusta.

Ingenuity at Akron
John Stuart Martin

I think I can say without contradiction that the most significant change made in golf equipment since the inception of the game was the development of the wound ball, the steel shaft notwithstanding. Excluding such prehistoric objects as a round stone or a beechwood burl, there actually have been only three kinds of balls. The "feathery," which was used when the game was formalized in the eighteenth and early nineteenth centuries, was a peck of feathers packed into a leather cover. It was hard as a rock, difficult to get airborne until it was scuffed, and worthless when it got wet. The "guttie," made from the sap of a tree, was a glob of gum which had to be carried in an ice bucket in hot weather to prevent it from being knocked out of round. It was a short-lived follower of the feathery.

The wound ball had none of the problems of its predecessors and, although it has been around longer than any other item of standard equipment found in a golf bag, it remains the most important. Solid and two-piece balls introduced in recent years are actually throw-backs to both the feathery and the guttie, although their ingredients are much different.

Since it emerged on the golf scene around the turn of the century, the wound ball has been reduced and enlarged, its cover markings converted from convex to concave and from mesh to dimples, and its colour changed from white to orange and yellow; but basically it remains the same. It is an all-rubber ball except for its centre. It is the only ball the pros play despite the introduction in recent years of a plastic counterpart which defies destruction.

John Stuart Martin, a founder and former editor of Time *magazine and a one-arm golfer from Princeton, has detailed the evolution of the golf ball, including the amazing man responsible for conceiving the idea of the wound ball and the mechanical genius who made it possible. They were responsible for the biggest giant step in the progress of the game.*

THE GREAT BLIZZARD of 1888, three nights and three days of snowfall from March 11 to 14 that lethally buried the entire East, still looms like a grim tombstone in American history. Little noted at the time, but of far more lasting human significance, was a much smaller, happier event which took place in rural Yonkers, N. Y., exactly three weeks prior.

Washington's Birthday was balmy that year, and on it John ("Jock") Reid, a transplanted Scotsman who had made a modest fortune in plumbing fixtures (J. L. Mott Iron Works), entertained some gentleman friends at his Yonkers country home. He had planned his party for March or April, but the fine weather and his impatience to spring a surprise spurred him to advance the date.

The fact is Jock Reid was a "carrier" of that irrepressible parasite which was destined to infest his entire adopted country—the golf bug. A wiry, whiskery, tireless little sportsman who was never quite fulfilled by all his shooting, riding, and tennis, he had commissioned his fellow countryman, Rob Lockhart, to bring back from a visit to their home heath of Dumfermline a set of golf clubs and a few dozen guttie balls. Rob had obliged, and the object of Jock's holiday gathering was to demonstrate his wondrous Scottish playthings to his sporting cronies.

This he did so persuasively on that birthday of America's "father," in a cow pasture across the road from his mansion, that in time Jock Reid would be hailed as "The Father of American Golf."

The title is as debatable, if not quite so far-fetched, as Col. Abner Doubleday's to the paternity of baseball, or Adam's to the siring of all mankind. Yet it serves a like purpose, for every human pastime has to "start" sometime and somewhere. And the St. Andrews Golf Club (of Yonkers) which Jock Reid and his friends organized later in that year of the Great Blizzard was definitely germinal. More demonstrably than any other early claimant it precipitated that fallout of golf balls which, sporadic at first and confined to rich men's acreages, has swirled up into today's white maelstrom of 10,000,000 *dozen* golf balls flying off the clubs of 10,000,000

enthusiasts day in and day out the year long all over the continent.

The St. Andrews (Yonkers) Golf Club was moved and its layout altered four times before it took final root at Hastings-on-Hudson. Actually, it was preceded as an American ground where golf balls were formally struck, followed, cursed at, and prayed over by "courses" dating back a century and more.

A few incorrigible Tories laid out and played some golf holes in 1786 at Charleston, S. C., and at Savannah, Ga., in 1795. Large, muscular Charles Blair Macdonald of Chicago came home from his schooling in Scotland in 1875 and at once went to hitting balls into tin cans sunk on an old Civil War parade ground. (Other Chicagoans thought he was daft.) Even Kentucky (1883), West Virginia (1884), and New Hampshire (1885) have priority claims, to say nothing of Montreal (1873). And so, most definitely, has Foxburg, Pa., north of Pittsburgh at the junction of the Alleghany and Clarion Rivers. Here, in 1884, Joseph Micklen Fox of the old Philadelphia Quaker family laid out some holes on the lawns and meadows of his ancestral summer estate; and then, in 1887, designed a formal little nine-holer, complete with clubhouse (St. Andrews, Yonkers had but a tent), to which his neighbors came and played at $1 per annum. That Foxburg course has remained in continuous play ever since.

But St. Andrews (Yonkers) was closest to the country's financial, social, and sporting capital, whence its influence and traditions radiated soonest and widest. Within a very few months, similar playgrounds for men (and some women) of wealth, leisure and energy mushroomed on Long and Staten Islands, at Tuxedo, at Newport, in New Jersey, and around Boston and Philadelphia. The World's Fair of 1892 in Chicago brought some Britishers who helped bristling, dictatorial Charley Macdonald at last to establish golf near the Windy City, first at Lake Forest on Senator Farwell's lawn, then on a stock farm at Belmont, and finally on a grain acreage (the nation's first 18-holer) near Wheaton.

All the first sticks and balls had, of course, to be imported from Scotland and England; and then dozens of professionals to teach the game, to lay out courses, to make and repair more and more golf sticks, to mold and remold thousands of guttie balls. In 1894, after some intersectional squabbles over early rules and tournaments, the United States Golf Association was formed to govern the game country-wide. The speed of golf's ensuing growth in America can be judged by some turn-of-the-century estimates: 100,000 players on more than 500 courses spending about $10 millions per year on the game.

Under such boom conditions it is not surprising that accurate records on the priorities of golf's birth and rearing in America, and the hot arguments thereanent, were disregarded at the time. Nor are these pages any place to debate them. But this chapter will now describe in close focus our young country's first basic contribution to the old game. The place was Ohio, that lively mid-sister between the urbane East and brash West—more specifically, the cities of Cleveland and Akron. The year was 1898, just ten years after the Great Blizzard.

By that time, both these places had golf courses—Cleveland's at the fashionable east end of town on the Lake Erie shore front, Akron's in sheep meadows around the old homestead of the late Abolitionist John Brown in nearby Portage. No golfers emerged thereabouts of a caliber to compare with the top Easterners and Westerners, but two players there made greater golf history than all their contemporaries put together.

Like his father before him, a chunky, energetic Akron youth named Bert (for Bertram) Work labored in the B. F. Goodrich rubber factory at Akron, of which the main output was tires for bicycles and the newfangled motor cars; also overshoes, rubber blankets, raincoats, and support garments for ladies and gents. It also handled gutta percha, some of which it supplied in bulk to professionals and enthusiasts of the newly imported pasture pastime. It made up a certain number of guttie golf balls in molds of its own.

By 1898, Bert Work had shouldered to the top at the rubber plant, and had taken up golf as much for social as for business reasons. Through

it he had formed a close friendship with one of his bicycle tire customers, a young New England sportsman named Coburn Haskell who had come to Cleveland in 1892 and married an heiress, one of the Hanna girls.

Until this book, the annals of American sport were singularly and deplorably devoid of information about this figure who was to make such a lasting mark. All golfers are indebted to his daughter Gertrude Haskell (Mrs. Brigham) Britton of Cleveland, for the following filial memoir she has written expressly for these pages:

"Dad was born in Boston Dec. 31st, 1868, son of William Andrew and Mary Coburn Haskell. He was raised there and went to Harvard, for I don't know how long, but he didn't graduate. He joined a light opera company that went on tour with Gilbert & Sullivan operas.

"From pictures of him in his younger days I thought he was very handsome and dashing— dark wavy hair and a face full of character and humor. When I knew him he was in his forties and fifties and quite portly.

"His main interests were horses and books and shooting. He belonged to the Black Horse Troop in the National Guard, the Gentleman's Driving Club (amateur trotting horse races in 4-wheel carts, part of the Roadside Club at the Glenville track), and he was part owner of the Pastime Stables. Their most famous horse was Lee Axworthy, who held a world's record for stallions.

"He was a good shot and belonged to the Cedar Point Duck Club near Toledo, and enjoyed the shooting in Thomasville, Georgia—quail, dove, turkey.

"He had literary tastes—collected rare books, read a great deal, and also collected original illustrations, including works by N. C. Wyeth, Arthur Rackham, Cruikshank, etc.

"His obituary in the Cleveland *Press* (he died Dec. 14, 1922, of cancer), said:

Coburn Haskell was 54 and had been ill many months. He retired from the M. A. Hanna Co. about 20 years ago, and was well known as a sportsman and horseman. He was a member of the Pastime Stables. He invented the golf ball.... He was with a shipbuilding concern before going to the Hanna Co.

"It was American Shipbuilding, very briefly, I believe. Also, according to my cousin Livingston Ireland, his father R. L. Ireland and mine went into a bicycle manufacturing business together while they were still young bachelors. Evidently his business career lasted only about ten years in Cleveland, and terminated when my mother contracted T.B. and they lived in Switzerland for a while.*

"He married my mother, Mary Gertrude Hanna, on June 4th, 1895, three years after coming to Cleveland. His father was a friend of Howard Melville Hanna (who was her father, and a younger brother of Mark), and that is how they met. After Dad's retirement they lived in three places—next door to our present address in Cleveland, in Thomasville in the winter time, and Blue Hill, Maine, for part of the summer. As newlyweds, they rented their first house from John D. Rockefeller, Sr., with whom Dad often played golf.

"By the time I appeared, the golf ball story was that he was the poorest player in his foursome. He thought how nice it would be if he could invent a ball that would sail out beyond everyone else's drive at the first tee, to amaze them—so he did that, with Bert Work's help and connivance."

Stories differ as to just how these two contrasting characters, the sporting dilettante and the factory superintendent, did chance to contrive the golf ball's second revolution. A popular version is this:

*Not understood by his descendants (or this writer) is how or why Coburn Haskell has often been mistitled "Doctor." The Dunlop company's publicity department has even referred to him as "a designing dentist," possibly confusing him with a dentist who did invent the wooden tee-peg. A doctor of no kind was Coburn Haskell, honorary or otherwise, unless perhaps in fun as "Doc" to his cronies, for having made a major scientific advance, or for his solicitous vetting of his horses, dogs, children, and self (he suffered from gout).

One summer day Haskell called for Work at the Goodrich plant to play a round of golf at the Portage links. Delayed at his desk, Work suggested that Haskell take a stroll through the shops. There, on a work table, Haskell saw some piles of elastic thread which the company was trying to fabricate into garters and suspenders. Fingering the stuff, testing its resilience, Haskell (his mind on the coming game) realized that this was the same material (rubber) that went into tennis balls, which were so much bouncier than gutta percha golf balls. When he rejoined Work, Haskell suggested winding up some of that rubber yarn into a golf ball. Goodrich workmen took over and—lo!—the rubber-wound wonderball.

Years after his death Haskell's eldest daughter, Katherine H. Perkins, quoted her father as saying that he first spotted in Work's office "a scrap-basket full of elastic band waste, which he started to wind into a small ball. The ball had become quite sizeable before a slip of the thumb started it bounding across the room. He started on another ball, using more tension, and when Mr. Work appeared he said, 'If you would cover this ball with gutta percha for me, I believe I could win some golf matches.' Mr. Work was impressed with the demonstration of zip and bounce, and told Dad to go ahead and get the idea patented, and that he would put the problem of developing a machine up to his engineering staff. It all worked out...."

In a third version, recorded by the late Dr. William C. Geer, who was Bert Work's brother-in-law and the Goodrich vice president in charge of research, Haskell gave up trying to wind a ball himself, so "some skilled girls were called in.... The thread spheres were sent into the factory and covered with gutta percha in a hollow mold. Haskell could scarcely wait for a train to Cleveland to try the ball on his golf course [the Lake Shore Country Club]. He at once found it to be longer in drive and truer in putting...."

Far more circumstantial is an account, preserved unsigned in the Goodrich archives, written by someone in Atlanta*, after a party there

*Bob Jones believes that the author was his own Boswell, the late O. B. Keeler, famed sports writer.

56

evidently about 1920, at which Bertram Work, president of Goodrich, was the guest of honor:

"...Mr. Work's account of the way the Haskell ball was invented was one particular story I'll never forget.

"It was along in 1898, says Mr. Work, that Coburn Haskell...was sitting in Mr. Work's office...

" 'You ought to be doing something besides just playing golf,' he told Mr. Haskell. 'You've got a lot of ability being wasted. Go ahead and make two blades of grass grow somewhere, or something.'

" 'No thanks,' said Mr. Haskell. 'Golf is all I care about.'

"'Very well,' rejoined Mr. Work, 'make a better golf ball. Do something for the game, if you love it so much.'

"Now, that was a hunch. Mr. Haskell began to think. After some fairly profound cogitation he said, 'If a good rubber ball could be developed—solid rubber—it would increase the range of the shots.'

" 'Solid rubber won't do,' said Mr. Work, who knew as much about rubber as anybody in the world. 'Too soft. It would yield too much to the blow.'

" 'How about compressing the rubber?'

" 'Can't compress rubber, any more than you can water,' was the objection.

"Mr. Haskell pondered some more. Finally he said: 'Well, if you made the rubber in strips, and stretched the strips, and wound them into a ball in their stretched condition, you could get a ball as hard as you wanted, couldn't you?'

" 'NOW you have said something,' Mr. Work told him, and added that he had better get off his coat and waistcoat and prepare for toil. Mr. Work sent for a hank of rubber yarn, and Mr. Haskell set to work.

" 'It was a funny sight,' said Mr. Work reminiscently. 'There was Coburn Haskell, perspiring at every pore—it was a hot day—and winding away at the slowly growing core of stretched rubber strands. And just as he would get it about the size of a marble, the blamed thing would slip and the rubber yarn would fly about like a clock-spring released. And he would swear and scramble around on the floor and wind

it again, and then it would break loose once more.'

"Mr. Haskell, luckily for golf, was persistent, and toward evening he proudly and wearily presented to Mr. Work a fairly round ball of rubber strands, under considerable tension. It felt firm and solid. 'Now then,' said Mr. Work, 'this thing will have to be covered in some way. The first punch on the exposed strands will set the thing unravelling all over the place.'

"And that was Mr. Work's job. He evolved the cover, of gutta percha then, of balata now, and worked out a plan for heating a slab of 'gutty' and pressing it on to the first rubber core. And when that first ball was finished and painted, Mr. Haskell took it out to his golf club and teed it up, and summoned the professional, Joe Mitchell.

" 'Hit this ball for me,' he requested of Joe. The ball looked exactly like the usual ball, the cover having been pressed in the same mold, and Joe took his stance and walloped it with never a thought that he was assisting at the making of history.

"Out across the fairway of the first hole was a bunker which never had been carried by anybody. It was so far from the tee that only an occasional tremendous poke with the old 'gutty' would send the ball rolling into it, in dry weather. And it was right over the middle of that bunker that Joe's drive with the new ball sailed, high in the air, landing yards beyond.

"Joe Mitchell stood watching the ball with eyes and mouth wide open. Then he let out a yell and began a sort of dance. Then he began to implore Mr. Haskell to tell him if he was dreaming and if not, what was in that ball.

"So that's the way it started.... Mr. Haskell may have passed up the notion of making two blades of grass grow where one grew before, but look at what he did for the golfing duffer. He made a hundred thousand grow where one grew previously. And they still are growing."

None of the foregoing accounts gave credit to two Goodrich workmen who actually brought the Haskell ball out of the idea stage and into being.

Emmet R. Junkins is, at this writing, still alive at ninety in an Akron nursing home. It was he, not Haskell, who hand-wound the very first ball to be covered and tested — presumably the ball first driven by Joe Mitchell; and it was he who then taught some nimble-fingered girls how to carry on.

The second workman was John Gammeter, then the genius of Goodrich's tool shop. It was he who figured out a substitute for the girls.

As disclosed in 1951 by Kenneth Nichols of the Akron *Beacon Journal*: "He (Gammeter) was asked by Work if he could invent a machine to wind the balls. Gammeter shifted the wad of tobacco in his mouth and replied, 'Sure.' He was — and is — a sort of Dizzy Dean of mechanics, with full confidence in his own powers.

"Working in a locked room and with the utmost secrecy, Gammeter produced his machine. Its success depended on the use of a core, or center, on which to start the winding."

Before John Gammeter, neither Haskell nor Work had thought of this starting step, but they mentioned it when they applied for their patent on August 9, 1898.

What they claimed was "a new and useful improvement in Balls...for use especially in the game of golf." Letters Patent No. 622,834 were granted to them jointly on April 11 the following year. They described a ball of rubber thread "wound under tension...upon itself" or on "a central-core-section of relatively non-elastic material," and encased in a gutta or balata shell.

"(The ball) shall possess the essential qualities of lightness and durability and...the property of being comparatively non-resilient under the moderate impacts incident to its use, but highly resilient under the stronger impacts."

Translated from the meticulous prolixity of patentese, this language about "impacts" meant simply that the ball should fly swiftly off the club when hit hard, but not rebound too gaily when it struck the ground or was putted.

Two other essential characteristics of all rubber-wound balls to come were also mentioned: "...It is an essential feature...that the core shall closely fill the interior of the shell and desirable that (it) be confined therein under some compression."

No mention was made of any winding machine because, at the time of the ball patent application, John Gammeter had not yet unlocked his workroom door and brought forth the gadget that would truly and lastingly revolutionize golf. Without it, the hand-wound balls would have failed miserably, through their scarcity and eccentricity.

When Gammeter did show what he had wrought, eyebrows must have elevated. The thing was about three feet high and three feet long. It looked more complicated than a 365-day cuckoo clock. It contained more than fifty parts, most of them moving, which it took Goodrich's patent attorneys eight mechanical drawings and seven pages of patentese to describe.

There were "two rotating cord-winders mounted on two concentric circular tracks... on opposite sides of a circular frame...secured in a vertical position to a bed plate...Each track consists of a cylindrical flange...

"The proximate edges of each flange...and associated ring...are beveled, whereby there is formed a circumferential V-shaped groove which serves as one part of a ball-race, the other part...being formed by a V-shaped groove in ...the ring-shaped winders...mounted on ballbearings...These mesh with two pinions ...secured to the two concentric shafts...

"To these two shafts are respectively secured the beveled gears which engage...a beveled gear fast to the drive shaft...These two winder rings are rotated in opposite directions. Each...carries a spool whereon the cord to be used is wound. A needle is pivotally connected to each winder...to guide the cord into what I term the 'winding plane'...in which the cord is wound upon the ball...in a great circle.

"...The free ends of both needles lie close together, resting upon the ball...where they are held, as the ball grows in size, by the pull of the two cords which are being wound upon the ball...The tension device...is a small grooved sheave, rotatably mounted...It is subjected to more or less friction, tending to resist its rotation by means of a coiled spring...

"The ball is held in the axial line of the two winders...and it is turned to change its position by...two parallel rollers...The ball is held with its center in said winding plane between four rollers . . . mounted in pairs . . . These movements of the ball are alternated and thereby the ball . . . is constantly changing its position . . . with the result that the ball is wound into spherical form."

In other and fewer words, John Gammeter did it the hard way. Instead of spinning on just one he spun on two rubber threads at once, turning the ball constantly in place while applying the threads to it under tension, in a pattern for which his term "great circle" would become a key phrase in the industry.

The whole contraption whirred and growled and gently clanked. Ralph Perkins, who was to become one of Coburn Haskell's sons-in-law and who for a time worked in the Goodrich plant operating a Gammeter ball winder, later recalled: "Imagine, if you can, a machine that would produce a ball of equal and changing radii from a continuous rubber band under equal tension. If the ball ever escaped the four cylinders that kept it revolving, it flew around the shop in a dangerous and unpredictable manner!"

But the thing worked; and it would be years before other geniuses understood it, let alone improved upon it. Gammeter was awarded a patent April 10, 1900 (just 364 days after Haskell's) which he assigned to his employers, for whom it long earned royalties.

Until the Gammeter machine was completed, and duplicated many times, golf ball production at the Goodrich plant was painfully slow, limited to the digital efforts of Emmet Junkins' female task force. But even before mass production could be got rolling, the happy inventor displayed and dispensed his creations far and wide. In the Foreward to this book, Chick Evans relates one bit of Coburn Haskell's salesmanship, at the Edgewater club north of Chicago. Haskell was also a member of the Chicago Golf Club, where Jim Foulis was the presiding pro. And it was here that a grave deficiency of the early Haskell balls was accidentally discovered and remedied by Foulis.

The early Haskell was, as noted by Evans, "a fitful ball, going abruptly and irregularly." Although its gutta percha cover was pressed on in the same grooved molds as used for most gutties of the day, it exhibited the same tendency to duck and dart as the earliest smooth gutties had done, before they were grooved.

Jim Foulis happened to possess, and to prefer, a guttie mold of the improved brambled "Agrippa" pattern, which raised blackberry bumps on the ball instead of graving narrow, shallow meridians. One day in his shop at Wheaton, when he was remolding a batch of old gutties, Foulis chanced (without noticing it) to include and to bramble a used Haskell. In play, this ball performed so prodigiously that Foulis cut it open, and discovered what had happened. Unwittingly he had given the Haskell ball the kind of surface its liveliness required to make it fly far and true. Thereafter, all early Haskells were called in to be brambled, and the ball of the future was truly on its way.

America's Guest
Dan Jenkins

I have found that one of the postdated joys of attending any major golf tournament is to pick up a copy of Sports Illustrated *a few days later and read an account of the tournament by Dan Jenkins. A transplanted Texan from Fort Worth who easily fits into the New York scene as a smart, savvy personality, Dan has brought wit and a special kind of irreverence to writing about golf. His quiet, unobtrusive manner belies one of the most uproarious talents I've ever had the pleasure of knowing.*

A near-scratch golfer and a former captain of the Texas Christian University golf team, Dan's broad knowledge of the game is well founded. So is his uncanny sense for the unusual and the amusing, which any reader of the magazine will attest.

Dan has not confined his talent to writing only about golf, either. He has several books to his credit including Semi-Tough, *which made the bestseller list for weeks on end. It was Jenkins at his best, a tongue-in-cheek treatment of pro football done in the Texas idiom of which he is a master. Hollywood made a movie of it starring Burt Reynolds, and the success of that first novel, I am sure, inspired Dan to write* Dead Solid Perfect *and* Baja Oklahoma.

Jenkins's bright, brash style is evident in everything he writes. "The Dogged Victims of Inexorable Fate" — a title inspired by a phrase from the writings of Bobby Jones — is no exception. It is from a collection of articles Dan wrote for Sports Illustrated *in the sixties which did much to establish his reputation as a humorous writer and as an astute observer of golf and the players and personalities connected with the game.*

"America's Guest" describes one of the real characters on the golf scene. In the hands of a writer less skilful than Jenkins, George Low would have to be characterized as indescribable. Not so with Dan, who brings Low and his unique association with golf to life in this remarkably accurate portrait.

IN PROFESSIONAL tournament golf the club-house veranda can often be a noteworthy blend of rumble seat, wax museum, promenade deck, theater wings and courthouse steps. As the tour moves from one Crystal Rancho Happy Avocado Creek Country Club to another, the verandas undergo some severe botanical changes — a palm will beget a pine, or a eucalyptus will beget an oak — but the human plantlife will remain practically changeless. Except for the occasional intrusion of a spectator fully equipped with binoculars, periscope, chair seat, transistor, program, pairing sheet, camera and hot dog, and the almost invariable presence of at least one young female in form-fitting slacks, huge dark glasses and a straw bonnet, the regular veranda standers comprise a remarkably homogeneous and identifiable part of golf. They are the hanging-in, cooling-it businessmen of the game. And as they spread across the lawn, gazing toward the nearest leader board while a tournament progresses, they are not unlike a cluster of military commanders observing the glow of shell-fire from a distant valley.

To almost anyone in the 1960's who knew the difference between a Ben Hogan driver and a shooting stick the faces of these fringe personalities looked as familiar as casual water, but only the true insider was able to identify them by name. There was the stocky, pink-faced man in the dark blazer, his hands usually folded behind him, the one ready with a Sam Snead anecdote or a story about the 1937 Ryder Cup team. That was Fred Corcoran, Snead's lifelong agent and the tournament director of the International Golf Association. There was the tall, blond fellow in the white shoes, a briefcase in one hand and Winnie Palmer's arm in the other. That was Mark McCormack, a Cleveland lawyer and manager of Palmer, Jack Nicklaus, Gary Player and most of the ships at sea. And there were several others, forming a sort of corporate blur, spaced equidistantly among the umbrellas: J. Edwin Carter of the World Series of Golf, Jack Tuthill, the PGA tournament supervisor, Bob Rickey, a Brunswick-MacGregor vice-president, Ernie Sabayrac, an equipment distributor, Bob Drum, a hulking writer, Joe Wolfe, the Wilson clubmaker, Darrell Brown, Palmer's pilot, Doc Giffin, Palmer's personal secretary, Malcolm Hemion, a TV director for ABC, and, finally, the most familiar figure of all, that of a man called Bubble Head, a man who was always there, never doing anything.

On or off the verandas, Bubble Head, or George Low, was (and still is) the stand-around champion of three decades. He is, all at once, America's guest, underground comedian, consultant, inventor of the overlapping grip for a beer can, and, more importantly, a man who has conquered the two hardest things in life — how to putt better than anyone ever, and how to live lavishly without an income.

For thirty years George Low has been the vaguest, most mysterious man in all of golf. Outwardly solemn and immobile, he stands like an urban renewal project on the verandas in a plaid jacket and an open-collared shirt, deeply tanned, granting interviews only to the bookmakers and forcing grins only toward those who might seem inclined to buy him lunch or a cocktail. It has been said that if George Low is not on your veranda the tournament simply hasn't started yet. When the Western Open was held at the Field Club in Pittsburgh in 1959, for example, George did not reveal his two hundred forty pounds until the final round, whereupon a friend on the committee scolded him for being tardy and nearly giving the event a bad name.

"Well, you got to understand that a man who don't have to be back to his office for thirty years is sometimes gonna be lax," said George.

The only office that George Low has ever had is the trunk of someone's automobile, preferably a Cadillac, which, if he borrowed it for long began to look like a rummage sale of golf clubs, clothes and photo albums. George has no age. His lungs are one hundred, his stomach is one fifty, and his soul is two thousand, says he. The body has been fifty-four or so for a while. For most of these years, at any rate, George's home has been a car seat, a convertible couch in someone's living room, a roll-away bed in a friend's hotel room, or, when he's going good, the vacant wing of a friend's mansion. But always these places have been where the sunshine is — either on or near the PGA tour. He is also very comfortable in Palm Springs, Scottsdale or Miami

Beach, whether the tour is in the vicinity or not, or at Saratoga, Santa Anita or Gulfstream.

"I go where some rich guy's got a bed and a kind heart," George says. "Most guys are if-come in this world, but there's a few that ain't phony, and they like having me around. They understand that I got to be where it's warm 'cause I can't afford no overcoat."

To the person who is "strung out," as George puts it, which means he has a steady, respectable job, it may seem that Low's existence is mostly a matter of survival. But George has never thought of it quite that way. On the contrary, George Low has usually lived comfortably, and often far better than the strung-out fellow who rides a commuter train or drives the freeways to work, who is paying off a divan and a Frigidaire and who has to purchase a daily ticket to a golf tournament, not admissible to the clubhouse.

The main reason why George Low has been able to survive in reasonable splendor is that he has one of those personalities that appeal to gentlemen of means. He has a rare sense of humor that makes him one of the superb put-down artists of his time, an unobtrusive manner for being around and not bothering anyone and a crashing honesty, all of which can add up to good company. Aside from these things George knows as much about golf as anyone, and a lot of gentlemen of means like to play golf, apparently while being put down unobtrusively, honestly and without being unduly bothered.

If he *does* have to work he does that on a putting green in Palm Springs or Miami Beach, mainly, where he is apt to putt with a wedge or with his shoe against a wagerer using a putter, and come out all right.

"Put me on a putting green in Miami for a week," says George, "and I'll kill more tourists than the Fontainebleau."

Among the celebrities who have demonstrated that they enjoy George's company and have, therefore, been his happy hosts, are, just to touch on four different sports, Jimmy Demaret, Willie Shoemaker, Horace Stoneham and Del Miller — a golfer, a jockey, a baseball owner and a harness racing mogul, respectively. George has visited with Stoneham in Phoenix during November, he has spent Christmas with Demaret

in Houston and he has devoted a lot of weekday drop-ins to Shoemaker in Los Angeles and Miller in Pennsylvania. It was Paul Grossinger of the resort by that name in the Catskills who once labeled George "America's guest."

"After which he came up with a freebie," says George.

Another associate, Bob Johnson, once the president of Roosevelt Raceway outside New York City, may have summed up George perfectly — at least it delights George — for all of his hosts one evening as Low kept badgering Johnson for another hundred dollars to buy drinks for everyone at a Palm Springs party.

"Just loafing with George is better than having a Dun & Bradstreet rating," said Johnson.

All of this helps make absolutely clear George's uncomplicated philosophy of life, or rather his blueprint for leading a life of ease.

"There ain't no use hanging around a broke 'cause nothing falls off," he says. "The only time I pick up a check is to hand it to somebody."

This, for George, sharply divides the world into two distinct categories of people — those who "come up," or pay, and those who "plead the fifth," or don't pay, when a tab appears.

Since most everyone who knows George knows him well enough to keep his pocketbook either handy or hidden, there are never any surprises or embarrassing situations. If George strolls by you prepare to pay or you prepare to leave. "It's an honor to pick up my check," he says. "How many true celebrities do you know? Anyhow, if you plead the fifth I'll go find a live one somewheres."

Low has a carefully thought out term for the man with a reputation for being something less than a wild spender. A very cautious student of the dollar, George calls him. Like Sam Snead.

"When I dine with Mr. Snead he always suggests that I order as if I was expecting to pay for it myself," says George. "I have known many great destroyers of money, but Mr. Snead is not among them."

Anyone who might happen to stand near George on a veranda at a tournament is likely to be treated to a comic routine. It oozes out naturally from his husky voice and always with a cynical tone. Most of the competitors have learned to feed George straight lines just for the pleasure of picking up a new expression.

Al Besselink came by one day at Pensacola and said, "Loan me fifty, Bubble."

Staring straight ahead at a sheltering palm Low said, "Loaning you money is like sending lettuce by rabbit."

Another time, as George rested himself against the trunk of an elm at Colonial, Billy Maxwell good-naturedly said, "Wish I had your energy, George."

"I wish I had a rock in each hand," said Low.

When Mark McCormack began packaging and selling Arnold Palmer, a close friend of Low's, in ways that no one had ever thought of before and practically printing money in the process, it gave George a lot of ammunition for his veranda standing. If someone were to ask Low if he had seen McCormack lately George would reply, "Yeah, he was sticking up a supermarket about an hour ago."

Mark learned to approach Low delicately, but it would never do any good. George would only tell McCormack, "Driving your getaway car is the best job in golf."

Bing Crosby once told George, who had insinuated he needed a room during Bing's tournament, that he could probably fix him up at the Del Monte Lodge and probably for a good rate.

"Thanks a lot," said George. "Can I loan you a dime to mark your ball?"

The Crosby has never been famed for drawing large crowds to the Monterey Peninsula for two reasons: it is inconveniently located on a 17-mile drive from Earth, and the weather is nearly always deplorable. When Crosby seemed rather excited one year by what appeared to him to be a better than average turnout Low remarked, "I seen more people on the back of a motorcycle."

Though George might frequently have a hangover gaze about him, his mind remains quick. Roasting in the Las Vegas sun one afternoon during the Tournament of Champions, when it was still being held at the Desert Inn course and when Wilbur Clarke was still alive, George noticed something unusual going up on the scoreboard. Arnold Palmer had just posted a nine, a seven and a five, in that order. Turning quietly to Clarke, Low said, "That's twenty-one. Pay him."

One of the better verandas to stand around on is that of the Augusta National Golf Club during the Masters. It has two big shade trees, some crawling wisteria, a scattering of umbrellas and tables and, always, George Low. He will move from a table to a bench to a tree trunk to a slope in the sun and back again, covering his steps, mumbling comments about the wretched state of the world and how many brokes there are in it. One year George arrived fresh from having spent a weekend sharing a hotel room with a friend, Bob Drum, who was then a writer for the *Pittsburgh Press*.

"How do you like rooming with Drum?" George was asked.

"It's okay," he said. "If you don't mind taking a shower with your money in your hand."

And there was the time at Augusta that George was hearing about Oscar Fraley, a former columnist for UPI, getting into a minor argument in a bar and causing some mild excitement. As the tale was being related by someone who had witnessed it, Fraley happened to stroll by. George interrupted the story and called to Oscar. "I hear you didn't start no fight last night for a change," he said. "Where'd you stay? In a room full of nuns?"

George Low may not have been born bourbon-faced or angry, but he was certainly born "energetically lazy" to use his words. "He was born retired," is the way Jimmy Demaret has put it. The event of George's birth occurred before World War I, that much is known, and not three hundred yards, a stout Nicklaus tee shot, from the pro shop at Baltusrol Golf Club in Springfield, New Jersey.

"I like to say I was born in the 19th Hole — the only one I ever parred," Low says.

He was the son of a rather famed Scot, George Low, Sr., who was runner-up for the U.S. Open championship in 1899, and who became the resident professional at Baltusrol. As one of those Scots who came to America to teach the game to an intrigued continent, George, Senior, numbered among his pupils a couple of renowned White House slicers, William Howard Taft and Warren G. Harding.

"There were poor guys like that all around Baltusrol," George remembers. "The Toppings and them kind of charity cases."

Despite the fact that George grew up near the 1st tee of a golf course, he did not try to learn the game until he was fifteen. And this after his father had retired and taken his son back to Scotland. George *had* to play golf in Scotland, he felt.

"What else is there to do over there? Wear a skirt?"

Try as he did to avoid playing golf, two things came naturally to George. A good swing and a deep, nagging feeling about the game. These attributes combined—conspired, more probably—to bring him back to the U.S. in the early 1930's. But in those days George returned as more than just an assistant pro at a variety of clubs in the upstate area of New York. For instance, there was one summer when he was working at a club in the Catskills when he was struck with a get-rich scheme. He found a friend who owned a Ford Tri-Motor airplane and together they dreamed up the idea of shuttling newspapers from the cities to resort areas.

Soon, they decided they could make their business even more profitable by shuttling more than papers. Like booze, this being during Prohibition. And at the same time, on weekends, they staged what could only be described as the world's worst air show featuring George Low parachuting out of the Tri-Motor.

"I didn't exactly jump," he says. "I'd open the door of the plane, and then I'd open the chute and let it pull me out. Who the hell wants to jump if he don't know the chute's gonna open?"

All of this came to an end one cold evening during a shuttle flight when the plane somehow drifted into a small mountain.

"Me and the pilot got out safe, but the booze died," George says.

It was also during these early, formative years that George developed a special fondness for Saratoga and thoroughbred racing itself. In August during the Saratoga meeting, he got acquainted with the sport by becoming a runner, one of those guys who found out what the swells in the box seats wanted to wager and then ran to the betting tables to get it down for them.

"I knew all the rich guys," he says. "Most of 'em were empty suits."

To this day, George has a knack for going to the tracks in style. As recently as the summer of 1969 George was back at Saratoga, quite comfortable in the home of Harry M. Stevens III, a young Stevens of the family that invented the hot dog, the straw, the paper cup and now caters no fewer than forty-one tracks and stadiums around the country. Sitting on young Henry's porch one evening, George was asked by his host if he wanted to pitch coins at a line for cash.

"Now what would I do with a catering business?" said George.

But let's retreat back to those 1930's again, to the days when Low honestly felt he could make it all the way from his assistant pro jobs into a handsome living on what had become a burgeoning PGA tour.

George started out on the tour determined to make his way as a champion, but, well, it was just too much fun in those days. Card games all through the nights—pitch and bridge, that kind of thing. And there were all of these characters to pal around with—Demaret, Jimmy Thomson, Leo Diegel, Craig Wood. "And that Indian," he says. Which was Ky Laffoon.

"Laffoon is the only man who ever beat me outa something on the putting green," says George. "At the old North and South Open at Pinehurst we got into a game that lasted day and night. I should have known I was in trouble when we putted at night. Laffoon was an Indian and Indians can see at night. I didn't get in that jackpot no more."

Low made an attempt which might generously be described as feeble to win the British Open of 1939. The idea of returning to semi-native soil gripped him, one reason being that he might be able to redeem himself for the last round he had played in Scotland. A long time before, in the British Boys' championship at Edinburgh, George had been beaten 8-7 by a cross-handed Scot, and he was so disgusted about it he heaved his clubs out of a train window. So George and Johnny Bulla sailed on the *Transylvania* in the summer of '39 for England.

The trip abroad took too long for George. Struggling to occupy his time on board ship, he got into a high-stakes game of shuffleboard with a gentleman of nobility, and he lost so much money that he was forced to delay his arrival for the British Open. Instead of going straight to St. Andrews he went with the earl or count or whatever he was to Perthshire. There they would bowl on the green.

"My bankroll looked like an elephant slept on it when I got off the ship," George explains. "Took me three weeks bowling on the green to get it back."

Low finally got to St. Andrews but not in time for a practice round. And he isn't altogether clear on how well he played. "I think I missed the cut—if I teed off at all," he says. "I forget. In those days, me and Clayton Heafner had a bad habit of being withdrew."

Where are the characters on today's tour? That's one thing George would like to know. Where are the fun-lovers, the withdrews? "All you got out there is a bunch of authors and haberdashers," he says.

"All you got to do to write a book is win one tournament. All of a sudden you're telling everybody where the V's ought to point. And them that don't win, they're haberdashers. They sell sweaters and slacks and call themselves pros."

Says George, "There ain't many of 'em knows how to repair a club in a shop. They can bend 'em, but they can't work on 'em until they know what's right. Most of 'em couldn't win consistently if they had Dick Tracy for a partner. I do a little club work for a few of 'em, but there's not too many who'd give the ducks a drink if they owned Lake Mead. They'll pop for a handshake, but those I got plenty of."

One of George's last flings as an active tour player came in 1945, and history confirms that he went out beautifully. Among the more remarkable facts of golf is that George Low helped end the fantastic winning streak of Byron Nelson. It happened in the Memphis Open that summer. Nelson, the Mechanical Man, had won eleven straight tournaments when he got to Memphis to try for the twelfth. Nelson finished third at Memphis behind Amateur Freddie Haas, who shot 270, and none other than George Low, who shot 276.

"Haas win the tournament, but I win the front money," says George. "I was the first pro to beat Nelson. Look it up."

Very shortly after that Low retired to the putting greens forever.

So many legends and half-truths have been written, spoken and whispered about George Low's putting ability, he ought to be a folk song. There are wild tales of George putting with a rake, a shovel, a pool cue and a broom handle and defeating others using a legitimate putter. There are stories of George kicking the ball with his foot and acing five out of nine holes in one round on the putting green. Other stories say that George has given putting "secrets" to Arnold Palmer, Bing Crosby, Willie Mays, all sorts of celebrities who turn up in his photo albums with their arms around his bulky shoulders. And there are stories that in the old days George took so much money away from tour winners on the putting greens that he should have been given a speeding ticket.

Low only forces a sly grin when the stories are put to him.

"They get started because I live good," he says. "I spend $50,000 a year of somebody else's money, that's all."

Oh, there are a few things George could talk about if he wanted to get himself in some kind of jackpot, as he says, but it isn't worth it. Sure, he can kick the ball with his foot and get it down in two from almost anywhere. For example, at Las Vegas a few years ago he was walking around in a practice session with Bo Wininger when Bo plopped a ball down on the 16th green at the Desert Inn and said, "Three cases of beer to two you can't get it down in two from here." The putt was seventy-five feet long. George called it, put his shoe to the ball and rolled it up within two inches of the cup. And George *can* beat you putting, even if he uses a wedge. "Don't ever try him," Byron Nelson has warned.

"I shall have to admit, in all modesty, that I'm probably the greatest putter who ever lived," says George. "At least I'll try anyone for a nominal fee."

There is a simple reason why George Low is the greatest putter who ever lived. "I've done more of it than anybody else," he says. "Back in Scotland, in Carnoustie, there was a thirty-six-hole putting green right outside our house. I putted for three or four years, eight, ten, twelve hours a day, before I ever started playing golf. I've always been able to do things with my hands anyhow. Build things. I have feel in them. So I putted and putted before I ever played golf, and then I've done nothing but putt since I quit. I can beat anyone on the tour because they have to worry about getting to the green. I'm already there."

George is not keen about giving away his putting secrets — not for free, at least. But he can offer a little advice.

"Everybody has a different problem putting," he says. "The best thing you can have is a quick left wrist. That makes you take the clubhead back on the inside. Most of your weight ought to be on the left foot for good balance. Another important thing is to keep both thumbs squarely on the top of the grip for the right feel."

He goes on, "The feel of the club may be the most important thing of all. When you reach in your pocket for a coin the last thing that touches the coin is your thumb. You use it to roll out the coin. It's the most sensitive finger. That's why you grip the putter with both thumbs on top of the handle."

And on, "After you get the feel of the club the thing to do is be sure you get a good, solid rap on the ball when you hit it. And there's only one way to be sure of doing that. Take the club back on the inside, like opening a door, and then bring it forward. When you open a door you take it back slow. When you close the door, that's the way the putter should meet the ball."

And on, "The worst way for the beginner to putt is to jab at the ball. You'll see some of the pros jab at it, but it's their own method they've worked out, which they think is good for all of the bad greens they putt on. There are a couple of 'em that jab the putt on any kind of green. Billy Casper, for instance, and Bob Rosburg. They're pretty good putters, but there are exceptions to everything. Besides, they jab the same way every time, which is the real key to good putting. Consistency."

And finally, "That's why I'm gonna beat everybody. I'm gonna hit the ball the same way every time, and you're not. And if we putt long

enough for the luck to scare off, I got to be the winner."

George Low might be a more mysterious figure than he is if it had not been for Arnold Palmer. When Palmer won his second Masters in 1960, Low's name burst into print as some sort of weird genius of the greens — and all because of a remark Arnold made to the press. That year Palmer sank dramatic putts for birdies on the last two greens to win, not only before the thousands in Augusta, but before millions more watching television. And later on, in an interview, when asked about those heroics, Palmer said, "The only thing I did on those putts was keep thinking what my old friend George Low always says: 'Keep your head down and don't move.'"

A short time after this Low's small but impressive notoriety resulted in an autograph-model putter, the George Low putter, a mallethead type with a marketing slogan that went "the putter with the built-in touch." It was made by a company called the Sportsman's Golf Corporation of Chicago. A few of the pros began using the Low putter, mainly Gary Player. And exactly one year later, back in Augusta again, Player, using the Low putter, won the Masters and George Low got even more publicity.

"But I was lucky," says George. "The putter started selling so well I got fired. It was a relief. With a lot of money in your pocket, it takes away the torment of where you're gonna sleep."

Along about this time another change took place in Low's career. A motel chain, Ramada Inn, hired him as a goodwill ambassador. His job was to follow the tour and guide as many pros as possible into Ramada Inns across the land. They gave him a Cadillac to drive — "the only Cadillac in the press lot" — and let him have free rooms in all of the Ramada Inns he could locate.

"It didn't feel right," he says. "I knew it wouldn't last. Something was missing. The daily challenge that I'd grown used to. The challenge of whether I'd be able to borrow Frank Stranahan's car and lose it to somebody in a coin flip or something. It got so bad for a while I almost bought a pair of shoes on my own."

That wouldn't have been right. George hadn't bought a pair of shoes in thirty years.

He'd got them all from Foot Joy. "I been a test pilot for Foot Joy forever. I test their sixty-five-dollar alligator models to see if standing in them for long periods of time in a bar brings them any serious harm. What effect spilling beer has on them."

Rarely is George anything in appearance but the portrait of prosperity. Foot Joy shoes, a handsome plaid jacket that he got from Joe Jemsek, a golf course owner from the Chicago area ("he wears my size") and a Western-tooled, monogrammed leather chair stool, courtesy of Bob Goldwater, Barry's brother.

"No if-come about him," says George. "Bob stands up."

There have been, sad to relate, times when George Low has insisted on paying up himself. Not often, but some. And only in these latter, more prosperous years. One such occasion was in Augusta in 1965 in a place called the Bull Bat Lounge, just off the lobby of the Town House Hotel. George was sitting with a few journalist friends he could trust, drinking beer and getting ready to go search for a cafeteria. He prefers cafeterias to elegant restaurants because they have a lot of vegetables. Anyhow, George was in the middle of an anecdote when an old friend appeared.

"Good to see you, Bubble," the voice said, the voice belonging to a Tampa car salesman named Madman Morris. "Where you been? I been all over. Pensacola. Miami. Everywhere. How come I didn't see you?"

"Madman," said George. "Either shut up or sit down and assume the financial obligation. I got my own lies to tell."

"Sure good to see you, Georgie," said Madman. "I know this guy thirty years. . . ."

"Are you gonna sit down and buy something, Madman, or just stand there looking like a buried lie in a bunker?" George said.

"I been all over, Bubble. Jacksonville. Pensacola. Miami. How come you wasn't anywhere?" Madman said.

"There's a rule in this joint that any guy stands around has to *buy* something," said Low. "Why don't you take your shag bag somewhere else and hit your shanks?"

"Whatta guy," said Madman Morris. "Same old George. I'd see this guy everywhere. Palm Beach. Orlando. Pensacola. Miami . . ."

"I can't get in no jackpot with an unplayable lie like this," said George, excusing himself, sliding out of the booth in the Bull Bat Lounge, paying the check and leaving to go look for vegetables.

There are also occasions when George Low can be persuaded to play a round of golf. Actually play. Naturally, the type of golfing companion George prefers is someone with money and questionable talent, an ego-inspired handicap, perhaps. "Give me a millionaire with a bad backswing and I can have a very pleasant afternoon," George says.

An afternoon like this occurred not so many winters ago at the posh Seminole Golf Club in Palm Beach. George got into a game with the Duke of Windsor and the late Robert R. Young, the railroad magnate. An earl or a duke or a count could always entice George into a game of something. George's putter was good to him this day as it usually is when more than laughs are involved. The other shots he could hit well enough from memory. George came out in good shape, don't worry. Except that when the round was finished Low didn't notice the Duke straining to get in his pocket.

They were all sort of strolling toward the clubhouse — to the veranda, of course — slowly, amid a rather awkward silence. George cleared his throat a couple of times. They stopped and chatted about the nice day, how lovely the course looked this time of year. George shifted his weight from one Foot Joy to another and cleared his throat again.

Finally, Robert Young discreetly took George aside and whispered something to him.

"Oh, by the way, George. I should have mentioned that His Royal Highness never pays money," said Young.

"He don't do *what*?" said Low.

"His Royal Highness never pays. It's custom with him. It's rather a privilege, you see, to play golf in his company."

"Mr. Young," said George Low, the only George Low there ever was or ever will be in golf. "You take care of your railroads and I'll take care of my dukes."

"Nipper" Campbell Takes the Stand
James Reston

James Reston certainly is one of the more distinguished journalists to have contributed to these pages. During his continuing long association with The New York Times, *mainly as its chief Washington correspondent in addition to being a vice president of that great newspaper, he has accumulated a staggering array of awards. Included are a Pulitzer Prize, the Overseas Press Club and the George Polk Memorial awards, several honorary college degrees and decorations from two foreign countries. And he has been most deserving of them as one of America's most outstanding political pundits for forty years.*

Reston is known as "Scotty" and he rightfully comes by his nickname as he was born in Clydebank, Scotland, and spent a good part of his childhood attending a boys' academy in Alexandria. Naturally, being Scottish and living there until he was eleven, he played the national game. And Scotty plays it very well, as his reputation as the best golfer in the Washington press corps attests.

"'Nipper' Campbell Takes the Stand" was written by Reston nearly fifty years ago when he was just starting his newspaper career in Ohio.

The subject of Reston's piece is an interesting study. He was one of the early missionaries of the game who came to this country at the turn of the century to work as a professional at a time when a major requirement for that pursuit was to speak with a burr. Campbell also was on hand when the great transition from wood to steel-shafted clubs was made, and his observations concerning the change-over and the effect it had on playing the game certainly are worth recalling.

Reston has gone on to more important assignments in his chosen field, but he certainly proves he was a golf writer par excellence — I hope you will excuse the pun — and a master of transcribing the speech characteristics of one of his native countrymen.

I HAD THOUGHT of golf only as a very enjoyable game until I met Alec "Nipper" Campbell. To him it is something entirely different. It is something by which to live materially and spiritually. It is his philosophy.

Golf in the United States was still at the lisping age when, in 1899, Alec came from St. Andrews to be professional to The Country Club at Brookline. A nineteen-year-old boy, a kind of a golfing engine, he was brought to Boston by Mr. G. H. Windeler, one of the fathers of the game in America. Today, Alec Campbell, waggish and whimsical, is the professional at the Moraine Park Country Club course, which he built, in Dayton, Ohio.

Though the glamour of his competitive days has slipped away, Alec brings the enthusiasm of a boy to the game, a contagious enthusiasm which beggars description. In mid-winter he seldom misses a day at the course. At fifty-three, lithe and small, he walks hatless across two miles of frozen ground to the course. Once there, he works in his shop or wanders over the course, club in hand. Alone, contented, his is another world.

What, then, after thirty years in competitive golf in America and Britain, has this man to say of the game?

On the difficulty of teaching:

"Y'know it's hard to teach the game. Man's like a narrow-moothed whiskey bottle. He can only tak a word or two at a gulp. Ye have to tak it slow. But the American's a guid pupil. He's studyin' the game. Tak the Governor! [Former Governor of Ohio James M. Cox, Democratic candidate for the presidency in 1920.] There's nae nonsense wi' him. He'll see ye doin' somethin' an' he'll ask ye how ye did it.

"An' when ye tell him, he'll work at it till he masters it. He may have to change it to suit his style, but he gets the notion an' he uses it. I'm no tellin' ye he's the average, for he's no', but the Yank's workin' along the same lines, thinkin' his way through. An' that's why he's doin' sae weel."

Are there any new ideas regarding the golf swing or the ways of teaching it?

"It's the ways o' sayin' 'em that's new: no' the ideas. The auld caddies on the ither side knew 'em all before a lot o' these people touched a club. But that's no' tae say the new ways o' sayin' and describin' things is no good. A man can understand 'keep your chin back o' the ball' when ye'll jist muddle him by tryin' to describe swayin' to him. But this 'forward press' business they're bletherin' aboot is as auld as the hills. Only we call it the 'delay.' An' the 'drag' they talk aboot is no' much different. They're done for the same purpose — to make ye start the club back richt."

What is the most important fundamental?

"The grip. An' I'll tell ye why. The golf swing's the same as onything else. Start it richt, an' chances are ye'll end it richt. But if ye're wrong at the start, ye're a goner. If the grip's guid, the first foot o' the back swing'll be guid, an' there ye are. Now I'm no' sayin' that means the overlappin' or the interlockin' grip. When Sarazen was a bad gripper, it was nae because he was lockin' his fingers. It was jist because he did nae have his hands the gither."

Why have the British golfers slipped?

"They've no' got a model, an' they're no' takin' the pains wi' it. The war hurt 'em. They're no 'footerin' wi' it the way they used to."

How about Sarazen's proposal to enlarge the golf cup to eight inches?

"Y'know, I had Nancy, ma wife, save me some tin cans an' I tried 'em oot. I had 'em in the greens there. The only thing I like aboot 'em is the sound. My, they've got a grand sound!

"They'll hang Gene if he talks aboot 'em on the ither side.

"If they really want to give 'em a try though, let 'em play a tournament wi' 'em, an' have the pros play thirty-six holes to the eight-inch cups an' the amateur to the four-inchers; an' then let 'em change on the last thirty-six an' see what happens."

Have there been many changes in golf course construction in the past twenty years?

"They're jumpin' frae piller to post on the course buildin'. For a while they were tryin' everythin'. I was lookin' for 'em to run ventilation shafts up the trees afore long. But they're gettin' more sensible in their auld age. When I first came to America, all the par-four holes were bunkered in back. The Chicago Golf Club course is an example. A fine course, but it penalizes the bold player. We've learned to stop that, to give the man wi' courage the advantage. That's why ye see nae bunkers in back o' my two-shotters at Moraine.

"They're only learnin' how to make bunkers. Ye see so many that are nae bunkers at a'. A bunker should be put down only where it'll make ye play a grand shot in order to save a stroke. Otherwise, it's meant to cost ye. These things ye can slap the ball out of are nae bunkers.

"There was a tendency to build courses only for the best players a while ago. An' that's no richt. Courses should be built specifically for the average club member with tees so situated that you can push the scratch player back. The best course is the one that's built into the landscape ye've got."

What did the steel shafts to do the game?

"Plenty. They changed the correct use of the club from a *swing* to a *hit*. We slug the ball now. They give more distance with the wooden clubs. But there's nae comparison through the fairway.

"The steel shafts changed the professional's life entirely. Once he was a craftsman, a mechanic. In the old country, he learned the trade jist like a carpenter, an' often he went before a notary an' signed a contract before he got the job. It was part o' his work to season hickory, to cut the heads right oot o' the block, an' to know how to balance a club.

"Everything's ready-made now, an' when there's any repairin' to be done, back it goes to the factory. Club-makin' is a lost art. An' do ye see what that has done to the pro? He has nae anythin' to do wi' himself. He sits aroun' the shop when he's no' teachin', because he's fed up wi' playin'. What's to become o' him? What's he to do when the tournament days pass? He'll be sick o' the game an' he'll have naethin' to fa' back on.

"Wi' me it's different. I'm always experimentin' wi' somethin': a new clubhead, or some new kind o' grass for the fairways, or the rough. An' that's anither thing. The pro's goin' to have to learn how to take care o' the course. It'll be part o' his job in the future.

"There's nae question, the pro killed the goose that laid the golden egg. He made pennies and lost dollars when he boomed the steel shaft. He made some money all at once, but now that he's got a' the ricks jinglin' wi' steel, he's no gettin' any repairin' to do, and he can't re-sell the same members on the fact that they should throw away their one-hundred-dollar sets jist because he proved that he was wrong."

What is the future of golf?

"It's jist beginnin'. The boys are swingin' golf clubs in the streets in these days instead o' baseball bats. Public course golf should get to a greater number o' people a' the time. I think maybe we'll have more golf at the golf courses in the future an' less social life."

Alec's is an interesting history. Raised on the sea-born turf at Troon, he accepted golf as he did the mist of Scotland's hills. It was part of the landscape. It was more important than school and far more interesting. So every day he walked for a mile along the beach to the course by the sea, and this he did from the time he was old enough to carry the sticks.

Every night he visited the burn at Black Rock (the second hole on the Troon course), for there he had concealed in the mouth of a drain a piece of fishing net ("which ol' Mr. Cameron, a fisherman, gied me") which yielded its weekly supply of gutties. Then, with only the plover and the wild duck for companions, with fishing nets laid out to dry upon the fairways, he played with a sense of possession.

These nightly rounds bore fruit. One of the dramatic stories in Scottish golf history concerns fifteen-year-old Alec Campbell, a "wee laddie with an amazing short game," who beat the best players in his section of the land in the first tournament he entered. All Scotland heard of this feat, and everyone was astonished. But not Alec. "I told ye I'd win, Mither," he shouted as he rushed into the house after beating Stewart Garner, two and one, in the final. His mother gave him "tuppence" (four cents), "an' I went to Troon on a jaunt!"

Four years serving his time, a year of which he spent in worshipping Harry Vardon, and a few months as a journeyman at St. Andrews, elapsed before he came to the United States in 1899. And this boy dreamed. He did not realize then how the small man was handicapped by the guttie ball. But always it managed to beat him.

Fortune robbed him of the United States Open title in 1907 in one of the strangest cases in the history of the game. Playing at the Merion Cricket Club course in Philadelphia, Alec was leading the field as he stood on the fourth tee on the last round. He was using a new ball which had just been invented, the "silk-pneumatic" ball, and the "Nipper" was being paid to play with it. When he hit his drive on the fourth, part of the air gave out of the ball and it fluttered into a trap. A comparatively easy hole, the fourth cost him a seven. His nerves shaken by his misfortune, he took fives at the next two holes, dropping strokes to par at both. At the finish, he was two shots behind Alec Ross, now profes-sional at the Detroit Country Club.

It is impossible to estimate the influence of Alec Campbell on the game. For example, the shy, quiet lad "who lived jist aff the twelveth fairway" at Brookline, the boy who watched Campbell's every movement, was no other than Francis Ouimet, who was to come to Alec, in his famous match with Vardon and Ray, for encour-agement and counsel.

His swing is still a picture of studied ease, a "fast-and-faster" swing with great flexibility of the wrists. "Ye can niver turn awa' frae that ba' too far on the backstroke," says Alec, and his own swing demonstrates this point. But it is not the swing nor his knowledge of the swing that marks this man. It is the man himself and his knowledge of other men.

The Port-O-Let Guy
George Plimpton

George Plimpton has brought to life the Walter Mitty who exists in all of us. An Ivy Leaguer (Harvard, class of '48) who by appearance and manner seems more at home in a drawing room, he has become a national figure by writing about his experiences as a temporary "jock."

George was not the first to risk life and limb in such hazardous pursuits: Paul Gallico, when he was sports editor of the New York Daily News, *boxed with Jack Dempsey; and Dennise McLuggage tried parachute jumping on an assignment for the old* New York Herald-Tribune. *But George has been the most tenacious.*

Plimpton's Not In My League, *concerning his tolerated, inept efforts to play major league baseball, was so well received that he was able to venture into the violent world of professional football as a fear-ridden, fumble-prone quarterback with the Detroit Lions. The resultant* Paper Lion *was a bestseller and established him as an observer of sports from an extremely personal and unusual angle.*

Fortunately, Plimpton also devoted his attention and great talent toward the PGA Tour and the gilt-edge nomads who make up that non-violent element of the sporting scene. George became one of them for a winter season and was able to tee it up often enough in the pro-ams which precede a regular tour event to experience the catalogue of frustrations that beset every golfer, even those who play the game for a living.

This excerpt from The Bogey Man *concerning one hilarious situation serves as the kind of first-hand insight that can be brought to a sport by one who dares ignore both caution and his own inadequacies.*

ALL THE GOLFERS I talked to on the tour agreed that the most unfortunate position out on the course was to play immediately in front of Arnold Palmer and his Army. If one had to play in front of one of the superstars, Jack Nicklaus was the golfer one would hope for, because he was slow, so that however large a following he had, one could move on ahead of him and open up space between his gallery and one's own group. As for playing *behind* golfers like Nicklaus and Palmer, well, that was simply a matter of patience—waiting until their cohorts had moved their easy, elephantine meanderings beyond range.

At the San Francisco pro-am, I and two other amateurs were to be partnered by the professional Rod Funseth. I noticed in the evening papers, which published the starting times for the next day's play, that our foursome was scheduled to tee off immediately in front of Palmer's group.

It was overcast the next day, but Palmer had a big crowd with him. As I had been led to expect, golfing that day was not like playing in a tournament at all, but rather like being in a migration, the Great Trek, during which, because of some odd ceremonial ritual, one was asked to carry along a golf club and strike at a golf ball from time to time. One stepped out from the multitude to knock the ball along the line of march, standing and concentrating on the shot while the oblivious crowds rolled along beside the fairway, like the slow flow of a stream around a rock in a riverbed. There was only one person they had come to see hit a golf shot, and that was Arnold Palmer.

On the 14th at the Harding Park Golf Course I was nearly engulfed by the Army. The hole is a long par 4. On the golfer's left as he stands on the tee the fairway slopes sharply into gullies covered with heavy brush, and after a bit the hill drops off abruptly to Lake Merced, sparkling far below. When I stepped up to drive, the advance elements of Arnie's Army were streaming along the fairway, the mass of them on the right getting themselves into position for his appearance immediately behind us. I hit my drive off the heel of the club, perhaps compensating, wanting to keep my ball away from the crowds on the

right, and it shot off at an angle and into one of the gullies on the left, not more than 50 yards or so from the tee. I sighed and went down there with my caddy to look for it. The rest of the foursome, Rod Funseth in the fore, continued down the fairway. I called to them that I would catch up if I could. My caddy and I both took clubs out, smacking through the underbrush in the hope of uncovering the ball.

In the meantime, Palmer and his group had finished the 13th and they had come up on the elevated 14th tee. I found my ball after a long search, and I was thinking about how to play my shot when I happened to glance back up at the tee behind me. There was Palmer looking intently down the fairway. I was so far down in the gully that I could only see the upper part of his torso. From the set of his shoulders I could tell that he was braced over his ball and that the rest of my foursome was now far enough away for him to lace into his shot. He had not noticed me; if he had, I doubt he would have taken me for a member of the team in front, since by now Funseth and the rest of them were more than 300 yards away down the fairway. He would have taken me for a groundskeeper, perhaps, clearing out underbrush with scythe.

"Wait!" I called.

He looked down, almost directly it seemed, off that high tee, as if he were peering over the edge of a large container. I thought afterward that he had the abrupt look of someone sitting at his desk who sees something move in the bottom of his wastepaper basket.

I raised my driver and waved it, so he could identify me as a fellow golfer.

"Down here," I called. "I'm sorry." I shouted, "I'll be right out," as if in reply to someone pounding on a washroom door.

The caddy handed me a club. I settled over my ball, my back up against a bush, and was about to thrash at it when I discovered that the caddy, in his confusion and in the awe of the moment, had taken my driver and mistakenly handed me a putter.

I tossed it back to him. "An eight," I called. "An *eight* iron."

I took a quick look back up at the tee. Palmer was looking on, and behind him were the other members of his foursome and their caddies and a few officials and a back line of spectators, all grim as they stared down. I hit a shot that bounced up out of the rough onto the fairway.

"Let's go," I said. We ran up after the shot, the caddy trotting hard, the clubs jangling thunderously in the bag.

I barely got my feet set before hitting the next shot — ripping up and letting it fly on down a fairway by now thickly flanked by Arnie's Army waiting for his drive.

I hurried down between those lanes. Some cardboard periscopes came up from the back ranks of the crowd and peered. I could catch the glint of glass. A couple of hundred yards ahead I could see the rest of our foursome on the green. Behind, Palmer was still waiting. We were not yet out of range.

"Lord," I said. The clubs jangled furiously. Fleetingly I thought of a *Golfer's Handbook* record I had noted the day before — a speedy round by an Olympic runner from South Africa who was able to whip around the Mowbray Course in thirty-odd minutes.

"I'm going to pick up," I called to the caddy.

I scooped up the ball on the fly like a center-fielder bending to field a hit, and we veered and headed off the fairway for the Army, stepping in among them. There were a few stares but then the heads began craning for Palmer's shot. We walked along with the crowd and I joined the others on the 15th tee. Funseth and my partner looked up when I climbed over the restraining ropes to join them. I apologized and said I had picked up. I was doing so badly. They said, never mind; one of them had birdied the hole, and the team was all right.

I was telling a friend about the experience later that morning. "I didn't see what else I could do," I said. "Picking up, I mean." I described what had happened, playing the shots in front of that grim gallery on the 14th tee: Palmer and the rest of them — a tableau of generals, with their staffs, they might have been, surveying the pageantry of battle from a hill, except that immediately in front of them something had gone wrong: a soldier's drum had fallen off, rolling down a gentle slope, and he was rushing after it, his cockade askew, and the drum was beginning to bounce now and pull away from him . . .

"You did the right thing," my friend said. "Picking up."

"I think so."

"That was not a pleasant experience."

"It certainly wasn't," I said.

He cleared his throat. He said that well, nothing could compare with an experience *he* had had with Palmer and his Army. I've forgotten what tournament he said it was, possibly the Masters or the PGA, one of the great championships, for sure. He was a spectator on the golf course at a position where the big-name players were coming through. While waiting, on the side of the fairway, he had stepped into one of those sentry-box structures called Port-O-Let, chemical toilets that are set about courses during tournament week. After a while he opened the door, which made a shrill squeal, and he stepped out into the bright sunlight. When he had stepped into the Port-O-Let there had been quite a few people trudging by, the advance guard of Arnie's Army. Now, he said, with himself and the Port-O-Let at its apex, an enormous fan of people had materialized that stretched away toward the distant green, a double line of faces — thousands, it appeared — all straining to see. And there, not ten yards away, standing over a golf ball that he had hit nearly out of bounds, and getting ready to swing, was Arnold Palmer. At the creak of the hinges Palmer looked back, and he saw my friend standing in the door of the Port-O-Let.

"What did you do?" I asked.

"Well, my gosh," my friend said. "I stepped right back inside and pulled the door shut. It was the typical reaction, I mean, stepping out and seeing all those people. It was like slipping through a door and finding oneself alone on the stage of a fully occupied opera house. What happens is that your eyes pop and you back up right through the door you came out of."

"Of course," I said.

Royal and Ancient...and Antic
Peter Dobereiner

Peter Dobereiner is a tall, hulking writer from England whose rather hang-dog look masks a keen wit and a tongue-in-cheek attitude regarding the strictures and traditions of the game. He initially gained wide readership as "our golf correspondent" for the London Observer *and, since the retirement of Pat Ward-Thomas, has taken over in a similar capacity with the* Manchester Guardian. *As is his wont, he follows a back-breaking schedule of nearly forty weeks on the road with the European Golf Tour, forays to the United States for the major championships and an annual junket to one of the four corners of the globe for the World Cup Matches.*

His daily production of prose notwithstanding, Peter manages to write a monthly column for an appreciative American audience in Golf Digest, *plus numerous other editorial assignments for the major publications devoted to golf in England. In his more recent efforts seen in the United States, he has, in all good humour, been campaigning for a larger golf hole, fewer clubs and golf course hazards more in keeping with the capabilities of golfers of his ilk.*

Peter is a delight to read and, once one becomes attuned to his Midland accent, it is an extreme pleasure to listen to his recounting of life on the tour in Europe and the players and personalities who follow it.

It came as no surprise to me, when Peter got around to writing a major golf book, that his light touch would be evident on every page and that it would include some of the more bizarre and humorous aspects of the game which he and I have so assiduously followed for so many years. The chapter "Royal and Ancient...and Antic" is taken from his brilliant The Glorious World of Golf *which, to my mind, is one of the most engaging golf books I ever have had the pleasure to read.*

WHEN IT CAME to filling out his entry form for the British Open of 1965, Walter Danecki had a brief crisis of conscience. He had to state whether he was an amateur or a professional, and that was a difficult decision for forty-three-year-old Walter, a mail sorter from Milwaukee who played weekend golf on a municipal course and who proposed to take a holiday in Britain. He also proposed to play in the Open. This was straightforward enough: Walter's amateur status was unstained. As he later explained, he did not charge if he gave a lesson. On the other hand, Walter believed he could beat Arnold Palmer and, what's more, he was determined to win the Open. "I wanted the crock of gold, so my conscience made me write down 'professional,'" he said.

Walter had made inquiries about joining the PGA and had been put off the idea because of the stipulation of a five-year apprenticeship. "What I'll do is win one of the big ones," he told himself, "and then they'll have to let me in." Boy, would his friends be impressed when he came home with the trophy. And if perchance some unforeseen catastrophe beyond his control should rob him of his triumph, putting him in second place, say, or even third, then the whole venture would be his little secret. Nobody at home need ever know. So, true to the spirit of the rules of amateurism governing "professional talent," Walter filed his entry as a pro, and the R. and A., which at that time did not scrutinize credentials very closely, accepted it.

Walter was drawn to play the prequalifying rounds at Hillside, just over the fence from the Birkdale championship course. Hillside is generally reckoned to be a few shots easier than Birkdale. Against the par of 70, Walter and his playing partner reckoned that two 75s would be good enough to qualify. Walter went round in 108. Officials of the R. and A. thought that Walter would quietly fold his tent and creep away after this debacle. They arranged for a substitute to play the second round with his partner. Next morning Walter presented himself on the tee, not a whit abashed. "I don't like to quit. I like to golf and that's what I came to do," he said. This time he had a considerable gallery in attendance. He started with two 7s and an 8

and then settled down with two solid bogey 5s. Then a 7 and a 9 were followed by two more 5s to put him out in 58. Perhaps that total unnerved him, because he started back 9, 6, 10 before he got it going again for an inward half of 55. Round in 113, or 43 over par, to make a two-round aggregate of 221. He missed qualifying by just 70 strokes. But the indomitable Walter wasn't making any excuses. Far from it. "I want to say that your small ball is right for this sort of course," he said. "If I had been playing our bigger ball I would have been all over the place."

God bless you, Walter. The world would be a poorer place without people like you. Happily, golf is full of Walters. No game is as rich in human eccentricity as golf, and its foibles are carefully recorded in *The Golfer's Handbook*. This work, which is published in Glasgow every year, is basically devoted to golfing records and useful information, but the best of it is a section headed "Interesting Facts, Feats and Extraordinary Occurrences in the Game." There follows a great number of subdivisions under such headings as "Spectators interfering with balls," and "Balls in strange places." The entries, which cover more than a hundred pages of fine print, are presented in deadpan, almost telegraphic fashion, although occasionally the editors reveal a flash of personal opinion. For instance, under "Freak Matches," there is an item reading, "In United States competitions with nondescript hazards, such as suspended barrels to be played through and gates played around, are frequently held" — and here one can detect a pursing of the puritanical lips — "to provide what are supposed to be amusing variations of the game."

For the most part this section is a casebook of golf lunacy. Here an eminent violinist plays a match attired in a suit of armour. "He was beaten by 2 and 1" the item adds, which we cannot help feeling served him right. A millionaire travels between shots by helicopter and another rare spirit plays a round by divebombing a course in a light airplane and hurling golf balls at the greens. He completed 18 holes in 29 shots. Golfers challenge archers, javelin throwers, racquets players, and flyfishermen and hardly a day passes, it seems, without somebody attempting a speed round or a cross-country marathon.

The editors reserve their greatest enthusiasm for disasters. The lady who required 166 strokes at a short hole gets a fat entry, and fatal accidents on the course are recorded in morbid detail. The carnage caused to fish, birds, and animals by golf balls gets a separate section. But aficionados of these golfing curios were dismayed by recent editorial pruning of the section "Hit by ball—distance of rebound." In earlier editions this was a rich treasury of tasteless trivia. The record was held by an unnamed South African caddie who, on September 28, 1913, was struck just above the right temple by a ball driven by Edward Sladwick. The rebound was measured at 75 yards. This shattered the record. See here, the longest rebound in the book is Barton, playing at Machrie, beaned a caddie named John McNiven. Out came the tape measure to record a rebound of 42 yards, 2 feet, 10 inches. We can imagine the excitement as Mr. Barton and his friends consulted *The Golfer's Handbook*. "We did it! It's a new world record. See here, the longest rebound in the book is thirty-four yards, set up way back in August, 1908, at Blairgowrie at the ninth hole." How transient are such moments of triumph. Just twenty-seven days later the title went to Mr. Sladwick. Still, Barton retains the British native record.

It is now useless to consult the *Handbook* if you should have the good fortune to catch a caddie flush on the forehead. The records have been withdrawn. You will be all right if you step into a bunker and sink waist deep. You will find such deeds in an appropriate section, but you are doomed to disappointment. On July 11, 1931, at Rose Bay, New South Wales, Mr. D. J. Bayley MacArthur did the same thing, only he sank to the armpits. If your ball impales itself on a hatpin without dislodging the hat, or pierces a spectator's topper, or lodges in a donkey's ear, or drops down a chimney into a pot of Irish stew bubbling on the hearth, you may make it among similar examples. But rebounds are out.

As for freakish scoring, you will have to do something really spectacular to qualify. It's no good starting off 1, 2, 3, 4, 5, 6, for instance, because it has been done already. If your opponent holes out with his tee shot you should not delude yourself with the heady thought that it would be quite unprecedented to do an ace yourself and halve the hole. It has happened before. Several times. Almost commonplace. What about a hole in one at successive holes? Sorry, it's been done: in 1971 during a PGA tournament in the British circuit. John Hudson, making a rare tournament appearance as a break from his duties as a club pro, holed out at a short hole at Norwich golf club. The next hole, played from an elevated tee and partly blind from a stand of trees, measures 311 yards. Hudson cracked one with his driver, although most of the field was playing discreetly short because of the tightness of the approach to the greens and holed out.

For sheer luck it would be hard to surpass the experience of the golfer who sliced his drive at Prestwick's first hole. The ball flew out-of-bounds, hit the railway line, and rebounded into play. He sliced his approach shot. Again it carried the O.B. fence, again it hit the railway line, and this time it rebounded onto the green and rolled into the hole. Fair enough, but a similar incident had an unhappy sequel at Los Angeles in 1950. Bob Geared sliced his tee shot at the 425-yard second hole and his ball bounced on the road and landed in a passing truck. The driver tossed the ball back by the green and it went into the hole. The committee heartlessly ruled that he should have played another ball off the tee under the O.B. rule.

Not every curious incident finds its way into the *Handbook*. Possibly because they do not have a subsection for "Sexual Deviants on the Links" the editors missed, for instance, the Effingham affair. A foursome of lady members was playing on the exclusive suburban course at Effingham, near London. They were putting out when a man wearing a bowler hat and nothing else sprang from the bushes. Undaunted, the lady captain demanded sternly, "Are you a member?" and receiving no satisfactory reply—it would hardly have done to offend, say, an influential committee chairman—dispatched the intruder with a sharp blow from her eight-iron. All golfers will understand why she did not risk damaging her putter on such an unyielding target.

In the normal course of events sex has very

little association with golf. That statement may provoke boisterous laughter in ten thousand clubhouses, and I quite understand. Every club has its scandals from time to time, but this is essentially *après*-golf and has no direct connection with the game. On the course men and women tend to avoid each other's company, no matter what they may do later. The golf is the thing at the time. Among the professionals a few, such as Walter Hagen, could cast an appraising eye over the galleries and chat up a dolly while playing an important match. But, generally, the pros keep their minds on the game. What they do later is their business and no lurid revelations will be made here.

In one part of the world sex and golf do coexist. The wealthy mandarin golfers of Taiwan have evolved a local custom which may surprise visitors. When two western businessmen were invited to join two merchants for a round, they were only too glad and readily agreed to play for "the usual stakes," thinking this would mean a $5 nassau or something of that order. They won, rather easily, and accepted an invitation to play again the next day on the same terms. They won again and the Chinese said they would send the winnings round to their hotel. That evening the businessmen were duly paged and found in the hotel lobby fourteen giggling girls who announced that they had come to give the golfers their bath. Somehow it is difficult to imagine the practice spreading.

Women generally have been the second-class citizens of golf. Although there is abundant evidence of their interest in the game, they were less than welcome in many clubs for many years. Only in the United States, even today, have women golfers won equality. There are a few men-only clubs in America and some lesser examples of discrimination can be discovered, but generally speaking American women golfers have achieved a freedom that is the envy of their overseas sisters. If they occasionally feel slighted, they might reflect on the situation elsewhere. In Australia, for example, the woman golfer is even denied her womanhood. Oh, she can join a club right enough if she is prepared to accept the condescending label of "associate." This is the word which marks her cramped and

relatively inferior quarters in the clubhouse. And that is how she is called by the men — "I got held up at the ninth by a couple of associates" — as if she were a different species of lesser being. At that, she may be in a happier situation than her English counterpart who is dignified by the title "lady" — and by not much more in some clubs. Emancipation is spreading slowly in Britain but the process is fiercely resisted in certain bastions of male reaction where women are suffered, and themselves suffer.

In extreme instances, women are permitted to play the course, provided they stand meekly to the side of the fairway (preferably getting right out of sight) and allow any male match to go through with unimpeded progress, and provided they change their shoes in the car park and on no account attempt to set foot in the clubhouse. The more usual restrictions consist of a kind of golfing purdah with the women confined to their own cramped quarters, forbidden to play at certain times, and subject to rigid rules of how they may dress. Some clubs maintain ludicrous regulations such as forbidding women to use a certain flight of steps in front of the club. Restrictions on the times when women may play are still fairly general. Most men see women's golf as a slightly frivolous, and miniaturized, version of their own game. And every golf club which permits women members can provide examples to support that smug theory. At the same time the theory is false. As in life, so in golf: Women are different. Mostly they play for different reasons. Psychiatrists are not notably reticent when it comes to talking rubbish, but none has yet suggested that women's golf involves an urge to display their virility. Women have no need to flex their muscles in public, and so from the very outset their basic reasons for playing golf are different. The appeal of the game lies in what it provides them — release from the domestic scene, companionship, fulfillment of the competitive instinct, and a congenial way of filling the waiting hours while husbands are at work. If that sounds patronizing, it is not meant to be. Once women become addicted to golf and set their minds seriously to it, they become highly proficient at the game.

Making due allowances for the disparity in

horsepower, it is probably fair to say that the best women golfers achieve a higher level of skill at golf than the best man. At the professional level, and here we are talking mainly but not exclusively about the American women's golf circuit, the players at the strongest end of the scale are just about the equal of the shortest hitters on the men's tour.

But once the drives have been struck, the effective difference becomes progressively less marked through the range of clubs. A good woman player can use her four-wood to match the shot of a man playing the same distance with his four-iron. And once we get into the area of "touch shots" around the green, the women stars are not just the equals of the men but possibly their superiors. Where women golfers are at a disadvantage is in the controlled application of explosive power — as in bunkers and heavy rough — but they normally avoid such situations better than men because of greater accuracy.

Such a judgment must be generalized. It cannot be stressed too strongly that the distance a golf ball may be hit is governed less by sheer strength than by the speed of the clubhead. And clubhead speed can be generated by timing and technique in the hands of a physically frail woman, provided — and it is a proviso which is almost universally misunderstood, or ignored — that the weight of the club is reduced. It can be safely asserted with a mass of scientific proof that women's golf is grotesquely handicapped by the use of clubs which are totally unsuitable in weight. For confirmation we have only to watch women at golf. Control of the club is clearly essential. Yet when you see women playing golf it is obvious that very early in the stroke the club is swinging the woman rather than the other way round. Clubmakers do employ women advisers, but they are famous players and as such exceptional. If women's golf is to be liberated, the battle must be waged on a much broader front than the area of male prejudice among club committees. They must get into the factories and insist on rational research and development. Burn your bras if you must, dear woman golfer (although *that* is probably the last garment for a golfer to discard), but for true liberation cast off the shackle of those 13-ounce drivers.

The search for improved performance on the golf course — and it should be made clear that we now are off the subject of sex — has strained the ingenuity of man to the limits of absurdity. Both the R. and A. and the USGA maintain black museums of illegal clubs which have been submitted by hopeful inventors. Nearly all are designed on fallacious scientific theory. Most of them are weirdly contorted — the clubs, that is — and grossly violate the rule that clubs must conform to conventional shapes. It was in that spirit that the R. and A. banned the center-shafted Schenectady putter after the Australian-born American, Walter Travis, won the 1904 Amateur Championship at Sandwich with a putting display that was positively inhuman in its accuracy. Possibly there was an element of pique behind the decision since Travis, a man of waspish disposition, took no pains to conceal his animosity after being shabbily treated by the pompous officials. It was nearly fifty years before the center-shafted putter received official blessing.

The USGA was on rather firmer ground with its first decision concerning the form and make of golf clubs. In the inaugural U.S. Amateur Championship, won by the mighty Charles Macdonald, one of the competitors had a novel idea. Richard Peters insisted on putting with a billiard cue and was duly disqualified.

Many golfers have had the same idea since then and have tried to devise a putting method which uses the billiard-cue principle. It is, after all, the easiest way, some might even say the only way, of directing a ball at a target with any degree of certainty. One solution to the problem of getting the hole, the ball, and the eyes in a direct line was the shuffleboard putter. This came in a variety of forms, the favorite being a cylindrical head on a long shaft, up to eight feet in some cases. The technique was to place the clubhead on the turf behind the ball, take aim along that barrel of a shaft, and shove. It worked only too well, if not quite so effectively as a billiard cue, and the authorities duly ruled it out of court. Apart from offending against tradition, the shuffleboard putter could be indicted under Rule 19, which requires that "the ball must be fairly struck at with the head of the club and must not be pushed, scraped, or spooned."

The legal position was rather more moot when the croquet putter came into fashion. The club conformed to the center-shafted specifications, and the stroke itself, swung between the legs with the player facing the hole, did not offend against Rule 19. Many golfers, especially those whose nerves had become worn to shreds through years of putting tension, found a new lease on golfing life through the croquet method. Sam Snead, the most notable exponent among the professionals, has achieved some success with croquet putting. Although it helped some golfers, croquet putting was not a superior method, per se. No great championship successes were achieved by the croquet brigade, nor were any putting records broken. It was different but demonstrably not better. The croquet putter did not give its user an unfair advantage. All it did was to permit some golfers to compete on level terms again with conventional putters.

So, you may ask, why not leave well enough alone? The argument was persuasive—and advanced with great force and forensic skill at the time—but in the end the powers of tradition prevailed and croquet putting was banned. That is to say, rules were introduced forbidding a golfer to stand astride the line of his putt, and the specification of putter was altered to forbid the shaft to be sunk into the putter head exactly perpendicular. Sam Snead neatly got around the new regulations by facing the hole, as usual, but positioning himself beside the ball, instead of behind it. He called it his sidewinder style and found it no less effective than the old croquet method. Most of the other erstwhile croquet putters simply reverted to the conventional style. Although the authorities took a particularly ponderous steamhammer to crack this inconsequential nut, they were surely right to ban croquet putting. It most certainly was not golf. Above the tedious legal wrangling there remained the feeling that croquet putters were not playing the game as we had come to know it. The governing bodies are often criticized, and with justice, for their pettifogging legalistic attitudes, but in most cases they are motivated by a genuine desire to preserve the original forms of

the game. Their instincts are sound, as they proved when they brought in the fourteen-club rule. Professionals were sponsored by manufacturers on the basis of the number of clubs they carried (or, to be accurate, their long-suffering caddies had to carry). Absurdity was achieved when pros had thirty clubs in the bag and the idea was spreading through the ranks of club players that such a complement of ironmongery was "necessary." Some believe that the maximum limit could well be lowered further to eleven or ten.

Weird and wonderful clubs by no means exhaust the inventive genius of golfers. Patent offices are stacked with designs for devices to make golfers play better. Enormous contraptions fitted with pulleys and clanking cogs have been built to educate a golfer's muscles to perform a geometrically perfect swing. There is even a design for a pivoted tee from which the ball will be dispatched with magically induced extra energy.

The ball has not been neglected. Every possible variety of filling for the inner core has been tried, including porridge, with subsequent claims of almost supernatural qualities. Alas for us golfers, the main thrust of inventive energy in the field of golf equipment has been directed toward marketing and advertising. Very little valid scientific research has gone into golf. Those studies which have been undertaken suggest, indeed prove in some cases, that many of the accepted theories about the properties of golf clubs are scientifically unsound. Yet the makers continue in their old ways, preferring to employ a copywriter who can turn out effective scientific mumbo jumbo for their ads, rather than put a scientist to work to improve the product. It is all very sad, knowing that technical improvements could be made in our equipment, but at the same time it must be admitted that the most important quality a club can possess is the faith of the man who swings it.

The Irish professional Jimmy Kinsella hammered a second shaft inside the shaft of his driver. Scientifically, the idea is absurd. As Bobby Jones wisely observed, the shaft simply connects the hands with the clubhead and of itself imparts nothing to the shot. Of course it doesn't. It is nothing but dead weight. Yet because Kinsella believes in his double-shafted driver it works for him in the same way that Roberto de Vicenzo can play well only with a ball marked with a "4." A surprising number of golfers are victims of such superstitions. Some have lucky colors. Others perform odd rituals like kissing their putters before every putt. (Bobby Locke actually slept with his, but that was more to ensure that no one stole the precious wand than to keep it in a good mood.) Nearly every tournament pro likes to follow a set routine, which seems sensible enough until you realize that these preliminaries often include such irrational details as insisting on putting on the left shoe first. It is all harmless enough most of the time, but if circumstances arise to upset the *idée fixe*, then the golfer can be undone. If that lucky sweater is lost so is the player.

Occasionally superstitions produce ludicrous situations, as in a mixed-foursome competition some years ago. A woman had got into the habit of teeing her ball right up against the tee marker, within three inches of it. The habit began as an aid to break her tendency to an exaggerated in-to-out swing. The arrangement made her swing along the line of the shot, and it got so that she had to have the tee marker right by the ball whenever she used her driver. This time, aware of the crowd watching and playing with a famous partner, she was naturally nervous, and she missed the ball completely. So the next shot had to be played by her partner. That tee marker would have been disturbing enough to any golfer, but in this case it was worse because he was left-handed. All he could do was make a token pass which counted technically as another air shot so that she could have another go. The woman made contact with her second attempt but it was not much of a shot.

No golf club is complete without a reproduction of a portrait showing an early golfer in his splendid uniform of scarlet jacket. In our enlightened way we tend to find the thought of a uniform for golf slightly amusing. "Fancy getting yourself up in an outfit like that to play golf" we tell each other, without realizing that we ourselves are hardly less given to peacock finery on the links. These old golfers inherited the tradition of uniforms from the archery societies whose colorful coats performed the same valuable function as the red jackets which modern hunters are encouraged to wear. They identified the wearers and saved them from being shot at and did likewise for golfers. Even today on one London municipal course in a deer park, the patrons have to wear red shirts or sweaters.

However, the impulse to dress up, and thereby make leisure activities more enjoyable, is a basic human instinct. The only special article of dress we actually need for playing golf is a pair of studded shoes, and even then a player who is properly balanced does not require anything like the full set of destructive studs of a modern golf shoe. (The studding pattern of golf shoes is one area which has been neglected by researchers. Yet if the teachers of golf are to be believed, a right shoe with studs only under the ball of the foot and the inside of the sole ought to ensure correct leg action. And any arrangement which reduced the number of studs would be a boon to greenkeepers. In a four-day tournament over a million studs pierce the surface of greens and make putting difficult in the closing stages.)

Yet we sheeplike creatures wear special clothing for our game, and what is more we allow ourselves to be persuaded that the trademark on a golf shirt affects our game. Today's golfer believes that by buying clubs with Arnold Palmer's name stamped on them he is purchasing some degree of his skill. The assumptions in this subconscious train of thought are too foolish to enumerate, but the effect is a powerful marketing force. In the same way, but even more absurdly, Bill Casper shirts, Lee Trevino hats, and Gary Player slacks are jujus to us sophisticated golfers. Protest as we may to the contrary, the idea of reserving special clothes for golf proves that at best we are sheep following the flock and at worst we are superstitious sheep who imagine that we are turning ourselves into tigers.

When there is no advantage to be found in clothing or equipment, there is always the leverage inherent in a judiciously offered bet. The tradition of having a little "interest" on the side must be nearly as old as golf itself; in moderation a little flutter is harmless enough. As to what constitutes "little," this depends. The safe rule is never to gamble for more than you can afford to lose without flinching. As soon as a golfer goes in over his head he can be quite sure that his game will suffer. The hustlers know this and use their knowledge to advantage. And there are more than a few unscrupulous characters about, mainly operating resort courses, who are all too anxious to take the unsuspecting golfer for his roll.

The usual American convention is the nassau, which means three bets: one on the first nine holes, one on the second nine, and one on the match. A $10 nassau thus involves a total liability of $30. In addition, there is the four-ball system of corners, $10 a corner on the match. Here the novice should establish clearly what is meant. Usage varies. Sometimes a $10 corner is taken to mean that each of the two losers pays $10 to both winners. Sometimes it is taken to involve a total liability of $10 from the losing side to be shared by the winning pair. More correctly, this is a bet of $10 a side, but it is good to be sure of the liability before the match starts. For match play there is the extra complication of the press bet. That is, when one player (or pair) falls two holes behind he can "press," start a new match on the remaining holes for half the stake (as well as continuing the main bet, of course). Further complications arise over byes. When a match is finished, say by four and three, the remaining three holes can be played as a separate match, or bye. Thus it is possible to get a complexity of bets going at once, with the match and its bye, the first press and its bye, and the second press and its bye, and so on. Few golfers have the mental agility to keep track of all these transactions and the safe rule is to note all the scores and bets on the card for a grand reckoning at the end. But what sounds like a straightforward $10 match can easily involve $100 changing hands, so it is wise to be wary.

On the subject of hustling, even greater caution is required. Hustlers usually operate singly, although they occasionally hunt in pairs. A golfer on vacation is the favorite quarry and the operation normally begins with an affable invitation for a game with a small stake. The object is to assess the quality of the opposition and to let the vacationer win. This is a process known as salting the pigeon and produces an obligation for a return match. This the vacationer is usually all too happy to provide. He may be allowed to win again, for a bit more interest. He is being set up, and once the psychological moment arrives there follows some casual remark such as, "I had a good night at the tables and I might as well lose it to you as give it all back to the roulette wheel. Shall we raise the ante?" It is at this point that the wise vacationer suddenly develops a chronic attack of rheumatism.

The madness of golfers takes two general forms. There are the idiosyncrasies the player brings with him when he takes up the game; the irrational examples we have been discussing fall mostly into that category. Then there is the rather more insidious form of disorder which comes from long exposure to the mind-bending game itself.

For instance, take the singular experiment of the three golf balls and the effect it had on its victims. At the time when the USGA and the R. and A. were pondering the possibility of a uniform golf ball for all the world, a number of examples of the suggested compromise ball fell into the hands of an evil newspaper golf correspondent.* In the interests of the golfing public he took himself off to try out some of the new-size balls. After hitting several shots he began to think he was losing his reason. Being a Machiavellian fellow, he thought that rather than send himself mad it would be vastly preferable to inflict this fate on the members of his club. He knew that, given a uniform shot, the small, British-size ball 1.62 inches in diameter would go farther than the 1.68-inch American ball and that the medium-sized compromise ball of 1.66 inches would perform somewhere between the two extremes. And this is exactly what happened, in accordance with the immutable laws of dynamics.

However, when he collected up all the balls and threw them down in haphazard fashion, there were instances when he could not distinguish which balls were which. When that hap-

*The author.

pened, and he did not know the size of the ball he was hitting, the results changed. There was no pattern to the shots. Some of the big balls went just as far as the small ones, and vice versa. The middle-size balls' behavior was similarly capricious. The cynic will say that the explanation was simple: He was a lousy golfer who couldn't hit a consistent shot and, as a matter of fact, the cynic would be right. But why, in that case, did the small ball go farther in the first experiment? A number of club members were summoned, some of them players of no mean skill. Just to make sure, the pro was included among the guinea pigs. The same thing happened. When they did not know which ball was which, the golfers performed much the same with every shot. Some went farther than others but the outcome was entirely random without any relationship between distance and the size of the ball. Yet when they tried again, this time being told which ball was which, the results conformed almost exactly with expectations. Disregarding obvious mis-hits, the small ball outdistanced the 1.66, and the big ball came last. (The exception to that norm was the pro who, knowing the ball sizes, hit the big one consistently farther than the other two sizes. He explained that since he always played the big ball—as required by the British PGA—he had developed a technique which was especially suited to it.) The effect on the ordinary players can be imagined. Believing for years that their small ball gave them 15 yards extra on their drives, they now had proof that notwithstanding the laws of nature they played just as well with the 1.66 or the 1.68. In fact, the size of the ball had the same significance for practical purpose as the number 4 painted on Roberto de Vicenzo's ball.

Even more traumatic experiences await the golfer. Nongolfers are frequently puzzled by the extraordinary rituals which pros perform as they face up to a 3-foot putt. "Why is he going through that song and dance over that tiddler? Why I could knock it in with one hand."

And so he could, once or twice, or maybe ten times. Then he would miss one and his troubles would start. For the pro the importance of the occasion makes the difference. Apart from that, golfers acquire a personal case history of disaster which can affect them almost as strongly as a physical jog on the elbow at the critical moment. Imagine the residual damage caused by Walter Hagen's experience of twitching a putt out-of-bounds, which itself may have been the result of past disasters.

Brian Barnes, the British Ryder Cup player, was in contention for the French Open at Saint-Cloud in 1968 and was going well when he came to the 8th hole in the second round. It is a par-3, and a short one at that, with no special difficulties. Barnes bunkered his tee shot and his recovery left him a long putt. Still smarting at his poor recovery, Barnes proved again the old saying that an angry man never hit a good shot. His approach putt was 3 feet short and with the old red curtain coming up over his eyes he lipped out the 3-footer. He raked at the ball and missed and by now he was lost. He patted the ball to and fro and by the time it dropped, what with penalty strokes for hitting a moving ball and standing astride his line, his playing partners reckoned him to be down in 15. Not surprisingly Barnes made a hurried exit from the scene. Who can tell what scars that experience left on his subconscious long after the incident was forgotten?

Tommy Armour was just one golfer who allowed his stubbornness to get the better of him. The week after he won the U.S. Open he was feeling that he could make the ball do anything he liked. He came to the 17th hole of the Shawnee Open and decided that the best way to play was to hit a long draw off the tee. The difference between a draw and a hook is, all too often, the out-of-bounds fence and that's just what happened. Armour was determined to play that draw shot and fired away off the tee, only to see ball after ball soar over the fence. His card was marked with a 21 for the hole, but afterward Armour disputed the figure. He insisted it should have been 23. It just proves once again that golf cannot be conquered.

After a lifetime of daily application, the game still has the power to turn and rend the complacent golfer. In realistic terms the game of golf defies success. Over some forty years, that is to say something like twenty thousand rounds by the world's most accomplished players, the ringer score, or eclectic, for the best eighteen holes at Augusta in the Masters is 38 strokes. Potentially that figure could be reduced by four more shots and doubtless will be in time, as players have the luck to hole out with approach shots. We can say, then, that a score of 34 would represent perfection at Augusta. The course record is 64, which demonstrates that the finest golf by the world's best players is a long, long way from perfect. We are all doomed to failure when we take a golf club in hand. The height of anyone's ambition can only be that his failures be modest. And it is here, surely, that can be found both the source of golf's lunacy and its sanity.

Almost everything in golf is a paradox. The learner discovers through distracted trial and error that in order to make a ball go upward it must be hit downward, and that if the ball is to be hit far it must be struck with a slow swing. At every turn in the game these paradoxes occur.

We tell ourselves that golf is a microcosm of life itself, but in truth it is life through the looking glass, life in paradox. And so we come to the comforting thought that the madness which manifests itself in every golfer is really, in our back-to-front world, quite normal. The man who devoted an entire room as a shrine to Arnold Palmer becomes by this interpretation entirely rational, as does the man who has created a large lawn from collected debris torn from golf courses by the clubs of the stars.

By the same token we who shoulder our clubs and seek to master what we know can never be mastered, are perhaps not so irrational as we sometimes fear. For what we are doing is to chase the bitch-goddess Failure. That is golf's ultimate paradox and it could be that we only appear mad from the other side of the looking glass. Maybe we are really the sane ones. And if not, never mind. Golf is fun and that, when you get right down to it, is all that matters.

Up the Tower
Henry Longhurst

Henry Longhurst is best known in North America as a television golf announcer who added a new dimension to that profession in that he was not averse to noting when a shot was less than was desired. He also was one who, judging by his performance, did not believe in superfluous commentary. He relied, instead, on the picture for the telling of the story and he used his "voice over" comments to add a short, intelligent note to enhance the viewer's enjoyment. His style was in sharp contrast to the platitudinous "pap" inflicted on viewers by most of his American counterparts. Henry was the first esteemed English golf writer to become affiliated with an American network.

Long before Longhurst came to the U.S. for television commentating, he was a legend in his own country as a master of the written word and as the successor to Bernard Darwin as golf columnist for The Sunday Times, *an assignment which gave him a continuing pleasure for twenty-one years. Besides being highly regarded as one of golf's most respected observers, Henry had the distinction of serving two years in the British House of Commons, and of authoring a book on oil for which no less a personage than Winston Churchill wrote the foreword.*

I was one of Henry's many friends and admirers and relished the rare occasions when our paths crossed. He was a raconteur of great charm, and I always was delighted when he took the time to tell me of the latest happenings in golf on his side of the Atlantic. One of the great moments we shared together was when Tony Jacklin won the United States Open at the Hazeltine National Golf Club near Minneapolis in 1970: Henry, because it was the first triumph by one of his countrymen in that championship in fifty years; myself, because I was responsible for the golf course.

Henry's inimitable style of writing, incorporating several personal anecdotes plus a few asides of interest, was never more evident than in "Up the Tower," in which he describes his introduction to radio broadcasting, then television on the BBC *and, finally, American* TV.

LIFE IS A MIXED BAG—chances offered and taken, more often chances missed or not even noticed. Successes are sometimes to be scored by honest toil and solid worth, more often by happening to be standing somewhere, thinking of nothing, at exactly the right time. In the latter category may be placed my entry into broadcasting, which for about thirty-five years has been one of the most pleasurable activities of my life.

Television is, by comparison with radio, a pushover. In television—I am talking, of course, of golf—in times of local difficulty, which means quite often, you can always intersperse what Sydney Smith, referring to the loquacious Macaulay's conversation at dinner, called "brilliant flashes of silence," and, indeed, as I hope to show in due course, this may gain you much merit. In other words, you can always sit back and let them look at the picture. In radio, if your mind goes blank for three seconds, they think the set has gone wrong. It is essential, therefore, in an emergency to possess the ability to "waffle on," and with this from the first I never had any great difficulty—on the radio or anywhere else, come to that!

I believe I can claim to have done the first "live" outside radio broadcast on golf when the BBC (British Broadcasting Corporation) set up a glass box on stilts at some vantage point far out on the Little Aston course outside Birmingham, overlooking two greens and three tees. In a way we were not unsuccessful. We saw plenty of play, chopping and changing from one hole to another, and had an added piece of good fortune when a past British Open champion, Arthur Havers, completely fluffed a short approach shot in front of our window. Perhaps he was unnerved by the thought of being on "live" for the first time in history.

Then the BBC brought in a portable apparatus with which it was to be possible actually to follow the golf, and here the initiator, at the English Amateur Championship at Birkdale the year before the war, was the doyen of our profession, Bernard Darwin. He set off onto the course accompanied by two engineers, one carrying a portmanteau-shaped apparatus strapped to his back with a long aerial sticking up vertically behind his head, and the other lugging around the batteries. I naturally listened with professional interest, having been invited to carry out a similar venture at the Amateur Championship at the Royal Liverpool Golf Club at Hoylake later on.

It was soon pretty clear that the venerable Darwin was finding it heavy going and it was no surprise when he declared, on returning to the clubhouse, that golf, so far as he was concerned, did not lend itself to this type of broadcasting.

At Hoylake on the morning of the Amateur Championship quarterfinals, we tried to follow the play but soon came up against the elementary stumbling block that in order to describe the play you had to see it, and in order to see it you had to be within range of the players, and they could therefore hear what you were saying, which was not only extremely embarrassing but led to persistent cries of "sshhhh" from the silent spectators. For the afternoon semifinals, we set ourselves up on a knoll beside the fifth fairway, well out of the way but with a reasonable view of the distant play. It seems incredible today but the signal for us to start was to be the lowering of a white handkerchief by an engineer perched on the roof of the Royal Liverpool clubhouse.

The exact hour of the broadcast in those days had to be printed in advance, so there was no flexibility in time. The first semifinal came to us and passed, then came the second. At this point the engineer raised the white handkerchief and we were under starter's orders. He lowered it briskly, and we were "off"—whereupon the second match vanished from sight, leaving our little trio silent upon a knoll in Hoylake, unable to move since our range was only a mile. I state with confidence that I gave an absolutely splendid and dramatic eyewitness account of the play, understandably interspersed with a good deal of the "Wish you were here...lovely view across the bay" sort of stuff, and I could not help feeling that not everyone could have waffled continuously or to such effect for ten whole minutes about nonexistent play. I thus returned to the clubhouse feeling that a congratulatory hand or two might well be extended. Instead, we met the engineer. He was most apologetic. "We had to fade you out after a minute or two," he said, "on account of a technical hitch."

Much as I respect the club, Hoylake has never been my happy hunting ground for either radio or television. In 1936, when golf on the radio was comparatively new, the engineer and I were stuck in a tiny, glass-fronted box situated among the guy-ropes at the back of the refreshment tent, with barely room for ourselves and a suspended microphone. Firstly, one day's play in the Open was cancelled on account of a snowstorm — in July — and I had to do three ten-minute pieces on a program going out across the British Empire, filling in for a whole day's play that had never taken place. Then a couple of friends espied me from afar and with schoolboy delight advanced upon our humble box.

I was in full spate when they came and made rude two-fingered gestures outside the box, pressing their noses against the glass and generally carrying on as though provoking a monkey in a cage. Finally, when once again we were in full flow, a waitress came out behind the refreshment tent carrying an enormous pile of plates. The strange spectacle in our little box so distracted her attention that she tripped over a guy-rope and sank with a crash that reverberated throughout the Empire. I explained what it was and gather that it gave innocent pleasure as far away as New Zealand.

The first serious attempts in Britain to televise live golf were directed by Antony Craxton, who used to do the queen's Christmas broadcasts. Many were from Wentworth, which, in summer, with the trees in fully glory and a shirt-sleeved crowd moving from hole to hole enjoying themselves in the sunshine, can present a magnificent picture. I remember Craxton saying how golf even then attracted quite a large "rating" by comparison with what had been expected, and how many housewives on housing estates said that they knew nothing about it but liked to watch because "it seemed such a lovely place." Nowadays, of course, this holds good to a much greater extent and some of the scenes in color — on British television so much superior to the American color, for once, due to different "line" standards — can be really heavenly.

For myself I always thought the "beauty shots" and the little irrelevancies — though we seem to have time for few of them these days — added to the appeal of golfing programs: the 360° panorama of, say, Turnberry, with the Clyde and the Isle of Arran and the long encircling arm of the Mull of Kintyre and Ailsa Craig; or Muirfield, with the distant tracery of the two great Forth Bridges and the Kingdom of Five on the other side of the Firth; or St. Andrews and the bay and the snow-capped Cairngorms; or, again, the small boy at the eighth at Wentworth who, immediately after the last match had passed by, emerged from the undergrowth and started fishing in the pond; or the lark's nest focused upon by an alert cameraman at Muirfield during the Open. The producer had to sacrifice this camera for quite a while before the mother lark returned to the nest to feed the young, and there were many who afterwards said that this was the best bit in the program, never mind Jack Nicklaus. The same cameraman's roving eye and telephoto lens discerned a couple on the sand hills, just outside the course and it was nip and tuck whether their subsequent union would appear, live and in color, for the first time on this or any other screen. If only the producer had been under notice from the BBC at the time, he might have risked his arm and given the world a most entertaining exposure — and I sometimes wonder what I should have made of the commentary.

What we put up with in the early days of TV golf never ceases to surprise me. For a Walker Cup match at St. Andrews I was stuck up on a tall tower out by the "Loop," where the holes crisscross over each other at the far end of the course, making it almost impossible on a small monitor to detect who is playing which hole and who is crossing over playing a different hole. Once again the wind howled in, direct from the North Sea and twice as strongly at forty feet up as on the ground, and soon it was so cold that one became numbed. Nor were the senses quickened by the fact that the British team lost every match on both days. For the second sitting I borrowed a fine, fur-collared flying coat from the barman at the Scores Hotel, but once again I gradually froze, to such an extent that I eventually found myself huddled over the blurred picture, thinking how poor it was and that there wasn't even a commentary. It was quite a time before the penny dropped. I suppose I can claim the doubtful distinction of being the only BBC commentator who has actually forgotten to do the commentary.

Another time, at St. Andrews, it was the picture that failed and I heard frantic voices from London saying, "Tell him to do a sound commentary till we get the picture back." This was really like old times and the "lovely view across the bay" stuff came back as naturally as though it were yesterday. In fact, at St. Andrews, there *is* a lovely view across the bay. I kept this up for about twenty-five minutes till eventually we got going again, and at the end of it all strolled back from my perch at the seventeenth to the Royal and Ancient for refreshment, which I felt had been well earned. As I got inside the door, the porter handed me a telegram. It was from the Nore Golfing Society. FIRST RULE OF ELECTRONICS, it read; IF IT DOESN'T WORK, KICK IT.

What can be the mentality of the man who actually rings up the BBC during the course of a transmission, as did a doctor during the playoff for the British Open between Peter Thomson and Dave Thomas at Lytham? We were in full voice when the producer came in with: "There's a doctor who has just rang the BBC in London with a message saying, 'Tell Longhurst there is no "p" in Thomson.'" This is a moment for instant decision. The answer comes immediately to mind, but do you give it? Do you say, "I understand a doctor has just rung the BBC to say there is no ''p'' in Thomson, and if it is of any interest to him this is by no means the only thing in which the p is silent' — or don't you? I didn't, but I still have a sneaking wish that I had.

Gradually it came to be appreciated that, if you wanted to "show the winner winning," the thing to do was to concentrate, as the Americans were already doing, on the last five holes, together with any "bonus" holes that the same cameras might be able to cover elsewhere — as, for instance, at St. Andrews, where the first five and the last five all share a common strip of ground.

It was also realized, as was really known all along, that the commentator need not be able to see what he was talking about, since his first task is to watch the monitor, the cardinal sin being to talk about something the viewer cannot see, thus driving the latter into absolute frenzies of frustration. Thus at last we began to be pitched nearer the clubhouse rather than miles out on the course, and up only one ladder, and the hand of civilization was extended towards us in the shape of little glass boxes to sit in.

It was to producer Ray Lakeland, and to the fact of happening once again to be in the right place at the right moment with my mouth open — literally, and with the right elbow lifted, at that — that I owe another experience in television which has given me more delight than I can say and has turned out to be a compliment not only, if I may say so, to me but also to "us." Lakeland was for some reason at the 1965 Carling tournament at Pleasant Valley outside Boston. I was also there but, having no work to do until the Friday, was idly sitting around having a drink, when he informed me that CBS, who were televising the event, wondered if it would interest me to go up one of their towers, it being their rehearsal day, and "see how they did it." I was naturally intrigued, and did so, joining John Derr, one of their announcers, as they call the commentators in the U.S.

So far as I remember I only said a few words into their microphone, but to my astonishment I got a note from the producer, Frank Chirkinian, inviting me to do the sixteenth hole next day. This turned out to be a long short hole of some 210-odd yards, where the players drove from an elevated tee down between two bunkers and onto a huge green, behind which we sat under a big parasol on a tower no more than 20 feet high.

"After all I've been through," as my mother is fond of saying, I soon discovered the luxury that is the lot of the American television announcer by comparison with home.

Firstly, we ascended our little tower by a broad set of steps instead of a death-trap ladder. The next luxury was the thought of having only one hole to pay attention to, and a short one at that, so one did not even have to watch drives as well as second shots.

At any rate, at Pleasant Valley I did all I was called upon to do, which heaven knows did not seem very much, naming the players and their scores correctly as they came up to the tee, which one could hardly fail to do in view of the fact that a very efficient young fellow had already put a piece of paper in front of one's nose containing the information, and occasionally adding some commonplace comment before being told to "throw it to fifteen."

It transpired, however, that completely unwittingly, I had managed to cause two minor sensations in our limited little world. One was when, towards the end, a young golfer named Homero Blancas came to the sixteenth hole with the prospect looming before him of picking up, if everything went right, the equivalent of some ß12,000 ($33,000). It proved to be a little much for him and, taking a two-iron, he hit the shot that a good many of us would have done in the circumstances; in other words, he hit it right off the sole, half topped, and it must have stung like the devil. "Oh, that's a terrible one," I said instinctively. "Right off the bottom of the club." In fact, it scuttled down the hill and finished on the green, but that wasn't the point. I had said it was a bad shot — which of course, it was — but no one, it transpired, had ever said such a thing before, at least in such downright terms.

This, though it took some time for the penny to drop, and I can sometimes scarcely believe it still, was the first "sensation."

The second took even longer to dawn on me. Golf being, like billiards, a "silent" game — that is to say that silence is expected while a man is making his stroke — it had never occurred to me from the very beginning that one should do other than remain silent while the golfer was actually playing his shot, so that "talking on the stroke" had always seemed to be one of the cardinal sins of golf commentating, even though, heaven knows, I have found myself often enough guilty of committing it. This had not been, up to that time, the accepted principle in America it has since become, and the "brilliant flashes of silence" turned out to be the second "sensation."

Also, of course, the most commonplace little expression in one man's country may seem strange and catch the attention in another's. Towards the end of this (for me) momentous day, for instance, I announced that the eventual winner, Tony Lema, later so tragically killed in a private plane accident, had a very "missable" putt. This, I was told, was greeted with much applause by the crowd watching in the locker room: "You hear what the old guy said? He said, 'He's got a missable putt.'" For some extraordinary reason this commonplace and self-explanatory expression seemed never to have become part of golfing language in America.

Anyway, it was all good for trade, and not only was I invited again by CBS, this time to the Masters at Augusta, which must have a separate mention of its own, but also by ABC who handle such "prestigious" events as the U.S. Open and the PGA championships. This has meant not only a minimum of four visits to various parts of the States each year but also a whole host of new friendships among the general camaraderie of television, which, though I hope it does not sound pompous, is the team game to end all team games, since there are so many links in the chain between the original product and the viewer's screen that a single incompetent or bloody-minded link can ruin the whole enterprise.

In a modest way, too, my name has gone into the language of television, for by the time we all met in America I had already grown portly enough to wonder what I was doing, climbing these ladders at my weight and age, and made so bold as to wonder whether it would not be possible to somewhat civilize this mode of ascent. From that time onwards a form of staircase, complete with handrail, has been the order of the day, for which I and all my successors may be truly thankful. What I am really proud about, though, is the fact that, in the directions to the scaffolders who erect the towers, these staircases are ordered by ABC under the name of "Longhurst Ladders."

Such is immortality!

As a result of the pleasant episode at Pleasant Valley, CBS, as I have said, invited me the following April to cover a hole at the Masters at Augusta, Georgia, and for years I have had the honor, to say nothing of the aesthetic pleasure, of sitting on a little tower at the back of the sixteenth there, too. It is once again a short hole and clearly, I should have thought, among the first half-dozen in American golf.

Who christened this tournament "the Masters" no one seems quite to know, nor is it certain that the pious founders would ever have started it at all if they had known what eventually they would be letting themselves in for. However that may be, the tournament they created remains unique. No advertisements are allowed to disfigure the scene either inside or outside the grounds—except when some supporter of Arnold Palmer (not, we may be sure, the great man himself) hired an airplane to fly noisily over the scene all day trailing a banner with the words GO ARNIE GO. Nor is any mention of filthy lucre permitted, and this really is something when you consider that the "leading money winner" seems to be the chief focus of interest in American golf. All the television directors and commentators have to submit to a solemn lecture forbidding mention of any tournaments other than the U.S. and British Open and Amateur championships and the American PGA (other tournaments on the professional tour simply do not exist) and especially forbidding them to mention money in any form. No prize money is announced beforehand and none presented at the time, it being held sufficient for the winner to have won the Masters and to have been invested with the traditional green blazer, which, thenceforward, even though he be a millionaire, he wears with justifiable pride. Only later is it revealed that the first prize came to $40,000, or whatever it may be.

Perhaps I may add one final comment on my own modest operations in television, namely that, whatever you may say, it is nice to be recognized, even if only by one's voice. This is not vanity. It adds much to the pleasure of a taxi ride (as well as to the tip!), for instance, if the driver says, "I'd know your voice anywhere," and starts talking about golf. Only the other day, hailing a cab opposite the American Embassy in Grosvenor Square, I said, "I wonder if you could take me to Cricklewood Broadway?" to which the man replied, "I'd take *you* anywhere."

Like so many London taxi drivers he was an avid golfer—they have a golfing society of their own—and actually had a golf magazine beside him in the cab, open at a picture of Arnold Palmer, who once, he said, the biggest day of his golfing life, he had driven in this very cab. All this is not, however, the irrelevance to the subject of the Masters that it may seem, for my peak was reached, and you can hardly blame me for relating it, when, on handing in my baggage at Cape Town airport in South Africa, I had had time to say only, "I wonder if you could check in this shooting stick as well as the suitcase?" when a transatlantic voice behind me said, "Hey! Aren't you the guy that does the sixteenth at the Masters?"

Golf in Los Angeles:
Part Royal and Ancient, Part Disney
Jim Murray

Having lived in New Jersey most of my adult life since coming to this country from England as a boy, and considering my home is only a few short miles from the headquarters of the United States Golf Association in Far Hills, I have to be considered part of the Eastern establishment, in golf and in many other ways. This would explain why, despite my travels, I only occasionally am able to indulge myself in reading the wonderful writings of Jim Murray of the Los Angeles Times. *Although he's syndicated nationally, no paper readily available to me carries his column.*

I sincerely regret this as I always have found Jim's style to be bright and breezy, with a rare flair for recognizing the absurd. He has a marked ability to amuse as well as to inform. Reading him whenever I can, I have come to realize he has a broad knowledge of all sports and an almost patented ability to extract the humorous from the serious for the enlightening entertainment of his readers.

Golf is no exception. Jim has an insight into the sport which stems from a long exposure to the game and to the foibles and failures of those who play it and who serve to provide much of the grist for his riotous columns concerning golf. He is no idle witness to the sport, either. My son Bobby, who lives on the West Coast, tells me that Jim plays the game with a vengeance, to which he added, "I have learned to my regret."

"Golf in Los Angeles: Part Royal and Ancient, Part Disney" is typical Murray at his laid-back best. For those of us who live on the other seaboard, it is a thoroughly amusing insight into golf in and around the city where leisure suits, Gucci loafers and convertibles are more in evidence than Brooks Brothers suits, rep-stripe ties and snow tires. It also is a rare look at many of the people in show business and how they disport themselves when they are not portraying larger-than-life images.

GOLF IN AND AROUND Los Angeles tends to be—like the rest of the landscape—unreal...part Royal & Ancient, part Disneyland. The Good Ship Lollipop with 4-irons. You expect a director to come walking out of the woods on 18 in puttees and with his cap on backward yelling, "Cut!"

The stuffy types at Blind Brook or Old Elm or The Country Club would never understand. There's a gaudy impermanence to Golf Hollywood that would shake the walrus mustaches right off the portraits in those staid old clubs. Remember, we're talking about an area where a chain-saw manufacturer bought the London Bridge and had it shipped over to provide a crossing over desert sand. They bought the Queen Mary and turned it into a chop house. They could buy St. Andrews and stick it up at La Quinta.

You get a running start toward understanding palm-tree waterpipe golf if you listen to that old joke about the sport in Los Angeles. Seems a man named Frank Rosenberg, a Texas oil man, wanted to get into Los Angeles Country Club, the West Coast version of the stodgiest and most exclusive club in the world. It is said eligibility for membership is a Hoover button, a home in Pasadena and proof-positive you never had an actor in the family. Once, when a member proposed Jimmy Roosevelt for membership, they not only blackballed the Roosevelt, they kicked out the member.

Rosenberg was rejected out of hand and the membership committeeman politely suggested he try Hillcrest. Hillcrest is a golf course which was founded by a movie man who was snubbed at a Pasadena course because of his religion. It has fewer gentiles than a kibbutz.

Rosenberg was stunned to be rejected by LACC and he so confided to a friend. "Oh," suggested the friend, "they probably thought you were Jewish. The club is restricted."

So Rosenberg applied at Hillcrest. "Fine, we'll take your application and wait for the first opening," he was told. "Fine," said Rosenberg, "but there's one other thing I want you to know—I'm not Jewish."

The committeeman looked at him and said softly, "Oh dear, I'm sorry. We don't admit gentiles." "Well, I'm an s.o.b.!" exploded Rosenberg. "If you can prove that," the committeeman told him, "you can get in Riviera!"

Riviera may be the most beautiful of the L.A. area courses. But it's a monster. It is the *only* Southern California golf course ever to host the Open. Hogan won it there in 1948. It's a demanding 7,100-yard, par-71 track no weekend player should be abroad on. Its rolls list mostly ruthless golfers, not cardplayers, not social members, but guys who can shoot in the 70s anywhere in the world.

It used to be a hustler's paradise. The stories are legendary (also libelous) of the dentists, Philippine generals, European counts, carefree movie stars and moguls who got fleeced on its not-so-broad fairways. It was Titanic Thompson country. You could get a bet on the color of the next dog coming up the fairway. It is Dean Martin's happy hunting ground as this is written and Dino is usually marauding on its tees and eucalyptus trees in division strength. It looks like Hitler's armor coming down the back side. Martin usually has three or four foursomes (or fivesomes) of pals, usually including one name pro (Devlin, Floyd, Bayer or Bolt), and the bets flow two or three holes back. Barry Jaeckel, French Open winner and son of a movie star, used to *caddie* for Dino, who has a reputation for having lost a fortune at the game. If so, he did it some time ago. Dean now is recognized around Riviera as a guy you give strokes to at your own peril. All the same, the trading is livelier among those golf cars than it is on the Paris Bourse. I know a lot of people who would like to cut 10 per cent of it and retire to the French Riviera after one season.

So, if golf is your bag, get in Riviera. They don't care what your religion or background is there. But they hope you have money and are willing to risk it. Mac Hunter, the pro there, was once considered a better prospect than Arnold Palmer and may hold the record for a club pro making cuts in the U.S. Open. His dad won the British Amateur and his son just won the California Amateur at Pebble Beach. If a guy says he's from Riviera, be sure to say, "We'll adjust at the turn," or you may go home in a barrel.

L.A. Country Club, apart from its exclusivity, is noteworthy because it sits athwart what must be the most expensive cluster of real estate in the world. It is almost in the center of Beverly Hills and its two golf courses have nearly a mile of front footage along Wilshire Boulevard. It is a 2-iron from Saks Fifth Avenue, I. Magnin, Tiffany's and the most expensive furriers and jewelers and boutiques in the world. The Beverly Hilton Hotel hangs over it. Imagine a golf course on either side of Fifth Avenue from 38th Street to the 80s and extending for 250 acres in all directions, and you have a notion of the Big Rock Candy Mountain that is LACC. Some *countries* couldn't afford to buy it.

If Riviera is the club for golfers and L.A. the club for oil, orange and railroad barons, Bel-Air attracts the management end of the broadcast and movie media. There are more station managers, network West Coast brass and their satellite advertising agency account executives (with a sprinkling of used-car dealers) at Bel-Air than at any other club in America.

It once was a club for L.A. Country Club rejects. It, too, sits astride some of the world's richest real estate, and it used to be a sandbox for the movie rich. Bing Crosby once belonged here. Fred MacMurray, Ray Bolger, Andy Williams play here and the Show-Biz types, the *talent*, shower downstairs. The upstairs locker room is, fittingly, the executive suite. The talent *handlers* — directors, agents, press agents, producers, ad men and network veepees shower up here.

Dean Martin was a daily communicant at Bel-Air until a greens committeeman cut up the greens to "improve" the course, a venture that was to prove long and, therefore, costly, because Dino had dozens of others quit in protest at having to play temporary greens. The departure of a Dean Martin from a golf club is comparable to a nearsighted millionaire leaving a crap game in a smoky room.

Lakeside has a charisma all its own. Here, in the salad years, the movie greats gamboled... Laurel and Hardy, W. C. Fields, Crosby, Hope, Jack Carson, Dennis Morgan, Gordon MacRae and Johnny Weissmueller drank here. Across the street from Warner Bros., it was a happy hunting ground for Warner's stars, who were not of the same magnitude as MGM's in those years but were a whole lot more festive. A requirement at Lakeside was that you be able to hold your booze. This was the club of the hard-drinking Irish and, the gag was, a standard for admission was that you had to be able to kill a fifth in nine holes.

Disc jockeys, industrial press agents, radio announcers (radio!) still dot Lakeside's membership rolls. The Old Guard is almost all gone (Buddy Rogers and Richard Arlen still play, for you trivia buffs). Only Bob Hope remains and fits in a fast nine holes on the infrequent occasions he is at home. Crosby keeps a locker but hasn't used it in years. The hard core of Lakeside is made up of guys who made it in the Big Band Era. It's THE club to belong to if you live in the lace-curtain sections of the Valley. Like Bel-Air, it has a slightly more modern step to it, as reflected in its clubhouse and dining areas. It's a golf course for the well-heeled suburban types. Unlike the muttonchop sideburns courses like L.A., it has no trouble making the bar and restaurant pay off but, like them, its club flag is at half-mast too often these days.

Wilshire Country Club is almost in downtown L.A. This makes it accessible to judges, lawyers, business executives, railroad and bank presidents. Color it dull gray.

The city's most celebrated golfers long were Hope and Crosby. Crosby in his prime was a solid 2, but he has drifted away from the grand old game in favor of bird-shooting and game-fishing. But not before he was hitting a few practice shots off the 10th tee at Bel-Air one afternoon (Bel-Air has no practice range) and a member of the greens committee came out and stuffily ordered Der Bingle to cease and desist. Crosby looked at him with that cold look a friend once described as "Arctic blue," the look that could stave in the bow of the Titanic. And Crosby gravely packed his clubs, emptied his locker — and has not been seen at Bel-Air since. He occasionally shows up at the more raffish Lakeside (which has a practice range), where the members don't much care where or for what purpose you hit the ball. W. C. Fields was fond of playing the course sideways with his pal, Oliver Hardy. He liked being in the trees where he could drink without scandalizing the natives.

Mickey Rooney holds the unique distinction of being thrown out of Lakeside. The Mick was a solid 3 in his best days, but he was not only a club-thrower, he threw whole sets. He once played the front nine with a new set and, at the turn, junked them and bought another new one for the back nine.

Playing with Mickey is like playing in the middle of a rehearsal for a Broadway musical. Mickey will sing the score, act the parts. He will do Judy Garland and Professor Labermacher (an old Jessel routine). He showed up on the first tee one day proudly announcing that Jack Nicklaus, no less, had straightened out his swing. As he moved flawlessly through the first three holes, he purred with praise for the new set of stiff shafts he had purchased. He dispensed tips with a lavish hand for the rest of the foursome. By hole 5, the swing began to disintegrate. By hole 9, the Mick was looking darkly at his new set of clubs and beginning to question Nicklaus' credentials to be teaching golf. By the back side, Mickey was holding the clubs aloft to anyone who would listen and demanding, "I ask you! Just look at these things! Look at the hosel! How can a man play with implements like these!" If you're a Mickey Rooney fan, you're rolling behind the trees, helpless with mirth. Mickey's funnier when he's not trying to be. But the members got tired of ducking in the showers when Mickey came through looking for a game, and they told him to empty his locker.

At Hillcrest, the game is "Can-You-Top-This?" and I don't mean a golf ball. There is a table at Hillcrest that is a shrine of Show Business. George Burns, Jack Benny, George Jessel, Eddie Cantor and Al Jolson used to lunch in a shower of one-liners. Every noon was a Friar's Roast. Danny Thomas represents the Catholics at Hillcrest. In the days of the Dusenberg-Bugatti-leopard-on-a-leash Hollywood, more picture deals were set here than at neighboring Twentieth Century-Fox, which is just across the street and is gradually giving way to a high-rise subdivision. The opulence of Hillcrest is Hapsburgian. The chandeliered dining room makes the Queen Mary foyer look like a lunch counter. The Marx brothers (save for Groucho, who disapproved of golf courses because there weren't enough girls) were the best players in the comedians' flight.

Brentwood, referred to as "Hillcrest East," plays host to the newer crop of comedians — Joey Bishop, Don Rickles, Don Adams (who also belongs at Riviera) and the generation of stand-up comics who came along in the television-Las Vegas era. Brentwood is not as severe a test of golf as LACC's North Course or Hillcrest, but successive renovations have given its clubhouse more and more of a Taj Mahal look.

Brentwood is important historically, because it was to have been the site of the 1962 PGA. The California attorney general threatened legal action because of the PGA's "Caucasian only" clause, and the PGA in 1961 jerked the tournament to friendlier climes at Aronomink in Philadelphia. But later in '61 the offending phrase was removed from the by-laws and the way was paved on tour for the Charlie Siffords, Lee Elders and George Johnsons.

Los Angeles probably has more "celebrity" tournaments per square foot than any golfing area in the world. Any golfing actor worth his marquee value would rather be caught without his makeup on camera than without a favorite charity. As Jerry Lewis once complained, "By the time I arrived, all the diseases were taken." George Jessel once observed that all that was left for the newcomers was gonorrhea. Chuck Connors has a tournament. A Tim Conway, a Bob Stack and even character actors have tournaments of their own. Even the tour fixtures have reached out to embrace celebrities. The venerable L.A. Open was the last to capitulate and become the "Glen Campbell L.A. Open." The slightly less venerable San Diego Open is now the Andy Williams SDO. The celebrities trade guest appearances at each other's tournaments, and the star power attracts the Kansas City wheat merchant to pay out a grand to tee it up with some crooner or TV tough guy in the pro-am.

Humphrey Bogart, it may surprise you to know, was very nearly a scratch golfer. Once a journalist drinking buddy of his put this reputation down to side-of-the-mouth braggadocio. Bogey, who rarely made one, took his pal down to

94

Tamarisk and proceeded to rip off an impeccable 73 after not playing for two months.

It's a game for all seasons in California. You can play golf 365 days a year. Every private club is awash with entertainment giants and sports greats. You might bump into a Jerry West (but not in the rough) at Riviera or a Jim Brown at Western Avenue (a flat muni-type club where the membership is largely black). The Dodgers' Don Sutton will be at Oakmont in the off-season, as will half the franchise. The Rams are addicts.

It's not a game uniquely suited to a community famed for its happy endings. John Wayne ducked the game throughout his career, even though his whole stock company, including Grant Withers and Ward Bond and Forrest Tucker, was scattered around Lakeside, where Wayne had a membership. The official reason was that "a golf ball just isn't Duke's size." The screenwriter, James Edward Grant, had a better explanation: "How could a guy who won the West, recaptured Bataan and won the battle of Iwo Jima let himself be defeated by a little hole in the ground?"

The Qualities of Greatness
Pat Ward-Thomas

For anyone but Pat Ward-Thomas, attempting to define the qualities of greatness might be a near-impossible assignment, like trying to capture smoke in a bottle. But Pat's unerring eye and his ability to transmit his observations have served to bring sharply into focus those qualities that place certain golfers on a higher plateau than others—a plateau reserved only for the enduring champions.

As a long-time admirer and good friend of Pat's, I also would place him on a plateau reserved for a few chroniclers of the game. Despite the fact he was middle-aged before he seriously turned his hand to such a creative endeavour, Pat has become one of the most highly-regarded golf writers in the world. Actually, he did not get started until he was thirty-seven, but he started at the top—as golf correspondent for the Manchester Guardian. *He was the first and only writer to bear such a designation until his retirement from daily assignments in 1978. Pat has not been idle since then. He continues to contribute his beautifully descriptive articles to* Country Life. *Two years ago he compiled a detailed and comprehensive history of the Royal and Ancient Golf Club at St. Andrews—*Royal and Ancient. *More recently, his highly unusual autobiography,* Not Only Golf, *was published.*

Anyone familiar with golf writing in the United States and Great Britain knows that writers in the two countries have a markedly different approach to the subject. In the U.S., the writers "tell it like it is"; overseas they give more of a commentary, and the writer is wont to give his personal views and interpretations of the events that happen, coupled with sometimes critical appraisals of a golfer's performance or lack of it.

Such a piece is this one by Pat, which clearly demonstrates his rare and gifted insight into the qualities of a handful of great champions who have warranted his critical delineation.

THE ART OF HITTING a golf ball well is not so very difficult given a measure of aptitude, a sound swing and the time and application to practise. Thousands of golfers the world over are thus qualified; many of them, professional and amateur, devote much of their lives to the game but few enter the reckoning on the great occasions and fewer still become champions. Only a minute company in every generation reach an absolute peak of supremacy and ensure themselves a lasting place in history. To do so demands uncommon qualities of character and temperament. They make fascinating study far more so, to my mind, than that of technique.

The winning of championships, not once but many times, is not solely a matter of consistent striking and controlling the ball under all conditions of climate and pressure of competition. If it were so the game would be an entirely automatic process that any highly trained dullard could master. Insensible men have achieved considerable success but the greatest rewards invariably escape them, and always will because ultimately golf is an examination of a man's mind and heart and nerve.

The qualities that set the great champions apart from their fellows are the abstracts of judgment, self-discipline and resilience of spirit that enable them to make the most of good fortune and the best of bad; the command of absolute concentration on the task in hand; the ability to analyse a situation and weigh the chances, the knowledge of when to gamble and when to play the percentages; the nervous control that under the severest strain will ensure the preservation of rhythm and timing; the gift of positive thought and the courage to face and overcome the prospect of victory. Fear of success is the greatest single destroying factor in golf.

Every great player has had these qualities, and others besides, in varying measures, but above all they have had the ambition to win and go on winning; the ambition that neither money nor fame will readily appease, the ambition to conquer for the sake of conquest, to prove themselves superior to everyone else in the world. This is the absolute essence that moulds all the other qualities into a single consuming force.

Whenever I think of this the name of Hogan comes to mind.

It is fitting to write first of Hogan. There is little doubt that he has been the most accurate golfer, and probably the most formidable competitor that ever lived. Comparison between the ages is invidious, no man can achieve more than absolute supremacy in his own time, as young Tom Morris, Vardon and Jones did in theirs, but I cannot imagine that anyone ever had greater or more exact control of a golf ball than Hogan. I asked Gene Sarazen once who was the finest player he had ever seen. He answered without hesitation that "no one ever covered the flag like Hogan," and Sarazen has known and played with all the great ones since the First World War.

Now I doubt that Hogan was born with a greater genius for golf than most of his contemporaries. Nor had he any advantages, either financial or physical, at the outset, but he was possessed with a well nigh inhuman determination to succeed. This overcame poverty, long years of disappointment and struggle in the 'thirties, the accident that almost destroyed him, and bred a desire for perfection of technique that few golfers have ever approached. I have often wondered whether he ever played a round that really satisfied him; it was as if the challenge of the game and the course exceeded that of beating the field. This probably accounted for the large margin of many of his victories. Jones said once that Ben was so good at finishing the job. Once he was ahead in his great years the rest of the field might as well have packed up; there was no quitting, no weakness, no faltering in sight of victory. Hogan had command to a greater degree, more often than any modern golfer.

To say that Hogan is reserved would be an understatement. In conversation he is not forthcoming and one learns little of the man himself from his own lips. This may be due to a defensiveness, bred in the tough years of youth, that he has never been able to shed; there is, too, a coldness about him, for all the gentle, polite manner and the broad smile, that suggests an almost frightening self-sufficiency, as if he has little need of the ordinary warmth of human contact, so essential to other men.

To meet Hogan is to be aware immediately of a personality of compelling strength, and yet every time I have talked with him I have had an impression of rare modesty, even humbleness. At Augusta during the 1964 Masters I was unable to make him agree that his golf was still good. The next day he played the huge course in 67, without putting particularly well, and in other events that summer his golf proved beyond doubt that, even at fifty-two, he was still the most accurate player in the world from tee to green. This modesty, no small part of Hogan's strength, is not uncommon in great players. Few have any conceit about their golf. They have learned that the game is greater than they are, but I am sure that Hogan strove harder than any golfer in history to become the exception.

Not the least interesting aspect of any study of the great players is that they are men of widely differing personality, education and background. It would be hard to find two more contrasting types than Hogan and Arnold Palmer, but they have many qualities in common. If one was asked to describe Arnold in a word I think it would be "responsive." The foundation of his huge success as a golfer is the strength of his response to challenge and competition, and as a person the genuine, unaffected warmth of his response to everyone with whom he comes in contact. Over the years I have had the pleasure of being with Palmer on many different occasions, and yet no matter what was in prospect — conversation, a drink, dinner, flying, bridge or simply doing nothing very much — I have rarely known him not to respond instantly. Even in times of frustration and disappointment, and for all his success he has had his share of these, the tremendous urge for living, the humour and good nature are never stilled for long. The life force runs strong in Palmer. It is the awareness of this and the man's expressiveness and freedom from affectation of any kind, apart from the exciting nature of his golf, that are the secret of an extraordinary appeal to the crowds who swarm in his wake.

Palmer's greatness as a competitor stems from his reaction to challenge in any form. The difficult recovery, the telling putt, the long dan-

gerous carry, the desperate situation when all seems lost; any form of adversity is adrenalin to him; with a hitch of the pants and a grim smile he gets to work; his attitude is that of a man fighting and loving it — as indeed he does. Occasionally, however, the reaction is not so obvious — as at Troon in the Open of 1962. No golfer, especially an American, could have been enamoured of the links as it was that year, but Palmer, save in private, kept his opinion to himself while others grumbled. I am sure that the condition of the course was the inspiration for his wonderful scoring. The fact that it offered a ready-made excuse for lesser mortals was sufficient to call forth a supreme effort from Palmer, just as it would have from Hogan.

Their reaction to circumstance was equally great but somehow different. Hogan's approach was that of the coldly efficient, superb technician, achieving mastery by the ruthless production of perfect strokes; the whole operation planned with surgical care and precision. Emotion and inspiration would seem to play little part, although undoubtedly they did to some invisible degree, whereas one could not fail to be aware of these in Palmer, whose golf is much more a matter of mood than Hogan's ever was.

Hogan came closer to de-humanising the game than anyone else has ever done. With Palmer the human element is abundantly strong, even now when he is so mightily established, and the old surging rushes from behind are infrequent, the strategy of his golf is ever based on attack. The two golfers are as dissimilar in manner as the commander of a mechanised army and the leader of a great cavalry brigade, as the rifle to the broadsword.

In the beginning the fires of Hogan's ambition may have been lit by force of circumstance but those of Palmer's must always have been smouldering. He was not driven by extremes of necessity, like that which existed in the depression, and neither by any means was Jack Nicklaus. Never has immense achievement come so easily, so swiftly to a young golfer. Long before he was twenty-four he had won the American Open and PGA championships, the National Amateur twice, and the Masters. His earnings for the first three years as a professional must have reached a million dollars and that is evidence of an exceptional young man. In the opinion of his rivals, he clearly was born with far more than his share of what it takes to make a champion; notably immense power and confidence.

Power is an undisputable advantage, almost a necessity, to win in modern golf, but for all the mighty strength of Nicklaus, his success has been greatly due to an apparently impregnable confidence. I have not known its like in any other games player. It is alive in every move of the solid frame, in the urgency of his walk, the crisp unhesitating speech, the set of his strong, clean-cut features and the directness of his gaze. Nicklaus has few, if any, of the doubts and fears that sabotage others; instead he has a tremendous belief in himself.

Long ago in the *Art of Golf*, one of the first classic books on the game, Sir Walter Simpson wrote that a "secret disbelief in the enemy's play is very useful." Nicklaus has this in no small measure; even when I first knew him as a young amateur there was no sign of awe and hero-worship of great players. I think he has always believed, and this is no idle conceit, that he is the finest golfer in any field. Nicklaus accepts victory simply as the natural outcome of the event. His manner shows less of joy and relief than that of other men, and conversely failure never disturbs his remarkable equilibrium and self-assurance. Obviously he hates losing; there never was a worthwhile champion who did not, but the only effect is to harden his determination. There is no trace of dejection, no loss of poise and never a hint of excuse; there is no self-deception in the philosophy of Nicklaus.

Rarely indeed does one hear the great players excusing failure, explaining it, yes, but not blaming it on misfortune. Such an attitude of mind leads to defensive thinking. A man who seeks excuses is unlikely to be a champion. In the long run the gods are fair in their distribution of chance and the good generally balances the bad. Realisation of this is the measure of a fine competitor; Palmer and Nicklaus certainly have it.

Nicklaus has yet another gift—that of detachment. Golf may occupy a great deal of his life but I doubt that it will ever become an obsession. I have spent many hours with him when he has not introduced the subject at all; Palmer is the same, and relishes many other things in life, but never gives the impression that his detachment is absolute. He is thoroughly absorbed in golf, every aspect of playing the game, whereas Nicklaus's approach to it is far less complex, less emotional and less expressive. It is astonishingly free of complication.

The ambition to be the best is the ultimate driving force that sustains the form and position of the great players long after financial security has been achieved. Sadly it seems to be rare in British golfers since Cotton commanded the scene in the years astride the Second War. There never was a more ambitious golfer than Cotton, nor one more absorbed in all the manifold ways of golf as a profession. He devoted himself to the cause of technical perfection and success with an intensity that even Hogan hardly surpassed.

Even now as he approaches sixty it is impossible not to be aware of the man's enthusiasm. It shines in his eyes and rings in his quick eager voice, and I never cease to wonder at the depth of his passion for the game. His mind is always alive, ever progressive and searching for new ideas and the fresh approach. Such qualities are born not acquired, and Cotton is blessed with a livelier intelligence and imagination than almost any other professional golfer. Many have envied his magnificent skill, that has had few peers, and his success in the business of golf, but these were not easily achieved.

There was nothing of the prodigy about Cotton; he worked and worked to make himself strong, to create a method that would and did endure throughout a long career; to master a highly strung sensitive temperament that often must have caused him untold anguish; to develop his personality and presence so that he compelled attention to a degree that no British golfer of modern times has approached. In this last he was shrewdly aware, as he said to me once long ago, that to be a champion you must act like one. To this end he not only set himself high standards but demanded higher prices than anyone before him, and profited enormously thereby. Cotton has been the complete professional in every conceivable sense of the term. No man exemplified the qualities of a champion more vividly.

The more I watch first-class golf the more convinced I am that rhythm is the most important single factor in playing it successfully. Once a sound, repeating swing has been developed the essence of consistent striking thereafter is the preservation of a constant rhythm. All the great players have this in common but I doubt that there will ever be a finer example than Bobby Locke.

Rhythm is one of the hardest qualities to acquire unless a man be naturally gifted because it is directly related to his temperament. Anxiety, temper, frustration, even elation, can sabotage it all too easily. One sees instances in every tournament and thus keeping an even rhythm often demands mental control of a high order. In the years when Locke was one of the world's finest competitors I marvelled at the self-discipline that maintained his measured pace when things went amiss. As everyone knows there is a great temptation after a poor stroke to hurry the next one, usually with fatal results. I cannot recall a single occasion when Locke did so. If anything he would take a little more time but generally his pace was as unchanging as the tide. There was an impression of eternal serenity about his golf. Nothing, absolutely nothing, ever seemed to disturb him and in this respect, the secret of his greatness, he remains unique in my experience of champions.

Any mention of rhythm inevitably brings to mind the legendary figure of Samuel Jackson Snead. So far in discussing the qualities that make champions no count has been taken of the purely natural physical gifts. No golfer in history could have been more richly endowed in these than Snead. He was blessed not only with great strength but with remarkable suppleness that made possible an effortless turn of the shoulders and body without any loss of control or balance, and a marvellous sense of rhythm. The result was a natural swing, matchless in its grace and beauty and power. Some, like Nicklaus, may have hit the ball further; one or two as consistently, and there have been many swings that were a delight to watch but there has never been one more beautiful than Snead's—or one that has retained its superb quality for so long.

Winston Churchill said once that balance was one of the outstanding traits in the British character. It is true of most of the great players of games in the mental as well as the physical sense. There have been many distinguished golfers with unstable temperaments, capable in some moods of great deeds and extremely vulnerable in others, but I cannot think of a great one who was lacking in balance.

It is a remarkable feature in both Palmer and Nicklaus, considering the phenomenal success that would have turned the heads of many another and I have always thought that Peter Thomson is an uncommonly balanced golfer, not alone in his beautifully orthodox, simple swing and the athletic poise of all his movements, but in his attitude. Thomson has always seemed to make success and failure effortless; he is never excitable, never prone to talk overmuch about golf and able, to a marked degree, to disassociate his own play from any discussion. Like Nicklaus he has the priceless quality of detachment. Although the whole process of success may not have been as free from strain as his manner invariably suggests he has had balance to a rare degree. Without it no man's golf can endure long enough to achieve lasting greatness.

(1965)

The Triumvirate
Bernard Darwin

Golf has long captivated the English-speaking world, and we in golf are fortunate that there have been writers who have left us stories of the past and of the players who contributed to the vitality of the sport in distant years. Foremost among these chroniclers would have to be the legendary Bernard Darwin, who wrote for nearly half a century as our golf correspondent for The Times *of London, for* Country Life *and as author of a half-dozen books relating to the game.*

Herb Wind unabashedly called Darwin "the greatest writer of golf the world has ever known." That is high praise coming from one who has himself been similarly regarded by his contemporaries. Darwin was the grandson of Charles Darwin, the great naturalist who propounded the theory of evolution. Educated at Cambridge for a career in law, Bernard forsook that profession to follow the fairways and to report, in a literary and lucid style, on a game in which he never lost his interest.

This was evident to me in 1951 when I met Darwin for the first and only time, at St. Andrews. The occasion was the "driving in" of Francis Ouimet as the first non-British Captain of the Royal and Ancient Golf Club. It was an honour which Darwin himself had received previously as Captain of the R & A in 1924. As a writer, he enjoyed this distinction as much as his membership on the first team ever assembled for a Walker Cup Match, in 1922 at the National Golf Links of America at Southampton, New York. The Great Britain-Ireland team was defeated, but Darwin contributed one of the four points it won.

"The Triumvirate," which is included here, is Darwin at his best. It is a highly personal appraisal of J. H. Taylor, James Braid and Harry Vardon, incorporating a pleasant mix of their respective techniques and styles plus a commentary of the time as it related to the game. Although it was written more than sixty years ago, the piece always will be evergreen to those of us who cherish the great contributions of Bernard Darwin.

THERE IS A NATURAL LAW in games by which, periodically, a genius arises and sets the standard of achievement perceptibly higher than ever before. He forces the pace, the rest have to follow as best they can, and end by squeezing out of themselves just a yard or two more than they would have believed possible.

During the last year or two we have seen this law at work in billiards. Lindrum has set up a new standard in scoring power and our players, in trying to live up to him, have excelled their old selves. The same thing has happened from time to time in golf, and those whom we call The Triumvirate undoubtedly played their part in the "speeding up" of the game.

Taylor, though by a few months the youngest of the three, was the first to take the stage, and it has always been asserted that he first made people realize what was possible in combined boldness and accuracy in playing the shots up to the pin. Anything in the nature of safety play in approaching became futile when there was a man who could play brassie shots to the flag in the manner of mashie shots. Mr. Hilton has suggested that this raising of the standard really began earlier and was due to another great Englishman, Mr. John Ball. It may well be so, for it is hard to imagine anything bolder or straighter than that great golfer's shots to the green, but Taylor, being the younger man and coming later, burst on a much larger golfing world than had Mr. Ball. Moreover, he was a professional who played here, there and everywhere, and so was seen by a large number of golfers, whereas the great amateur, except at championship times, lay comparatively hidden at Hoylake. Time was just ripe when Taylor appeared: golf was "booming" and the hour and the man synchronized. Though in the end he failed in his first championship at Prestwick, he had done enough to show that he was going to lead golfers a dance to such a measure as they had not yet attempted. In the next year he won, and for two years after that the world struggled to keep up with him as best it could.

Then there arose somebody who could even improve on Taylor. This was Harry Vardon, who tied with him in the third year of his reign (1896) and beat him on playing off. There was an interval of one more year before the really epoch-making character of Vardon was appreciated. Then he won his second championship in 1898 and was neither to hold nor to bind. He devastated the country in a series of triumphal progresses and, as in the case of Lindrum, there was no doubt that a greater than all before him had come. To the perfect accuracy of Taylor he added a perceptible something more of power and put the standard higher by at least one peg.

And, it may be asked, did Braid have no effect? I hardly think he did in the same degree though he was such a tremendous player. He took longer to mature than did his two contemporaries. Of all men he seemed intended by nature to batter the unresponsive gutty to victory, and he won one championship with a gutty, but his greatest year, his real period of domination, came with the rubber core. He cannot be said to have brought in a new epoch except to this extent perhaps, that he taught people to realize that putting could be learned by hard toil. He disproved the aphorism that putting is an inspiration for, after having been not far short of an execrable putter, he made himself, during his conquering period, into as effective a putter as there was in the country. By doing so he brought new hope to many who had thought that a putter must be born, not made, and had given it up as a bad job.

Presumably everybody thinks that his own youth was spent in the golden age, and that the figures of that period were more romantic than those of any other. At any rate I can claim romance and to spare for my early years of grown-up golf, for I went up to Cambridge in 1894 and that was the year of Taylor's first win at Sandwich. Moreover, The Triumvirate were then, I am sure, far more towering figures in the public eye than are their successors of today. It was their good fortune to have no rivals from beyond the sea. They were indisputably the greatest in the world. Then, too, they had so few ups and downs. Today a professional is in the limelight one year and in almost the dreariest of shade the next, but these three, by virtue of an extraordinary consistency, always clustered round the top. Finally their zenith was the zenith of the exhibition match. They were constantly playing against one another and no matter on what mud-heap they met, the world really cared which of them won.

It is partly no doubt because I was in the most hero-worshipping stage of youth (I have never wholly emerged from it), but it is also largely due to the personalities of those great players that I can remember quite clearly the first occasion on which I saw each of them. It is a compliment my memory can pay to very few others. Taylor I first saw at Worlington (better, perhaps, known as Mildenhall) when he came almost in the first flush of his champion's honors, to play Jack White, who was then the professional there. I can see one or two shots that he played that day just as clearly as any that I have watched in the thirty-seven years since. I had seen several good Scottish professionals play before that, including my earliest hero, Willie Fernie, most graceful and dashing of golfers. I thought I knew just what a professional style was like, but here was something quite new to me. Here was a man who seemed to play his driver after the manner of a mashie. There was no tremendous swing, no glorious follow-through. Jack White, with his club, in those days, sunk well home into the palm of his right hand, was the traditional free Scottish slasher. He was driving the ball as I imagined driving. Taylor was altogether different and his style reminded me of a phrase in the Badminton book, which I knew by heart, about Jamie Anderson and his "careless little switch." One has grown used to J. H. long since, but the first view of him was intensely striking, and I am inclined to think that in his younger days he stood with his right foot more forward than he does now, so that the impression of his playing iron shots with his driver was more marked. He was not appallingly long, but he was appallingly straight, and he won a very fine match at the thirty-fifth hole. Incidentally, the memory of that game makes me realize how much the rubber-cored ball has changed golf. The first hole at Worlington was much what it is today, except that the green was the old one on the right. Now the aspiring Cambridge undergraduate calls it a two-shot hole and is disappointed with a five there. On that day—to be sure it was against a breeze—Taylor and Jack White took three wooden club shots apiece to reach the outskirts of the green, and Taylor with a run up and a putt won it in five against six.

My first sight of Vardon came next. It was on his own course at Ganton, whither I went for the day from Whitby, and he had just won his first championship. He was playing an ordinary game and I only saw one or two shots, including his drive to the first hole. Two memories vividly remain. One was that he was wearing trousers and that from that day to this I have never seen him play except in knickerbockers, an attire which he first made fashionable amongst his brother professionals. The other is that his style seemed, as had Taylor's on a first view, entirely unique. The club appeared, contrary to all orthodox teaching, to be lifted up so very straight. Even now, when I have seen him play hundreds and hundreds of shots, I cannot quite get it out of my head that he did in those early days take up the club a little more abruptly than he did later. The ball flew away very high, with an astonishing ease, and he made the game look more magical and unattainable than anyone I had ever seen. For that matter, I think he does so still. In view of later events it is curious to recall that a good local amateur, Mr. Broadwood, who was playing with him, talked then of his putting as the most heartbreaking part of his game, and said that he holed everything. I only saw one putt and that he missed.

It must have been a year later that there came the first vision of the third member of The Triumvirate, who had hardly then attained that position. This was at Penarth, where there was a Welsh championship meeting, and Taylor and Herd were to play an exhibition match. Taylor could not come; at the last moment Braid was sent for to take his place and arrived late the night before. I remember that he did in his youthful energy what I feel sure he has not done for a long time now; he went out early after breakfast to have a look at the course and play some practice shots. His enemy, by the way, had come a whole day early and played a couple of rounds. I have almost entirely forgotten the Penarth course, and the shots I played on it myself; the one thing I can vaguely remember is the look of the first hole and of Braid hitting those shots towards it. Here was something much more in the manner that one had been brought up to believe orthodox, but with an added power; save for Mr. Edward Blackwell, with whom I had once had the honor of playing, I had never seen anyone hit so malignantly hard at the ball before. Mr. Hutchinson's phrase about his "divine fury" seemed perfectly apposite. One imagined that there was a greater chance of some error on an heroic scale than in the case of Taylor and Vardon, and so indeed there was, but I remember no noble hooks that day, nothing but a short putt or two missed when he had a winning lead so that Herd crept a little nearer to him.

From the time when I was at Cambridge till I sold my wig in 1908, my golfing education was neglected for, if I may so term it, my legal one. I played all the golf I could, which was a good deal, but watched hardly any. Therefore I never — sad to say — saw Vardon in his most dominating era, nor the great foursome match over four different courses in which he and Taylor crushed Braid and Herd, chiefly through one terrific landslide of holes at Troon. However, in the end I managed to see each of the three win two championships, Braid at Prestwick and St. Andrews in 1908 and 1910, Taylor at Deal and Hoylake, 1909 and 1913, Vardon at Sandwich and Prestwick, 1911 and 1914. I suppose the most exciting was in 1914 when Vardon and Taylor, leading the field, were drawn together on the last day, and the whole of the West of Scotland was apparently moved with a desire to watch them. Braid, too, played his part on that occasion, for had he not designed the bunker almost in the middle of the fairway at the fourth hole? And was it not fear of that bunker that drove Taylor too much to the right into the other one by the Pow Burn, so that he took a seven? No wonder J. H. said that the man who made that bunker should be buried in it with a niblick through his heart. Yes, that was a tremendous occasion, and Braid's golf in 1908 — 291 with an eight in it at the Cardinal — was incredibly brilliant; and Vardon's driving when he beat Massy in playing off the tie at Sandwich was, I think, the most beautiful display of wooden club hitting I ever saw; but for sheer thrilling quality give me Taylor at Hoylake

in 1913. There was no great excitement since, after qualifying by the skin of his teeth, he won by strokes and strokes; but I have seen nothing else in golf which so stirred me and made me want to cry. The wind and the rain were terrific, but not so terrific as Taylor, with his cap pulled down, buffeting his way through them. There are always one or two strokes which stick faster in the memory than any others, and I noticed the other day that my friend Mr. Macfarlane recalled just the one that I should choose. It was the second shot played with a cleek to the Briars hole in the very teeth of the storm. I can still see Taylor standing on rocklike feet, glued flat on the turf, watching that ball as it whizzes over the two cross bunkers straight for the green. There never was such a cleek shot; there never will be such another as long as the world stands.

It is surely a curious fact that, though these three players dominated golf for so long, and the golfer is essentially an imitative animal, no one of them has been the founder of a school. They made people play better by having to live up to their standard, but they did not make people play like them. Here are three strongly marked and characteristic styles to choose from, and yet where are their imitators? Vardon had one, to be sure, in Mr. A. C. Lincoln, an excellent player who belonged to Totteridge; he had at any rate many of the Vardonian mannerisms and a strong superficial likeness. There is George Duncan, too, with a natural talent for mimicry; he remodeled the swing he had learned in Scotland after he first saw the master. Imagine Duncan slowed down and there is much of Vardon. Beyond those two, I can think of no one in the least like him. It is much the same with Taylor. His two sons, J. H., Jr. and Leslie, have something of the tricks of the backswing, but nobody has got the flat-footed hit and the little grunt that goes with it. Braid, with that strange combination of a portentous gravity and a sudden, furious lash, seems the most impossible model of all. I know no one who has even copied his waggle, with that little menacing shake of the clubhead in the middle of it. Each of the three was so unlike the other two that the world hesitated which model to take and ended by taking none. American players look as if they had all been cast in one admirable mold. Ours look as if they came out of innumerable different ones, and as if in nearly every mold there had been some flaw. It was part of the fascination of The Triumvirate that each was extraordinarily individual, but now it seems almost a pity for British golf. If only just one of them could have been easier to imitate! In other respects, of course, they did all three of them leave a model which could be imitated. By all the good golfing qualities of courage and sticking power and chivalry, by their modesty and dignity and self-respect, they helped to make the professional golfer a very different person from what he was when they first came on the scene. Their influence as human beings has been as remarkable as their achievements as golfers.

Harry Vardon
Charles Price

I think I can say without contradiction that I am one of the few people in golf still around who had the pleasure of watching Harry Vardon play. It was a long time ago to be sure, sometime during the summer of 1920 when he, along with Ted Ray, made his third and last trip to the U.S. to play a series of exhibitions prior to the United States Open at Inverness in Toledo which, incidentally, Ray won.

Vardon and Ray played against Walter Hagen and Jim Barnes and, despite the thousands of golfers I have seen since, I would be hard put to cite four players with more dissimilar styles. Hagen swayed at the ball, Ray lunged at it and Barnes, because of his height, swung from a decided crouch. Vardon, without a doubt, was the true stylist of the group. He also was the worst putter of the four. Today we would call him a "spastic" who jabbed at the ball in contrast to his otherwise smooth shotmaking. Despite their obvious differences, it was one of the most titled groups ever assembled for a one-day stand. Combined they had won, or would win, a total of twenty-four major championships in the United States and Great Britain.

Regrettably, I cannot remember their individual scores or which side emerged as the winner. I guess, as a first-year caddie at the Country Club of Rochester, New York, where the exhibition took place, I was too overwhelmed by the excitement of the occasion and the presence of such "giants" to fix such details in my mind.

Fortunately, Charles Price has never been one to be overwhelmed by an assignment, especially one which required meticulous research and an acquired understanding of the life and times of a subject. Charley has written what I believe to be the best and most comprehensive study ever made of Vardon by a modern writer.

THERE WAS THIS golfer—so goes a weary story that has been kicking around locker-rooms for half a century—who was so unflaggingly accurate that he couldn't play two rounds in the same day over the same course; his tee shots in the afternoon kept falling into the divot holes he had made in the morning. No one ever seems to have asked why so accurate a player could not have missed the divot holes purposely.

The story is usually told in reference to Harry Vardon and is typical of the sort of tales his golf inspired. So many absurdities have been pinned on Vardon, in fact, that in some circles today there is doubt the man even existed. As the years have gone by and the stories about him have grown more fantastic, he has turned into a kind of golfing Paul Bunyan—more myth, actually, than man.

Vardon's size, for one thing, has been grossly exaggerated. One would get the impression today that he was some gargantuan golfer who could handle a club as though it were an obedient extension of his mind. Actually, he was far from Bunyanesque physically. He stood exactly five feet, nine and one quarter inches and, during his prime, he weighed a hundred and fifty-five pounds. His hands, though, were large enough to have belonged to a man twice his size. With them—for Vardon's power emanated almost totally from his hands—he performed feats of golf seldom seen before or since.

Separating what actually was seen from what only was heard of Vardon has always been a task. But there are some reasonably authentic anecdotes that can be plucked from the almost endless apocrypha of his life. Here are three.

In a grudge match for one hundred pounds against Willie Park, Jr., just before Vardon became Open Champion, Vardon halved ten straight holes against the then invincible Park, and, in the process, dropped his tee shots within a few clublengths of Park's on every hole. The stalemate was broken on the eleventh fairway when, after Park's tee shot had come to rest, Vardon's ball hit it *on the fly*. Visibly shaken—as well he might have been—Park never managed to win a hole.

On another occasion, Vardon sank a mashie (about a five-iron) on his second shot to a par-

four hole. For those in the gallery who thought the shot might have been due entirely to luck, Vardon managed that afternoon to sink another mashie shot on the same hole.

While engaged in a lengthy exhibition tour of the United States in 1900, Vardon was hired to display his form by hitting balls into a net at Jordan-Marsh, the Boston department store. To relieve the monotony of what Vardon thought was an inane way to show off his skill, he amused himself by aiming at the valve handle on a fire extinguisher that was projecting through the netting. Since the handle was no larger than a silver dollar, hitting it at all would have to be classified as quite a feat. Vardon hit it so often that the floor manager begged him to stop for fear that the store would be flooded.

Harry Vardon was, to state the situation mildly, a hell of a player. For more than twenty years, or a third of his life, he dominated competitive golf not only in his own country but throughout the world. He was to win the Open Championship a total of six times, a record that has never been approached. No accurate count of his lesser tournament wins exists, but it is known that in one stretch he won fourteen straight.

Vardon won the United States Open in 1900 during his triumphant exhibition tour and tied for first in 1913, only to be beaten in the play-off. In 1920, at the age of fifty, he came close to winning the title again despite two past seizures of tuberculosis which seemed to have left him without even a vestige of his putting stroke. "At that time," recalls Gene Sarazen, who played in that championship, "Vardon was the most atrocious putter I have ever seen. He didn't three-putt, he *four*-putted."

Harry Vardon was an utterly natural golfer. He never asked anyone to give him a lesson and nobody ever had the audacity to offer him one. With all his native talent, he nevertheless knew in his mind what every muscle in his body was doing. He was the first of the long line of so-called "mechanical" golfers who bring off bullet-like shots with the consistency of a press printing tomorrow's headlines. While the consistency of many of these has often reached monotony, Vardon added a fillip to his shots. He "typed" them, cutting the cloth, so to speak, to fit the pattern of the hole. Depending upon the architectural characteristics of a hole, he would draw the ball or fade it and, if the wind so dictated, loft it high or punch it low in the process. "I first saw Vardon at Brookline during practice rounds for the 1913 Open," Walter Hagen once said. "He was practicing mashie shots off a downhill lie, and he was fading every one of them. The groove in his swing was so obvious you could almost see it. I was so impressed that during the last round, when my swing started to leave me, I started imitating his. And it worked, too. Fact is, I almost caught him with his own swing."

Unlike most mechanical golfers, Vardon was a swinger in the classic sense who was not above employing alterations in form that he thought were worth while. For example, he advocated John Ball's open stance for every shot in the bag because, as he explained, "there is nothing to impede the clubhead in coming through first." Even on his drives he assumed a stance more open than most pros today use on pitches, positioning his left foot at least six inches behind the right and pointing it almost directly down the intended line of flight. Addressing the ball, he then executed his swing with such consummate grace that you had the impression he might very well have played the same shot, if need be, while standing barefoot on a cake of ice. "To accuracy," says Bernard Darwin, "he added something more of power which put him for a little while in one class with all the other golfers in another. He could reach with two shots greens which asked for two shots and then a pitch from nearly all the rest, and his brassie shot was likely to end as near the pin as did their pitches."

Vardon's power is one of the few aspects of his game that has not been exaggerated out of all proportion to what it actually was. The reason for this may be that he played most of his exhibitions while paired with Ted Ray, an Englishman whom few men could keep up with off the tee but a player with only a fraction of Vardon's talent. "Vardon always played well within himself," says Sarazen. "He always kept ten yards of his power in reserve and there were times, when he hit the ball flat out, that he could add as much as thirty yards to a drive."

Considerable though they were, Vardon's physical talents formed only a part of his genius. His demeanor was perfectly attuned to the rigors of competitive golf. Few players since have been as capable of comprehending the potentialities of a golf course, of understanding when and where a course ought to be treated with respect, and then, knowing this, going out and trouncing it, not just with power, but with more skill than its architect bargained for and more cunning than nature could have devised. He was the epitome of confidence. Often, he would play a shot and then replace his divot before bothering to see where the ball had gone. He didn't have to see. He knew. Imperturbable, taciturn, he seldom smiled on the course, but then he seldom scowled either. He never threw a tantrum, never gave an alibi. He just came to play.

Bobby Jones once recalled being paired with Vardon during a qualifying round for the 1920 National Open at Inverness, near Toledo. On the seventh hole, a short dog-leg to the right, Jones topped a simple pitch to the green into a bunker. Embarrassed, he turned to Vardon on the next tee. "Did you ever see a worse shot in your life?" he asked.

"No," Vardon replied.

Emotionally, Vardon had the equanimity of a plowhorse. "If a dog crossed the tee in front of him while at the top of his swing," wrote Andrew Kirkaldy in his autobiography, speaking of Vardon, "he would be able to judge whether the dog ran in any danger of its life. If it did, he would stop his club; if it didn't, he would go through with the shot, without pulling or slicing."

Harry Vardon was born on May 9, 1870, in Grouville, a whistle-stop on the channel Isle of Jersey, just off the western coast of France. His father was a gardener. Harry had two sisters and five brothers, two of whom also became professionals. Harry and his brothers took to golf by caddying at a nearby course which had been constructed by some visiting sportsmen from England. He was then eight years old. For fun, he and his brothers and some other caddies built a course of their own, consisting largely of fifty-yard holes. They fashioned clubs by using oak branches for heads, with strips of tin for faces, and black thorn branches for shafts. Marbles were used in lieu of golf balls.

As his father had before him, Harry became a gardener in his teens. His first job was with a retired army major who was a fanatic on golf. He encouraged Vardon to play and gave him his first set of clubs. Through one of his brothers who had become a professional, Harry secured a pro berth at the Studeley Royal Golf Club in Ripon, Yorkshire, while in his early twenties. In 1896, at the age of twenty-six, he won his first British Open by defeating J. H. Taylor by four strokes in a thirty-six hole play-off at Muirfield. He won the championship again two years later at Prestwick, repeated in 1899 at Sandwich, his favorite course, and returned to Prestwick in 1903 to win again. After the first of two major battles with tuberculosis, Vardon managed to win his record fifth British Open at Sandwich in 1911. He topped this off with a sixth win in 1914 at Prestwick.

Vardon first visited the United States in 1900. He drew vast galleries by the standards of the day. During his appearance at Jordan-Marsh in Boston, large enthusiastic crowds, only a few of whom had ever played golf, were moved to applause just at the sight of him effortlessly smashing balls into a net. The store sold out its entire stock of clubs in a matter of hours. While in the United States, Vardon played dozens of matches against all comers and lost only one. This was to Bernard Nicholls in Florida. The defeat was considered a baffling upset. Out of what he considered fairness, Vardon took on amateurs two at a time, playing their better ball. At the Country Club of Atlantic City he played against H. M. Harriman, who was then National Amateur champion, and Findlay S. Douglas, who had been runner-up to Harriman and champion in his own right the year before. Vardon closed them out on the twenty-eighth green, winning nine-and-eight.

Like most of the players of his day, Vardon played with only a putter and six clubs: a driver, a brassey, a cleek, a driving mashie, an "iron," and a mashie, as they were called in the parlance of the day. These were equivalent, in today's terms, to a driver, a brassie, a shallow-faced two-iron, a three-iron, a four-iron, and a five-iron, the last of which he used for recovering from bunkers by laying open the face. Later in his career Vardon added three clubs, one of which was a left-handed five-iron which he used when fences or trees interfered with his normal stance. There are those who say there was no perceptible difference between the results of his left-handed mashie and his right-handed ones. He was capable of tearing the flag out of the hole with either.

Vardon dressed for a round of golf by wearing hobnailed brogues, a necktie, and knickerbockers, establishing the fashion for the latter over trousers. These he supported with suspenders rather than a belt. "Braces seem to hold your shoulders together," he explained. By the same token, he advised against playing without a coat, even on the warmest of days.

One of the popular misconceptions about Harry Vardon is that he devised the overlapping grip, which even today is more often than not referred to as the "Vardon grip." Actually, he did not and, furthermore, never took nor expected any credit for devising it. Almost until the time he won his first British Open he used the palm grip, or what is commonly referred to in America today as the "baseball" grip. He abandoned this grip because it had a tendency to make him overpower his shots with the right hand.

"Golf is a two-handed affair," he once said in explaining why he switched to the overlapping grip. "The clubhead and the hands, wrists and arms should be considered as parts of the club, all working together as one piece of machinery."

To Vardon, everything about golf was strictly "mechanical." Every shot had its logical cause and its logical effect. "As you get on in golf," he once wrote, "you know that every good shot and every bad shot was absolutely of your own making; the whole thing happened according to laws of exact science. You may be unfortunate in having a bad lie, or in having a specially difficult shot presented, but so far as the shot itself is concerned it is all in the hands of the player to make of it what he will. The old golfer realizes that. But the young golfer is apt to think it is largely due to fate — something quite inevitable and not worth bothering about."

Harry Vardon was, it is plain to see, an absolute realist about the game. With this attitude he was able to develop a set of mechanics for golf—a unified grip, a graceful pivot, dazzling footwork—by which anybody could improve his game. Until Vardon, playing golf well was largely a job of perfecting one's own peculiarities, and the individual styles of all the great players were marked by all sorts of idiosyncrasies. Hilton hit the ball with a lunge, Taylor cut most or all of his iron shots, Ball held onto the club as though it were a ham sandwich. It is to their credit that they played as superlatively as they did.

But with Vardon came a style so effortless and simple that it seemed the most logical thing in the world to imitate it rather than to hobble along with one's own eccentricities. To this easy style he added not just power or finesse, but both, and in such equal measure that there did not seem to be any shot, however long or however short, that he could not play as well as anyone else. It is to Vardon's everlasting credit that so free was his game of any weaknesses—excepting a tendency late in his career to jab short putts—that it was conversely never known for any particular strength. His whole game was strong. He could drive, pitch, chip and putt to such a degree that his record in winning the British Open—the oldest, most prestigious contest in golf—has not been approached in half a century.

The Professional: Walter Hagen
Fred Corcoran with Bud Harvey

What a parley, Walter Hagen and Fred Corcoran! I recall many colourful memories of these two old friends. Hagen, of course, was a flamboyant personality who opened the clubhouse doors for all those who followed with a PGA card in their pockets. He also was my first idol, a bronzed, handsome figure driving a white Packard convertible, a man whom I first viewed with awe from the standpoint of a twelve-year-old caddie at the Rochester Country Club.

He was a Beau Brummel, a bon vivant and an international celebrity when most of his pro contemporaries were hidden in golf shops no bigger than closets. He was a character bigger than life who practised what he preached: "I don't want to be a millionaire, I just want to live like one." And he could play—eleven majors and five Western Opens when the latter was second only to the U.S. Open in importance.

I knew Walter well, but not as well as did Fred Corcoran, a smiling Irishman originally from Boston. Fred started as a scoreboard keeper—it was he who introduced the use of red ink to indicate under-par scores—and went on to become one of golf's premier promoters. He served stints as Tournament Director for the PGA in the critical thirties and for the LPGA in the fifties, when the latter organization was just getting started. He also was Hagen's manager and he was affiliated in a similar capacity with Craig Wood, Sam Snead and Tony Lema, in addition to baseball great Ted Williams.

Fred was a source of a million golf stories and was a walking encyclopedia of the game. His almost total recall and inherent news sense saved many a sports columnist from a disaster at deadline. If it ever happened in golf, Fred remembered it.

Hagen was more than a happening; he was an era, and Corcoran has chronicled that period and the man who made it so, like no one else. See if you don't agree as you read this chapter from Unplayable Lies, which Fred wrote with Glynn "Bud" Harvey, another ex-Bostonian and former Publicity Director of the PGA of America.

LET'S MAKE AN IMPORTANT distinction right here. There are golf professionals and there are professional golfers. The two terms are not necessarily synonymous. The golf professional is a man who sells you golf balls and, when the occasion calls for it, prescribes for your golfing ills. The professional golfer plays golf for money.

Walter Hagen was a professional golfer, although he may not have been the greatest professional golfer who ever drew breath. I'd have to go along with Ben Hogan in this department, because he owns just about every record in the book, plus a dozen you won't find there. But Hagen was the first professional to make a million dollars at the game—and the first to spend it. If Hogan was the king, Hagen was the prince, and the darling of the people. Where Hogan walked the fairways looking neither to the left nor right, Hagen—in his own words—met a million persons.

He was the corporal of the color guard. No question about it. He had that magnetism, the electric quality, that fired the imagination. He lived the life lesser men dream about as they plod back and forth every day between their offices and the subway.

I suppose I've told more stories about Walter Hagen than about any other sports figure I've ever known. And not because I was that close to Hagen. I wasn't. But only because Hagen himself is a living legend and the sports world is filled with curiosity about him.

The strange part of it is, the legend has distorted the actual portrait. True, Hagen loved life and people. And he hated to go to bed because sleeping seemed like such a waste of time. But the picture of Hagen flashing through life with champagne bubbling out of his ears is a false one. The Hagen of his golden years took excellent care of himself. He was the world's champion hider of drinks. Walter always had a full glass in his hand. But after the ball was over, the sweeper would find a dozen drinks lined up behind the piano where Hagen had slyly stashed them during the revels.

That first year on the PGA tour, I met Walter at San Francisco during the Oakland Open. He was embarking on a world exhibition tour and I had just been named manager of the American Ryder Cup team. We discussed arrangements for handling the team which would be selected that year to play in England. Walter, who was named the nonplaying captain of the American side, said he was planning his itinerary to reach London in time to meet us.

True to his word, Hagen was standing on the station platform in London when the boat train arrived from Plymouth at two AM. And I remember so clearly the picture he made standing there as fresh and debonair as if it were nine AM.

While the luggage was being sorted and the hatboxes were being loaded aboard taxis, he drew me aside.

"You'll have to help me identify these wives," he said. "Some I know, but most of them I've never met."

He didn't offend any of them. As they stepped off the train he gave each one a little hug and called her Sugar.

This was so typical of Hagen, this thoughtfulness. He always seemed concerned for the sensibilities of others. I'll never forget his acceptance speech at the end of the matches. When the American team won, Walter began writing memos to himself and stuffing them in the pocket of his polo coat.

"We want to make sure we don't forget anyone," he kept repeating, and down would go another note, perhaps a reminder not to forget an accolade for the assistant greenkeeper.

So he had a pocketful of paper when he took his seat for the presentation ceremonies. Unfortunately, he tossed his polo coat over a chair at the far side of the dais and when the time came for him to accept the Ryder Cup, he reached in vain for his verbal ammunition. Walter sighed and stood up.

"You have no idea," he began, "how proud I am to captain the first American Ryder Cup team to win on home soil..."

Several voices in the throng interrupted him at this point to shout: "You mean *foreign* soil, Walter!"

Hagen shrugged. His face broke into a wide smile and he said:

"You can't blame me for feeling completely at home over here, now can you?"

That was all he had to say. The crowd loved it, and loved him for it.

The matches were played at Southport where Hagen saw Snead for the first time. Sam, you'll recall, burst on the golf scene that year like a meteor and had played his way onto the Ryder squad. Walter watched Snead for a few practice holes and marked him immediately as a great player. Yet, he didn't play Sam in the foursome matches and he told me why.

"He's never played an alternate shot affair, has he?" Walter said. "I don't believe I'll play him the first day. It wouldn't be fair to him. He's strange to the game and not familiar with the rules."

So he limited Sam to the singles matches and Sam crushed Richard Burton by 6 and 5.

I first saw Hagen play in the U.S. Open at Brae Burn in 1919 when he beat Mike Brady in a play-off. I was working the scoreboard for the USGA, my first assignment of that kind. Hagen was only twenty-seven years old, but already a sports page celebrity and well on his way to becoming the legend he is now, a bronzed fine specimen of a man who strode down the fairway with his head high. Hagen always walked with his head in the air as if, subconsciously, looking over the heads of ordinary mortals.

He came up to the last hole of regulation play needing a pretty good putt to tie Brady who was already in. Impeccable as always in his traditional white silk shirt and silk tie, Hagen lazily drew his putter and surveyed the putt. Then he looked up with a smile and called, "Where's Mike?"

He wanted Brady out there watching while he stroked home the tying putt. It would give Mike something to think about for the next twenty-four hours.

The play-off round wasn't much of a golfing exhibition. Neither played well. But the turning point came at the 17th hole where Hagen took command with a typical Hagen combination of brains and skill. He put his tee shot into a peat pocket where it lay virtually buried. Then, as now, there was a penalty for playing the wrong ball, so equity permitted the lifting and cleaning of the ball for purpose of identification. Hagen asked the officials to have the buried ball identi-fied. Naturally, when it was dropped again, the lie was improved considerably. Hagen then put his next shot on the green, holed out in four, and went on to win—a patented Hagen finish.

In 1940 I met Monsignor Robert Barry, a low handicap golfer himself, who was having lunch at the famed Thompson's Spa, across the street from the Boston *Globe*. He said, "Tell me, how is Walter Hagen?" I told him Walter was fine when I had last seen him.

"You know," said the priest, "when I was going to the monastery I would drive a couple of hundred miles on a weekend just to watch him play. There is something about the man I found fascinating. I enjoyed watching him...the way he dressed...his actions...his wonderful golf...everything he did was so dramatic. Tell me about him."

Well, what do you tell one man about another? I suppose, instinctively, you try to relate him to the mainstream of the other's life.

"You know," I said, "Walter is not a religious man. I know he believes in God, but if I ever wanted to go looking for him I wouldn't start with a church." I thought a little and added, "I have an idea he's broken eleven of the Ten Commandments, but I'll tell you something else, Father, I think I'd like to be with Hagen wherever he goes when he dies..."

Monsignor Barry's eyes were following me closely and he was nodding silently. I went on.

"Now, another thing. He's done more for people than anyone I know. For instance, he always takes good care of his caddie. If the boy needs a lift into town, Walter remembers. He always remembers to give the boy a little gift. And he's like that with the other players. Always giving...not only his money, but himself..."

"Now," I said, "I'd like to ask you this: How are we going to be judged?"

The monsignor didn't hesitate a moment.

"I'll answer you, Fred, by saying the Walter Hagen you have just described has the quality we all must have to earn Heaven. That's charity."

Faith, hope and charity, he pointed out, abideth. And the greatest of these, as the Gospels tell us, is charity.

Well, I found this conversation very interesting and, the next time I saw Walter, I reported it.

Hagen sat quietly for a moment, looking down at his feet, then he said softly:

"I'm not a very saintly person, I know, but I've tried my best to go through life without deliberately hurting anyone..."

Hagen was the first true American golfing internationalist. He enjoyed meeting new people and seeing new places. He was an authentic citizen of the world.

In 1942 I was going to England as a Red Cross volunteer and Hagen made me promise to stop at the Savoy, his favorite London haunt.

"And be sure to ask for Karl Hefflin," he said. "He's the manager. Give him my regards and tell him I asked him to take good care of you."

So I arrived at the Savoy in due time and asked for Mr. Hefflin who met me in the lobby with a puzzled frown. When I identified myself and extended greetings from Hagen, the puzzled frown vanished.

"Oh," he said, "the boy must have misunderstood you. He thought you said *you* were Walter Hagen. And, you know, we've had three bombing raids in the past month and, as I was coming down to meet you, I was asking myself, 'How can I take these air raids *and Walter Hagen, too!*'"

But he said it with affection, and went on to inquire about Walter who, over the years, had become his favorite American guest.

Until Hagen and Gene Sarazen came along, American golf existed in a vacuum. American golfers stood with their backs to the Atlantic and either didn't know or didn't care that the game had any roots. Hagen and Sarazen turned our faces back to the wellspring of golf. Walter was never happier than when, as a player or a captain, he was leading an American team of professionals over to Britain. He believed every American professional worthy of the name owed it to himself and to the game to play in at least one British Open championship. Or *the* Open, as he called it.

Sam Snead, with the other American Ryder Cuppers, had played in the 1937 Open at Carnoustie, following the matches that year. But he hadn't played well at all, and he never went back. In 1946 I entered Sam in the British Open which was going to be played at St. Andrews,

shrine of golf and home of the Royal and Ancients.

But during the last round of the Inverness Four-Ball tournament and on the eve of his scheduled departure for Britain, Sam came to me at the 9th hole and said, "Fred I'm not going. I'm just not putting well and there's no point in me going over there if I can't get the damn ball in the hole..."

Well, our plans were all made. He was supposed to fly that evening to New York and take off for England the next day. I remember going into the clubhouse and the first person I met was Walter Hagen. I told him Snead had decided not to play in the Open.

"What's the matter with him?" asked Walter.

"He says he isn't putting."

Hagen said, "Oh, what a shame! And with his touch he'd putt those greens at St. Andrews as if they belonged to him."

When Snead came off the course, Walter was waiting for him. He drew Sam off to the far end of the locker room and said, "Sam, let me see you putt." He watched Sam stroke a few balls, then he stopped him.

"Raise your blade just a little, Sam," he told him. "Try to slap that ball just above the equator. All you want to do is get it rolling...rolling... rolling..."

Over and over, he had Sam stroke balls on the carpet until Sam was snapping his putts with a new crispness. Then he stopped him and said, "All right, you've got it now. Go ahead over there to St. Andrews and win it."

I duly told the newspaper boys about the episode in the locker room and the next morning the local paper carried a sports page headline: "Snead to Play in British Open—Takes Putting Lesson From Walter Hagen." This was all right. But, at the same time, Snead was syndicating a series of instruction pieces and the gospel for the day was set up in a two-column box next to the main golf story. The headline over here read: "How to Putt, by Sam Snead"!

Any good story has to have a happy ending, and this one does. Snead went to St. Andrews and won the Open. He never putted better.

The only time I can recall Walter Hagen losing his poise was in his epic match with Gene

Sarazen for the 1923 PGA championship. This might well be classed as the match of the century. Hagen and Sarazen were great rivals. They were unquestionably the two outstanding golfers of their day, and I suspect Gene always felt Hagen got the better of it in their daily battle for sports page space. This gnawed at him, and he took a special delight in whipping Hagen.

The 1923 PGA final dingdonged along through 37 well played holes. On the 38th, Sarazen pulled his tee shot and it appeared to go out of bounds. In fact, to this day, Hagen insists it *did* go out of bounds and was tossed back in play by "an outside agency"—one of Gene's partisan fans who lined the playing limits at the Pelham Country Club, in the heart of "Sarazen country."

Satisfied that Gene's ball was out of bounds, Hagen played his tee shot comfortably down the middle of the fairway. Under the penalty code of the day, a ball out of bounds at this point would spell complete disaster. Sarazen could never have recovered from the penalty and all Hagen had to do was play safely to the green and hole out.

But Gene's ball was found lying in the tall grass, well within the boundary stakes. Sarazen, playing with icy courage, hit a magnificent gambling second shot that carried across a dangerous elbow to the green, within a foot or two of the hole. Hagen stared at Gene in dismay and shook his head in disbelief. Then, obviously shaken, he proceeded to put his second shot in a trap, short of the green, and that was the match.

The Hagen legend has created a myth of invincibility. This isn't so, of course. Hagen lost his share of matches and tournaments and, in fact, was beaten pretty badly on occasion. I remember especially his International match with Archie Compston in 1929. Hagen had just stepped off the boat and was pretty rusty. He hadn't swung a club in weeks. Compston defeated him in a 72-hole match by 18 and 17!

After the first couple of holes, it became clearly apparent that things weren't going well for Hagen. Then he seemed to chuck it entirely, apparently totally unconcerned about the outcome. He seemed more interested in making adjustments to his swing. It was a curious attitude, but he explained it later and I'll never forget his words.

"If you're going to get beaten," he said, "it doesn't make any difference if you lose by one hole or by ten. It was a wonderful chance to get a lot of bad shots out of my system at once."

Two weeks later, at Muirfield, Hagen won the last of his four British Open championships with a 292, matching his best score in this championship which he cherished above all others.

Walter never showed any great enthusiasm for the marathon practice sessions that have become part of the working day for the modern tournament pros. I remember standing with him at the Colonial Club in Fort Worth, watching the players hammering away on the range. We watched Byron Nelson for several minutes while he hit a steady barrage of flawless iron shots. Hagen sighed.

"What a shame to waste those great shots on the practice tee," he said. "What are they doing out there anyway? Those guys already know how to hit a golf ball. They don't have to do that. I'd be afraid to stand out there and work at my game like that. I'd be afraid of finding out what I was doing wrong."

We turned back to the club and Hagen talked on.

"You know," he said, "I used to go out to the practice tee and hit four or five balls—just to relax and get the feel of it. I always planned to make any adjustments on the course. I always figured to make a couple of mistakes on the first few holes. But mistakes don't hurt you at this stage. It's those mistakes you make on the last few holes that kill you. I always figured to have my game under control by then..."

He jerked his head back to the firing line.

"That," he said, "is nothing but corporal punishment."

I'm reminded of the time at Augusta, when Sam Snead spent an hour on the practice tee. When he came in I asked his caddie how Sam was hitting them. The boy grinned and said, "I dunno if we're gonna win the tournament, but man! we sure won the practice tee championship!"

A typical Hagen story is an account of his match with Joe Turnesa at Dallas in 1927. Hagen was the master of applied psychology and always said he liked the head-to-head character of match play. He said he always knew exactly where things stood.

On this occasion, Walter arrived at the clubhouse thirty minutes late and was sharply scolded by the tournament officials. Hagen knew he was wrong. He apologized humbly and hurried off to dress.

On the first three holes he grandly conceded putts of varying lengths and Turnesa quickly went three up. Then Hagen said, "There, that makes up for the thirty minutes I was late. Now we'll play . . ."

Well, the match rocked along until they reached the 17th hole — the 35th of the match — and Joe had a fairly easy putt. But Hagen made no gesture of conceding it. In fact, he was elaborately helpful to Joe in lining it up. Joe missed it and the match was all even.

They came to the last hole and Hagen put his second shot off to the right in some tall grass, partially screened off from the green by some trees. Turnesa was in good position in the middle of the fairway. Walter studied the line of flight, paced back and forth several times, tentatively drew three or four clubs from his bag. Then he turned and waved Turnesa back into the gallery.

"Joe," he called, "I may have to play this safe." Later he chuckled, "I could have driven three Mack trucks up to the green through those trees."

Then he settled down and played his shot, sticking the ball within twelve feet of the flag. Turnesa, kept waiting and watching this strange performance, finally stepped up to his easy shot and dunked it in the trap flanking the green — and Walter had won his fifth PGA championship.

Curiously, Hagen's grandstand performance thoroughly delighted Turnesa, as it did the gallery. One of the remarkable things about Walter Hagen was the fact that, even in their defeat, his opponents all had a tremendous affection for him. In fact, Joe Turnesa tells this story with complete admiration for Hagen.

There's the famous story about Walter turning up in the lobby of the hotel in the wee small hours before his championship match with Leo Diegel. Somebody remarked to Hagen that he shouldn't be on the town at that hour with a big match staring him in the face in the morning.

"Look at that Diegel," argued the well-intentioned adviser. "He's been in bed asleep for five hours."

To this Hagen replied, "Diegel may have been in bed for five hours, but he's not sleeping . . ."

Hagen, on the other hand, could sleep like a kitten — literally. That's how he slept, all curled up in a ball. I was with Ty Cobb early in the evening in Detroit and he wanted to visit Hagen. So we went over to the Detroit Athletic Club where Walter lived, and asked for him. The clerk said Hagen was sleeping. Cobb refused to accept such a preposterous answer and said he'd see this phenomenon for himself.

So upstairs we went to Hagen's room. His door was open and we walked in. There was Hagen in bed. Cobb shouted, "Walter! Walter! Wake up!" But Hagen didn't move a muscle, just went on snoring peacefully. And Hagen, incidentally, snores pretty good. Cobb studied the sleeper and shook his head in admiration.

"There's the most relaxed man I ever saw," he commented. "See how he sleeps all rolled up in a ball? Anytime you have trouble sleeping, just try it. It's complete relaxation . . .

Bob Harlow, who played full-time manager to Hagen, used to say, "One thing about Walter, he wouldn't spend your money any faster than he spends his own . . ."

I'm reminded of this remark by stories Tommy Armour tells about Hagen. Armour, a great champion in his own right (U.S. Open champion in 1927, PGA champion in 1930 and British Open champion in 1931), loved and admired Walter Hagen as he did no other player in the game, unless it be Jones. But Armour's natural Scottish instinct for financial responsibility was outraged at times by Walter's extravagance.

He and Hagen traveled to England together in 1929 to play in the Open.

"I gave Walter two hundred dollars before we landed," Tommy recalled, "and we went directly to the Savoy where we unpacked and I took a bath and shaved. When I came out of the bathroom there was a case of Scotch, a case of gin and a case of champagne neatly stacked against the wall. A *case* of champagne, mind you! You don't buy champagne by the case. You buy it by the bottle — chilled!

"I turned to Walter and said, 'What's all this for? Are you expecting Parliament to declare a national prohibition law overnight?'

"Hagen spread his hands and smiled. 'But we'll be having people in and out.'"

Hagen got ready for the warm-up match with Compston we spoke of a few pages back, and Armour pleaded with him to cancel out. Walter hadn't swung a club in a long time and one practice round left his hands blistered. But Hagen insisted on playing. He met the inglorious 18 and 17 defeat we have already described, after which he went on to win the Open.

"After that," Armour relates, "we crossed over to France where we split up. I went down to the south of France where I had a couple of exhibition matches at Aix-les-Bains and somewhere else. Hagen stayed in Paris to play in the French Open and in some exhibitions. We met again a couple of weeks later to return to the United States.

"Now Walter had picked up about $2,800 for his exhibition with Compston," he went on, "and he took first money in the Open. He got a couple of exhibition fees in France and won that tournament purse over there. But, do you know something? I had to loan the son of a gun another $200 to get off the ship in New York!"

Typical of Hagen's legendary disregard for basic bookkeeping is what happened when the Hagen memoirs were published several years ago. The press run was 15,000 copies. Of these, Walter ordered several thousand for personal distribution. He was giving books away faster than the booksellers could find customers!

Walter was amazed and indignant when he received a bill from the publisher. He flatly refused to pay it. The idea of paying for copies of his own book struck him as the height of absurdity. The disillusioned publisher finally had to bring Hagen in for an accounting.

But that was typical of golf's most majestic and beloved personality. The daily scramble for coins in the marketplace wasn't for Walter. He lived above the tumult and the shouting. And the pixie in him wouldn't let him have any special regard for the formalities of social banking. There was the grand party he and a dozen Hollywood personalities tossed for themselves in San Francisco one year. When the waiter fi-

nally trotted around with the reckoning, Richard Arlen, the actor, demanded to pay it. But Hagen wouldn't hear of it. He snatched the tab and strode over to the cashier's desk where, with a flourish and a broad wink to several others in the party, he signed Arlen's name to the check!

Meanwhile, back at the table, the movie star was delivering an oratorical tribute to the boundless generosity of Hagen, pausing in midsentence to throw a salute across the room at Walter, who smiled broadly and waved back.

I remember, along in the early 1940s, I met the Duke of Windsor, then serving as Governor-General of the Bahamas. I proposed, in the course of a Florida conversation with him, that I would bring to Nassau for a Red Cross benefit exhibition match the four men he had seen win the British Open: Hagen, Armour, Sarazen and Jones. The Duke was delighted with the prospect.

I flew to Nassau in advance of the match to complete the arrangements and we sat on the lawn of the Government House, the Duke and I, chatting about golf and golfers. He asked especially about Walter and I told him one story after another.

Then I mentioned Hagen's philosophy of life. It went like this: Never hurry and don't worry. You're here for just a short visit. So don't forget to stop and smell the flowers along the way.

The Duke's eyes widened and he snatched a pencil from his pocket.

"Oh, I say," he exclaimed, "this is just priceless! Priceless! Let me write that down . . ." And he scribbled it on the back of an envelope. Then he jumped up.

"I've simply got to read this to the Duchess," he said, excusing himself. "I'll be right back."

With that he sprinted for the house and went bounding up the stairs, waving the envelope and shouting for the Duchess.

Somehow, every time the name of Walter Hagen comes up in the conversation I always think of that afternoon on the lawn of the government residence at Nassau—and of the king who had given up his throne, racing off to recite the Hagen philosophy to his Duchess.

(1965)

117

The Grand Slam
Herbert Warren Wind

I make no secret of my fondness for Bob Jones. The ultimate golfer, sportsman and gentleman, he certainly was the greatest golfer of his age, and one who is ranked with the best of all time. It was more than my good fortune to have collaborated with him in making changes to the Augusta National Golf Club course and in the development of the Peachtree Golf Club; it was an honour. He was kind, considerate and one of the most understanding individuals I have ever met. I cherish his memory.

Although it was accomplished more than a half-century ago, his Grand Slam still remains as the single greatest achievement in golf. It is one which I am sure never will be equalled. Of that heroic attainment hundreds of accounts have been written, but none is more complete or informative than the one written by Herbert Warren Wind, included here. Relative to Bob Jones winning the four majors, Herb concluded: "There were no worlds left to conquer for Bobby Jones."

Bob Jones did achieve new heights, however, but in an entirely different way. That was in his establishment of the Masters which, in addition to serving as an annual, living memorial to his greatness, stands unsurpassed as the epitome of excellence in a golf tournament. And because of the majestic site on which it is staged and the flowers which bloom on almost every hole, it is the most beautiful of all golf gatherings. It is a pageant in the pines.

IN 1930 BOBBY JONES won the British Amateur, the British Open, the United States Open, and the United States Amateur Championships. Jones' clean sweep of the four major titles — what George Trevor neatly termed "the impregnable quadrilateral" — was, of course, the crowning achievement of his career, and, very probably, the greatest exhibition of skill and character by any individual athlete, bar none, since the beginning of recorded sports history.

In the winter of 1930 as he conditioned himself for his annual campaign, Bobby Jones had no presentiment that he was embarking on a historic year. His feelings about his potential in any one tournament season were about the same as they had been in 1927 when, in collaboration with O. B. Keeler, he had published his autobiography, *Down the Fairway*. The chapter on 1926, when Bobby had won two major crowns for the first time, was entitled "The Biggest Year." He was overjoyed with having trounced the percentages in 1926 "because I'll never have another chance to win both the British and American Open Championships in the same year."

Bobby, however, was looking forward to 1930 with more than his usual enthusiasm. It was a year when the Walker Cup Match was scheduled to be played in Great Britain, and this meant that after two years of strictly domestic activity, Bob would have another shot at the British events, and particularly the British Amateur, the one major championship that had eluded him. During the winter Bobby, who put weight on rather quickly, kept in trim by playing "Doug," a combination of tennis and badminton evolved by Douglas Fairbanks, who had sent his friend the paraphernalia. From the first day that he began his light workouts on the golf course, it was evident to everyone who watched him that, for one reason or another, Bobby had something that he had never had before. Noteworthy, too, was the fact that, departing from his habit of tuning up informally, he entered two minor tournaments, the Savannah Open and the Southeastern Open, held at Augusta. At Savannah Jones finished second with 279, a stroke behind Horton Smith, the winter wonder. But at Augusta, Jones' 72, 72, 69, 71 for 284 was not only tops but thirteen full strokes ahead of Hor-

ton, the runner-up. After taking in Bobby's display at Augusta, Grantland Rice, who had studied the Georgian closely over a long period of years, expressed the opinion that Jones was playing discernibly better golf than ever before, and Bobby Cruickshank exploded with an indecently accurate prediction: "He's simply too good. He'll go to Britain and win the Amateur and the Open, and then he'll come back over here and win the Open and the Amateur. He is playing too well to be stopped this year."

Never one to enthuse about his own game, Jones confided to his intimate friends that he felt much more confident than in any previous year, that he was hitting every shot in the bag. Even those little pitches between 50 and 125 yards that had frequently displeased him were behaving properly. Psychologically, as well, Bobby was fit. His strong showing against Espinosa in the playoff for the Open the year before had not by any means erased from his mind the near-disgrace of kicking away a six-stroke lead on the last six holes and leaving himself a 12-footer to tie. The memory of Winged Foot would be a salutary spur. He was also rid of that mental block about eighteen-hole matches. At Pebble Beach he had lost the one he had been frightened of losing for years, and now he could go into the British Amateur free from any defensive phobia.

In Britain, before the stars of two continents convened at St. Andrews for the Amateur, Jones shot some of his best stuff in the Walker Cup Match at Sandwich. Partnered with Doc Willing, he won his foursome 8 and 7 and took his singles from Roger Wethered 9 and 8. As the captain of the American team, Jones could have placed himself in the number-one singles spot, for which his record logically qualified him. It was typical of Jones that he awarded the honor of playing number one to Jimmy Johnston, the Amateur Champion, and dropped himself to the second slot... And then on to St. Andrews and the one championship he had never been able to win — the British Amateur.

Right off the reel Bobby walked into a match he could have easily lost. Syd Roper, an ex-coal miner from Nottinghamshire without a clipping to his name, played one 5 and fifteen 4s over the sixteen holes of his match with Jones. On the very first tee Bobby seemed to divine what was coming on, for he got right down to business and knocked in a 20-footer for a birdie 3. He added a 4 and a 3, and on the fourth he holed out a 150-yard spade-mashie from Cottage Bunker for an eagle 2. Bobby's 5-under-par burst for the first five holes gave him only a three-hole lead, and this was the extent of the impression he was able to make against the amazing Mr. Roper.

In the fourth round Jones came up against Cyril Tolley, the defending champion, and a bitter battle ensued. Tolley's topped drive off the first tee was about the one mistake the long-hitting Englishman made for eighteen holes. At no time was either player able to edge ahead by more than one hole. They were all even as they came to the seventeenth, the famous Road Hole, a dogleg to the right that ordinarily required two good woods to reach unless the player elected to risk cutting the corner over Auchterlonie's drying sheds and carrying the deep out-of-bounds elbow. Neither Tolley nor Jones thought this was the day for flirting with the straight-line route. Both drove out safely to the left, Jones far to the left. The shot Bobby elected to play for his second was a high spoon, cut just a fraction so that it would hold after landing on the back edge of the green. It didn't quite come off. The ball carried the vicious Road Bunker that guards the entrance to the middle of the green from the left, but instead of plopping itself down obediently, it kicked up like a colt and might have run on into trouble had it not struck a spectator standing on the back fringe. With this timely assist from Fortune, Jones was able to get his 4, and he needed it, for Tolley pitched two feet from the cup after playing short of the green with an iron on his second. They halved the eighteenth in 4. The match moved into extra holes. Both got off the 19th tee well but Tolley clubbed his approach off-line and it cost him the match. His chip was not stone-dead and Bobby, putting up on his third, laid Tolley a stymie he was unable to negotiate. (The entire population of St. Andrews seemed to stream from the town onto the links whenever Jones was playing, and on the day of the Jones-Tolley match the town was so deserted the novelist Gerald Fairlie selected that afternoon as the time when the villain in one of his mysteries committed murder in downtown St. Andrews and, though marked with the stains of his crime, was able to make his way unnoticed down the empty streets.)

Had it been Jones who had been confronted with jumping a stymie on the 19th to keep the match alive, there is every reason to believe that he would have done it successfully. A confirmed fatalist in his attitude toward golf tournaments, at St. Andrews Bobby was visited by the strange and wonderful feeling that he simply could not lose, whatever he did. After the Tolley match, in which Jones had been outplayed but had gotten the breaks, O. B. Keeler was beginning to share this queer sense of fatality, and as the tournament moved on and Bobby escaped from two more ferocious matches that could have gone either way, Keeler was convinced that some large and intangible Providence simply would countenance no other person's winning the 1930 British Amateur. It was an odd way, a very odd way, to feel about a golf tournament, but for Keeler there was no other explanation for the things that were taking place at St. Andrews. In several of Jones' matches a single bad shot at numerous junctures could have changed the entire picture, but as O. B. remarked, Bobby stood up to the shot and performed what was needed with all the certainty of a natural phenomenon. By the semi-final round, the feeling that Jones' triumph was mystically inevitable had communicated itself to many of the spectators. When Jones was 1 down to George Voigt with only three holes to play, Sir James Lieshman, a Scottish fan, declared, "His [Jones'] luck is as fixed as the orbit of a planet. He cannot be beaten here." On the very next tee Voigt drove into a bunker and lost the hole.

The struggle with Voigt followed a distressingly close scrape in the sixth round with Jimmy Johnston. Jones was 4 up on Jimmy with five to play, but Johnston won two of the next three holes and took the Road as well. A win for him on the eighteenth would have forced the match into extra holes, and Jimmy came within a hair of doing it. Both players took precautions to hit their approaches firmly enough to carry the Valley of Sin, and both ended up on the very back edge of that huge green, Johnston about ninety feet away from the pin, Jones not much closer. Playing the odd, Johnston putted up beautifully, inches from the cup, for a sure 4. It was up to Bobby to get down in 2 to save the match. His first putt began to slow down as it took the final dip toward the hole and died eight feet short, leaving Jones with a nasty sidehiller. He holed it precisely, just as Von Elm and Ouimet, watching from the balcony of the Grand Hotel, knew he would.

In the semi-final, Voigt, playing the finest golf of his life, sticking his irons inside of Jones' and putting very well indeed, had accumulated a two-hole advantage as he and Bobby prepared to play the fourteenth. There is an old golf fable that the man who is 2 up with five holes to play will lose the match. More often than not, the fable folds, but it holds up just often enough to perpetuate itself. Voigt, 2 up with five to play, cut across his tee shot, and the strong wind blowing from left to right tossed it out-of-bounds. Jones played safely down the left and won the hole. The fifteenth was halved. Up first on the next tee, Jones, who knew St. Andrews as well as he knew East Lake, played his drive fifty yards to the left of the center of the fairway to make certain he avoided the bunkers. Voigt, aiming for that patch of fairway to the left of the Principal's Nose, once again underestimated the force of the cross-wind and was blown into the bunker. Jones' hole. Hauled back to even now, Voigt made a brave countercharge on the seventeenth. After two splendid shots had carried him to the front edge of the green, George all but holed his approach putt. To halve Voigt's 4, Jones had to hole an 18-footer. The weird sensation that someone was taking care of him was never stronger than when Bobby bent over his ball. He felt that no matter how he hit it, the putt would go in. It did. On the home green Voigt failed to get down his 6-footer for a par and Bobby had won the match from an opponent who had been 2 up with five to play.

Roger Wethered was Jones' opponent in the final and faced the hopeless task of staying with Jones when Bobby was in one of his most determined moods. There was only one moment during the match when Jones was not patently in command. On the very first hole, after his drive had set him up with the easiest of pitches, Bobby looked up on his shot and missed it so badly that it didn't even make the burn cutting across the fairway twenty yards ahead. He chipped up close with his third, went down in one putt for his 4, and took nothing over a 4 until he squandered a miraculous recovery from the Road Bunker on the seventeenth by muffing a 2-footer. He finished the morning round 4 up.

Francis Ouimet, who walked back to the Grand Hotel with Bobby at lunchtime, could not figure it out when Jones began pacing his room, obviously burned up about something.

"What in the world has got into you, Bobby?" Ouimet finally asked. "You're four up."

"Did you hear what that official said on the first tee?" Jones asked.

Francis thought a moment and then remembered that before Jones had teed off, an official had remarked that in all the years that the greatest golfers in the world had been playing the Old Course, no one had ever succeeded in going around with nothing higher than a 4 on his card.

" . . . And I," Bobby said in disgust, "I had to go and miss a two-foot putt to be the first man ever to play St. Andrews without taking a five."

Bobby had turned an innocent conversational sally into a personal challenge. He had been playing St. Andrews rather than Wethered.

In the afternoon, the scent of victory, that long-awaited victory, was sufficient to insure a continuation of Bobby's aggressive play. The strain began to tell on Roger and he began missing the 4-footers. Jones added one hole and then another to his lead, and the match ran itself out on the 30th green. Then, fifteen thousand mad Scots, who had been waiting all week for this moment no less anxiously than Jones, converged on their idol. In the wild stampede Henry Lapham was knocked into a bunker and converted into a trestle; the crowd attacked the policemen guarding Jones with the fury of bobby-soxers; and the band that was to play the victor in was scattered in the mêlée and played not a note. Keeler finally made his way to the side of the young man whom he had followed for fourteen years through twenty-four championships. "Honestly, I don't care what happens now." Bobby smiled at O. B. "I'd rather have won this tournament than anything else in golf. I'm satisfied."

There was no mysterious presence walking hand in hand with Bobby Jones at Hoylake. Jones won the British Open by the normal expedient of bringing in the lowest four-round total in the field. He did it the hard way, as he had at Lytham in '26, outscoring through sheer stick-to-itiveness a handful of fine golfers who were on their game when Bobby was not. He was neat around the greens. He was lucky in playing his bad shots when they hurt him least, and he managed to pull off the best shots in his repertoire at the critical moments. St. Andrews had been touched with destiny. Hoylake was manual labor.

The understandable contentment he derived from his victory in the British Amateur made it hard for Jones to buckle down to belligerency as the date of the British Open approached. He had twice before won the British Open. Furthermore, he had no Grand Slam on his mind. Bobby was taking things easy, and his indifference brought back to Keeler the similarly flat frame of mind Bobby had acquiesced to when he was preparing for the United States Open at Oakmont in '27. Then, he had never been able to rouse himself and had floundered into his worst showing in a major tournament since he had first become a champion. The English critics had no Oakmont as a touchstone, but they noticed the letdown in Jones' attitude and in his game. He looked stale.

Once the practice and qualifying rounds were over and the championship proper was underway, a change came over Jones. His desire to win reasserted itself. It drove him to an opening round of 70 and a second round of 72, although his game remained as imprecise as it had been when Bobby hadn't cared. "I simply don't know where the darn ball is going when I hit it," he said impatiently to O. B. "I guess I'm trying to steer it, and of course that's the worst thing in the world to do. But what can I do? This is a tight course. You can't get up there and slam away and trust to freedom of action to take care of the shot. You simply have got to exercise some control of the ball. And it's the most hopeless job I've ever tackled. I've never worked so hard before." Jones' 74 in the third round began with a par on the first when he escaped a bunker by inches. He went 1 over on the second, and instead of getting that stroke back on the 480-yard third, an easy birdie hole, Bobby took a 6 and lost another stroke. Then he settled down and fought. 3-4-4-3-4-4 gave him a 37 for the out-nine, and 3-3-4-3 braced him for the killing finish at Hoylake, five holes averaging 457 yards. 5-5-5-5-4 was not too sharp—another 37 for a 74, which dropped him from first to a stroke behind the pacemaker, Archie Compston. Compston had led off with a devastating rush of 4-3-4-2 and completed as fine a round as has ever been shot at Hoylake in 68.

Jones set out on his last round fifty minutes before Compston was called to tee. Bobby began with a par 4, and then on the 369-yard second sliced his drive hectically to the right. The swerving ball bounced wildly off the head of a steward and careened a full forty yards forward into a bunker off the fourteenth fairway. Considering where the drive would have ended up without the intervention of the petrified stewart, it was an incalculably lucky break; Bobby was fifty years off-line but only 140 yards from the green and lying well in the bunker. He stroked a pitch onto the center of the green, holed his 20-footer, and had come out of the hole with a birdie 3 when he would have settled for a 5. A short while after this had happened, Compston was striding across the first green full of confidence. A putt of eighteen inches would give Archie his regulation 4, an adequate opening for the bright round the rawboned giant felt was coming on. Compston tapped his wee putt, and, in almost the same motion, bent over to pick the ball out of the cup. It wasn't in the cup. It was still on the lip. Compston straightened himself up and stood staring at the ball, bewildered and unbelieving. He was never the same afterwards. His confidence had been cut away before he reached the second tee, and lurching like an injured vessel, he needed fourteen strokes more than he had taken in the morning to get around the same course. Nothing could snap Archie out of it, not even the early report that on the eighth, a 482-yard 5 that Jones was expected to birdie, Bobby had blown himself to a big 7. Just off the green in

2 with a prosaic chip up a bank to the green, Jones stubbed his chip short, was ten feet away on his fourth, slid a foot by on his fifth, and missed that 12-inch kick-in. Bobby's 38 meant nothing to the broken Compston, but the reports of this wobbly first nine filtered back to Diegel and Mac Smith and pricked up the ears of those two great hard-luck golfers.

Bobby battled his way home. Two 4s on the short holes didn't help. Then into that back-breaking final five. A 4 and a 5. So far, so good. A 4 on the 532-yard 70th, thanks to a great out from a trap by the green with the 25-ounce niblick Horton Smith had got for him. Another 4 and a final 4. A 37. A 75. It could have been worse, a great deal worse, but would it be good enough to win? Bobby relieved his exhaustion with a good stiff drink. He sat nervously in the clubhouse, using two hands to steady his glass, as he sweated out the news on Leo and Mac.

Diegel, two strokes off Bobby's pace at the 63rd, turned it on. He picked up a stroke on Bobby on the first short hole coming in, picked up another on the second short hole. He came to the 70th, tied with Jones. Throwing every ounce of his power into his shot off the tee, Leo smashed out a long, hard drive. The direction might have been better. The kick might have been, too. The ball caught the corner of a trap. Leo did not give up, even after he had missed a short putt for his 4 on that hole, but it was no use. The Dieg couldn't do it.

Nor could Mac Smith. Starting six strokes behind Jones, the grim old bloodhound had made up four of those strokes but, to tie with Bobby, Mac had to play those last five holes in one-under-4s. It was an impossible task. Mac's chances for a tie at length simmered down to holing a pitch for an eagle 2 on the eighteenth. As that pitch danced past the pin, Bobby took one hand off the glass he was holding.

At Hoylake Bobby had won through patience and guts and philosophy and instinct.

The United States Open was played in early June at Interlachen in Minneapolis. A hot sun beat down on the parched fairways where $40,000 worth of perspiring fans—it wasn't so much the heat as the humanity—walked restively after Bobby Jones. There was no question about Bobby's goal, now that he had won the two British championships. He had his sights set on a Grand Slam now. This would be the tournament. If Bobby could get by the pros at Inter-lachen, only the Amateur, the comparatively placid Amateur, would remain.

In many an Open Bobby had led off with fast rounds and had shaken off all but one or two of the pros before they could get going. At Interlachen Bobby started well with 71-73 for 144, but the big names were right along with him at the halfway mark—Horton Smith in front with 142, Cooper at 144, Mac Smith at 145, Armour at 146, and Hagen, Farrell, Golden, and others still close enough to pull out in front if they could get in a blazing third round.

It was Bobby who played the great third round. One of the earliest starters, he went out hard and handsomely, making no errors of commission or omission until he slipped one over par on the ninth. Even with that bogey, he had shot the first nine in 33 and was well on his way toward achieving the objective he had set for himself: to play so hot a round that he would demoralize the opposition and take a comfortable margin with him into the final eighteen. At Interlachen there are seven holes of the drive-and-pitch variety, and Jones was flicking his mashie-niblicks right at the pin. Three times he came within inches of holing 100-yard pitches, the ball, directly on line, pulling up less than a foot from the hole. Six strokes under par for sixteen holes, Jones could not maintain that pace over the last two, the 262-yard seventeenth and the 402-yard eighteenth. He went a stroke over par on each of these holes, but his 68 was sufficiently low to have the desired harassing effect on his rivals.

The news of Jones' 68 quickly reached Horton Smith, Tommy Armour, Mac Smith, and the other contenders. It sent them off on the hunt for birdies, forced them to go for everything. These tactics cost them more strokes than they saved. Mac Smith's 74 put him seven strokes behind Bobby; Horton's 76 put him six strokes behind. Jones started on his final eighteen with a five-stroke lead over his nearest rival, Harry Cooper, who had added a relatively low 73.

Nine to ten thousand well-meaning, annoying fans, the largest gallery that had ever hounded a golfer in an American championship, shrieked and groaned and sometimes applauded as Bobby went to the turn in 38, added three orthodox pars, and then played the last six holes in a bizarre blend of beautiful and bad golf. He went two over par on the 194-yard 67th, his second double-bogey of the round on a short hole. He rallied with a birdie 3 on the tough 444-yard 68th, parred the 69th, and got himself another birdie 3 on the 70th after a pin-splitting approach. Then, almost home, almost completely safe from the gallant last-round challenge of Mac Smith, who had picked up four strokes and was still coming, Bobby again messed up a short hole, the 262-yard 71st. He hit his tee shot on the heel of his club and the ball sliced off in a dipping parabola and skidded into the water hazard past the rough. A penalty stroke, a chip, two putts — his third 5 of the round on a par-3 hole. Now it was imperative that he play the last hole right.

Bobby pulled himself together. He took a nice full cut at his drive and sent it down the fairway toward the large home green 402 yards away. His iron was on nicely. He holed a 40-footer. 75.

That final birdie clinched it. Mac Smith, the only challenger who did not wilt, finished with a 70, one of those supremely elegant rounds Old Mac could always play when it was too late, but it still left him two strokes off Jones' mark of 287.

By nightfall the radio and newspapers had carried the good news to the fans in the countless Atlantas from Portland to Portland who had been fidgeting like first-time fathers. The wait was harder on the Jonesmen living in foreign countries who had to go until the next morning before learning of the outcome. Bernard Darwin's ordeal was characteristic of the plight of thousands. Bernard came down to breakfast, and his heart stopped beating when he caught sight of the morning newspaper lying on the table. He ripped it open as fast as he could to the sports section — for good or for bad, he would know soon. This would be the page . . . Phew! The old boy had done it . . . Bernard settled down to a slow, wonderful breakfast.

Two months after his burst in the third round had won the Open for him, Bobby Jones headed for Merion Cricket Club and the Amateur. Merion — it looked like a good augury. Fourteen years before, when Bobby had been a pudgy, club-heaving fourteen-year-older, he had played in his first national tournament at Merion and given the golfing world a startling preview of the shape of things to come. Six years before at Merion — Bobby had won so many titles between 1924 and 1930 that the Amateur of '24 seemed like paleolithic times — the Georgian had marched to his first Amateur Championship. It was historically right that Merion, which had twice served as a milestone in Jones' career, should be the battlefield for Bobby's climactic performance.

Three down and the Amateur to go! What had appeared impossible five months before was now palpably achievable. Bobby could do it, the golfing world was sure . . . if he survived the qualifying round . . . and didn't run up against some unconscious stripling in the two rounds of eighteen-hole matches . . . and had the stamina to play Jonesworthy golf in his big matches. He was so close now on the eve of the tourney that these and other trepidations annexed themselves to the fervent hopefulness of golf fans, the way the lurking danger of a lucky hit tightens up a baseball crowd that has been in on a no-hitter for eight innings. Multiply the tension of the no-hitter by fifty. There have been many no-hitters. There had never been even the prospect of a Grand Slam before. No-hitters are spun in less than three hours. Jones had been working for four months on his Grand Slam, on two continents, in all sorts of weather, in all sorts of form.

Each evening Americans squirmed in their chairs by the radio waiting for the word from Merion.

Tuesday evening: Jones had qualified. More than that, he had won the medal with a record-equaling 69–73 — 142 and would have broken the record had he not overpitched the last green with his spade-mashie. Bobby was evidently in good form. Five former champions — Johnston, Guilford, Marston, Egan, and Herron — had failed to qualify, and this was strangely comforting news. One of them might have given Jones trouble.

Wednesday evening: Bobby had got by his eighteen-hole matches safely. In the morning against the sound Canadian stylist, Ross Somerville, he had turned in 33 and had run out the match 5 and 4. That was the same count by which he had eliminated another Canadian, Fred Hoblitzel, in the afternoon. Bobby had played a wavering first nine of 41, but had started in 4-3-4-3-4. He seemed to be pacing himself intelligently, playing mediocre but winning golf when his opponent was playing downright poor stuff, stepping up his game when his opponent began to find himself. A bit of a relief, too, that some of the men who had the best chance of beating Bobby had run into some hot golf. Doc Willing, Phil Perkins, Francis Ouimet, and young Goodman had fallen in the first round. Voigt had been stopped in the second, and so had George Von Elm, a real threat, after he and Maurice McCarthy Jr. had battled stubbornly and brilliantly for *ten extra holes*.

Thursday evening: Yes, Bobby had won his first 36-hole match, defeating Fay Coleman of California 6 and 5. He had the match securely under control all the way.

Friday evening: And he had got by the semifinal round. Jess Sweetser had been far off form, and Jones had coasted to a 9 and 8 victory without having to shoot his best golf. But he might have to in the final, for Gene Homans, the lean, ministerial-looking chap who would be opposing him, had played very well in defeating Lawson Little and Charles Seaver (Tom Seaver's father).

It was much cooler on Saturday morning than it had been all week, and a gusty wind blew over Merion. It was apparent from the outset that Gene Homans was nervous, decidedly uncomfortable that he now represented the one obstacle between Jones and the Grand Slam. Gene went six holes before he played his first par, and it was surprising that Jones, wind or no wind, had picked up only three holes. When Homans settled down, Jones, as he had in his previous matches, accelerated his own game. Bobby played the second nine in 33 and boosted his lead to seven holes. It was no longer a question of whether or not Bobby would win but how soon he would win. In the afternoon he climbed

to 8 up, to 9 up, and then, believing that he had built up a formidable reservoir of holes, permitted the deep tiredness he felt to show through in his play. He three-putted the 25th and took two shots to get out of a trap on the 28th, but Homans could win back only one hole and Jones was dormie 8 as they came to the 29th tee. The thousands of spectators, sensing that the great moment could be postponed no longer, fought for positions of vantage around the 29th green. Both Bobby and Gene were on in two. Bobby laid his approach putt up close to the cup. To keep the match alive, Homans would have to hole his long one. He stroked it carefully but as soon as he saw it swerve off-line, Gene started over to be the first to congratulate Jones.

Before Homans reached Jones, the first standard shrieks and howls had crescendoed into a mighty, heartfelt roar. The cheers of thousands were not for the Homans match. It had been a dull contest, an irritating, drawn out anticlimax. And the cheers were for the Amateur Champion only inasmuch as the Amateur was the last quarter of the stupendous whole — the Grand Slam. The cheers were for May, June, July, and September, for St. Andrews, where the Grand Slam had several times hung by a thread, for Hoylake, where courage and perseverance had nurtured a faint possibility into a fair probability, for Interlachen, where Jones had risen to his full powers on the third round and scattered the field with his 68. And yes, dull match or no dull match, tame tournament or no tame tournament, the cheers were also for Merion, where Jones had not only completed the last leg of the impregnable quadrilateral but had done it with such concomitant authority that never once did he allow an opponent or a break or the strain of four months the smallest opening to destroy the chance of a lifetime.

Protected by a Marine bodyguard, which had dashed onto the green the second the match was over, the authentic hero walked thoughtfully to the clubhouse, acknowledging as best he could the respects his thousands of rejoicing subjects were paying him, unable to digest the fact that the Herculean task he had set himself was actually accomplished, tired, very tired after pushing himself all week, and happy, so very happy, that at last it was all behind him. The walk to the clubhouse seemed to take days, and it seemed weeks before the hordes of friends and admirers were finished shaking his hand and telling him how overjoyed they were, but at length, everyone had the good sense to clear out of the locker room and give Bob a few minutes alone with his dad, the old Colonel. The great friends let themselves go completely, and in the furious outpouring of heart and head, Bobby finally washed himself clean of the strain he had been carrying around for months.

There were no worlds left to conquer for Bobby Jones.

(1948)

Jones, The Soul of It
Furman Bisher

Furman Bisher has caught the feeling of the ambience of the Masters in "Jones, The Soul of It." More importantly, he has caught the spirit of the man responsible for it in his extremely accurate portrait of Bob Jones in his comprehensive book, The Masters, Augusta Revisited: An Intimate View.

Bisher, in the best tradition of Grantland Rice, O. B. Keeler and Ed Miles, is one of the South's most respected and authoritative writers, whom I look forward to meeting every April when I go to Augusta. His unusually close association with the tournament for more than a quarter-century has given him an insight and an appreciation of it and its founder that sets him apart.

ROBERT TYRE JONES, JR., made his first association with golf at the age of six. A man named Fulton Colville, practicing chip shots in front of the boarding house where the Joneses had taken summer quarters on East Lake, noticed him sitting on the porch steps watching and addressed him: "Would you like to hit some, sonny?"

After a few attempts, made shyly and awkwardly, for he was a scrawny child, little Bobby was favored with a gift. Fulton Colville drew an old cleek—that's something between a putter and a two-iron—from his bag and handed it to him, and so the legendary voyage into golf was launched.

Fulton Colville's role in it was only as a walk-on, but Bob Jones later said, "Something inspired him to give me that club. I didn't have any interest in golf before then."

It wasn't long before the Jones boy was out on the golf course at East Lake Country Club banging his little cleek around along with his parents. East Lake is only six miles from the center of Atlanta, but in those times it was a summer retreat for the cityites, a colony surrounded by forest and enveloped by solitude, perhaps a setting you would expect in one of Scott Fitzgerald's vintage stories. Businessmen placed their families in quarters for the season—the Joneses chose a Mrs. Meador's—and joined them by trolley that ran out from downtown. It was there, under the guidance of an immigrant Scottish golf professional named Stewart Maiden, that little Bobby Jones learned the fundamentals of the game that transformed him from a scrawny kid into an epic of sport and an international personality, a blessing for which he paid his dues to game and society times over.

He became at one and the same time the symbol of the Southern Gentleman and the American Sportsman. Clifford Roberts has said of him, "We never have had an athlete who came close to matching Bob Jones in popularity." It was this popularity that became the cornerstone of Augusta National Golf Club and the Masters golf tournament. It bordered on a kind of sainthood, unofficial but unwavering.

Author Paul Gallico turned his back on sportswriting for fiction with a bitter-sweet fare-thee-well. He wrote a book which bespoke his disillusionment with the games and the people he had covered, but one of these was not Bob Jones, of whom he said, "I have found only one who could stand up in every way as a gentleman and a celebrity, a fine, decent human being, and one who never once since I have known him has let me down in my estimate of him."

Robert Tyre Jones the Golfer was not a "Jr." in the technical sense of familial procedure. His father made him so in defiance of custom because Robert Purmedus Jones regretted not having been named for his father. He passed on to his son the name of his grandfather, staunchly oblivious to the rule that dictates such a christening falls under the heading of "II."

They were the Joneses of Canton, Georgia. They originated in that small town 40 miles north of Atlanta and were in the mercantile business, graduating into textiles before the family became dazzled by the city lights of Atlanta. There, offspring Robert P. became an attorney. For many years he served as general counsel for Atlantic Steel Company. Being an only child, little Robert and his dad became great pals. Mutual admirers. "The Colonel," Bob called him, as did most of those close to his father. And The Colonel was always there in the gallery when Bob was playing one of his major tournaments. Young Bob dedicated his book, *Golf Is My Game*, to his father and elaborated on their relationship later on. "One of the greatest gifts golf gave me was the enjoyment of many years of playful association with my father," he wrote.

And he DID write it. It was HIS book. Bob Jones would not stand still for a writing "ghost," any third person–first person relationship. When a title once was proposed to him for the *Saturday Evening Post* with a by-line that would read, "By Bobby Jones as told to . . . ," he sniffed. "Makes me sound like a damned illiterate who can't write his own name," he said, and refused.

He was indeed an excellent handler of the language. His literary talent bordered on the Oxonian, finely fundamental and excellently rhetorical. His breadth of interests is brilliantly illustrated in the way he went about his education. He earned a degree in mechanical engineering from Georgia Tech, studied English literature at Harvard, and later whisked through law school at Emory University in a year and a half. He could have been most anything he chose to be, except a sprinter. His feet moved considerably more slowly than his mind, and he often made jokes about his slowness. But then you don't have to run fast to play golf.

As a gentleman sportsman, Bobby Jones was a mountain among hillocks. First, though, he had to learn his lessons himself, and the miracle of it is that he survived to adulthood through a petulant youth of club-throwing, pouting, and childish tantrums that embarrassed partners and rivals. And once, if you can believe it, stalked out of a tournament at the holy of holies, St. Andrews. But once reformed, his reformation was as enduring as it was drastic.

In one of the U.S. Opens he entered a forest to play one of his errant drives. Emerging a few minutes later, he signalled that he was penalizing himself one stroke. The ball had moved as he was addressing it, and the rule clearly calls for a penalty, whether the player is being witnessed or not. It was a matter of honor with Bob Jones, and he was flabbergasted when the act drew such a wave of admiration.

"Well," he said, "you might as well have praised a man for not robbing a bank."

When he beat Watts Gunn for the U.S. Amateur championship in 1925, much was made of the fact that it was the only time two members of the same club had ever advanced to the final round. (And it has never happened again.) The fact is, Watts Gunn was there only because Bob Jones had talked his parents into allowing his younger friend to accompany him and The Colonel to Pittsburgh to play the tournament. Even lesser known was the story of an interception that took place on the back stairs of the clubhouse at Oakmont, where the two friends were staying. Watts had met a young lady in Pittsburgh who had aroused his interest. On the night before the championship match, Bob came upon his friend trying to slip down the back stairway for another date with his new friend. "Oh, no, you don't," Bob said. "You're going to march right back up to that room. You'll need all the sleep you can get for tomorrow." And Watts Gunn's date was suddenly broken.

The competitive part of Jones' life came to an abrupt close in 1948, after which he never was able to play golf again. Struck down by some dastardly fate that was of such a cruel disposition as to reach out and trip a mortal it seemed to have judged to have given too much. The ailment that invaded his person was a rare one that with a creeping mercilessness took away his ability to manipulate his limbs and eventually shriveled him to a withered ruin of the Adonis that he had once been. "Syringomyelia" was its medical name.

Almost 20 years earlier, however, he had assured himself a place in the roll call of golf's immortals. There is no other achievement in sport comparable to winning the U.S. Open, the British Open, the U.S. Amateur, and the British Amateur championships all in the same year. In fact, this Grand Slam has become, at least by the perceived limits of foreseeable years, the Feat Impossible. The economics of golf have seen to that. Amateur players no longer carry that status any longer than it takes to qualify for the professional tour. There is no longer the lure to remain amateur that existed in Jones' day, when the golf professional was still only a few steps removed from the choreman of the shop. But Jones, fortunate to be backed by a well-to-do father, as an amateur accomplished the Grand Slam. Since his time, not one of the professional players has been able to achieve even the "Pro Grand Slam" by winning the Masters, the U.S. Open, British Open, and PGA championship of the U.S.A. in one year.

Shortly after Bob Jones completed the improbable foursome by sinking the putt that defeated Eugene Homans on Marion Cricket Club's 11th green, it being their 29th hole of play in the finals of the U.S. Amateur Championship of 1930, his retirement took effect. Retirement had been lying in the back of his mind since 1926, to be executed only when he could find the proper stopping place. Here he was, barely out of college, retiring from competition in golf at the age of 28, removing from the center ring of the game its stellar attraction. The next four years of American golf were to be low in interest without him. For Jones it was simply the halftime in his life.

Those were times when society rode high and the living was opulent. The estate life and Gatsby's era. Sprawling hotel resorts and the rise of the American Plan. Endurance flying and flagpole sitting. Flappers and Clara Bow. The budding of radio and Atwater Kent. Gloomy Gil Dobie and "Hurry Up" Yost. The Volstead Act and gin made in a bathtub. Sinclair Lewis and the Spirit of St. Louis. Yale-Harvard and Albie Booth against Barry Wood. The Charleston and rooftop ballrooms. Crooning. The Stork Club. Electric fans. And hickory shafts.

Clifford Roberts drove up to Knollwood Country Club one day in the middle of the Roaring '20s, presumably in his Pierce-Arrow or Franklin. Knollwood was located in Westchester County, where New York's wealthy went to the country for the weekend. He was a member. Bobby Jones was playing a friendly match at the club that day, and Roberts was pointedly "dropping in" to take a look at this young man of whom he had heard so much. Other details of the day grow vague, but the two were introduced and discovered they had mutual friends, among them an innkeeper named Walton Marshall, who divided his years between the Hotel Vanderbilt in New York and the Bon Air Vanderbilt in Augusta. Neither had the faintest glimmer of a notion at the time, but with this meeting the first seed of the Augusta National Golf Club was sown.

"Our paths crossed several times after that. I saw Bob play in several tournaments. One I recall distinctly was the National Amateur at Baltusrol when he lost in the final round to George Von Elm," Clifford Roberts said. It happened that Roberts was present that year of the Baltusrol Golf Club, near Springfield, New Jersey.

Roberts dealt in investments and securities. Therefore, his life ran to the monied interest, and he turned up at those fashionable addresses frequented by outstanding figures of finance, industry, letters, and politics. One of these was the Bon Air Vanderbilt in Augusta, which in those times registered the finest clientele in America, it is said. As testament, President Taft and J. P. Morgan were frequent guests.

"I had tried Pinehurst two times and had the terrible luck to run into snowstorms both times. Augusta had never heard of snow, and I was encouraged to try this location. It was a choice wisely made, not only for the golf and the climate, but because of the accommodations. Walton Marshall was a notch above your average innkeeper, and the Bon Air was beautifully run. Everyone who came to Augusta stayed at the Bon Air invariably, but, by God, you had to get your reservations in a year in advance. January and February were the height of the season. It was closed in the summer," Roberts said.

"You see, people traveled by train then. Florida was too far, actually wasn't even developed to any great degree. The main purpose of people who came was golf, and Augusta came to fit our needs perfectly. You can step right outside the clubhouse here at Augusta, and you're just 150 feet above sea level. The climate was temperate and the courses were good, and that was the reason Bob spent a good part of his winters over here, playing golf. Conditions were so much better than in Atlanta, which is about one thousand feet higher."

Wherever Bob Jones played, it amounted to an exhibition, as that friendly match at Knollwood had turned out to be. People came out to watch. It was so at Augusta as well. He appeared often at the two courses of prominence then, the Augusta Country Club and Forest Hills, but he simply couldn't play a round of golf in privacy.

Augusta National, as it turned out, was the product of impulse. Roberts knew that in the back of Jones' mind was the idea of building a golf course to his own specifications and his own taste some time, some place. As they talked of it one day, Roberts blurted out, "Why not here in Augusta?"

A beautiful blend of the minds took place on the spot. It was simply a matter next of finding the proper location, a piece of property that Jones would approve. In the fall of 1930, shortly after Jones had accomplished his Grand Slam, Roberts arrived in Atlanta with a lay of land in mind, requiring only Jones' visual approval and a plan of membership.

There is next this vision of Bob Jones walking from the doorway of the old manor house, which is block-shaped like a fortress, and standing for the first time on the grassy overlook that has since become the terrace lawn of the Augusta National Golf Club.

"The experience was unforgettable," Bob Jones wrote later. "It seemed that this land had been lying here for years just waiting for someone to lay a golf course upon it."

What they had come upon was a gentle, rolling spread of hill and valley with a spring-fed stream that only a near century of preparation could have put in such perfect condition to receive a golf course. The moment of Bob Jones' first view of it came in December, 1930. By the next spring, having heard its ultimate call, the 365 acres of land began to come alive.

While America was still a wilderness, Indians had camped upon this land, attracted by the spring that is the course's source of water, that feeds the lakes and Rae's Creek. De Soto and his marchers are said to have passed through it in their search for the Mississippi River. What the prospective founders of Augusta National Golf Club found there was a former nursery not so tenderly attended for several years. A family of Belgians had settled the property in 1857, and the nursery they created there was the first known in the South. They were of noble heritage. Baron Prosper Jules Alphonse Berckmans, motivating force behind the nursery, was a man of many splendors. Scholar, horticulturist, landscape architect, botanist, and artist. He had arrived in this country in 1850, having taken his leave of Belgium for political and religious reasons upon which there is no elaboration. He was followed into the nursery business by his two sons, Prosper Jules Alphonse, Jr., and Louis.

The Berckmans' nursery made vast contributions to American horticulture, and the Augusta National Golf Club has gone to great effort to preserve and showcase that bonus that came with its purchase. For instance, all the thousands of miles of privet hedge that grow in the United States can be traced back to the mother hedge that still thrives directly back of the practice tee near where all the monstrous wagons and trailers gather in a television community each week of the Masters. The wisteria vine that seems to writhe out of the ground at the corner of the clubhouse on the terrace lawn is said to be the oldest in the country. The massive oak that stands guard like some arrogant sentry over the entire spread, from clubhouse down the gentle hill to the focal spectating point where the 2nd and 7th greens and the 3rd tee abut, is over 200 years old. Markers are found about the grounds identifying the botanical significance of all the growth of historical note — tree, shrub, and flowering plant.

Old Berckmans had remarried, and at the time of his death in 1910 he willed the property to his young widow instead of the two sons. P.J.A., Jr., and Louis soon left the area and relocated elsewhere. The young widow, having no interest in the nursery, eventually sold the property and its commercial name, "Fruitlands," and for about 15 years prior to its discovery by Clifford Roberts and friends, the acreage had suffered for lack of attention.

One of Augusta's most distinguished industrialists, Fielding Wallace, was appointed to handle the purchase for the Club and eventually became its first secretary. Also, he later became president of the U.S. Golf Association. (Around Augusta, his designation by the man on the street was unique: "The man who runs the Chinese hair factory," for his company imported the hair of Chinese women by the bales and produced mattresses and other products from it.)

As the membership was being formed, one of the first moves made by Clifford Roberts and his group was to search for and locate the two Berckmans sons and induce them to return and spend the rest of their lives on the old family place. P.J.A., Jr., became the Club's first manager. Louis, having fared more prosperously, was able to become a dues-paying member and was appointed the Club's first treasurer. In the process, they made great contributions to the horticultural rejuvenation of the grounds. And so we have a story beginning with a happy ending, and all the peripheral segments of one broad narrative coming together in the fruition of the dream of one man and the vision of another, and for a poignant side effect, the reunion of two brothers with the old soil on which they once bounded about on shoeless feet.

We take our fade-out as Bob Jones makes his

solemn pronouncement as to the nature of Augusta National Golf Club and what it was all about at its origin.... "Our aim is to develop a golf course and a retreat of such nature, and of such excellence, that men of some means and devoted to the game of golf may find the Club worthwhile as an extra luxury where they may visit and play with kindred spirits from other parts of the nation."

It has been achieved, never veering from course.

"Unless I break down, I hope to participate every year, regardless of how I am putting or where I finish" — Bobby Jones at the first Augusta National Invitation Tournament (which would not become "Masters" officially for four more years), March, 1934.

He WAS the tournament, especially that first year. He made out the first invitation list himself. His name brought the highest price in the Calcutta pool. He made no move but what journalism reported on it. Wherever he went on the course, those men covering the tournament were always close at hand; but it was a different kind of star-media relationship than has developed in the age of television. First, the press entourage was significantly smaller, and Jones knew nearly all of them personally. Also, those writers were privileged to follow close at hand down the fairway and chat with him between shots. When Grantland Rice arrived, their official dean was at hand, and as O. B. Keeler reported in the *Atlanta Journal*, "He [Rice] ruled the tournament as of even greater importance than the National Open." After all, it was the only place in the world where the public could see Bobby Jones play golf anymore. That, as it developed, had not been achieved with ease.

"I had an awful time convincing Bob he should play at all," Clifford Roberts said. "He wanted to be the host and an official. I told him he couldn't invite his friends to a game of golf and not play with them."

People responded. The opportunity to see Bobby Jones play again at $2 a head drew them out in numbers estimated at 3,500, even exceeding expectations. Most of them were gathered around the 1st tee as Jones made his first drive, and they cheered loudly. He wore a checked blue sweater above knickers, with socks to match. Paul Runyan, with whom he was paired, was dressed in a tomato red sweater and matching socks. Jones out-drove the little professional by 40 yards.

"Jones Off in His Putting as Masters Starts." The headline in the *Atlanta Journal* drove directly to the point. Just as Jones had feared, his conduct on the green was erratic. He was playing with an unusual handicap. His treasured companion of all those great years was missing. "Calamity Jane," his putter, had been misplaced, and he'd had to send to Atlanta for a substitute. He three-putted each of the last three greens. His score was 76 on the first round.

Jones finished that first tournament in thirteenth place, tied with Denny Shute, a PGA champion, and Walter Hagen, U.S. Open, British Open, and PGA champion, and the most flamboyant professional of his time, with a score of 294 for the 72 holes. It was to be, as history turned out, Jones' best finish in the tournament created about and for him. Of all the rounds he played in 12 Masters never once did he break par. The scores of his final year, 1948, indicate a deterioration of the game that a man who demanded so much of himself could not long bring himself to tolerate. He shot 75-81-79-79 and finished out of sight at 314. By this time the press had mercifully turned its head and left him to his peace, such as he could find.

During the four years between his retirement from competition and his return in the Masters, Bobby Jones had managed to fill his hours with gainful ventures. Warner Brothers, the film producers, contracted him for a series of instructional shorts with a story, or gag line, including some of the movie idols of the time such as Richard Arlen, W. C. Fields, and Guy Kibbee. The Listerine Company sponsored him in a radio series of golf and how it should be played, teamed with his Boswellian companion, O. B. Keeler. He was syndicated in another instructional form through a regular newspaper column. And the A. G. Spalding Company made his involvement complete when he was contracted to serve the manufacturer of sporting goods for many a lucrative year as a designer and consultant on a line of golf clubs that bore his name. When his career on the course came to an end, he was not, then, left bereft of activity. He also had contacts in the legal profession to develop, and later he bought two Coca-Cola Bottling outlets. And always, always, there was the Masters.

"One of the miracles of it is that a town of some 65,000 can absorb all these people with so little ripple" — Clifford Roberts, 1975.

For several of the earlier years of the Masters, the Bon Air Vanderbilt served the tournament, served Augusta National, and continued to serve a continuing clientele of America's social elite. It was the center of tournament living. Fare was $5 per day, American Plan. Formal dress for dinner was required. Walton Marshall managed on. He was not one to break with, or even allow warpage of, tradition.

Curiously, though, as the golf tournament made gains in popularity, the hotel's prestige lost ground. In no way were these changes of stature related, except for the inescapable fact that expansion of facilities at Augusta National surely siphoned off some of the Bon Air's regular patronage. When World War II broke loose upon the nation, Augusta's face began to change, and many of the old standards and traditions changed with it. Resort hotels began losing guests to the burgeoning "second-home" movement. Americans began moving about by air. That brought Florida nearer in time, and as the palms, the beaches, and the balmy air became more accessible, so did it become more attractive. The tourist boom broke out, driving the alligators and the Seminoles deeper into the marshes and mosquito country. The piney woods atmosphere of the mid-Southern resorts lost some of its appeal.

The military had taken over the Forest Hills Hotel in Augusta and its golf course during World War II, and civilians never got them back. The Bon Air's demise was less abrupt and dreadfully more painful. It was an awful thing to watch, year to year, its death by deterioration, neglect, and flighty management. It sat there on its hill, a huge white ghost, seeming to cry out for someone to save it. In its halcyon years, natives "down the hill" had gazed upon the Bon Air with awe, watching the great people of America, tycoons, presidents, men of letters and nobility, come and go in their chauffeured livery. Now all barriers were down. The gasping old hotel begged attention. The townspeople moved about its premises with freedom, but found themselves disillusioned, for all the attractiveness and the lure of the glittering personalities were no longer there.

Forest Hills Hotel has now become Oliver General Hospital, a branch of the Veterans Administration. The Bon Air still sits in its crook of Walton Way at the top of the hill, but the world races by it unnoticing. It has become a residential home for senior citizens.

The Hotel Richmond sprang to the fore as the Bon Air began to fade. It was located downtown on Broad Street at the war memorial monument, a place where drummers stayed when the Masters wasn't on. Making no pretense of trying to take the place of the Bon Air in the social life of Augusta, it provided only four walls, a bed, a place to eat, and the necessities of life found in the typical commercial hotel. The Barringers owned it at the time it was cutting its widest swath as a host, but death and estate problems brought it down eventually, too. Now it is closed and has been succeeded by a stunning new modern hostelry called the Executive House. Otherwise, Augusta has become a motel town. The visiting patrons are now decentralized, strung out from Interstate Highway 20, which crosses Washington Road two miles west of Augusta National, to North Augusta, across the Savannah River, and all the way to Aiken, South Carolina.

Then we have the latest form of itinerant resident. He rents. Not a room, but a whole house. He blows in for the week of the tournament. The landlord and family leave town for the week and take a vacation, generously bankrolled by the rental fee. The one-week resident brings in his family, friends, business accounts, or shares with another family. Or as in the case of a tournament player, another golfer and family. Sometimes the house is a classic, one of the columned residences out Walton Way. Sometimes it's a subdivision house without pretension. Sometimes it goes for $1,500 for the week. Nearly every afternoon smoke from charcoal cookery casts a blue pall over the backyard. A few drinks, a steak, to bed, and out to the course early in the morning for the player. For the watcher, a long night, a midmorning brunch, an afternoon of gallerying, and a party in the evening, maybe the annual church Southern Bar-B-Q at the old lodge on the lake Saturday, or the loftier and more formal atmosphere of dinner and dancing at Augusta Country Club.

House rental became popular when the Augusta Chamber of Commerce took this course to satisfy the rooming demands in the years when Augusta was being transformed from a hotel to a motel town, and quarters were short. It has stuck. Some of the tournament players have been renting the same house or in the same residential section for years. Look out the window and Gary Player may be jogging by. Arnold Palmer may be backing out of the driveway. Jack Nicklaus may be standing at the mailbox talking to a one-week neighbor. Just typical American family living with stars in the roles.

People drive by that place every day never knowing of its share in the history of golf. It is a silent landmark, saying nothing, revealing nothing of its secret that Bobby Jones once lived there. The address is 3425 Tuxedo Road, dead center in the section of Atlanta where the heart of old Northwest Side society beats. On a turn behind a white spiked fence, the columned mansion sits back from the street, almost out of sight of eyes that would be curious. Where Mr. Jones lived, a Mr. Brown lives now, an implied pseudonymic procession of occupancy as if the address itself seeks its own anonymity. When the Joneses lived there, the mailbox bore a simple black-on-white plate that said "Whitehall." It is not there anymore.

There were three children: Robert III; Clara, named for Bob's mother; and Mary Ellen, named for her own mother. To them "Whitehall" was home, though the name itself had no meaning whatsoever in their lives.

"Dad bought the house from a Dr. Childs, and the name was on the mailbox when we moved there. Dad just never did bother to take it down." Mary Ellen Jones, now Mrs. Carl Hood, wife of a banker, mother of one daughter, car-

pooler, member of Lovett School PTA, speaks from a wing chair in the parlor of her home in that part of Atlanta known as Buckhead. "After his operation, we made it a habit to visit him every Saturday afternoon at five o'clock. Have a drink and talk to him about friends and things outside that he had an interest in. We'd go by every afternoon after a Georgia Tech football game and tell him how the team looked and how the new players were working out. He never lost his interest in Georgia Tech, but going to games was out of the question. On the other hand, he kept going to his office nearly every day until about a year before he died."

Mary Malone Jones was in charge of the religious affairs of the family, and being of Irish descent, the children were reared in the Catholic faith. Little Mary Ellen attended parochial school at Christ the King, and one day in her first grade class all the children were asked by their teacher, a nun, to stand and tell of their fathers and what they did. When it came Mary Ellen's turn, she stood and said, "I don't know, but he has an awful lot of blue ribbons, so he must have won something; but my brother and sister have a lot of blue ribbons, too, and they rode horses."

Bobby III and Clara rode in horse shows at summer camp. Kid stuff. Mary Ellen never had such an inclination, nor toward any kind of athletic games, for that matter.

"I never was a golfer, but when Dad was involved in building the Peachtree course, he hired Stewart Maiden, his old teacher, as the professional," Mary Ellen says. "Then he decided Stewart Maiden needed some customers and that I should start taking lessons. So once a week for about a year, I took a lesson from Stewart Maiden, who was not inclined to be very gentle with his instructions. To his outspoken disgust, I was a very poor student. To paraphrase the title of Dad's book, 'Golf Was NOT My Game.'

"I played golf with him one time in my life, Dad and I against Mother and my brother. A two-ball foursome at Peachtree. The course was still rather new and in an unrefined condition. It was a dreadful experience for him. I put him in poison ivy, honeysuckle, thickets, and brooks, places where he had never been on a golf course.

Finally, I was so tired of it all I hauled off without caring and hit a drive on the 4th hole, a par three, and the ball stopped about two feet from the pin. He sank the putt. I said, 'I retire, I quit. I'm finished,' and walked back to the clubhouse."

Of course, most of Bobby Jones' golfing battles had been fought by the time Mary Ellen was born. The Grand Slam had been won. He still played the Masters, but that was not one of the wars, more a walk through the park with old friends and old foes. None of the great conflicts is any part of Mary Ellen's memories. The public's steadfast reverence for her father was there, but even this made no deep impression because she grew up with it.

"They took me to California when I was three months old, when Dad went out there to make those movies. My nurse told me of all the famous movie stars I had met, but I remember none of that." Being the daughter of a celebrated father has made few waves in her life, in other words. "With a name like Mary Jones," she says, wryly, "you can get by without stirring up much attention.

"It was not that way with my brother. Bobby had something to live up to, being the son of Bobby Jones, the great golfer. He always had that shadow hanging over him. It was like being the son of Red Grange and playing halfback. Bobby played well, but never good enough.

"Dad always had this desire for him to qualify for the U.S. Amateur, then finish in one of the positions that would earn him an invitation to the Masters. So one year he qualified for the U.S. Amateur. He flew out to Colorado for the tournament, full of fire and enthusiasm, ready to take that old tiger by the tail. Who does he draw in the first round? A kid named Jack Nicklaus. Bobby never made it to the Masters."

If nothing had yet certified for her the international esteem of her father, his notability, the near sainthood bestowed upon him, the confirmation came in October, 1958, when Mary Ellen was invited along to St. Andrews to witness his acceptance of the Freedom of the City. Just right off, no one was quite certain of the caliber of the honor until it came to light that only one other American had ever received it—Benjamin Franklin. The Joneses flew to London on a flight that almost became a disaster. The plane lost an engine and had to turn back to Gander, Newfoundland, as it approached the point of crisis over the Atlantic. They reached St. Andrews a day behind schedule.

"It was one of the great experiences of my life. The ceremony was a moving thing. I was stunned. Younger Hall was just jammed. We were taken in through the back entrance and seated on a stage. I'll never forget Dad, how he got on that stage and up to the lectern with his two walking sticks. He was determined to do it without any help. It was painful to watch him. I thought he'd never make it, but he did.

"He had worked hard on that speech of acceptance, and it was beautiful. It became quite emotional at the end, and then he and the Provost were seated in a golf cart and they drove down the aisle through the hall. People were crying and reaching out to touch him, and to touch even us, my mother, my brother, and me. I felt like the Queen of England. Then almost in unison, purely spur of the moment, I think, they began singing 'Will Ye No' Come Back Again?' well knowing that he never would. We walked down the aisle behind him, and I can still feel the tingles in my spine. It was moving."

As for the Masters tournament, it was only a glimmer out there on some distant horizon to Mary Ellen. She heard of it, read of it, knew of it as some peripheral event concerning her family, but her attendance was rare. "A good deal of the time, especially when Dad was still playing, I was away at college. Then I was married and had other interests and responsibilities. I do remember one year a bunch of us in our 20s rented a railroad car and went to the Masters, but that was more a big party than it was a junket of golf. I can't even tell you who won it that year."

Four years before he died in December, 1971, so crippled he could no longer endure a journey of even 165 miles to the Masters, Bob Jones and his Mary gave up the responsibilities of householding for an apartment on Peachtree Street. Most of the last 20 years of his life he required fulltime attendants who served as valet, hand servant, nurse, and chauffeur. His man's man at the end was one of distinguished bearing and manner named Hoyt. Being virtually immobile at this point, Jones required constant attention. Hoyt moved along with him to the apartment, there to watch over him as he awaited his appointment with death. Three days before he passed on, Bob Jones told a close friend, "If I had known it would be this easy, I wouldn't have been so worried about it."

On a cold Saturday morning in December, Robert Tyre Jones, Jr., died. Two years later, almost to the day, Robert Tyre Jones III, only 47 years old, lurched forward and died of a heart attack in Nashville, Tennessee. In May, 1975, Mary Malone Jones passed away. Now only the two daughters are left, and some destiny has drawn them close. Clare and Mary Ellen live not more than two blocks apart, and "Whitehall" is not more than a mile away.

(1976)

28 Holes in 100 Strokes
Gene Sarazen with Herbert Warren Wind

Gene Sarazen has been one of my favourite people in golf ever since he graciously agreed to play an exhibition to dedicate the Valley View Golf Course in Utica, New York, in 1941. He did it as a favour to me as I had been responsible for the design of the course. Since then our paths have crossed frequently and he and I have remained close friends. Gene is one of golf's great success stories. A product of the caddie yard, he has achieved the heights as one of the game's most indomitable champions through hard work, unquestioned ability and more than his share of luck. He also has been one of the game's great innovators, as the first to use the interlocking grip and as the inventor of the sand wedge and the weighted practice club.

 Although he was the first professional ever to win the four major championships — Masters, United States and British Opens and PGA — Gene is best known for the double eagle he scored in the 1935 Masters: he holed out a second shot on the par-5 15th hole to make up 3 strokes on frontrunner Craig Wood and then went on to beat Wood in a 36-hole playoff.

Lesser known is a shot Gene made in the 1973 British Open at Troon in Scotland which I had the good fortune to witness. The tournament, which ultimately was won by Tom Weiskopf, initially was noteworthy because it was to be Gene's fiftieth anniversary and farewell appearance in that oldest of championships. Never one to hide his talents on such a historic occasion, Gene stole the headlines the first day when he holed a 5 iron for an ace on Troon's 8th, the famed "Postage Stamp."

That was only one shot of dramatic impact, whereas this selection from Thirty Years of Championship Golf, which Gene wrote with Herbert Warren Wind, details one hundred he made in his dramatic rush to his second United States Open Championship. It was one of the most sustained drives in the history of the game and, as this account proves, one of the most exciting.

IKE MOST ATHLETES I know, I have always played hunches and cultivated my superstitions, consciously and unconsciously. I entered 1932, for example, certain from the first day of January on that I would enjoy a banner year. After my rapid climb to the top in 1922, I had adopted 2 as my lucky number. It also did nicely for me at the roulette tables. On the golf course, I came to interpret a birdie 2 as an omen of a hot streak, luckier than a birdie 3 or a birdie 4. A 2 on the 69th ignited my sub-par dash at Agua Caliente, and 2's appeared in numerous other tournaments when I was looking for some sign that Sarazen was supposed to win. The year 1932, I had a hunch, might be another 1922.

I was right on the stick that winter, as Daniels would say. Through patience and practice I had mastered my grip and grooved a swing that I knew was compact, correct, and natural. I knew myself a bit better. I felt that I had a tighter rein on my impetuousness. In the twenties I had repeatedly made the mistake of trying to redeem a bad hole by forcing foolhardy miracle shots on the next, which only dug my grave deeper. I also had the sand-iron now and could stand up confidently to any trap shot, clean, half-buried, or buried. I had the game, I thought, to win the National Open at Fresh Meadow and the additional advantage of knowing every yard of that course. I'd been the pro at Fresh Meadow for six seasons, from 1925 through 1930.

One of my reasons for leaving Fresh Meadow was the old golf superstition that a pro can never win a tournament held on his own course. I had come face to face with that superstition and found that it apparently held true in my case. Fresh Meadow had been host to the 1930 PGA. With my club members cheering me on I had made my way to the final, where I met Tommy Armour. I must have been inside of Tommy on four out of every five holes, and yet I couldn't shake him off. He finally squared the match on the 35th when he played an incredible four-iron from a knee-deep lie in a Chinese vegetable garden. On the 36th tee, however, Tommy hit a bad smothered hook. A straight tee-shot and I had him. I missed my opening, my drive following Tommy's into the large trap at the left. We were both on in three, Tommy 35 feet away, myself 10 feet inside him. Before he even took his line on the cup, I knew Tommy would sink that putt. He tapped it in. I missed mine, as I knew I would. I was the home pro. Weak golf had as much to do with my defeat as strong superstition, I realized, but when I learned that the 1932 Open was scheduled for Fresh Meadow, I decided that I ought to get myself another job and give myself a fair chance to win that Open. I became the home pro at Lakeville.

In the winter of 1932, as I gave my hunch about the Open every chance to grow, I began to think about the New Orleans Open. In 1922, previous to winning the National Open, I had led the field in that earlier version of the New Orleans Open, the Southern Open. Might not be a bad idea, I reflected, to nourish the parallel between 1922 and 1932 by winning at New Orleans. I crossed it out. That was pushing things too far. Two days before the New Orleans Open was set to begin, I was lounging around my home in New Port Richey, Florida, discussing possible itineraries for a hunting trip with my old friend Lester Rice of the *New York Journal-American*. All of a sudden I was seized by an indefinable restlessness. I paced up and down the living room, trying to figure out what was bothering me. I cornered it. "Lester, pack your bag," I said, snapping my fingers. "We're going to New Orleans. I've got a hunch that if I can win that tournament, I'll win the National Open again this year." Inside of a half hour, we were on our way. We drove the eight hundred miles to New Orleans non-stop, taking time out only to feed ourselves at roadside diners.

I won at New Orleans. On the last hole I snagged the 4 I needed by playing my second shot onto the green with my driver. I play a driver off the fairway very rarely, but I had used that club on my second shot on the last hole at Skokie in 1922 to set up my winning 4. Replaying my last round as I drove home from New Orleans, I wondered whether I had purposely played the driver on the 18th because I had remembered Skokie, or if the odd similarity between the two finishes had popped into my head only after I had made the shot. It wasn't worth quibbling about, I decided. Either way, I liked it.

In June something went wrong. I won the British Open. That made it confusing. I hadn't won that championship in 1922, and so it hadn't entered into my plans for 1932. It was obvious that I had slipped up somewhere, misinterpreted some augury from which I should have been able to divine that it was the *British* Open and not the *United States* Open I was meant to win. If that was the way it was supposed to be, okay, I had no kick coming. I am not a choosy man. I'll settle for either of the two Opens any year.

All superstition aside, I did not think I had much of a chance to win our Open when I returned from England about a week before the field was due to tee off at Fresh Meadow. The British Open had left me worn-out and nervously tired. The last thing I wanted to do was subject myself to the strain of another championship. I discovered, however, at the wonderful victory dinners my friends gave me, that I was expected to duplicate what Jones had done in 1930—win both Opens in the same year. I dragged myself out to Fresh Meadow, feeling like a businessman who had slaved for weeks so that he could take off on a short vacation and then had been called back to his office from the Maine woods. My game was listless. A week was too short a period, anyhow, for it to regain the sharp edge it had in England.

Fresh Meadow was not a great course, but it was a tough one to score on. Like nearly all the courses designed by A. W. Tillinghast, it featured bottleneck greens guarded on both the right and the left by unusually deep bunkers. Unless my will to win was suddenly rekindled in the fire of competition, which I very much doubted it would be, my best chance in the Open, I thought, was to follow safety-first tactics. I decided that I would play for the pin only when the position of my tee-shot gave me the true opening to the pin. If it didn't, then I would play my approach cautiously to the front edge of the narrow opening to the green and take my chances on getting down in two putts once I was on. Sand-iron or no sand-iron, I didn't want to tangle with those brutal traps any more than I had to. The greens, I knew from six years of practicing on them, presented no such headache. Uniformly flat and unsubtle, you could get down in two on them regardless of the length of your approach putt.

I adhered faithfully to this calculated plan of attack, or non-attack, on my first two rounds. I was puzzled when it rewarded me with two mediocre scores, a 74 and a 76, which left me five shots behind the pacemaking total of 145 posted by Phil Perkins, the ex-English ex-amateur. Moreover, I had played shabbier golf than my scores indicated. I could have been three or four shots higher on each round if I hadn't been putting like a Hagen. I made up my mind, nevertheless, to stick with my conservative tactics on the third and fourth rounds. There was an awful lot of trouble on Fresh Meadow, as the high scores testified. Only two men, Perkins and Olin Dutra, had broken par, 70, on either of the first two rounds.

On the morning of the final day, as I was leaving our house to drive to the club, I stopped in the front hallway, sensing that I had forgotten something I might need. I ran through the list of possible omissions: Car keys? Wallet? Fresh underwear and socks? Cigars? No, I had them all. Oh, I knew what it was! I tiptoed back into the bedroom where Mary lay sleeping and withdrew from the clothes closet the gabardine jacket I had worn for the presentation ceremonies at Prince's.

I fell farther behind the leaders on the third round, losing a stroke to par on four of the first eight holes. The one club in the bag I was playing with decisiveness was my putter, a Calamity Jane model that I had sawed off at the neck and rewelded to gain a shade more loft. For the rest, my game had degenerated from cagey conservatism to downright timidity. I was amazed to learn from Jack Doyle, the betting commissioner, that even when I stood seven strokes off the pace after the first eight holes of the third round, my old club members at Fresh Meadow and other old friends were still placing bets that I would win, without bothering to inquire what the odds were. That was blind faith, if ever I saw it. When I stood on the 9th tee, I had a 3 for a 39.

On the 9th tee I made a couple of impulsive

decisions. I asked the two motorcycle policemen, who had appointed themselves my private bodyguard, to hit the road. "I don't care where you go, boys," I told them. "Go to the races at Belmont. Go to the beach. Go any place. You fellows are a jinx." And there and then I made up my mind to chuck my dainty safety tactics. Maybe they paid dividends for other golfers, but I'd given them a fair trial and they suited me like a cage does a robin. I smashed a seven-iron 12 feet from the pin on the short 9th and ran my putt down for a birdie 2. That was more like it. From that hole on, I threw caution to the winds. I belted my drives harder. The harder I hit them, the straighter they went. I rifled my irons right for the flag — to blazes with the bunkers. I began hitting the greens, and close enough to the hole to have a good crack for my birdies.

I started back with four straight pars, the easiest kind of pars. On the 14th I dropped a putt for a 2, gathering precision with every hole, and made it three birdies in a row with a 3 on the 15th and a 4 on the 587-yard 16th. Two clean-cut pars on the 17th and 18th rounded out a 32 back and a 70. I walked over to the score board to see what good, if any, my comeback had done. Well, I had picked up four strokes on Phil Perkins and five on Dutra. Perkins was still in front with 219 for his three rounds, but I was breathing down his neck now with 220. Diegel was also at 220, and Dutra and Bobby Cruickshank were a stroke behind. Bobby had played a 69. There was a fighter to admire. Bobby's home club had folded just a few weeks before the Open, and he really had to win prize money. His valiant 69 followed a 78 and a 74.

When I am battling for an Open crown I want to concentrate, and I have no patience with the golf pests who slap you on the back and ask you if you don't remember how they bought you a Moxie at Worcester in '25, or the time they acted as marshal at an exhibition in '27 at the Old Rough and Ready Country Club. I can't help being short with these intruders. There are times for social conversation and there are times when you ought to have enough sense to leave a man alone. I wouldn't barge in on a businessman in the middle of an important deal, and it beats me how some galleryites cannot realize that a golfer is a man at work when the chips are down in an important championship. Other athletes are luckier than golfers. I can think of no other sport in which a spectator is permitted on the playing field where he can touch the hand and bend the ear of a player who is in the throes of competition.

I know who my true friends are by the consideration they show me when I am under that all-encompassing pressure, as I was with eighteen to go at Fresh Meadow. Tom and Frances Meighan and my other friends from Lakeville and Fresh Meadow just said hello and wished me luck when we passed each other, understanding my preoccupation. Al Ciuci had a guard posted at the locker-room entrance to keep out the autograph collectors and the advertising agents scurrying around to sign up anyone who looked as if he could win. This locker-room guard was stumped when an elderly person who looked neither like an ad man nor an autograph hound requested permission to speak to me. "He's an old gent in a black suit and a stiff collar," the guard reported. "Oh, that's Mr. Wheeler," I said, smiling through my seriousness. "That's one man I always want to see." Archie walked in and shook my hand warmly. "I'll only stay a minute, Gene," he said. "I wouldn't have intruded now except that I don't want to bother you when you're playing. Here," he said, removing a small package from his pocket, "is a little token of the tremendous pleasure you gave me by winning the British Open. That was an excellent performance, Gene." I had scarcely thanked Mr. Wheeler for his gift, a set of platinum-and-sapphire cuff links, when he was shuffling his way out of the locker-room.

I enjoyed a relaxing lunch with Bob Jones and a friend of his, Reg Newton, although we were interrupted from time to time by human radar sets bursting in with reports on the front-runners. As I told Bob, I was stumped by the way everyone seemed so eager to tell me that my rivals were burning up the course. I remember that I toasted Perkins as I started draining my second bottle of beer. It was the first time I had ever toasted an opponent while the battle still raged, and I didn't know exactly why I had done it. Long before I learned for a fact that Perkins had turned in 35 and Cruickshank in 33, I sensed that I would have to be 68 or better to beat their marks. I was the last contender to go out.

The wind was blowing slightly with the players on the 1st hole. That was a good sign. It meant that the wind would be with me on the 6th and 8th and the other rough holes. I started with a par on the 1st, 437 yards long, playing my second on with a two-iron. I missed my par 4 on the 2nd hole — 395 yards, a sharp dog-leg to the left — when I shoved my drive into trouble on the right and dumped my recovery into a trap. I got that stroke right back with a birdie 3 on the 3rd, and then went below par by adding a birdie 2 on the 4th. I hit a very satisfying two-iron there, 9 feet from the cup on a hole that played longer than its 188 yards because of the gusty cross-wind. I slapped two straight woods up the 5th, a 578-yard par 5, pitched on about fifteen feet away, missed my putt, and took a 5.

In my books, the most dangerous hole at Fresh Meadow was the 6th. It was 428 yards long and menaced from tee to green along the left by a stout line of trees. This tight left side placed a heavy premium on straightness off the tee, but that was only half the battle. To carry the pond that nosed well into the fairway on the right, you had to bang a tee-shot that carried 220 yards. Because of the frequent high scores I had blown myself to on this hole, I used to rate it a par 5, a psychological dodge that did me as much harm as good. I must have played that hole well over a thousand times, but I never played it better than I did on the afternoon of June 25, 1932: a solid tee-shot well over the pond, a two-iron that split the pin all the way and sat down 4 feet from the cup, and a firm putt that hit the back of the cup and dropped for a birdie 3.

As I walked to the 7th tee, for the first time during the tournament, I was struck by the feeling that I *could* win. The front nine, in my opinion, held far more terror than the second, and I was past the danger zone on that first nine, alive and kicking and two under par. If I could strike a happy medium between brazen boldness and over-caution, hit my shots hard and crisp but only after I had thought each shot out clearly, there was no reason why I couldn't keep pace with par the rest of the round.

To finish 4-4-3 on the first nine was not hard for a player who knew the course as well as I did. Placement of the tee-shot was the key to the 7th, a slight dog-leg to the left, 412 yards into the wind. Birdie-hungry players always tried to cut off a little of the corner, but I couldn't see the percentage in fooling around with the tall trees and the trap at the break. I played down the right-hand side of the fairway and had a six-iron for my second. The pin was on the left side of the green, but I didn't go for it, although the opening was inviting. I aimed for the center of the green, playing the percentages. If I missed my approach shot to the right, I figured I would wind up in a trap, but there would be a reasonable amount of room between that trap and the pin in which to control my explosion shot. However, if I erred to the left and found the trap on that side, I would leave myself a much smaller area of the green, and consequently a much more difficult explosion shot. I played my six-iron 20 feet to the right of the flag and got down in two comfortable putts for my par 4. On this approach putt and my others I didn't gun for the hole. I tried to roll the ball up nice and gently so that it would die about a foot past the cup. If it caught a corner, chances were that it would drop. If it went by, I wouldn't be left with a sizable putt back. Those three-footers back knock the stuffing out of you in a tournament, even if you get them.

The wind was with me on the 8th and that helped. It changed that 425-yard 4 from a drive and a long iron or spoon into a drive and a pitch. The trouble off the tee was on the right here, rough grass and young maples. Plenty of room on the left. I played a right-to-left tee shot, aiming for the center of the fairway, knowing I would have a shot to the green regardless of how much I hooked my drive. I got it out there a very long ways, about 300 yards, I would guess, and in any event, just a moderate six-iron from the pin. Once again the pin had been tucked on the left side of the pear-shaped green to bring the long trap on the left into play. I lofted a pitch with adequate backspin to the center of the green, putted up close and made my 4.

The 9th was a short short-hole, 143 yards. The green was typically Tillinghast, bounded on the left side by one long trap, built up at the back, and with a circle of traps fringing the right. I punched a seven-iron 15 feet past the pin, in the center of the green. On this hole I deviated from the roll-'em-close putting strategy I had adopted for this crucial round. I went boldly for the cup with my putt, and knocked it in. The reason why I could afford to gamble on that green was that I knew every inch of it cold. It was right next to the pro shop, and during my years at Fresh Meadow it had served as my practice green. I must have spent two hundred hours all told on it, and what I didn't know about that green, Churchill doesn't know about oratory.

As a man whose lucky number was 2, I took full cognizance of the fact that my second 2 of the day on the 9th gave me a 32 for the first nine. I was confident and assured as I started the long voyage home. My guess was that a 68 would be good enough to win, and I felt that I had a 36, one over par, in my system. I was concentrating well. I know that as my gallery swelled by the thousands I was not conscious of their numbers, their movements, their cheers or their groans. I set my sights on starting back with a 4 on the 10th (385 yards), a 4 on the 11th (413 yards), and a 3 on the 12th (155 yards).

Looking down the 10th was like greeting an old friend. I had laid out the fairway traps. The trap on the left was 220 yards out, the one on the right, 240, so the sensible thing to do was to stay away from the right. I deliberately aimed for the trap on the left, as I was sure I could carry it and had no qualms about playing my second out of the rough. My drive sailed over the right-hand corner of the trap, fading perfectly to suit the contour of the fairway. I was 15 feet below the hole with my approach, a seven-iron. Down in two for my par 4.

The 11th was not a difficult hole. It demanded nothing more than a straightaway drive and a straightaway second to a punch-bowl green. My tee-shot traveled on a line a shade to the right of the center of the fairway. I was playing my drives on definite fairway points, allowing for a slight draw. If the draw didn't take, as it didn't on this drive, I had nothing to worry about. If the draw did come off, there would be ample room on the left to handle it. I was playing those right-to-left tee shots with

ease, really moving into the ball. The pin on the 11th was well to the back of the green. I could have used a mashie for my approach but I settled on my six. I didn't want to go over that green or even be past the pin and have a downhiller coming back. I made the center of the green my target area once again, and hit it. My approach putt from 18 feet died a few inches beyond the hole, and I got my regulation 4.

On the 12th I met my first shock. I elected to play a right-to-left iron to the green, 155 yards away. I half-missed my mashie, it fell short on the right-hand side of the entrance to the green, and I was confronted with a shot that gave me the shakes. I lay 40 feet from the pin, positioned on the slippery right deck of the green barely ten feet beyond the far edge of the trap. I couldn't afford not to play for the pin and sacrifice my par. I wanted a 3 desperately. If I could drop the ball delicately over the edge of the trap, I'd have a holeable putt for my 3 . . . but I'd have a possible 5 if I choked the faintest fraction. It was a gamble I had to take. I asked my caddy for the sand-iron and prayed that my many hours of practice with that club would enable my reflexes to function perfectly under the enormous pressure I felt. I did nip the ball just right. It cleared the sand trap by three scant feet, backspin slowed it down abruptly, and the ball spun itself dead 2 feet from the hole. I sank my 2-footer for my par. Whew!

The 13th, 14th, and 15th—I found I was planning my play three holes at a time—were rugged, testing holes. The 13th fairway, 448 yards from the tee to a staunchly trapped green, was hemmed in by woods on both sides. If you hooked or sliced, all you could do was to play safely, almost at right angles, back onto the fairway and be prepared to accept a 5. I didn't even think of the trees, I was that confident on the tee. I took the route down the right side of the fairway to open up the shot to the green. The approach called for was a long iron and it had to be straight. It might have been a three-iron, but discretion prompted a four. My ball hit and stuck 20 feet below the pin. Again down in two for my par, my fourth consecutive par coming back.

I matched par once again on the 14th, a stiff short-hole measuring 219 yards. I took a spoon and played as fine a shot as I did during the entire tournament. It buzzed on a beeline for the pin, landed on the front edge of the green, and rolled to within 16 feet of the cup. I putted up and got my 3. I was feeling very, very confident at this point. Wild Bill Cushing, my old Florida caddy who was acting as my spotter, brought in a final report on Perkins and Cruickshank. They hadn't slowed down. Phil had taken a 70, which gave him a total of 289. Bobby had tied that total with a 68. I did a little figuring before stepping onto the 15th or the 69th tee. I would need a 69 to tie, a 68 to win. . . . I was three under par, and par was 70. . . . I could drop one stroke to par on the last four holes and still edge out Perkins and Cruickshank. Well, I wasn't going to think in those negative terms. I was going to keep right on marching, hitting my shots full, thinking out each hole and each shot intelligently.

The 15th, which bent a bit to the left, was purely a tee-shot hole. Deep traps banked the green on this 424-yard 4 and there were traps about thirty yards in front of the green, but as long as you hit a sturdy tee-shot down the middle, you didn't have to worry too much about those green hazards. The place to miss your tee-shot, if you were going to miss it, was down the right. There was trouble on that side, trees, but nothing compared with what you had on the left—out-of-bounds and a cyclone fence. If you got up against this fence, you could use up a lot of strokes. Dutra had the day before. I cracked my drive down the right-hand edge of the fairway, and here I got a break. Had my ball carried ten feet farther, it could have ended up in the rough behind a tree. It landed on soft ground and stuck, a foot inside the fairway. As I studied my approach, for the first time memories began to spin around in my mind. Here was the hole where I had let Armour get off the hook in the PGA two years earlier. I had played my second rashly and had taken an unnecessary 5. Armour had got down in two from a trap, and had pulled out a hole I had counted on winning. I studied my approach carefully. I wanted nothing to do with that heavy-lipped trap on the left. I was going to be short, if anything. I played a seven-iron for the apron. My ball landed shorter than I had wanted it to, but it got a fast bounce off the worn-out turf and skipped up the green 10 feet

from the cup. I holed it for a birdie, a very lucky birdie. I had gained an insurance stroke I hadn't deserved. Luck may be the residue of careful planning, as the wise men say, or it can be just plain luck.

The course was playing very short on this last round but getting home in two on the 587-yard 16th was out of the question. I split the fairway with a right-to-left tee-shot and its overspin gave it a long roll. I decided I would use my driver instead of a brassie or spoon for my second. It wasn't so much a desire for distance as my concern about the shallow trap on the right-hand side of the fairway about one hundred yards from the green. If I happened to push the shot to the right, the low trajectory I would get with the driver would give my ball a better chance of running through that trap. I really tagged that second. It landed just before the trap, shot over on one big bounce, and rolled to within forty yards of the green. The pin was on the right, too close to a bunker to be tempting. I made no attempt to get a 4. A sand-iron shot took me to the center of the green on my third, and I holed in two from 15 feet. That was another helpful par. I needed only two more of them now.

The 17th at Fresh Meadow was only 373 yards long, a drive and pitch if you kept away from the heavy rough, the stone wall, and the out-of-bounds on the left. I played my drive over the trees on the right—there was lots of room—and had a simple sand-iron shot to the plateau green. I dropped it on, hole-high and ten feet to the right. I rolled my first putt to the lip and tapped in the two-incher I had for my par.

The 18th, 404 undulating yards, was a robust finishing hole. I was glad the wind was with me. As I was teeing up, my thoughts suddenly darted back to the Armour match again. I had hooked my drive off the 36th sharply into the trap on the left. I was determined not to repeat that error. A good drive and I couldn't lose. I had a 7 to tie Perkins and Cruickshank.

I waited until the marshals had herded the swarming gallery away from the right-hand side, the safe side of the fairway. I aimed down the right and brought my tee-shot in from right to left. I had been concentrating on direction but I must have hit that ball. I had just a seven-iron left to the green and I couldn't remember ever having played that hole with a seven-iron before. And then, with victory in the palm of my hand, I had to go and push my approach into the treacherous trap on the right. How I played that shot into the trap is something I still don't know today. One point I can clear up, though: I did not purposely play my ball into that trap, a fable that has gained considerable circulation. I had great confidence in my sand-iron, yes, but it would have been stupid to have deliberately played into trouble. I could have landed in a footprint or buried myself in the wall of the trap. Actually, I was disgusted with myself for hitting such a brainless, careless shot.

I was all set to march into the trap with my sand-iron when I heard Paul Gallico, the sportswriter, shouting anxiously to me, "Gene, Gene! Wait a moment! Wait until they get that crowd back! For Pete's sake, don't play that shot until that green is cleared!" I felt very cool and capable. I couldn't understand how Paul could be so upset. "Don't worry, Paul," I called back to him. "I'm not playing this shot. My sand-iron is. It'll take care of me." The spectators were still shushing each other and milling on the fringe of the green when I took a peek at the hole from the trap and flipped the ball with my sand-iron 8 feet from the cup. Then the marshals lost complete control of the gallery, which spilled onto the green and formed a tight twenty-foot circle around my ball and the hole. I didn't need the putt. I just tried to get it up close and was pleasantly surprised when it went in — 66. My 286 was three strokes lower than Perkins and Cruickshank.

The gallery, which had been rooting hard for me on every shot, broke loose with such a demonstration of joy and affection that I got very excited. I was finally rescued by the two motorcycle cops whom I had sent away on the 9th tee in the morning. They had been checking the heavy beach traffic when they heard over the radio that I had come back and was on my way to victory. They had jumped on their bikes and had arrived at the course as I was coming up the 18th. That accounted for the sirens I had been hearing. The boys escorted me to the locker-room. I had a drink there with Tom Meighan while I changed into my presentation jacket — now I knew why I had brought it along — and knotted the green tie with the white question mark I had also worn at Prince's. And then I remember Hagen approaching and throwing his arms in the air. "Gene, you've broken every record that I know of!" He placed his arm around my shoulder. "Gene, I don't think you know what you did. You played the last 28 holes in 100 strokes." It was the first time I had realized it.

(1950)

Lord Nelson After Pearl Harbor
Al Barkow

For the millions who were introduced to golf by television a couple of decades ago, when ABC definitely was the third network and sought to fill its unsold time on Saturday and Sunday afternoons with "live" telecasts of about twenty-five tournaments a season, Byron Nelson was a most familiar figure. He was the "playing expert" who offered critical comments regarding the techniques of the golfers from high atop a tower behind the 18th green, as anchorman Chris Schenkel would explain. Nelson was not unlike Tom Landry, the Dallas football coach, in that his comments were delivered in a Texas twang and he always wore a hat. ABC since has prospered and now confines its golf telecasts to major championships and, the fortunes of television being what they are, Nelson has been replaced by Dave Marr, a "mod" Texan.

But for those of us whose knowledge and association with golf predates TV, Nelson was more than just an image on the tube. He was a player entitled to be ranked with the very best. But because most of his unsurpassed accomplishments were realized during World War II, there has been a tendency to regard them as something as bogus as the ersatz golf balls which were in use at the time.

Nothing could be further from the truth, and Al Barkow has set the record straight with his chapter devoted to Nelson and his accomplishments in Golf's Golden Grind, *which traces the pro tour from its precarious, nickel-and-dime beginnings to its present structured multi-million dollar migrations. Nelson's domination of the golf tour, admittedly, was during a time when competition was limited, but even that cannot dim the magnitude of his performance.*

Barkow, a scratch golfer who played in the 1971 United States Amateur, is one of golf's bona fide authorities. He formerly was chief writer for Shell's Wonderful World of Golf. *He also was editor of* Golf *magazine before settling down to write the first definitive history of the professional golf tour.*

DURING WORLD WAR II, the British dug wide trenches across the fairways of many of their golf courses to keep German aircraft from using them as landing strips. And because German bombers would sometimes attack golfers at play, a set of war rules was drawn up. One allowed that "in competition during or while the bombs are falling, players may take cover without penalty for ceasing to play." Good show. Not all the rules were as lenient, though. "A player whose stroke is affected by the simultaneous explosion of a bomb or shell, or by machine-gun fire, may play another ball from the same place. *Penalty, one stroke*." Gee, guys.

Golf in the United States, much farther from the harsh realities of the war, did not go to such extremes, but there were definite cutbacks. The USGA canceled the official U.S. Open from 1942 through 1945. However, if you ask Ben Hogan how many U. S. Opens he won, his answer will be a curt, unequivocal "five." He won four official national opens, but in June 1942 the USGA, in conjunction with the Chicago District Golf Association and the PGA did mount a tournament to raise money for the war and called it the Hale America National Open. It was played in Chicago on the Ridgemoor Country Club course, which was not at all representative of U. S. Open courses, but Hogan counts it a U. S. Open. He won it.

Hogan had one round of 62 in the tournament, and next day the course-proud members had their greenskeeper cut the holes into any little knobs he could find on the greens. Hogan then shot 72. By the way, the Hale in Hale America is not an incorrect spelling. The tournament also promoted a national health program backed by John Kelly, father of actress Grace and Olympic rowing champion Jack. So Hale America, the double entendre an appropriate accident. There was also an auction after the event, the money going to charity. Hogan's putter fetched something around $1,500.

The USGA also suggested that, for the Duration, golf clubs turn portions of the rough on their courses into victory gardens. Could it be that from this such terms as *spinach, broccoli,* and *cabbage* became popular for off-fairway grass? Maybe not, since few clubs followed up on the idea.

As for the PGA and the tour, from 1943 through 1945 there was no count kept of total annual purse money, and the official record lists those years as "No Tour." But the people played golf, and there was a tour . . . of sorts. The government encouraged Ed Dudley, President of the PGA at the time, to keep the professional game alive, as a diversion from the war effort for the workers, by getting pros to play exhibitions at military hospitals and by staging tournaments to spur war-bond drives. Purses were paid out in war bonds. In addition, the equipment manufacturers, under their blanket organization (The Athletic Institute), put $20,000 into the tournament bureau in 1944 and 1945, $25,000 in 1946. The tour fire was kept flickering. Gas rationing kept the tournament schedule somewhat contained and limited, but it was something.

In one wartime event, the Knoxville Open, only eighteen pros entered. The prize list called for twenty money places, so those who played were assured of getting some of the "cheese," as Tommy Bolt calls it. All they had to do was finish — a sure thing. But there is no such thing, right? Lefty Stackhouse had entered this Knoxville Open and played the last round after a sleepless night. By the ninth hole, he was wavering like a thin reed in a hurricane. Fred Corcoran had brought Sergeant Alvin York, the World War I hero, out to the course, and when York, who had never seen golf played before, saw Stackhouse, he said to Corcoran, "I had no idea golf was such a strenuous game." Anyway, Corcoran told Stack to go into the clubhouse and have a nap, then come out to finish his round so he could pick up his war bond. But Lefty never saw the light of that day again, and finished out of the money. Incredible!

Almost all the top U. S. tournament pros went into military service, but there was no mass enlistment of pros in the cause of peace, as there had been in Britain during World War I. Ed Oliver was the first well-known U. S. pro to be drafted. Jimmy Thomson, the man who once hit a golf ball over 600 yards in two blows, entered the Coast Guard. The Navy got Demaret, Snead,

Lew Worsham, and Herman Keiser. Lloyd Mangrum, Jim Turnesa, Vic Ghezzi, Dutch Harrison, Jim Ferrier, Clayton Heafner, Horton Smith, and Ben Hogan were in the Army. Craig Wood was rejected because of a back injury sustained in an auto accident, Harold McSpaden because of sinusitis, and Byron Nelson because of a form of hemophilia.

As most name athletes generally do in the military, the majority of the pros stayed Stateside and were in Special Services, which is the military euphemism for playing golf with the generals. Jimmy Demaret was candid enough to say that he never got out of Sherman's, which was not a tank but a favorite bar in San Diego. Hogan and Smith were together in Army Air Force Officer Candidate School, in Miami Beach. They did drills on a golf course leveled for the purpose, but also found time to practice and play their golf. Lieutenant Hogan later served for a time as officer in charge of Army rehabilitation at the Miami-Biltmore hotel-golf-course complex. A bit of good luck in that assignment location. Hogan, Smith, Demaret, Snead, and others eventually got away to play in a few war-bond tournaments.

Five name pros went overseas: Keiser, Ghezzi, Heafner, Smith, and Mangrum. Mangrum was the only one to see real combat. He was wounded in the Battle of the Bulge and received the Purple Heart. No one will ever know how many potential Sneads and Hogans were lost in the war. The others undoubtedly missed some valuable time for their playing careers, but golf is a game that can be played at top efficiency for many more years than most games, and maturity often makes players even better performers. While Hogan was the tour's leading money winner from 1940 through '42, he did not win his first *official* U. S. Open until after the war, in 1948. Over all, none of the top pros lost peak years as did Ted Williams, for example, and they could not really complain of severe deprivations as a result of their military stints.

During the war years, though, professional baseball, and even football, which was not yet the new national game, could weather the Dura-

tion with less talented athletes or retired greats on the rosters, since they had a broader, deeper base of public interest. The St. Louis Browns had a one-armed outfielder, Pete Gray, and I recall seeing the fabled Bronko Nagurski play some football for the Chicago Bears and batter a goal post with one of his thunderous charges. Golf, however, was not that well fixed in the public mind, and even the periodic appearances of Hogan, Demaret, and Snead could not be enough to sustain interest in the game. The game and the tour needed, as they always seem to periodically, war or not, dramatic exposure to keep them from taking six steps backward. The drama would require an electric personality, or someone who could make eighteen straight holes in one. And, as it also always seems to happen in and for golf, there came Byron Nelson to keep golf and the tour on display. Indeed, Nelson would twice be named Athlete of the Year, in 1944 and 1945.

Nelson was not an electric personality. He was tall, expressionless, usually wore a white tennis visor, and always wore plain clothes. Neither did he make eighteen aces in a row. But he did accomplish something almost as unreal. In 1945 he won eleven straight professional tournaments. For the entire year he won nineteen times. These records are not ever likely to be equaled, much less broken. That is always a dangerous prediction, but I'll bet it holds. The years of World War II, in any case, belonged to Lord Byron Nelson of Texasshire.

Competitive records in sport made when a game is going through a format change, such as an extended baseball season or the depletion of the quantity of talent and the quality of competition by war, tend to get qualifying asterisks. The * is a favorite conceit among purists, who can be rather arbitrary. For example, when Roger Maris broke Babe Ruth's season home-run mark, his achievement was studded with a star—he played in more games. But has anyone seen Ruth's original record of sixty qualified by the fact that he was hitting the first "live" baseball? A ball, by the way, purposely goosed up so he could belt more round-trippers. So, records are often as much emotional as they are cold figures in a book, and Byron Nelson's skein of triumphs has invariably been qualified, if not with the ink-spot star, then with a diminishing pause in the minds of many.

The conditions placed on Nelson's run begin with the fact that he played against a grab bag of mediocre golfers. Then, too, he played those "dubs" on many short, fast-running roughless golf courses. Not only that; in a couple of instances Nelson played winter rules, which allowed him to move his ball onto a piece of good grass for fairway shots.

All is true, but the asterisks need exclamation points, nevertheless. His golf was just too good. Byron Nelson was one sweet and great golfer. Standing over six feet, Nelson took a swing that made maximum use of his height. It was straight up and down, his body not turning so much as moving laterally, an unusual action that has not often been seen. At impact he made a little dip of his knees, as most tall players do. Nelson once told me that a golfer cannot stand too close to the ball...before he hits it. I tried it for a season, getting up close to the ball at address, and hit my shots straighter than at any time in my checkered playing history.

The position forces an upright swing with the hands and arms remaining in close to the body, thus making them less apt to stray out of position. It is difficult to deviate from the swing plane. This position also produces a cramped feeling, however, one that brings a fear of, and sometimes a shockingly real, shank. Nelson himself occasionally slipped into this most discouraging of golf errors, known among those frightened by just the word as a lateral. Except for those rare lapses, Nelson was an incredibly straight hitter. He hit "frozen ropes," the ball seldom moving from right to left in flight or vice versa, unless he willed it so. He was not exceptionally long off the tee, but, like all great golfers, he had an extra fifteen yards on call when he needed it. He could also summon up the rest of his game when required. In an early round of a PGA championship match against Mike Turnesa, Turnesa had Byron down by four holes with five to play. Mike played those last five holes in one under par, and lost the match one down. Nelson

finished with four birdies and an eagle. He went on to win the championship.

Through Nelson's entire 1945 record run of victories, and even including the times he didn't win (he was second seven times, never worse than ninth), Byron averaged 68.33 strokes for a single round of golf. When he was thirty-three, Byron played 121 rounds in the year, usually the last thirty-six holes in one day, which gives him high grades for endurance alone. By contrast, in 1972 twenty-three-year-old Lee Trevino played 101 rounds of golf, eighteen a day, and had a scoring average of 70.89. In one stretch of nineteen rounds, Nelson was under 70 every time. Say what you will about courses, preferred lies, and all the rest, anyone who has ever made a serious attempt at the personal, inner-directed, inner-motivated game of golf will understand the magnitude of Nelson's performance.

The courses Nelson played were admittedly not up to the standards of difficulty of those played on the circuit now, but neither were they conditioned as today's velveteen carpets of grass are, and some allowance must be given Nelson for that. As for the winter rules, Charles Price, the keen-eyed American golf writer-historian, recalls that when Nelson did have the advantage of the preferred-lies rule he made the most minimal use of it, never moving the ball more than a turn or two from its original position to get it into playable turf, and then only with the club head, not with the hand. This in contrast to many who play field hockey with club and ball, not only improving the lie of the ball on the ground, but the angle of approach to the green as well. That's called Creative Rules Interpretation. Nelson didn't need it.

Byron's main competition in the first years of the war came from Harold "Jug" McSpaden, a prognathous Kansan who wore sunglasses, changed his clothes three times a day, and hit a powerful, controlled slide. He and Byron were longtime friends who traveled together and played as partners in four-ball tournaments. In a *Saturday Evening Post* article McSpaden by-lined in 1947, entitled "Nuts to Tournament Golf," the pro said that "the glittering cavalcade of tournaments made you famous but left you broke in spirit and poor in purse.... In 1944 I received $18,000 in war bonds. When I cashed them in I cleared $134.55."

McSpaden also had due cause to be broken in spirit. He once shot a couple of 64s in the closing rounds of a tournament and finished second... to Nelson. McSpaden's claim to fame, in fact, is being runner-up to Byron during the war years tournaments, which is always a demoralizing situation. At the beginning, Jug gave Nelson solid challenge. When Byron didn't win, McSpaden did. Through one set of ten tournaments, Nelson was sixty under par and Jug sixty-nine below. McSpaden's touch waned after that, and over all he was never a real threat in championship competition, although he did win some seventeen tournaments. He and Byron were called the Gold Dust Twins, but McSpaden saw more dust than gold.

Aside from McSpaden, when Nelson made his Electrifying Eleven and captured the sports pages, no less a player than Sam Snead was a regular on the tour. Snead had been discharged from the Navy with a slipped vertebra, but that did not hamper his golf. Sam won five times during the 1945 season, was twenty-one under par in winning the Pensacola Open, and beat Nelson in a play-off for the Gulfport Open. During a midsummer break in the tournament schedule, Snead and Nelson played a "World's Best Golfer" match—head to head at stroke play, then match play. Snead won the thirty-six holes of stroke play by one shot, then the next day Nelson took Snead in the thirty-six hole match play segment, winning 4 and 3. Snead broke his wrist playing baseball later that summer and did not compete in the last three of Nelson's streak of eleven, or in the remainder of the year's tournaments.

But by the end of that summer Ben Hogan was discharged, and with a public expression of vengeance at having missed a couple of years of regular tournament golf, and some prideful jealousy of Nelson's having taken over as the king of pro golf, Ben got his game geared up quickly. In the 1945 Portland Open, Hogan set a new PGA scoring record of 261 with rounds of 65, 69, 63, and 64. You would have to say that Lieutenant Hogan was doing a bit more than returning salutes while in the Army. Nelson had been playing an exceptional amount of golf that year, which can be wearying and damaging to a man's game, and for all his physical size, he was never a robust man. Yet, two weeks after Portland, Byron found the energy to break Hogan's mark with rounds of 62, 68, 63, and 66, totaling 259, with Hogan in the field. This score was made on a par-70 course, while Hogan had scored on a par-72 layout, but it was nevertheless brilliant golf. In short, golf tournaments usually become contests between two, three, or four of the best players in the field, particularly when such as Hogan and Snead are in the group. And Nelson won often with these two of the best players the game has had against him and playing quite well.

Finally, Nelson was not just a slightly-better-than-average golfer taking advantage of a situation. Byron was already an established champion before he went on his rampage. He won the Masters in 1937 and won it again in 1942, before most of the other golfers went into the military. In 1939 he won the U. S., Western, and North-South opens plus some lesser tournaments. He won the PGA crown in 1940 and again in 1945. Almost all his major victories came before anyone was off to the other war.

John Byron Nelson, Jr., began in golf as a ten-year-old caddie in Fort Worth, Texas. Ben Hogan was a fellow bag packer, and the two once tied for the caddie championship at Glen Garden Country Club. Many years later, when asked to compare himself with Hogan, who had actually turned pro six months before him, Byron said that he was simply more fortunate than Ben: He did not have to work as hard to perfect his golf. By the grace of the gods, or something, he had it sooner. Nelson turned pro in 1932, won $12.50 during his first ride on the tournament circuit, quit in something close to despair to seek another line of work, but came back to golf in 1934 to make some high finishes in winter-tour events. He took an assistant-pro post with George Jacobus, in New Jersey, and in 1936 won the Metropolitan Open, then a fairly big-time event.

Throughout most of his career, Nelson would be called by others and himself a club pro who played tournaments. Perhaps the chauvinistic influence of George Jacobus had a part in this, because Byron played an awful lot of tournaments. In any case, Nelson did become one of the most articulate "professors" of the golf swing, and has been credited with forming the considerable talent of Ken Venturi, a one-time U. S. Open champion, and Frank Stranahan, the outstanding amateur who won against the pros.

Nelson's ability to transmit golf instruction has never come through on televised golf, which he came to announce, but it was no fault of his own. When given fifteen seconds to "analyze" a golf swing, which cannot be adequately broken down in a month of Sundays, Nelson has been reduced to reminding everyone to "clear the left side in the swing." One gets the impression that if a golfer does not clear his left side, he can't play on television.

In the end, Byron Nelson made history, important history, for the tour, which had the good fortune of a remarkable talent coming, as it were, to the tour's rescue. As the war wound down and concluded, the nation was prepared to go on a cathartic spending and recreation binge. Much of that would be channeled into golf, and while Byron Nelson alone cannot be credited with the boom that came to golf after 1945, he did keep the channel clear, the lighthouse beacon burning, and made the passage to bigger and better things for the pros to come more navigable.

(1974)

Long Lags in the British Open
Sam Snead with Al Stump

The amazing Sam Snead has been around golf as a top player longer than anybody I know. Now over seventy, Snead considers any round in which he doesn't shoot his age or better as an off day.

Samuel Jackson Snead is a truly remarkable athlete and an amusing personality who, despite his constant exposure to golf and the sophisticated venues where it is played, in the U. S. and in more foreign countries than he can count, still retains many of his famous homespun characteristics acquired as a boy in the hills of Western Virginia.

Frankly, I think Sam works at retaining his hillbilly image. And I should know. Sam and I have been involved in several business ventures over the years, and I always have found him as astute in his dealings as he is in sizing up an opponent for a little nassau game, and as perceptive in reading a bottom line as he is in reading the line to the hole. If the legend is true that Sam keeps all of his wealth buried in tomato cans, the designated site must be an area as big as Fort Knox.

Some of Sam's homilies and his unwavering respect for the dollar are evident in this chapter from The Education of a Golfer, *which he wrote with Al Stump. The book is a remarkable autobiography as it includes the best of Sam's reflections on the first quarter-century of his career, combined with some easy-to-assimilate instruction from a player regarded as having the finest swing in golf.*

Some people forget that Sam was the first American to win the British Open after World War II, an accomplishment that caused only a ripple compared to the near tidal wave generated by a subsequent triumph by Ben Hogan in the same championship seven years later. Sam obviously did not regard his triumph as being of sufficient importance for him to return to defend it the following year. But here he reveals a number of other reasons why he did not go back.

BEFORE I WENT TO Scotland for the British Open of 1946, I'd never met anybody with a "sir" or "lord" in front of his name. So I still wonder how the London newspapers expected me to know it was a duke sitting across the aisle on the train to Edinburgh and the North.

Because of the duke, things got a little hot for me in British golfing society.

Down home in the woods, I wasn't short of ancestors and relatives myself. Mostly we were proud of Aunt Maggie Mathews, who gave birth to twenty children, including stillborns, and my great-uncle John. Big John Snead stood seven feet six, weighed 365, and died of fever in the Civil War after killing a few companies of Union soldiers with his bare hands.

We might have been plain people, but we were unusual. One of my great-grandmothers lived to be 106 years old and could still outshuck anybody in a cornfield when she was past 90. But no Snead ever ate tea and crumpets or got a look at royalty, except me — and in my case it was just a long-distance glimpse of King George IV when he'd galleried the 1937 British Open, which was my first trip out of the U. S. A.

In 1937 as a kid contender I'd finished tenth with an even 300 shots at Carnoustie, Scotland, in the Open. In 1946 I was primed to do better. But then along came the duke, and then a whole mess of more trouble.

Along with Lawson Little, I rode a gully-jumper train up from London. We passed places with names like Kirkintiloch and the Firth of Forth and then we slowed down past some acreage that was so raggedy and beat-up that I was surprised to see what looked like a fairway amongst the weeds. Down home we wouldn't plant cow beets on land like that.

"Say, that looks like an old, abandoned golf course," I said to a man across the aisle, tapping his knee. "What did they call it?"

You'd have thought I stabbed him. "My good sir!" he snorted. "*That* is the Royal and Ancient Club of St. Andrews, founded in 1754! And it is not now, nor ever will be, abandoned!"

"Holy smoke," I said, "I'm sorry." But how could I tell that I was looking at the most famous links in the world, the course that Bob Jones said

he respected most? Until you play it, St. Andrews looks like the sort of real estate you couldn't give away.

He was so insulted, this Duke Something-or-Other, that the British papers made a fuss about my remark and from then on I was dodging reporters who had the knife out for me. The only place over there that's holier than St. Andrews is Westminster Abbey. I began to think the whole trip was a mistake. In fact, I'd tried to avoid entering the British Open in the first place.

A few weeks earlier in New York, I'd met with L. B. Icely, the president of Wilson Sporting Goods Company. I used and endorsed Wilson equipment and drew top royalties for it, and Icely had a say-so about where and when I played. Icely listened to my arguments against going, then said, "No, Sam, we went you to enter. It's time you won a big title overseas. The prestige will be terrific."

What did I want with prestige? The British Open paid the winner $600 in American money. A man would have to be two hundred years old at that rate to retire from golf.

But Icely was firm about it.

"Have you seen me putt lately?" I argued. "It's awful. On the greens my mind just seems to leave my body."

"In this Open at St. Andrews the greens are double size. Big as a barnyard," said Icely. "They'll help you get your touch back."

I complained that a center-shafted putter, such as I used then, was illegal in English championships and that I hated to switch to a blade putter.

"Mr. Walter Hagen," came back Icely, "has done fairly well with a blade. He won the British Open at Sandwich, and also at Hoylake and Muirfield. I suggest you talk to Walter."

Hagen had the answer for my miserable putting when I saw him. "Just start hitting the ball above the equator," he advised.

"Goodbye, Walter," I said.

Hagen was no help. In advising me to hit the ball slightly above the center line, he was looking for end-over-end rotation, or overspin. But I'd long ago learned that too much overspin hurt me more than it helped. When the ball contacted the hole, whether on the right or left lip, it had a better chance of dropping without heavy top spin. I'd often discussed this with Ben Hogan. As Ben argued, "Given a lot of top spin, the ball retains too much energy at a point where you want it to die and often worms its way right out of the cup." Using Hagen's method, I'd seen many a ball go half in and flip out. And I'd topped far too many putts, also.

Whatever was wrecking my putting in 1946, it wasn't because I failed to try and catch the fat of the ball with a square action and apply a medium amount of overspin.

Once Icely had put down his foot, I went to England. And the jinx was on me all the way. Leaving New York, our Constellation sprang an engine fire on take-off and we stopped on the runway with smoke pouring into the cabin. All of us in there came popping out like ants. In London, which was still in bad shape from the war, you couldn't get a good meal or a hotel room. People were sleeping in the street. Carrying my golf bag, I knocked on the door of a private home in Kensington Road and asked to rent a room overnight.

"I'll be leaving in the morning. I'm going to St. Andrews."

"So I see," the owner said. "Having fun while the rest of us are on rations."

"Fun, hell," I said. "You should see me putt, mister." He slammed the door in my face.

At another house, a guy who looked like Boris Karloff with a monocle rented me a room for one hour for seven dollars. After one hour of sleep, I was kicked out and someone else got my bed. I slept in a depot and then caught the Edinburgh train. On the train, I began to get a light-headed, dizzy feeling. I thought it was from all the beans and porridge I'd eaten — there being no other food available. But an Englishwoman explained it. "You've been drinking a lot of our tea, haven't you?" she asked. "Well, it's quite strong these days, and undoubtedly you are suffering from a tea jag, which bothers most strangers. It's quite similar to being inebriated. Don't worry, in time it will pass."

Now I knew I'd putt myself out of the Open in the first eighteen holes.

Next came Duke Whoozis, and the insult I gave the Royal and Ancient course, without meaning to. After my remark that it was a pretty run-down old weed patch, the London *Times* gave me a good jab:

"Snead, a rural American type, undoubtedly would think the Leaning Tower of Pisa a structure about to totter and crash at his feet."

After that came caddie troubles. The way most golfers tell it, St. Andrews caddies are the world's best and can read the grass right down to the roots from Burn Hole, which is No. 1 on the Old Course, to Home Hole. Mine were a bunch of bums. I had four caddies in four days. One of them whistled between his teeth when I putted. After letting him go, I drew a fellow in sailor pants who couldn't judge distances or carry. On one hole he slipped me the 3-iron and said, "That's the ticket, mate." The shot left me 30 yards short of the green. The next hole he clubbed me with a 5-iron. This time I refused his advice, took a 7-iron, and even then landed over the green in a bunker. "Mate, you're sunk," I said, and gave him back to the caddie master. Then came "Scotty," guaranteed to be St. Andrews' best.

Scotty went to jail for drunkenness the night before the Open started, leaving me to figure the course for myself.

The gigantic double greens were a break for me. One of them measured almost two acres in size. I knew that nobody in the field, including the great Henry Cotton, Bobby Locke, Johnny Bulla, Dai Rees, and Lawson Little, would get close enough very often to hole out with one putt, which would help equalize my poor work around the pin. I thought that if I could beat them from tee to green, I had a chance to finish in the money. As it turned out, I never was longer off the tee. On No. 10, 312 yards, I drove the green three times in four rounds; on No. 12, 314 yards, I drove the green two out of four.

But it was the heavy-blade putter I was using that put me in a three-way tie for first place with a total of 215 strokes when the third round ended. I couldn't believe what was happening.

Later on I saw that a habit of mine on long putts had paid off. From 25 feet or more distance, I've never believed in going for the cup. On long-approach putts, any time you aim to make them you'll either overcharge by 10 or 15 feet or fall far short and wind up 3-putting, the reason being that from 25 to 75 feet no one can make a 4 1/4-inch cup his target with accuracy. From far out, I pick a line and adjust speed *to* the general area of the hole. Closer up, I go directly *at* it. I want my lag putts to die within easy second-shot distance of the cup.

There's another percentage involved here. A putt traveling fast enough to overrun by 2 or 3 feet must hit the cup almost dead center to go in, whereas a putt stroked up to the cup and no farther may fall in even if it's an inch or more off line from center.

A cup has a front and rear door and two side doors—four entrances. By not charging too hard, you take advantage of all of them.

Walter Travis, who was such an uncanny putt master that the British barred his center-shafted Schenectady mallet from their country for forty-odd years, didn't agree with that theory. He took dead aim every time. Billy Casper, one of the best putters today, does agree. Doc Cary Middlecoff thinks he can hole every long putt and goes for broke. Lloyd Mangrum, one of the half dozen best on the greens I've seen, tried to drop 90-footers but advised average golfers to aim for a 2-foot circle around the pin. There's little argument on this, but after the British Open I never questioned this part of the game again.

In the final round, a St. Andrews Bay gale made every putt a guess. It was so bad that balls jiggled and oscillated when you addressed them. Flory Von Donck, the Belgian, had a downhill 20-footer with the windstorm behind him. Von Donck turned his back to the cup, putted uphill away from the target, and then, as the ball rolled back down the hill, a sudden gust swooped it 15 feet past the hole. Others who tried to drop approach putts in that wind wound up chewing on their mufflers when their long rollers were blown every which way.

All I wanted was to be reasonably close and to lag for the safest possible position on my second putt. With the green sloping toward me (in any kind of weather) I'd rather be 3 feet short than over. It's 2-1 easier to make a 36-incher from an uphill lie than from a downhill or side-hill lie. Putting uphill, you take a firm, natural grip. Downhill, because of the extra momentum you'll get, you loosen the grip, and without realizing it you can get sloppy. On the No. 10 hole, from 20 feet away, I eased up to within 18 inches and dropped it for a birdie. On No. 12, from 30 feet, I did the same thing. With the 40-mph wind behind me, I stroked extra easy on those slick, dried-out greens. Against a cross-wind, I allowed for a big break, up to 6 feet on long putts.

On No. 14, Hell's Bunker, a Scotsman stuck his whiskers in my face and said, "You can shoot sixes from here on in, laddie, and win."

I checked this with Richards Vidmer, the New York *Times* reporter, who carried a walkie-talkie radio.

"No, six a hole isn't safe," said Vidmer. "But you can take it with fives. Cotton, Rees, and Von Nida have blown themselves out of it. But Bulla and Locke are still close."

With that news, I gambled a bit on an 8-footer at Hell's Bunker and got it for another birdie. At the par-4 sixteenth, some genius had placed the pin on a little shelf at the rear green guarded by a steep incline. My 30-footer climbed the grade, then rolled part way back to me. Next time I putted stiff to the flag, but the result was 3 putts, 5 strokes, and a bogey.

On the Road Hole, No. 17, the gale took my pretty 9-iron pitch, right on the flag, and swooped it 25 feet away. Again just lagging up, I was paid off for being cautious. The wind provided an extra few turns and in she fell—my longest putt of the tournament.

"He could use his bloomin' puttah on every shot and win!" somebody in the crowd shouted. That was music to my ears. Back home they'd been saying that I couldn't roll a marble into a manhole with both hands.

The Road Hole won the Open. All I had to do was play out No. 18 in 7 shots—and I took 4—to finish ahead of Locke and Bulla. I'd been half drunk on tea, and had gone without sleep and a good caddie, but my 290 score beat all four of Walter Hagen's best totals in this tournament, two of the three winning scores of Bob Jones, and the best by Tommy Armour, Jock Hutchison, and Denny Shute when they took home the cup.

The purse of $600 was such a joke that I decided then and there not to defend the title. My traveling expenses alone were over $1,000, and nobody but me picked up that tab. On top of that, all my hitting muscles "froze" in the icy wind at St. Andrews. For days I ached in every joint.

Then there was my caddie friend, "Scotty," who got himself sprung from jail and begged me to give him the winning ball. "Maun," he prom-ised tearfully, "I'll treasure it all my days."

That ball was worth some cash, and Scotty proved it. An hour later he sold it for fifty quid. So he made more off the Open than I did.

For years afterward, British and American writers panned me for passing up the British Open, but like I've always said—as far as I'm concerned, any time you leave the U. S. A., you're just camping out.

(1962)

Everything but a Victory
Merrill Whittlesey

The year 1912 was memorable for being the year that three of the true Legends of Golf were born: Byron Nelson in February, Sam Snead in May and Ben Hogan in August. All ex-caddies, they were pros from the time they first slung a bag over their shoulders. While Nelson and Hogan have long since hung up their competitive spikes and retired to other more sedentary pursuits, Sam, like Ol' Man River, just keeps rolling along.

He still tees it up with the "young 'uns" on the occasions when he is inclined toward faster competition than that offered by the PGA senior circuit, where he can more than hold his own. In 1979 he astounded the golfing world when he shot his age, 67, and two days later followed with a 66 in the Quad Cities Open. He finished tied for 36th against a field of players of whom most were young enough to be his grandchildren.

Ageless Sam has more tournament victories to his credit than any golfer who ever lived. But his staggering list of triumphs, including seven majors, does not include the United States Open, of which almost everyone is well aware.

In the year Sam became eligible for Social Security, Merrill Whittlesey did this comprehensive piece on the "Sweet Swinger." It gives a breadth and scope to his greatness, in addition to detailing his painful near misses in the Open. Merrill was witness to most of them as the golf writer for the Washington Star.

Whittlesey, a fine writer and a former champion of the Golf Writers' Association of America, was not one to follow Snead's perpetual golf quest. Merrill had the foresight to retire at age 65, two years before the outstanding newspaper with which he was affiliated for so many years folded.

AT ONE OF HIS increasingly infrequent tournament appearances shortly after reaching the age of 65 this spring, Sam Snead was on the practice tee pounding shot after shot with that heavensent swing, so fluid, so rhythmic—so perfect it approaches indescription.

As he loosened those marvelously supple muscles, the young men who dominate professional golf today occasionally paused to watch, all of them with some affection, some with awe, knowing that they probably will never again see so poetic a motion as Sam Snead swinging a golf club.

"Where's your wheel chair, Sam?" one of them called, grinning as he looked over his shoulder. Snead moved through impact on that flowing movement, and the ball seemed to explode as the club face met it squarely and sent it soaring into the dull gray haze.

"Come on, Gramps," another called. "Let's see you crank one up."

"No carts today, Sam. You'll never make it around."

It was all in fun, and every one of them stopped at one time or another to watch as Snead went through his bag, beginning with his wedge and ending with his driver. Every one of the younger men hit his practice shots farther than Snead, but they grunted and lashed and jumped at it; none approached Sam's graceful smoothness.

Finished, Sam flipped his driver to his caddie, paused to watch a swing or two, called some jeering comments of his own, gave a tug at his ailing back and walked off toward the clubhouse in that characteristic long, loose stride.

A hundred or so spectators had lined up behind the gallery ropes back of the practice tee, and when Snead left, so did they; they can see those others, and more like them, hit golf balls from coast to coast, from the winter tour through the major tournaments until year's end, but they may never again see a swing like Snead's, born as it was of a tree limb in the hills of Bath County in western Virginia.

The swing, mind you, is not quite what it was. Tendonitis has crept into Snead's left wrist, restricting the cock of the wrist and affecting his accuracy and his distance. He can feel it, and he has seen it in movies. He knows the swing has slipped a cog . . . but nothing goes on forever.

Snead's gifts are not limited to his ability to play golf shots; he owns a remarkable memory. In the 40 years since he won his first tournament on the professional tour—the Oakland (Calif.) Open of 1937—he has stored memories of the competitions, some of them shot-by-shot, hole-by-hole: the club he used, the yardage of the holes, the size of a clump of turf that deflected a chip shot, the wind, the rain, and the characteristics of the men he played against.

At the PGA Championship last year, Snead lounged in the locker room while a driving contest was going on outside. Someone asked how many driving contests he had won during his career. Jaws dropped when he answered.

"I used to win them all. I won my first one in 1937 at the Pittsburgh Field Club when I hit three drives 279 yards, 283 yards and 291 yards." Who else can recall the length of a shot hit 40 years ago?

Those kind of memories brought about another subject when Sam sprawled in another locker room this spring. Anyone who has ever taken even passing interest in this game knows that Snead has never won the United States Open. He's won everything else, of course—the British Open, the PGA Championship three times, the Masters Tournament three times, 84 regular Tour tournaments, 143 if you count some relatively minor competitions. But not the Open.

Snead, with a touch of affection, calls it "Big Daddy," and when he begins to talk of it you can see his mind replaying his failures, his near-misses, the bad bounces, the decisions that went against him, the luck of the draw sheet. Strangely enough he discusses the Open without apparent bitterness. He slumps in his chair, tilts his Panama hat over one eye, and with that disarming grin says, "The cow is out of the barn."

For those many disappointments Snead wears an asterisk beside his name in the minds of many of golf's archivists. It has cost him a notch in their accounting of the game's great players, dropped him a step below Ben Hogan,

Bob Jones, Byron Nelson, Gene Sarazen, Walter Hagen, and, of course, below Arnold Palmer and Jack Nicklaus. From the time he was runner-up in 1937, his first Open, until last year when he failed to qualify, Snead has been a dominant personality in the Open. Even as late as 1974, when he was 62, Snead, in the minds of many, had a chance to win at Winged Foot Golf Club in Mamaroneck, N. Y. We'll never know; he withdrew before the Championship began because of some injured ribs.

Each year for almost 30 years Snead's supporters kept hoping that this would be the year that Sam finally broke through. Over that span Snead was runner-up four times (only Arnold Palmer and Bob Jones have been second so often), and once he led after 70 holes but did not finish even second. At the Spring Mill Course of the Philadelphia Country Club in 1939, Snead lost four strokes to par on the last two holes and finished fifth.

Snead has played in 30 Opens and completed 72 holes in 27 of them, a figure that stands as an Open record. He played through all but one of them from the time he first entered in 1937 through 1965. He missed the cut in 1958 when Tommy Bolt won at the Southern Hills Country Club in Tulsa, Okla. The Open returns to Southern Hills this month, and Snead, Bolt and Julius Boros have been granted special exemptions from qualifying by the USGA Executive Committee.

Snead last played 72 holes in an Open in 1973 at Oakmont where he shot 295 and finished in a tie for 29th place. He qualified in 1974 but had to withdraw with his rib injury, missed the 36-hole cut in 1975 at Medinah, and last year he failed to qualify.

Through his career he has finished second four times, third once, fifth twice, and had five other finishes among the leading 10. As late as 1968, when he was 56, he finished ninth at the Oak Hill Country Club in Rochester, N. Y., where Lee Trevino won the first of his two Open Championships. In 115 Open rounds Snead averaged 73.37 strokes; for every 72 holes he averaged 293 strokes.

But he never won.

"I should have won seven," Sam muses, "and I could have won 12." Yet he maintains that his history of failure in the Open never once affected his concentration. "I guess I might have thought about it some when I was in bed," he'll admit, "but never on the golf course."

So many things have happened to Snead in the Open that he sometimes feels that he just wasn't supposed to win it.

"Maybe somebody in heaven had something to do with it," Sam says with a faraway look, "but, at the same time, I was the only one who had hold of that club, nobody tried to jerk it out of my hands. They used to say I couldn't win the big one, but I won the Masters and the PGA three times, and the British Open, and they're big."

As many another, Sam believes that had he won one of his early Opens, he might have won several.

Snead came out of the Virginia hills to the pro tour in 1936, raw and more than a little naive. It did not take long, however, for him to establish himself as something special. Early in 1937 he won the Oakland (Calif.) Open with four remarkable rounds, 69–65–67–69 — 270, and followed right away by winning the Rancho Santa Fe Open, which grew up to be the Bing Crosby Pro-Am some years later. By mid-June Jack Doyle, a New Yorker who ran a "winter book," listed Snead as the 8–1 favorite in this, the first Open Sam had entered. Snead made Doyle look good; he shot 69 in the first round to share the lead with Denny Shute, and followed with 73 in the second round for 140, two strokes behind Ralph Guldahl and Ed Dudley. In those years the final 36 holes were played on Saturday, 18 holes in the morning, 18 in the afternoon, and the pairings followed no particular pattern. Snead was among the early starters on Saturday, shot 70 in the morning round and 71 in the afternoon. He had a score of 283 for the 72 holes. In 1920 Chick Evans shot 286 at Minikahda Country Club near Minneapolis; 12 years later Gene Sarazen matched it at Fresh Meadow Country Club in New York. That record stood for 15 years until Tony Manero broke it in 1936 with 282 at the Baltusrol Golf Club in Springfield, N. J. Now Sam Snead, in his first Open, shot the second lowest score the Open had ever seen.

When he walked off the 18th green that afternoon it seemed certain that he would be the Champion. At about that time, though, Ralph Guldahl was on the third hole. He had begun that final round tied with Snead at 212 for 54 holes, one stroke behind Ed Dudley. He played the first seven holes in even 4s and then chipped in from off the eighth green for an eagle 3. He played a 2-iron onto the tough par 3 ninth hole and ran in a 25-footer for a birdie 2. He had played the first nine in 33 strokes, three under par, and now all he need do was play the second nine in one over par and he could beat Snead. He shot 36 coming in, giving him 69 for the round and 281 for the 72 holes, setting a new record.

No one thought much of Snead's luck that day; he was just 25 and with a swing like that he'd be certain to win the Open eventually.

Two years later, at Spring Mill, his day seemed to have arrived. It hadn't; instead this turned out to be the most tragic of all Snead's Opens. He opened with 68 and took a one-stroke lead, and then held on with 139 for 36 holes after shooting 71 in the second round. Johnny Bulla, a big, handsome guy with whom Snead traveled and shared both expenses and winnings for a time, shot 68 in the morning round that last day, and with 18 holes to play he led by one stroke with 211. Snead, Craig Wood, Denny Shute and Clayton Heafner were tied for second at 212. Bulla's game soured in the last round; he shot 76 and finished sixth with 287. Byron Nelson was playing ahead of Snead, but he began that final round four strokes behind at 216. Suddenly Nelson's game became remarkably steady and he played those last 18 holes in 68. He was in with 284, the best 72-hole score thus far.

When Snead reached the 17th he needed pars on the two finishing holes for 282, one stroke over the Open record set by Guldahl two years earlier. The 17th at Spring Mill is a good par 4 hole. Snead hit a tremendous drive, but his second shot went over the green into some clover. From there he chipped about five feet short and then missed the par putt by an inch.

Communication on the golf course then was not what it is today, and Snead didn't know what Wood and Shute were doing behind him, although he could hear an occasional cheer and draw some inferences. The bogey on the 17th made him a little nervous, and that, along with his lack of information on those behind him, caused him to believe he needed a birdie on the 18th.

This was the beginning of perhaps the most memorable hole in Open history. Snead had built his early reputation on his driving — he was probably the longest straight driver in the game at that time — and the fans flocked to him partly because of his power. Strangely, he didn't think his driving was the strongest part of his game; he considered himself foremost a good wedge player, then a putter, then a long iron player, and a bunker player. Driving, he said, probably was what he did fifth best. On the 18th tee at Spring Mill Snead hit a serviceable drive, all right, but he hooked it a little and it rolled into the rough.

He did not have a particularly good lie, and he was about 275 yards from the green, but he had heard those cheers behind him and he wanted the birdie. He tried to play his second shot with a brassie. The club selection was a disaster. The ball squirted back across the fairway into a bunker a bit short of the green by perhaps a hundred yards. The bunker had a steep face about five feet high. Snead could clear the face of the bunker with a sand wedge, but he might not reach the green with that club. Instead he tried to play an 8-iron. He didn't clear the bunker face; the ball hit and wedged between cracks on some freshly laid sod. Three shots used up now and still in deep trouble. From there Snead chopped at the ball through sand and sod, tore it loose and sent it careening into another bunker to the left of the green.

His next shot was on the green, but 40 feet from the hole. He putted three feet past and then left that putt short. An 8. All he needed was a par 5 to win, and instead he made 8. He was stunned, the gallery was stunned, and an awful hush settled over the crowd as Snead, numbed now, headed for the locker room. Women were in tears, and men patted him softly on the back; other players avoided looking at him to save him embarrassment. Instead of 70, which par figures on the last two holes would have given him, Sam shot 74; instead of first, he finished fifth. Shute and Wood later matched Nelson's 284, and Bud

Ward, an amateur from the Pacific Northwest, beat Snead's score by one stroke with 285. Nelson won the playoff.

This might well have been the most crushing experience anyone ever suffered through in an Open.

"If I had known all I had to do wăs make 5 and beat Nelson, I could have reached the green with three 8-irons," Snead reflected not long ago. "I was playing with Ed Dudley; he knew it but didn't tell me. Gary Nixon, my assistant at the Greenbrier, was following me, and even he didn't tell me."

Fred Corcoran, whose memoirs of the Open appear elsewhere in this issue, said not long ago that if he had been on the 18th tee, Sam might have won.

"He was worried about the guys behind him," Corcoran remembers. "If you want to win the Open you beat the score that's on the board, and that was Nelson. Snead could have beaten him with a par 5. If he had won that one, or the one where Guldahl made that late charge, it would have made a big difference in his career."

Sam was to have more chances in the Open. The war intervened in the early 1940s, and the Open was cancelled from 1942 through 1945. It was revived in 1946. Snead played indifferently after his opening 69 and tied for 19th place. The next year, though, he began with 72 at the St. Louis Country Club, and then strung together three rounds of 70. When Snead finished 17 holes of the final round, Lew Worsham was already in with 282, playing a loose 38 on the second nine after going out in 33. Snead had begun his final round raggedly with bogeys on the first two holes, but he made up those two strokes and was even par for the first nine. Sam began the home nine with a series of pars and then picked up a birdie on the 15th. If he could par in he would match Worsham. But no, he dropped a stroke on the 17th, the same hole Worsham had bogeyed earlier.

Now Sam needed a birdie 3 to tie, and this time he knew it. He split the fairway with his tee shot and played a lovely iron to the right of the hole, about 20 feet away. From there Snead rolled in his putt to set up a playoff the next day.

Playoffs are often anti-climactic; this one

was anything but. Both men played superb golf, and the finish is still among the best remembered incidents in the game's lore. Snead began with a birdie on the first and went two strokes ahead with another birdie on the fifth. Right away, though, Snead lost both strokes when he bogeyed the sixth as Worsham birdied. Two holes later Snead birdied and Worsham bogeyed to put Sam two ahead again. Then Worsham birdied the ninth, and as they made the turn for home, Snead held a one-stroke advantage. After both men played the 10th and 11th in par figures, Worsham birdied the 12th and the playoff was even once more.

Over the next three holes Snead picked up two strokes, first with a birdie on the 13th and later when Worsham dropped a stroke on the 15th. Now, with three holes to play, Snead seemed to be uncatchable. Surely he would not lose two strokes in three holes.

The 16th at the St. Louis Country Club is a par 3 of 188 yards. Worsham's tee shot rolled to the back of the green and he holed the putt for a birdie 2. Unless Snead could match it, one stroke of his lead would be gone. Sam played a good putt; the ball broke toward the hole, caught the lip but stayed out.

Both men played sloppy tee shots on the 17th. Worsham hit a big ducking hook that carried past the gallery and into the 18th fairway that runs parallel. Snead, playing a brassie because he couldn't control his driver, tried to bend the shot around the corner of a slight dogleg right and left the ball in the right rough. From where the two balls lay, Worsham actually had the better angle on the green, and he was able to hold the green with his approach. Snead's 8-iron hit the front edge, but it had nothing on it and rolled off the back, about six or seven feet into the rough. From there Sam chipped six feet from the hole and missed the putt. Worsham got down in two and Snead's apparently safe two-stroke lead had vanished. Tied once again, now with only the 18th to play.

Both men played reasonably good tee shots. Snead, outdriven all the way, played first and hit a gorgeous approach. His ball cleared a bunker that guarded the front of the green and came down about 20 feet from the hole. Worsham barely kept his second shot out of the rough that crowded around the green. He had to chip. Lew walked up quickly, played a very firm shot that rolled up to the hole, hit the edge and stopped less than three feet away. Snead, putting downhill, misread the speed of the green and left his ball short of the hole.

Now the drama unfolded. Snead walked up to his ball to play out the hole. Just then Worsham called for a measurement. As he explained later he thought he might be away and he wanted to putt first so that if he made the putt he would put added pressure on Snead. The putts were measured and Snead was away. His ball lay 30-1/2 inches from the hole, Worsham's 29-1/2. Snead would continue to putt.

He had by far the more difficult shot. To begin with it was downhill and Worsham's putt was uphill. Additionally, Sam had to play a left-to-right break. He tapped his ball a slight bit too lightly and the ball broke away, missing by about two inches. Worsham then rolled in his putt. Once again Snead was frustrated.

In the 30 years since that incident Snead and Worsham have become close friends, fishing together in Florida and hunting in the hills of western Pennsylvania, near Worsham's summer base, the Oakmont Country Club, near Pittsburgh.

"Lew was all charged up," Sam recalls today. "He was two strokes down with three holes to play and had come from behind to tie. It probably wasn't right to stop me after I had stepped over the ball, but it was the USGA official who was wrong for even making the measurement. As long as I didn't step in his line, I had the right to finish putting out."

His two other closest near-misses were not nearly as tragic as those of 1939 and 1947. Two years after his playoff loss to Worsham, Sam had another chance at Medinah Country Club, near Chicago, but he blames carelessness or bad judgment for that loss. Cary Middlecoff finished well ahead of Snead with 286, two above par. To match him Snead had to play the last nine in 33 strokes. With four holes to go, all Sam needed was four pars to tie. He made his figures on both the 15th and 16th, and now he faced the treacherous 17th, a massive par 3 over 200 yards across a wide body of water with a deep bunker in front of the green. It was all carry—no room for error. Snead hit a good looking tee shot dead at the flagstick but the wind held the ball up a little, and when it hit the green it drew back downhill about three feet off the putting surface.

Snead could either putt the ball or chip. He chose to putt, but he didn't notice that the ball was sitting in a little depression. He planned to hit down a little on the ball and let it skim across the apron, which should brake it somewhat. Instead, the ball popped up quickly, jumped across the fringe and rolled about eight feet past the hole. He missed his putt for a par, and now he needed a birdie on the 18th. His approach rolled over the green and his chip stopped about three feet short. He finished with 34 on the second nine and 287. Once again he failed.

The agony went on, but that was really Sam's last close approach to winning, although he was second once again in 1953, Hogan's greatest year. Hogan began that Championship by scoring 67 in the first round and 72 in the second. Snead shot 72-69 and he was then two strokes behind Hogan after 36 holes.

This was still the era of the double round the last day, and the pairings were still made without regard to how each man stood in relation to the rest of the field. Hogan was off much earlier than Snead; he played perhaps eight or nine holes ahead of Sam, but after each had completed nine holes of that morning round, Sam had a one-stroke edge with his 33, four under par. Hogan had played the first nine in 38. By the time Snead had put his 33 on the board, however, Hogan was almost finished 18 holes. Hogan played the second nine in 35, Snead played it in 37, and so with 18 holes to play Snead still trailed by one.

Before he teed off in that last round, though, Sam could see that Hogan was struggling. Hogan had bogied both the seventh and eighth and was one stroke over par. Snead could do nothing about it. He bogied both the third and seventh and had to birdie the ninth, an uphill par 5, to match Hogan on the out nine. After that it was no contest; Hogan played the last nine holes in 33, two under par, and Snead shot 38, three over par. Hogan won by six strokes.

Sam can look back on some other Opens where he believes he might have won, or at least threatened.

"At Cherry Hills in 1938 I remember I was a spastic with a putter. I think I could have won at Colonial Country Club (Fort Worth, Tex.) in 1941 if my back would have held out. I tied with Toney Penna for the first round lead at Canterbury (Cleveland) in 1946 and didn't win, and I had a shot at it at Baltusrol in 1954 when I played with Bobby Locke in the last two rounds."

It is often forgotten that when Jack Fleck and Hogan tied at the Olympic Club in San Francisco in 1955, Snead and Tommy Bolt tied for third place. They were, however, five strokes behind, Snead's chances ruined by a 79 in the first round.

His last great disappointment was at Winged Foot in 1974 when he had to withdraw in pain because he had cracked some ribs a few weeks earlier and didn't know it.

"My scores for three practice rounds were seven strokes lower than Hale Irwin's scores for three rounds," he said. Irwin won the Open that year with 287, seven over par. "I felt like I really had a chance until I hit a 3-wood out of the rough on the 11th hole of the last practice round. I felt this pain in my chest and I thought I had a heart attack. I managed to get back to the clubhouse, but when I climbed the steps I couldn't breathe. They took me to a hospital and gave me an electro-cardiogram test. A couple of attendants started to lift me onto a table, and I told them that I walked in that door by myself and I reckoned I could get up on that table without any help. The EKG was all right, but then they took X-rays and discovered two broken ribs. The doctor told me he might be able to tape me up so that I could swing, but as bad as I was hurting I didn't want any part of that."

Sam qualified for the Open at Medinah in 1975 and missed the 36-hole cut with rounds of 78 and 76, and then failed to qualify in 1976. "I played with Don January in the qualifying round, outplayed him over the 36 holes from tee to green and he was low qualifier and I didn't make it."

Snead claims he always thought positively about the Open, but in the next sentence he'll begin to talk of another tragedy of American golf.

"It's like Harry Cooper used to be about the PGA when it was match play. Harry was one of the greatest players in the world in those days, but in the PGA he would always say, 'One of those club pros is going to beat me in one of those 18-hole matches.' We'd try to talk him out of it, but Harry was convinced it would happen. Somebody always did."

In the five decades Snead has played in the Open, he has made some observations. For one thing, the courses are more difficult today.

"The Open was easier to win when I started," he believes. "Now they're setting up the courses so it's no longer any fun to play."

The physical strain of playing golf probably affected Snead less than almost any other player. He has never smoked, and he drinks only an occasional beer. And he exercises. Still he is beginning to experience some wear on the parts. He has had back problems over the years, and, in fact, withdrew after one round of the Masters Tournament in April because it bothered him so (he shot 84). "A doctor X-rayed my back and told me it looked like a clothesline with a load of wash on it," he says with a sly grin. He was involved in a minor accident in Florida last winter, and he has fought pinched nerves in his neck and others that deaden his left arm occasionally and cause his fingers to tingle.

When Sam first joined the tour he was such a long driver that he was often grouped with Jimmy Thomson, the longest hitter of his era, to give the spectators a thrill. Now Sam believes he is at least 30 yards shorter from the tee. "I used to hit a 7-iron 160 yards, and now I need a 5-iron."

What has kept Sam going so long? Jack Nicklaus has a theory:

"Where Sam excels is in being able to enjoy the game. He could play virtually every day without going stale, which is not true of most players."

Bob Toski played three rounds with Snead in the PGA Senior Championship during the winter.

"It was one of the greatest thrills of my life," Toski recalls. "One of the greatest players who ever lived; he loves to play every day, and he's enjoyed it longer than anybody."

This, of course, only increases the irony of

Snead's Open failures. He really liked to play in them.

He remembers particularly the 1948 Open at Riviera Country Club in Los Angeles when Ben Hogan won the first of his four Open Championships with a record score of 276.

"I started with an eagle," Sam remembers, "and I said to myself on the second tee, 'They'll never catch me.'" But they did, and quickly, on the second hole where, characteristically, he threw away some strokes. When he finished fifth, seven strokes behind Hogan, his consolation was a sympathetic word from Grantland Rice.

"If crying could help you, Sam," Rice said quietly, "I could flow a river." Remembrance of that remark still brings a sadness to Snead even 30 years after Rice consoled him. But, of course, tears couldn't help. Nothing could.

And now, 40 years after his first bittersweet disappointment, Snead will play in the Open for the last time. He won't win; he may not make the 36-hole cut, and it is also possible that he will withdraw before the Championship begins because of that tender back.

No matter what happens at Southern Hills, though, Snead's place in golf history is secure. He is without question the greatest golfer who never won the Open.

(June 1977)

Greatest Round Ever
Marshall Smith

It has been said that golf course architecture came of age in 1951 at the Oakland Hills Country Club when Ben Hogan won his third of four United States Open Championships. I have no dispute with this assessment, as I was responsible for the changes made to that golf course.

Previously, most of the major championships had been conducted on courses which had remained unchanged since coming into being save for extending a few teeing areas, letting the rough grow and shaving the greens. This was not to be the case at Oakland Hills where officials sought — and received — a transformation the likes of which would serve as a bellwether for the other courses that subsequently would host America's premier championship.

What had prompted their action was the two previous Opens played on the Birmingham, Michigan, course: in 1924, Cyril Walker won with a score of 297 — nine over par; in 1937, Ralph Guldahl won with a record 281 — seven under par. The advancements made in equipment — the steel shaft, a larger, easier-to-control ball and the wedge — coupled with improved playing techniques had dictated the need for a modernization of the Oakland Hills course, which had remained unchanged since its 1918 inception.

The remodelling of Oakland Hills was wholesale, as Marshall Smith of Life graphically describes in detailing how the Open eventually was won in 1951.

Despite the hue and cry by players about the changes made to the course, Oakland Hills produced a champion worthy of the title. It also served to give me a reputation as a "golf course doctor," which resulted in my performing similar operations on such other venerable courses as Baltusrol, Oak Hill, Congressional, Olympic, Southern Hills and Firestone.

To parody an old saying, "If you build a better sand trap, the world will beat a path to your door."

THE BRIGHTEST 18 holes in Ben Hogan's shiny career — probably the greatest golf round ever played — were shot on a calm and cloudless day at Birmingham, Mich. In the biggest tournament, the U. S. Open, before a gallery of 17,500, largest in golfing history, Hogan came from behind to win over 161 of the world's best golfers. But, more than that, his perfect round represented a triumph over a golf course — a green, bunker-pitted monster of a golf course that no living human was supposed to conquer.

The villain in architect's clothing who made the Oakland Hills course that way was Robert Trent Jones, a specialist hired especially for the purpose. Jones slapped bunkers on fairways at points where big hitters usually slapped their drives. He left targets to shoot at that narrowed to the length of a couple of billiard tables. Trying to hit them from 250 yards away would have been difficult with a .22 rifle, let alone golf balls. All told, 66 new bunkers were added. The greens, innocent enough at first glance, were more likely than not to have a "wrong side" that could cost a stroke if approached from any but the correct angle. As a finishing touch Architect Jones reduced par (from 72 to 70) and said smugly to himself, "Let's see them tear that apart."

Just the thought of it seemed preposterous to the pros. Oakland Hills discouraged the long, straight hitter, a thing golfers spend all their lives trying to become. They were forced to improvise and adjust their game to the course, play short off the tees and press extra hard on the second shot. The planning of every stroke suddenly became more important than its actual execution. Calculations on direction, distance, windage and nature of the target resembled those in the fire-control headquarters of a warship. The ability to swat a golf ball with the precision of a testing machine, a common talent among tournament golfers today, was not sufficient. The big thing at Birmingham was a commodity that seemed to have gone out of style with the wooden-shafted club: judgment.

In Ben Hogan's adding machine mind, judgment is not a product of guesswork or intuition. Five days of pre-tournament practice had photo-graphed the Oakland Hills course on the film of Hogan's memory. Yet, in the first day of competition, he fired a dismal 76. The six extra strokes were six errors in judgment. That night in their room at Detroit's Sheraton Hotel, Hogan said to his wife Valerie, "That was the most stupid round of golf I have ever played." It began on the very first fairway where he stood, hands planted on hips, debating whether to use a two or three iron to the green. The adding machine rippled through the approximately 48 factors involved in the shot — the choice of club, length of back-swing, allowance for hook or slice, whether to hit the ball low or high. There was only one right answer, and Hogan didn't get it.

He selected a two iron, waggled once and hit the ball 10 yards over the green. "Just bad think-ing," he explained later. "I used the wrong club." Other errors in judgment that first day were the result of firing for the pin instead of playing safe. "Like a stupid ass I'd be on the left side of the green instead of the right." Once he three-putted after leaving himself a long, downhill chance. Worst of all he was making the same mistake twice, unheard of for a man who had no patience with stupidity in either himself or others.

In the next two rounds he began correcting his errors, and when he came up to the final 18 holes he was only two strokes down to South Africa's Bobby Locke and Jimmy Demaret, who were tied for the lead. At lunch Ben Hogan was unaware of who sat beside him in the contest-ants' dining room and the food had no taste as he chewed and swallowed mechanically. He was struggling to get himself in the proper frame of mind to win the Open: restrained but not care-less. It was a manufactured mood that he had developed with much practice along with his swing. After lunch Hogan stepped out to the tee knowing by now exactly what he could do with Oakland Hills and knowing, moreover, that he would do it.

Off the tee he swung with all the business-like authority of a machine stamping out bottle caps. Hogan finally had all the answers to all the problems of the Oakland Hills course. To avoid trouble on tee shots he used a brassie instead of his driver, and once carried caution to such an extreme that he used a No. 3 wood off the tee. He went the first nine holes in even par. On the 10th Hogan went one under par after getting off what was undoubtedly the finest shot in all the tournament. His approach shot soared 200 yards straight for the pin, leaving him only a five-foot putt. That shot would have warmed anybody's heart. But not Hogan's. He refused the luxury of such emotions: "Man, I've got to restrain myself. I'm not in yet and I've got to restrain myself."

An Open champion, Hogan liked to say, is like a stew. Restraint was an ingredient that somewhere in 26 years of golf he had thrown into the pot. "You keep adding things, stirring and letting it simmer until it's ready to come off the fire." On the short 13th, with his third Open championship in four years within his grasp, Hogan bagged another birdie.

As he stepped up to the 18th tee, two under par, an almost solid wall of people circled the playing area from the tee to the green. In 17 holes Hogan had not made a single mistake that anyone could notice. He did not make one now. The question, how to play it, dropped into the gears of memory and knowledge. When his own private calculating machine gave him the answer, Hogan cleared the treacherous bunkers 250 yards out with a tremendous drive, then sent a six-iron shot floating over more bunkers. It came to rest 14 feet from the pin, and Hogan rammed home his putt for a birdie three. The greatest round of Ben Hogan's life—a three-under-par 67 at the "impossible" Oakland Hills—was complete.

In achieving his remarkable feat, the man that Ben Hogan should have been most grateful to was the man who made the course so tough. It put stress on brains, experience and fortitude, all long suits with Hogan. But Ben was not inclined to be grateful. He said, "If I had to play that golf course every week, I'd get into another business."

(July 1951)

The Greatest Year of My Life
Ben Hogan as told to Gene Gregston

There never has been a year like 1953 in the history of professional golf, and Ben Hogan was responsible for it. In 1951 he had conquered Oakland Hills in winning his third United States Open championship, a feat which many, myself included, regard as the pinnacle of his brilliant career. But that was a singular triumph which was subsequently dwarfed by his unprecedented "triple," scored two years later.

Ben was the first and only golfer ever to win three of golf's four major championships in a single season. He did it when he took the Masters with a record 274; the U. S. Open at Oakmont with 283, which was the first time par was ever broken there for 72 holes; and the British Open with 282, which included the course and tournament record for Carnoustie in Scotland. No wonder Hogan called it "The Greatest Year of My Life."

Although Ben would play for several years more, he never again would realize the heights of his banner years. In fact, he never again would win a major championship, although he came close in the U. S. Open in both 1955 and 1960.

Hogan was the most remarkable golfer I have ever known, especially after his near-fatal auto accident in February, 1949, which left him broken in body but not in spirit. It was an accident which could have terminated the career of a man lacking Hogan's determination. He fought back and, despite after effects of his injuries which required that he immerse himself in a hot tub and that he wrap his legs in elastic bandages to maintain proper blood circulation, he was able to re-establish himself as the greatest player extant at the time and one of the three best ever produced in this country.

Ben's physical limitations prevented him from giving any consideration to playing in the PGA, which then was conducted at match play. Had it been then as it is now, a stroke-play tournament, I am sure he would have been able to complete the "Professional Grand Slam" by winning all four majors. He was just that much better than his contemporaries.

CHIPPING OUT OF sand is the hardest shot in the world for me to make. But such a shot proved to be the turning point this year in my first bid for the British Open Championship. It came on the fifth hole of the final round at Carnoustie, Scotland, on Friday, July tenth. I was tied for the lead with Roberto De Vicenzo, of Argentina. Tony Cerda, also of Argentina, and Great Britain's Dai Rees were deadlocked at second, just a stroke back.

I had played the first four holes even par when Cerda, playing behind me, birdied the third hole. That made him one under fours. I knew he'd caught me. And I realized then that I had to get a couple of birdies some place and shoot a 70, or right around 70, to win.

At the fifth, a slight dog-leg to the right, my second shot hit the green, backed off and stopped in the fringe of a sand trap to the left and about thirty-five or forty feet from the pin. It hung on the edge of the bunker, held by two blades of grass. It kept moving, barely. Then it stopped, still on the edge.

I didn't know how much sand was under the ball or if it could have been blasted out. But I couldn't take a chance on that, for fear the ball might go over the green and leave me in real trouble coming back downhill to the pin. So I chipped with a No. 9 iron, something I ordinarily would never do. I've never been able to chip out of sand successfully — usually I either leave the ball there or hit it too far.

This time, as luck would have it, I hit it just right. It was nipped just enough for back-spin. The ball pitched against the bank of the green, skidded uphill to the pin, banged the back of the cup, bounced three or four inches into the air — then fell into the hole.

It was a birdie three, my first birdie on the final round. De Vicenzo had played nine holes one over par, so I felt I was in the lead by a stroke, the first time I had been able to get in front of the tournament. It had been a long, tiring road to that lead, and every step of the way reaffirmed my belief that no one does anything unless the Lord's with him. I think it was fate, and supposed to be, that I won this tournament. Otherwise, I wouldn't have won it or four other titles this year.

In a golfing sense this has been the greatest of my forty-one years, in that I have been fortunate enough to win five out of six tournaments. And personally it's been a tremendously satisfying year, if for no other reason than the homecoming celebrations given my wife, Valerie, and me in New York City and in our home town of Fort Worth on our return from Scotland.

Victory in the British Open was the climax of my 1953 tournament activity, and some have termed it the crowning achievement of my career to date. Yet the decision to undertake the trip had been difficult to make.

I told Valerie after the Masters Tournament in April that I thought I would enter the British Open — "if I win the U. S. Open." She wasn't excited at the prospect. She gets travel-sick regardless of the mode of transportation, and she knew what hardship the overseas trip would involve because we had made a similar journey with the Ryder Cup in 1949.

But all she said was, "I should think you'd want to play in the British Open if you didn't win the U. S. Open."

That's Valerie, a wonderful wife, partner, companion, trainer and adviser who deserves more credit than I can possibly give her for any success I've had. Her answer more or less settled the question between us, but it still was far from definite, and no one else was told of my intention until some time later.

"If I win the U. S. Open" — that was a mighty big "If." But it ultimately did not rest on that. My entry for the British Open was mailed before the U. S. Open was played, and I knew then that I'd go to Scotland whether I won my fourth U. S. Open or not.

I went to the British Open for several reasons. First of all, the trip was not undertaken merely to bring their cup home. Naturally, any tournament I enter I try as hard as possible to win, but the main reason for my going was to satisfy so many people's wishes that I play. I felt that if they had that much faith in me and wanted me to represent the United States in the British Open, I should reciprocate.

The second reason was that it was a challenge. I'd always heard about Carnoustie — pronounced "Car-NOOSE-tee" — being one of the finest courses in the world and one of the toughest on which to score. Then everyone told me the weather posed a problem we don't have over here. I wanted to try my hand at it. Also, I wanted to see how I'd fare with the smaller-sized British ball. I'd heard it said several times that I could not play the small ball with my deep-faced clubs.

Many comments to the effect that people didn't believe I could win under those conditions came to be secondhand, and I was somewhat determined to prove that I could. I think that's been one of my driving forces all my life, because over a period of years people have said I couldn't do this or that.

Even at Colonial, my home course in Fort Worth, several said this year that I couldn't win because I wasn't a very good wind player.

The third reason for the trip was that the United States Golf Association and the Royal and Ancient Golf Club of St. Andrews had made their rules identical, for the good of world golf, except the rule concerning size of the ball. The example of this standardization which most affected me was that the British agreed to permit use of the center-shafted putter after having banned it for many years. My putter, which has a brass-blade head made from an old doorknob while World War II was in progress and brass couldn't be obtained, is classed as center-shafted.

For another thing, the British Open this year came at a time when it didn't conflict with any of my commitments in this country. It seems silly to have that many reasons for going to a golf tournament, doesn't it? After all, I am a professional golfer and playing tournaments is my business.

But we've done a lot of traveling in nineteen years—more than those years show, perhaps. We knew this trip would be tough. In fact, I don't think Valerie believed me at first when I told her I might go. And I kept delaying sending my entry until the deadline of June sixth neared. Then, after mailing it, I began to feel a pressure that I've never experienced before about a tournament.

It wasn't that I felt I might lose a lot by going, yet I believed that if I didn't win, everyone would say, "I told you so." And I think if I hadn't won, the people over there would have thought, *Well, American players aren't so good as they're supposed to be, especially under British conditions.*

You know, a great many people have built up in their minds a mythical Hogan who wins whenever he wants to win. Well, it does not work out that way. That's just not true. If you win 1 per cent of the tournaments you play, you're very lucky.

Some have asked me if I set out to make this a banner year because of a comparatively poor 1952 showing and comments implying that I was "through." Well, that comes within the "driving forces" I mentioned previously. When I went to Augusta, Georgia, for the Masters in April, I felt that I was hitting the ball better than ever before. I'd practiced every day of the winter. This is no plug for Palm Springs, California, but the turf there is ideal for development of your swing. It's firm, and the sand underneath gives it a good cushion. I think my four rounds of 70-69-66-69 for 274 in the Masters were the best I've ever shot in the course of one tournament.

All this time Valerie and I had been making preparations for the trip to Scotland. My mother, remembering 1949, when I became ill in Great Britain and had to return home, didn't think we should go, for fear of repetition of that sickness. I did get a touch of influenza this time, but it wasn't serious.

It's true my mother tried to get me to give up golf when I was a boy, but there's nothing to the story that at sixteen years of age I told her that some day I was going to be the greatest golfer in the world. She never did approve of my playing golf, however, and I'm still not sure she approves of it.

When we arrived at Carnoustie I had my first look at the course. It was quite a contrast to the beautiful farms and fields of the countryside. It was extremely drab looking. The color was a mixture between brown and green. There were no trees. It was land that's never been developed since the Year One, I suppose.

We stayed at the Tay Park House at Dundee, about eleven miles from Carnoustie. This is the National Cash Register Company's guest house for use of executives and business people who come to Dundee, where the company has a factory. We had been offered accommodations there before we left the United States. We rented a car, a British Humber, and hired a chauffeur for our stay there.

A professional caddie named Cecil Timms, or Timmy, about thirty-three or thirty-four years old, who had worked for Harvie Ward and Dick Chapman, two of our top amateurs, in previous British events, asked me for a trial. He proved to be satisfactory, if a bit too nervous.

Naturally I was eager to begin practice with the smaller ball and get acquainted with the Carnoustie championship course, where the tournament was to be played, and the shorter Burnside course, where one qualifying round was to be played.

The practice area at Carnoustie is about a mile out on the course from the first tee. But it also is an army firing range. So help me, it is. About 200 yards away they'd be shooting machine guns, rifles and pistols, and you'd be trying to practice. The noise was terrific, so I moved to the more private Barry course between Carnoustie and Dundee.

My daily routine started with a breakfast of bacon and eggs. Then I'd drive to Barry for an hour or an hour and a half of practice, have lunch, then drive over to Carnoustie for a round of golf in the afternoon. After dinner, there wasn't much time left in the evenings, but Valerie and I did attend two movies while we were there.

I played two or three balls on every hole of my practice rounds. You can hit the small ball a mile! I'd say, conservatively, that it goes twenty-five yards farther than the American ball, and against the wind there is more difference than that. My biggest troubles were getting accustomed to the distance I could hit the smaller ball and learning to judge distances on the course.

I kept finding myself taking about two clubs less than we would with our ball, and, I suppose just subconsciously, I'd then hit it harder than I should. Since I never was able to trust myself to look and judge what club should be used, I memorized what it should take from various places on the fairway, taking the weather and other factors into consideration, and I played the tournament from that memory.

Their wind isn't any stronger than it is at some places in the United States, but it's a lot heavier and has a lot more moisture as it comes in off the sea. For instance, in my practice rounds I never hit more than a light No. 8 iron on my second shot on the first hole. But on the first round of the tournament I hit a driver and a No. 2 iron just as hard as I could nail them because of the high wind in my face. That's how much difference it can make over there.

And par changes with the wind. If you play a hole in the morning and you're going downwind, it's a par four. But in the afternoon, if the wind has changed and you're facing it, the same hole is a par five. They don't go by par, as we know it, however. They judge play on "level fours," a total of 72 for eighteen holes.

In the United States we play what I term "target golf." Our courses have boundaries, or borders, of trees, fences and hedges, and our fairways are well defined, easily distinguishable from the rough. Sometimes at Carnoustie it was almost impossible to determine from the tee where the fairway ended and the rough began because fairway and rough were identical in color.

When they build a course they just go out and seed a tee, seed a green, mow a fairway between them, and leave the rough the same way it's been for a thousand years and will be for two thousand more. They put sand traps everywhere. Traps on six of the holes were strategically placed in the middle of the fairway at the perfect driving distance required for those holes. You had to find your way around those traps because if you played short of them you could not reach the green on the second shot.

Normally, they mow the fairways about once a month and mow the greens about once a week. Since this type of course is easy to build and easy to maintain, golf is very inexpensive and everyone plays. The fee for a round at Carnoustie is forty-nine cents. It's unfortunate that we do not have a larger number of courses with similar fees, so more people could play golf over here.

Heather and gorse are abundant in the rough.

Heather, something like a fern, grows in clumps about eight inches to a foot high and is as thick as it can be. If you get in it, you have to hit the ball about ten times as hard as you would otherwise, and then most times it won't go more than ten yards or so. I was in it only once, thank goodness, and that was on a qualifying round. It was up close to a green and fortunately I came out of it all right.

Gorse is taller, sometimes waist- to head-high, and is a brambly bush. I don't know what you do if you get into it, and I never wanted to find out. I didn't practice getting out of the gorse or heather because I figured anyone who got into it frequently wouldn't have a chance anyway.

Every fairway is rolling and full of mounds, and you hardly ever have a level lie. It was bounce golf. I'd hit a shot and never know which way it might bounce when it landed. I do know that in seventy-two holes of the tournament I never bounced an approach shot "stiff" to the pin. By that, I mean close enough for what we'd consider a cinch putt. You'd think in seventy-two holes anyone would "luck" one up there that close, but I never did.

It was what I'd call a "burn-happy" layout too. There are two burns, or creeks — the bigger Barry Burn and Jockie's Burn — that play a large part in making the course difficult. In addition, there are several long ditches, or trenches, in the roughs. I suppose they're drainage ditches, but I don't know. In practice I tried to find all of them, not only because it was a certain one-stroke penalty if you hit a ball into one but because if I ever walked out into the rough I didn't want to fall into one and break my leg. They're about three feet deep, and I'm surprised there aren't a lot more one-legged golfers over there because of those ditches.

Their championship tees are called "tiger" tees. I thought this was because they were so far back in the heather and gorse that only tigers would be there. I didn't learn differently until my return to New York, when Bobby Jones told me where the name originated. The people call a golfer who plays from the back tees a "tiger," and the golfer who plays from the much shorter, front tees a "rabbit." I played several rounds at Carnoustie before I realized I was being a rabbit

part of the time. You can't find some of those tiger tees unless you have a caddie or partner who knows the course well.

While practicing, I formulated my plans for the tournament. My degree of sharpness at the time governs my attack and expectations for a particular tournament. A lot of things enter into this plan — the type of course, the weather, places where there's a possible need for sacrifice, and places where chances may be taken. I believed after two weeks of practice that the tee shot would be the most important because of the course and the weather, and thought that a score of 283 would win it.

You have to hit an extremely long tee shot at Carnoustie — the course measures more than 7200 yards from the tiger tees — and you have to keep your drive out of the heather, gorse and sand traps. Therefore, I did a lot of practicing with wood clubs, more than I normally do for tournaments.

In qualifying rounds I shot a 70 at Burnside and a 75 at Carnoustie, the 145 total qualifying easily. Many have asked if I coast along in qualifying rounds. Let's put it this way: I try, all right, but I just can't work up to as high a competitive pitch as in a tournament.

When I walked up to the first tee at Burnside for my first qualifying round and first official shot in a British Open, I didn't see anyone in charge, no one announcing players as we do in America. There was a little house off to the side and a woman sitting in it by herself. The twosome in front had teed off and played their second shots; still no one, not even my partner, Bill Branch, of England, who was a very quiet fellow, said anything to me about teeing off. So, when I thought it was about time, I walked onto the tee and put my ball down. Some people shook their heads negatively.

While I was waiting for some word, a train came up the tracks that ran alongside the first fairway. The engineer gave me three short blasts on his whistle, stopped the train and waved. I didn't shoo him away, as the news stories reported. I merely waved back to him. Then I heard his horn go "beep-beep." The woman in the little house had blown the horn, and that was the signal to tee off. All the people lining the fairway on both sides nodded their heads, indicating it was now all right for me to drive. Valerie said later that she could see I was about to burst with laughter, and I was. It was all new and funny to me, but, I guess, perfectly normal to them.

On that first qualifying round I also learned that my caddie, Timmy, is a very nervous fellow. He was a good caddie. He treated my clubs as if they were the crown jewels and kept them clean and shining all the time. He took my shoes home with him every night to polish them. But when things got tight on the course, he'd get extremely upset. And the more nervous he became, the more he'd talk. Each time, I'd stop and quiet him. Many times when I'd have a long putt he'd hold his head down between his arms and wouldn't look, indicating his lack of confidence in my putting. And most of the time I didn't want to look either. I putted poorly over there. I knew the greens were hard and I kept expecting them to be fast, but they never were.

Timmy was never wrong. I don't ask a caddie what club to use, but if I picked a No. 5 iron, for example, and the shot was short, I might comment that I should have taken more club. Every time I did this, Timmy would say, "Yes, I had me hand on the four-iron." He always knew — after the shot was made.

On the first day of the tournament the wind was blowing very hard. About five minutes before Ugo Grappasonni, of Italy, my playing partner for the first two rounds, and I were to tee off, Bobby Locke, of South Africa, finished his first round with a 72, and I had an opportunity to congratulate him.

I thought he'd shot a wonderful round in those weather conditions, and I thought he surely would be leading, or not more than one stroke back, after the first round. That proved to be wrong, however, because Frank Stranahan, our fine amateur, shot a 70 and took the lead.

I shot a 73. My play that day was satisfactory, except for my putting. Leaving the course afterward, I was somewhat tired, as I usually am after the first round. It seems as though the first is always the most tiring round for me in a tournament. And as I had lost some twenty pounds since February, my weight was down pretty fine,

as low as I wanted it to get.

The diet was restricted, of course, since they were still on rations, trying to recover from the war. Fruit was plentiful, though, and it helped me retain my strength. I also carried some candy fruit drops in my bag and ate them frequently for energy. At the start I gave Timmy a share of this candy, but on two rounds he ate all of his and mine too. Finally, after two or three warnings, he was convinced he'd better leave my candy alone.

I felt I played well in the second round, but again couldn't get my putts to drop, and scored a 71 that left me two strokes back of Britain's Dai Rees and Scotland's Eric Brown, who were tied for the lead at 142.

Rees, Brown and the other golfers from the British Isles played with much more confidence in their own surroundings and with their own ball. The transition was amazing; they play so much better over there than they do here. But just the reverse is true with our players, too, so I suppose it's like being more comfortable in your own home.

It seemed to me, however, that British golfers have a more leisurely approach to the game. Technically, their game is about the same as ours insofar as swing, stroke and method are concerned and most of them use American-made clubs.

The field was cut for the final thirty-six holes. I had learned on the first two rounds and, in fact, all the while I was over there, that the Scottish galleries, composed of people who came from all over the British Isles, are very respectful and know their golf well. They treated Valerie and me wonderfully.

I gained a tie for the lead in the third round of the tournament Friday morning by shooting a 70 for a total of 214, same as that of De Vicenzo. My partner for the last two rounds was Hector Thompson, of Scotland. Like Ugo Grappasonni, who could speak broken English, and Bill Branch, Thompson was a very quiet fellow.

It rained intermittently during the last three rounds of the tournament, but the wind wasn't as fierce as it had been on the first day. While eating my lunch before the last round, I kept thinking of the job at hand. I felt that my original plan had to be changed somewhat. As the tournament progressed, the pressure kept building up, and although I didn't feel well physically, having taken the flu the night before, the excitement of being tied for the lead with one round to go was offsetting my physical discomfort, and I actually felt stronger moving into the afternoon's final round.

I always do. My blood stream seems to get an extra shot of adrenalin from my body. Knowing that I hit the ball farther in the final round than I ever do in previous rounds because of this added strength, I purposely underclub each shot. For instance, where I normally use a No. 5 iron in the first to third rounds, a No. 6 iron would be used in the final round.

I might add right here that the only time I alter my original plan for a tournament is on the last round, as I was doing this time, when I'm in a corner and have to fight my way out. If you're in front, you can let the other fellow make the mistakes. This time I was tied with De Vicenzo, and Rees and Cerda were only one stroke back.

The husky De Vicenzo was the strongest man over there and a very long driver. He could carry over at least three of those sand traps in the fairways, and was always using two or three clubs less on his second shots than anyone else. I thought before it started that he'd run away with the tournament with any sort of luck on the greens, and he might have had he not knocked a ball out of bounds on the ninth hole of the third round.

Rees is a little fellow, but a fine player. Cerda is about my size, five feet, ten inches tall and 160 pounds or so. He's not so strong as De Vicenzo, naturally, but he has a fine swing and a well-rounded game.

De Vicenzo was about six to eight holes ahead of Thompson and me when we started the final round. Rees was in front of De Vicenzo, and Cerda was behind me. I had played the fourth hole in even fours when I heard about Cerda's birdie on the third. That's when I was fortunate enough to chip in from the sand trap for the birdie three on the fifth hole.

When I made that shot and heard that De Vicenzo was one over at the turn, I felt as the jockey must feel when he's finally poked his horse's nose out front of the pack in a Kentucky Derby.

I went through the first nine holes in 34. By then, I'd heard that Stranahan was in with 286 after shooting a great 69, and Rees had shot a 71 to tie Frank. De Vicenzo was playing the sixteenth or seventeenth and was still one over. The only thing I had to worry about was holding what I had and keeping track of Cerda right behind me.

But misfortune almost struck on the tenth hole. As I was taking my stance on the tee, out of the corner of my eye I saw this big black dog walk across the tee about ten yards in front of me. I thought I saw him walk in to the crowd, but as I hit a full driver the dog walked across. My ball didn't miss him two inches. If it had hit him, it probably would have killed the dog, could have messed up my score pretty badly and there might have been a different ending to this story.

I got my four on the tenth, though, and fours on the eleventh and twelfth. On the thirteenth I hit a No. 5 iron to the green and sank a twelve-foot putt for a birdie deuce, and that put me four under fours. De Vicenzo had finished one over for a 73 and a total of 287. I also learned that Cerda, who had stayed within one stroke of me through the eleventh hole, was now one over fours after his ball hit a spectator on the twelfth. I felt for the first time that I had the championship if I didn't do anything foolish.

Fortunately, I didn't. My good luck held and I finished four under fours for a 68, a total of 282 and victory in my first British Open. Someone informed me that the 68 was a new competitive eighteen-hole record for the Carnoustie course. I never had any thought of a record during the round, however, and I do not play to break records.

I play to win, and I think the Lord has let me win for a purpose. I hope that purpose is to give courage to those people who are sick or injured and broken in body.

(1953)

173

The Maddening First Hole
Arnold Palmer with William Barry Furlong

Arnold Palmer is a golfer who has interested me ever since he first gained prominence in 1954 by winning the United States Amateur at the Country Club of Detroit, a course which I had extensively remodelled in preparation for that championship.

Since then he has gone on to win sixty-one tournaments in the United States and nineteen foreign titles, including seven major championships. He has become a legend of golf and a millionaire many times over, but he has never lost touch with reality.

Because of his exciting, audacious style of play and his apparent disregard for the pitfalls such boldness can bring, millions have gravitated to his ranks as members of "Arnie's Army." His emergence on the scene more than a quarter of a century ago, coincidental with television's discovery of golf, were the prime catalysts for the subsequent "golf explosion" of the sixties and early seventies. There can be no question that he is the most popular golfer to play the game since Bob Jones. Even though he now is a senior, his popularity persists and his appearance in a tournament is a virtual guarantee of its success.

Palmer always has been the kind of golfer who radiates energy, especially so when he was a chain-smoking, pants-hitching prowler of the fairways ever on the hunt for pars, birdies and sometimes eagles to cap his 72-hole quest for a title. He was dubbed "The Charger," and rightly so, as his record is rife with tournaments he came from behind to win.

No better example of this is needed than his first-person account of his victory in the 1960 United States Open at Cherry Hills in Denver. Written in collaboration with William Barry Furlong, this memorable account reveals the kind of challenge that got his juices surging and inspired him to accomplish his goal of winning the championship.

THERE WAS A SHARP bite and sparkle in the mountain air. The Rockies loomed clearly in the distance—immense, clean, barren. I remember on the first hole at Denver, the sun was so bright that it hurt your eyes to look down the fairway. Standing on the tee, it was difficult to see the green without a pair of dark glasses. It took me four rounds to find it—but when I did, the whole thrust of my life was altered.

The time was 1960. The place was Cherry Hills Country Club. The event was the U. S. Open.

On the fourth round of that tournament, I tried a shot that I'd missed three times in three rounds. I tried it again not because I'd failed—or because I like failure—but because I was convinced that it was the shot necessary to win the tournament.

A bold shot?

Yes.

But you must play boldly to win. My whole philosophy has been based on winning golf tournaments, not on finishing a careful fifth, or seventh, or tenth.

A reckless shot?

No.

In eighteen years of tournament golf I feel that I've never tried a shot that I couldn't make.

On that summer day in 1960, I was young in what the world calls fame, but I was ripe in golfing experience. I'd been a professional golfer for five years, and up to then I'd won twenty tournaments. In those years, I'd learned something about the strategy of the game and its psychology and rewards. If there was any reward I treasured most, it was the way that the game responded to my inner drives, to the feeling we all have that—in those moments that are so profoundly a challenge to man himself—he has done his best. That—win or lose—nothing more could have been done.

My own needs were deeply driven ones: I could not retreat from a challenge. If the chance was there and if—no matter how difficult it appeared—it meant winning, I was going to take it. It was the "sweetness" of risk that I remembered, and not its dangers.

In looking back, I feel in these years I was learning something of the subtle dimensions of all this—I was learning the *meaning* of boldness as well as its feeling.

For boldness does not mean "recklessness" to me. Rather it involves a considered confidence: I *know* I'm going to make the shot that seems reckless to others. I also know the value of the risk involved: A bold shot has to have its own rewards—winning or losing the match, winning or losing the tournament.

But perhaps it was not until the U. S. Open at Cherry Hills that I put it all together, philosophically as well as physically. For not until that summer day in 1960 did it become apparent to me how boldness might influence not just a hole but an entire round, an entire tournament, and even an entire golfing career.

It began, really, on the first tee of the last round at Cherry Hills. On the face of it, there was nothing terribly subtle about this hole: You could see every mistake you made. It was downhill to the green; the tee was elevated perhaps 150 feet above the green. It was only 346 yards long, not a terribly long par four—and a terribly tempting birdie three...to me. It was guarded on the left by an irregular line of poplars and pines and on the right by a ditch that the membership had practically paved with golf balls. A nice direct hole for the strong driver, somebody who could—in that thin, mile-high air—get the ball out there 300 yards or so.

But there *was* one nasty little afterthought that had been provided for the U. S. Open: The grass was allowed to grow very long and become a "rough" right in the fairway, about fifty or sixty yards in front of the green. Moreover, the hazard was heightened by a treacherous bunker guarding the gateway to the green. It had grass in it that looked like it was three feet deep. If you got in there, you might never be found again. I mean it was the kind of place where you hunted buffalo—not par.

The idea, of course, was to penalize the strong driver, to threaten him with capture by the rough—and a difficult second shot—if he played to his own best game (a powerful drive) on his first shot.

The safe way to play that hole, for most golfers, was not to invite trouble—not to challenge the rough or the bunker in the first place. In that sense, the first hole was an authentic mirror of the entire course. For Cherry Hills was long in yardage (7,004) but not in reality: The thin air gave most tee shots a much longer carry than on a sea level course. But its greens were small and well guarded by bunkers and water hazards; there was an added danger that under the hot, direct sun and the afternoon winds they would become so dried out that it would be all but impossible to get the ball to stop on them. If you hit those greens with power, the ball would roll right over and off them on the far side. So it was a course that took accuracy, touch, and an unflagging concentration. It *looked* to many like a course whose yardage beckoned to power— Mike Souchak, a powerful golfer, led at the halfway mark of the 1960 Open with a remarkable sixty-eight, sixty-seven for a thirty-six-hole score of 135. But it was, in reality, a course that catered to placement more than to power—in that opening round of sixty-eight, Souchak had only twenty-six putts, nine or ten short of normal for an eighteen-hole round. So he wasn't up there scattering power shots; he was getting good placement with everything he did.

To focus on the first hole: It was the kind of hole that shaped your entire approach to the course in that it could reward you for power or for placement.

To the pretty good amateur golfer, it was an opportunity for a par four. He might put the ball out in the fairway pretty much where he could— far short of the rough—and then hope to get close to, or onto, the green with his second shot.

To the venturesome pro, it was an opportunity for a birdie. He'd use an iron to hit his shot off the tee, expecting to get enough accuracy from it (which he would less likely get from a driver) to drop the ball precisely in the fairway, where he'd have the ideal second shot. In short, he intended to place his first shot so that he could hit his second shot precisely to the cup— not just any old place on the green but *specifically* to the cup. For this was the kind of shot where the pro prefers—where he *intends*—to get his second shot so close to the cup that he'll need only one putt to "get down." So if he emphasized placement over power, he hoped to wind up with a birdie three, not a par four.

From my angle of vision—somewhat singular, I'll admit—this was an eagle hole, not a birdie hole. I figured that, with boldness, I could get down in two strokes, not three or four.

That meant being on the green in one shot, not two.

That meant getting into the cup in one putt, not two.

That meant emphasizing power over placement.

That meant using my driver, not my iron.

My intention was simply to drive the ball hard enough and far enough so that it would bound through the rough in front of the green and run up on the putting surface to a good position near the cup. To get a ball to stop precisely on a green, you must give it backspin, so that it bites into the grass when it hits and then stops short, or even hops backward. That's fairly easy to do when you're using an iron from the fairway that is fairly close to the green; you merely strike straight downward at the ball, taking a divot after making contact with the ball, and take a normal follow-through. But it is difficult to do while driving off the tee and ramming the ball through the rough. For one thing, on tee shots you may be hitting the ground a microsecond before you make contact with the ball. At least that's what I was doing with my driver back in 1960 (though since then I've changed my style somewhat). Then you normally give the ball a considerable overspin when you hit the ball dead center (or thereabouts) and make the big follow-through. Normally you want to give the ball some overspin when hitting off the tee with a driver. Overspin will cause the ball to roll a little farther after it hits the ground. So my tee shot would, I expected, be hitting those small greens without backspin. And if the greens were dry and hard, as I expected, the ball might never stop rolling this side of the Continental Divide.

So I was proposing to use a power club—the driver—rather than a placement club—the iron—on a hole that demanded placement as well as power. And I was accepting overspin, not backspin, on a green that threatened to be faster than the Indianapolis Speedway on Memorial Day.

"Boldness" is what my friends called it. "Insanity" is what they meant.

But I figured to have two things going for me when the ball hit the green.

If the ball went through the rough, not over it, the thick grass would cut down significantly on the ball's momentum, and very likely on how far it would roll, once it hit the green. Also, I'd be playing this hole relatively early in the morning on the first three rounds. (On the fourth and last round—because of the way the U. S. Open was run in those days—I'd be playing it in the early afternoon.) I knew that every green was being heavily watered at night, simply because the tournament officials were afraid that otherwise the greens would be hard and dry by the afternoon. So in the morning, the first green—obviously the first to be played—would likely be heavily laden with the water from the all-night sprinkling, and the water residue would slow down any ball hit onto it. That's another reason why the roll of the ball would be reduced.

(You didn't *really* think that I just went out there and hit the ball hard, without giving any thought to what would happen to it once it came down—now did you?)

The way I looked at it, all I had to do was pound the ball bouncingly through the rough and onto the heavily watered green. Then I'd one-putt and have an eagle. I'd have that course by the throat, and—as my fellow pro, Jerry Barber, once said—"shake it to death."

Only it didn't happen. Not on the first three rounds. That green was tough to reach with a rifle, much less a driver. In my first round I sent my tee shot into the ditch on the right. I didn't get an eagle or a birdie or a par on the hole. I didn't even get a bogey, for that matter. I got a double-bogey six—two over par, instead of the two under par that I'd aimed for. After that, things got better—but not much. I got a bogey five on the second round and a par four on the third round. So in the first three rounds, I'd

taken fifteen strokes on that hole, instead of the twelve strokes that playing it safe might have given me. And instead of the six strokes that—in wild flights of genius—my boldness might have given me.

More than that, starting off every round with a deep disappointment damaged my whole pattern of play. After three rounds, I had a total of thirteen birdies in the tournament, but they were so scattered that I'd never gotten any momentum out of them—no "charge," so to speak. The result was that I was in fifteenth place with a 215 after three rounds.

Just before lunch, and the start of my last round, I paused outside the vast white scoreboard outside the rambling, neo-Tudor clubhouse at Cherry Hills. There in the elaborate black and red numerals of golf, written in a manner as highly stylized as medieval script, I saw how the field lay. I was seven strokes behind the leader, Mike Souchak. But Mike wasn't the only hurdle. Between me and the leadership lay such great golfers as Ben Hogan and Sam Snead, Julius Boros and Dow Finsterwald, Dave Marr and Bob Goalby, and a twenty-one-year-old amateur named Jack Nicklaus.

By the time I sat down to a sandwich in the clubhouse, my mood was about as black as a witch's heart. Ken Venturi and Bob Rosburg, who also seemed to be out of contention, joined me, and a couple of newsmen stopped by our table to offer solace to the newly bereaved.

One of them was an old friend, Bob Drum, then of the *Pittsburgh Press*. He knew of my tribulations with that first hole and of my conviction that it was an eagle hole that would unlock the entire course to the player bold enough to attack it. He also knew that my failure in a daring power approach had—in an era of golf when meticulous precision was most admired—given a certain satisfaction to a few older hands around professional golf. "There are some guys out there who think you're just an upstart, a flash-in-the-pan," he told me. So when he began to console me, and hint that maybe it was time to play it safe and try to pick up some good also-ran money in the U. S. Open—since it was obvious I couldn't go from fifteenth place to first place in one round—the chemistry began working in me. Explosively.

"What would happen if I shot a sixty-five on this last round?" I asked, perhaps more aggressively than in the thirst for pure knowledge.

"Nothing," said Bob. "You're out of it." He was an old friend but a realistic one. Only one man had *ever* shot a sixty-five in the final round of the U. S. Open: Walter Burkemo in 1957.

But that got to me. And to my pride. Realism—and pessimism—I did not need.

"Well," I said, my voice lowering into my don't-tread-on-me tone, "the way I read it is that a sixty-five would give me 280 for the tournament. And 280 is the kind of score that usually wins the U. S. Open."

Bob gave me a startled look, as if he just noticed I had two heads.

"Sure," he said, "but you won't do it by taking another double-bogey on the first hole."

So there it was: I still looked at the first hole as a chance for triumph; Bob—and a great many others—looked at it as a place for patent disaster. I suppose they were right. If I'd played it safe on the first hole and teed off with my iron, instead of the driver, and gone for placement and par, I'd be three shots closer to the leaders after the first three rounds. If I'd picked up a birdie or two along with it, I might even be right on their necks. So the thing to do now was admit that the first hole had me beaten and go back to playing it like the other pros did—with an iron off the tee—and figure that by placing the ball and playing it safe, I might pick up enough strokes in the standing to avoid further shame.

But that's not the way I saw it. I wasn't playing golf to avoid shame. I was playing it to win championships. And the last round of a National Open is no place to start changing your whole style and philosophy of golf.

The way I looked at it, being fifteenth made it more *imperative* that I play boldly. It couldn't cost me much: The difference between being fifteenth or twenty-fifth or fifty-fifth is not terribly meaningful—at least to me. It's the difference between first and second that has meaning. And a considered boldness might—I was sure—still win me the tournament.

So when I got to the first tee, I reached for my driver. Even though it was now one-forty-five in the afternoon and the green figured to be dried out and it would take incredible accuracy to hit the green and hold it. One of my luncheon companions (not Bob Drum) had come along, and he looked as if there were nothing wrong with me that brain surgery couldn't cure. I addressed the ball as if it were my enemy—or my slave—and hit it with everything I could get into it. The ball went up and hung in the sharp, clear air as if it had been painted there. When it came down—with overspin—it leaped forward and ran through the rough and right onto the middle of the green.

Twenty feet from the hole.

Three hundred and forty-six yards and I'd not only driven the green but drilled it right in the heart!

Just like I'd been planning it all along.

Right? Right!

Okay—two putts. A birdie, not an eagle. But that didn't much depress me. For I'd shown that my idea *did* work—that boldness could conquer this hole. And that if it made the first hole yield, then the whole course could be conquered with boldness.

Suddenly my whole spirit, my entire attitude changed.

I charged onto the second hole—a 410-yard par four with an elevated green and trees right in the fairway. In two shots I was not quite on the green. But I chipped the ball from off the green right into the cup for another birdie three. I charged onto the 348-yard third hole and birdied it. I charged onto the fourth hole and birdied it with a twisting forty-foot putt. Four holes: four birdie threes. A par on the fifth, a birdie on the sixth, a birdie on the seventh: six birdies on seven holes. I finished the first nine holes in thirty strokes, just one short of a record.

"Damn!" I said to Bob Drum when he finally caught up to us. "I really wanted that twenty-nine." Bob exhibited deplorable self-control: "Well," he murmured consolingly, "maybe next time."

By the tenth hole, I was tied with Mike Souchak. By the twelfth, I was ahead of him. But it was not all over: There had been fourteen men between me and the lead, and before the afternoon was over, a half dozen or more held or challenged for the title. "This was, to put it mildly, the wildest Open ever," said *Sports Illustrated*. For me, the birdies disappeared, but the pars survived. The final five holes at Cherry Hills are a punishing finishing stretch: Ben Hogan, then forty-seven, felt it, and he faded here; Nicklaus was twenty-one, and so did he. I managed to play each of those last five holes in par and to come in with a sixty-five for the eighteen-hole round. Boldness had paid off: That surge at the start was, in the words of golf writer Herbert Warren Wind, "the most explosive stretch of sub-par golf any golfer has ever produced in the championship. . . ." I finished the tournament with a seventy-two-hole score of 280. That was enough to give me the U. S. Open championship and a certain hold on history.

For the "charge" didn't stop there. It was not, in the long perspective, to be confined solely to one round or one tournament. It became a sort of phenomenon that marked my career: In the period 1960—1963, I was to win thirty-two tournaments—and go on to become the first million-dollar winner in golf history.

(1973)

The Longest Year: 1962
Jack Nicklaus with Herbert Warren Wind

Jack Nicklaus has been such a dominant figure in professional golf, and for such a long time, that there is a tendency to forget his early career. During the fifties, he was hailed as "the greatest amateur since Bob Jones," and he fueled that assertion by twice winning the United States Amateur Championship, in 1959 and 1961, and by finishing second to Arnold Palmer in the 1960 United States Open with the lowest score ever made by a non-professional in the Open. During that period he also persistently denied any talk of his turning pro, but, after much soul-searching, he did so in late December, 1961. The rest is history. Seventeen other major championships and his vaunted status as golf's all-time leading money winner attest to the wisdom of that decision.

It is evident that Jack had some second thoughts about his decision, at least to the extent that he began to wonder if he ever would win on the pro tour. He confesses this in a chapter of The Greatest Game of All, *which he wrote with Herbert Warren Wind. He called 1962 "The Longest Year," as he described the life-style changes and adjustments he was required to make in his transition from amateur to pro. Jack dramatically proved himself a quick learner with his victory in the United States Open barely six months after the changeover.*

And he did it the hard way, beating Arnold Palmer in a playoff at Oakmont, one of America's most demanding golf courses, before a gallery which was overwhelmingly pro-Palmer.

I remember that playoff and the way Jack conducted himself as he unemotionally went about the task of beating one of golf's all-time idols in a manner characteristically Nicklaus — straightforward, nearly devoid of error and pointedly aimed at the heart of the matter — to win the title in his first attempt as a pro, a feat which I believe never had been accomplished before, at least not since the turn of the century.

THE TIME IT TAKES a year to go by, I gather, grows shorter and shorter the older you get. My mother, for example, tells me that when she sits down now to address her Christmas cards, it seems like only five months have elapsed since she sat down to do her cards the year before. While I am still too young to experience the sensation that the years are contracting, I do know that the longest year of my life by far was 1962. That was my first year as a professional, and during it I traveled so much more continuously than ever before, met so many new people, grappled with so many new thoughts, and faced so many new situations that it seemed like twenty-four months were packed into it.

Before turning pro, except for the Walker Cup expedition in 1959, I had never been away from home for an extended period, and I had never been on my own. My dad missed few tournaments I played in, but if he wasn't on hand, someone else was. I had really led a comparatively sheltered life. The only place I knew was Columbus. I had lived there all my life, I had gone to college there. At twenty-two, however, I was still so young that, all in all, breaking from my old Columbus groove wasn't a hard thing. In fact, I relished the challenge of trying to make good as a professional and the chance this would give me to widen my orbit. Nonetheless, as I sensed it would be beforehand, the itinerant life on the pro tour *was* hard in certain ways. From time to time Barbara came out and joined me on the circuit—later in the year when Jackie was old enough to travel, she brought him along—but there were long stretches when I was away from my wife and son, and I missed them deeply. My father also came out and watched the tournaments for a couple of weeks at a time, and I enjoyed his visits a lot. It wasn't that I was exactly lonely on the tour. I had known a good many of the pros before, and I found them hospitable and helpful. Mark McCormack, my lawyer and business manager, came out frequently to talk things over with the members of his growing stable. Then, too, at many of the stops, a representative of the MacGregor Company (with whom I had signed in January) was on hand to replenish my supply of golf balls, check with me on how I liked my clubs, and assist me with any small problems.

Transportation was no problem. Mark had worked out an arrangement whereby I had a Buick at my disposal whenever I needed a car. The Buick people, for instance, supplied me with one of their new models when I arrived in Los Angeles in early January, and I drove it to the tournaments in San Diego, Pebble Beach, San Francisco, and Palm Springs. I dropped it there and flew to Phoenix where another new Buick was waiting for me at the airport. The world of professional golf, I was discovering, was populated with companies and individuals who were only too happy to oblige a "name player." My chief regret was that I hadn't signed up with a good Chinese laundry and a nationwide we-pick-it-up-anywhere dry cleaning service. It seemed I was always either taking my soiled stuff out or else collecting it, and besides, the prices were steep.

One thing for sure—I had certainly chosen the right time to turn professional. Thanks primarily to television but also to Arnold Palmer's impact on the sports public, to the golf salesmanship of Ben Hogan and General Eisenhower before him, and to our steady national prosperity, tournament golf was entering a prodigious boom period. In 1962 the purses at most tournaments ran between $20,000 and $35,000, but the Lucky International, the Doral Open, the Indianapolis 500 Festival Open, the Buick Open, the Houston Classic, the Western Open, and the American Golf Classic were now offering $50,000 or more in prize money. As for the major tournaments, in 1962 the purse in the Masters came to $109,100, in the U. S. Open to $68,800, and in the PGA Championship to $72,000. Most significantly, in 1962 we had the first $100,000 tour tournament, the new Thunderbird Classic. Considering the millions that are spent annually on advertising and promotion by large companies such as the auto manufacturers, $100,000 was like a grain of sand in a bunker for them. But it was a lot of money for the pros to be shooting at, especially if you remembered that twenty-five years before no golfer had earned as much as $20,000 in prize money over a full season. Here we were now with a crack at $25,000 for winning a single tournament. The Thunderbird was the breakthrough. Five years later the $100,000 tour tournament had become almost ho-hum, a new record purse of $250,000 was established by the Westchester Classic, and the total prize money on the tour had climbed to $4,500,000. Along with this, when you take into account that a top pro earns at least the equivalent of his prize money from his subsidiary activities (golf club royalties, product endorsements, exhibitions, instructional articles, and so on), it was El Dorado. If a young man was going to turn professional, the 1960s were the time to do it.

In 1961, my last season as an amateur, the leading money-winner on the tour had been Gary Player. Gary's winnings, official and unofficial prize money combined, had come to around $68,000, some $3,000 more than Arnold Palmer's. When I joined the tour in 1962, however, there was no question whatsoever who was king—Palmer. He had been since 1960 when he had captured the Masters, the U. S. Open, and the excited admiration of the whole sports world. Arnold had solidified his position in 1961 by winning the British Open. In 1962 he was destined to have a remarkable season: apart from being the leading money-winner, he was to win eight tournaments in all, including his second British Open and his third Masters, and to win most of them with the dramatic closing charges that had become his trademark. I had known Arnold since 1954, when I'd met him at the Ohio State Amateur. Now that he had grown so much in stature, I didn't know quite what he would be like. I found he had time for everyone, including the rookie pros. He was always extremely nice to me—friendly and informal and enjoyable.

As a matter of fact, I found the touring pros as a group to be a great bunch of fellows. So many of them went out of their way to make me feel at home, it would be hard to list them all. Walter Burkemo, Stan Leonard, Bob Rosburg, Art Wall, Fred Hawkins, Doug Ford, Ed Furgol, Jack Fleck—they were all darn nice to me. So were Dow Finsterwald, Jay and Lionel Hebert, Billy Casper, Gary Player, Mike Souchak, Gene Littler, Jack Burke, Gardner Dickinson, Johnny Pott, Wes Ellis, and Mason Rudolph. Bo

Wininger was super. So was Dave Ragan. Really, it's difficult to think of anyone who wasn't cordial and pleasant. The veterans like Cary Middlecoff, Byron Nelson, Peter Cooper, Ted Kroll and Ben Hogan were, and so was old Tommy Bolt. So were the new pros—fellows like Dan Sikes and Bobby Nichols and my old sparring partner, Phil Rodgers. Tony Lema was most considerate. What pleased me as much, and surprised me more, was that I also found a very high level of what you might call "competitorship" on the tour. Each man regarded the men he was paired with as his equals. We were all out to make a living, and if you happened to be playing better that week than the next guy was—well, good luck to you. There was a minimum of pettiness and, I thought, a strong basic sense of fairness and sportsmanship. I don't think this has changed.

That winter I had the blinkers on. What I mean is that I thought only of two things: trying to make a successful start as a pro, and trying to do the right things as I learned the ropes in the new world. For all my precautions, I did have some trouble, minor trouble, with the press on the West Coast. Ninety percent of the sportswriters are first-class fellows, I have found, but there are always a few guys who have to attract attention to themselves and like nothing better than being controversial. For example, one California writer took as his premise that the pros "resent the intrusion of this highly publicized newcomer," and went on from there. I also made the mistake of saying in an interview, when I was asked how much money I expected to win, that I hoped my year's take would come to $30,000. After that appeared, I had to explain that I didn't think I was going to drive the established pros off the circuit and to make clear, past any misunderstanding, that I didn't have any particular money goal: I'd be happy to take whatever I won. Actually, I didn't think that aiming for $30,000 was having ideas above my station— I did win something more than that amount— but I learned quickly from this experience that you cannot be as honest or as spontaneous as you would like to be. You must always consider the circumstances.

Speaking not just in relation to my freshman

year on the tour but in general, I admire plain speaking in personal relations, and I am inclined to forget that public relations are different. As an amateur, I know, I was so forthright that if someone asked me how I was playing, it never occurred to me not to say, "Just great," if I was really playing that well. Sometimes this was interpreted as cockiness and brashness when all it was, in truth, was delight. You must have a certain style, I think, in order to get away with confident statements. I have in mind Gary Player's famous declaration to the press a few years back: "How am I playing? Actually I'm playing so well that I am positively embarrassed." Gary can be very amusing, and this being Gary at his Gariest, everyone took it that way. While diplomacy has never been my long suit, I believe I have learned to recognize its virtues. Today, if any young athlete were to ask my advice, I would counsel him not to be too slick, to be himself, and to try and temper honesty with tactfulness.... Now, if I can only follow this myself.

The opening tournament of the 1962 tour, the Los Angeles Open, was played, as it customarily was in those days, on the Rancho Municipal Golf Course. I had a 74 on my first round and added spotty rounds of 70, 72, and 73. My total of 289 was good for a tie for fiftieth, the last money place, which was worth $33.33. The winner, with a closing 62, was Mr. Philamon Rodgers, then in his second year as a pro.

At the next stop, the San Diego Open, held at the Stardust Country Club, I played a little better. A final 67, following a 72, a 69 and a 74, lifted me into a six-way tie for fifteenth. My check came to $550. (Tommy Jacobs was the winner, defeating Johnny Pott in a sudden-death playoff.) Next, the Crosby. There I ended up in a five-way tie for twenty-third and earned $450. (Doug Ford won out over Joe Campbell in a sudden-death playoff.) I was pleased with myself for finishing in the money in these three tournaments, but I was anything but happy with the brand of golf I was playing. I was driving the ball badly, and on the greens I had no touch at all. During our next stop, the Lucky International at the Harding Park Course in San Francisco, I went over to the Olympic Club to see if I could straighten out my driving. I found a good practice spot behind the seventeenth tee of the Ocean Course and hit out hundreds of balls. I decided there to change drivers. Beginning at L. A., I had been using a driver with an X (or extra stiff) shaft—I thought that now that I was a pro, I should be using a less-flexible-shafted driver than I had before. After fiddling around at Olympic, I went back to a driver with an S (or moderately stiff) shaft, the type of shaft I was accustomed to. I started using that driver in the next tournament, the Palm Springs Classic. I stayed with that driver, incidentally, the next four years.

The best that I had been able to do in the Lucky—71-73-73-73-290—was 16 strokes above Gene Littler's winning score and good enough only for a tie for forty-seventh and last money, $62.86. Once again, as in my first three tournaments, my putting had been atrocious. All in all, over those first 16 rounds, I managed only once to take less than 35 putts, which is about four more than a winning professional average. At Palm Springs I got some help. Jackie Burke, who knows as much about putting as anyone, played a practice round with me and studied my stroke closely. Jackie's diagnosis was that, instead of stroking through the ball with the palm of my right hand, I was dragging the club into the ball with the fingers of my right hand. He suggested I modify my right-hand grip. I had been setting that hand on top of the shaft, and Jack had me move it back a shade to the right so that the palm would be squarely behind the putter. I began stroking the ball better right off the reel and actually holed a few. One round at Indian Wells I got down to 33 putts, a real triumph. Once again, however, I finished way off the pace in the last money spot; this was worth $164.65 despite the fact that no less than nine of us were tied for that last place, thirty-second. After viewing me in action in this swing around California, very few established pros had packed their bags in panic and headed for home.

On to Phoenix. I made another change there. One day before the tournament when I was practicing at the Phoenix Country Club, I ran into George Low. George, a former professional, is a big, beefy, expansive fellow who for years has been one of the ripest characters who follow the tour. For a long while, the story had it, he had supported himself on the practice green: he was always ready to wager that he could outputt any pro, and it was rare when he didn't. In 1959 George had "gone straight." A company was formed to manufacture George Low-putters, and they sold very well. Be that as it may, I explained to George that I was having a lot of trouble adapting myself to the greens we played on the tour; composed of many different types of grass, the greens varied considerably in speed from one course to another. After watching me stroke a few balls, George told me that part of my trouble, quite obviously, was that the Ben Sayers model putter I was using was too light for the circuit greens. He went into the pro shop and returned with one of his Bristol models. This was a blade-type putter backed up by a pronounced flange—a sort of combination, you might say, of a mallethead and a blade. I liked its feel and decided to try it out in the Phoenix Open.

I proceeded to play my first good tournament as a pro. I drove well with my new driver, and thanks to Jack Burke's adjustment and the new putter, I had the ball rolling for the cup at a uniform speed all four rounds—69, 73, 68, 71. My 281 put me in a four-way tie for second with Bill Casper, Bob McCallister, and Don Fairfield, and it brought me my first sizable check, $2,300. I had never been in contention for first place, though, and, for that matter, neither had Casper, McCallister, Fairfield, or anybody else. Palmer, who had won at Palm Springs the previous week, was in absolutely brilliant form at Phoenix. He had led off with a 64, which put him 5 shots ahead of the field, and, piling it on, he eventually finished 12 full shots in front. How often do you see a tournament won by half that margin!

After Phoenix I went home for a week's rest, skipping the Tucson Open. After that second-place haul, I felt I could afford to do this. My game still wasn't right, but I thought that it was beginning to fuse somewhat better. During those first six weeks I had received quite an education, but one point stood out above the rest: Everyone on the tour shoots good rounds; the trick is to weed out your bad ones. That's easier said than

done, of course. When I rejoined the tour for the New Orleans Open, I failed to weed out an 80 on my second round, so although my other three rounds were respectable (two 71s and a 70), I finished a good ways down the list, sharing seventeenth with Mike Souchak and winning $650. The following week in the Baton Rouge Open, I tied for ninth. This was worth only $753.33, since Baton Rouge was a small $20,000 affair. The week after that, at Pensacola, I thought that my modest streak of having finished in the money in every tournament was over. Scores always run low at the Pensacola Country Club. Each day there are fifteen or twenty rounds in the 60s, so after a pair of 71s and a 74, I was miles back. Then on the last day — it was about time — I finally came up with a hot round, a 64. It shot me all the way up into a tie for eleventh, and I won $450. This was helpful, but what really mattered was knowing I had been able to come through with a good low round when I needed one.

The winter wore on. I passed up the next tournament, the St. Pete Open, and visited that week with my folks who were vacationing that year at Port St. Lucie. The rest of the time I spent with Jack Grout at his new club, La Gorce. I hadn't been satisfied with my short irons, so we worked mainly on them. Jack thought that the pattern of my swing in general looked okay, and he wasn't at all worried about the position of my right elbow. That was a big relief. After Phoenix, whenever I picked up a newspaper, it seemed that some authority or other was expounding that my less-than-sensational debut on the tour was due to the fact that I had developed a fatal flaw in my swing: my right elbow was not folding in toward my body on the backswing but breaking away from it. This "flying elbow," they said, was putting me into a position where I had to come into the ball all wrong. There was no question but that my elbow was not in the old-time classic position. Somewhere along the way, I had gotten into the habit of letting it break out, perhaps in my preoccupation with keeping the arc of my backswing as full as possible. (To go into the details a bit further, a golfer who has a conventional right-hand grip, in which the V points to the right shoulder, is less likely to move his elbow away from his side than a golfer like myself whose right-hand grip at that time was more on top of the shaft, with the V pointing at the chin.) Anyhow, after Jack had studied my swing, he told me not to worry about my elbow. "Your position on the backswing is perfectly all right," he told me. "You don't have a real flying elbow. That's a different thing entirely—at the top of the backswing the golfer's right elbow is pointing up, and the outward thrust of the elbow pushes the shaft of the club out so that it points far to the right of the target. At the top of your backswing, Jack, your elbow still points toward the ground—as it should. Your club's in perfect position—pointing right at your target. Now let's forget all that nonsense and play some real golf."

A session with Jack Grout always does wonders for me. I went out the next week in the Doral Open—the first Doral Open held—and finished third, two shots behind Billy Casper and one behind Paul Bondeson, who really should have won the tournament. My four rounds—69, 74, 69, 73—at Doral, a long and trouble-filled layout designed by Dick Wilson, added up to my best golf of the year. Aside from the transfusion from Grout, I was helped by the fact that Doral was in excellent condition—the first course on the tour that was. (A possible exception was Stardust in San Diego, where the turf was pretty good.) The other courses we played generally had wet, marshy fairways with high grass, or, if they were in the desert, bone-hard fairways with high grass.

Very simply, it was too early in the year for the average tour course to have had a sufficient growth of grass. On the other hand, despite the frequent winter rains, the greens had very little receptivity to them. When you are playing from tall wet fairways to hard bouncy greens, you have the toughest parlay in golf. On your approach shots, you must manufacture some half-punch compromise version of your usual swing, or otherwise all you'll hit is "fliers"—shots that sail well beyond your target area and keep on running when they land, since they have no backspin on them. (If your ball has a mild back rotation, that doesn't mean it has true backspin.) On those winter tour courses, you also get a high percentage of plain bad lies on the fairways. You have to gouge the ball out of them, and before you know it you're gouging everything out whether you have a bad lie or not. These were some of the items, anyhow, I found myself explaining when, passing up the Azalea Open, I went on to Augusta for the Masters and became involved in intricate discussions with Billy Joe Patton, Bill Hyndman, Charley Coe, Deane Beman, Ward Wettlaufer, and my other old amateur pals. After some practice rounds together, some of them thought I was hitting the ball sharper than I had before, but at least as many intimated politely that my swing wasn't as smooth as it had been—so there was a lot to talk about.

Probably because of my third-place finish at Doral, but also because the Augusta National is a course on which a big hitter has quite an advantage (as long as he is hitting the ball in the right direction), I was made a co-favorite with Palmer in the Masters. This seemed sort of ridiculous to me. I hadn't won a pro tournament nor had I been in a position to, except at Doral—I might have broken through there had I mustered a better fourth round than my 73. In this connection, I had a talk right after Doral with Jim Gaquin, then the director of the PGA tournament bureau, which had bucked me up a good deal. I had received a good-sized check at Doral, but Jim sensed my disappointment with my finishing round and my general frustration at failing to win on the tour. "One of these days," he said, "you'll go into the final round of a tournament and shoot a 34 instead of a 39 on the back nine, and you'll win one. Then it will be easier. Some of the fellows out here are content just to finish in the money and collect a nice check each week. Then there are fellows like you who are used to winning and who must play winning golf to be happy with themselves. Not all of them become winners, but, in my experience, most of them do."

However, I didn't think I was ready to win the Masters—I wasn't hitting the ball that well—but since this was the first major tournament of the year, I wanted terribly to play four strong rounds and show my friends (and my critics) that my game hadn't slipped and had, in

185

fact, matured in some ways. Well, I didn't show them much. In my three previous starts in the Masters I had come up with at least one 75 that had killed my chances then and there. I did once again. It came on the second round after an opening 74, and I was darned lucky to make the 36-hole cut. Since I started the third round 13 shots back of the leader, Palmer, no one was especially impressed when I finished with two fairly good rounds, a 70 and a 72. I couldn't blame them. I ended up tied for eleventh, which looks all right in the record book, but I was never a force in the tournament.

Palmer, by the way, won that Masters, his third, defeating Player and Finsterwald in a playoff. The day before, Arnold had tossed away a commanding lead, but being Arnold, he had bailed himself out at the eleventh hour with a birdie on the 70th (where he holed a wedge chip) and another on the 71st. Then he nailed down the playoff with a 32, four under par, on the in-nine. There was a man who knew how to win. Three weeks later, as some of you may recall, he went off on the most fabulous streak of his career. He won the Texas Open with a birdie on the 72nd. Then he won the Tournament of Champions by holing a 25-footer for a birdie on the 72nd. The following week he won the Colonial, at Fort Worth, beating Johnny Pott in a playoff with a subpar burst on the second nine. Most of these heroics were visible on television, and after this, Arnold, who had been a hero only to golfers, was a hero to everyone.

My own fortunes improved in the weeks following the Masters. After tying for seventh at Greensboro, I finished in a three-way tie for first with Bobby Nichols and Dan Sikes in the Houston Classic. The evening before the final round, when Dan and I were having dinner together, he said, "Jack, I've just got a feeling that one of the two of us is going to win this tournament." We came close, anyhow. In the playoff, Dan and Bobby had 71s—I had a glittering 76—and Bobby then defeated Dan on the first hole of the sudden-death overtime.

I skipped the next event, the Texas Open, but the week after that, when the fellows who had won tournaments were in Las Vegas for the Tournament of Champions, I joined the also-rans at the Waco Turner Open in Burneyville, Oklahoma. I tied for third there, and the following week was fourth in the Colonial. Then, in mid-May, I did a rather foolish thing. Earlier in the year, when I had been collecting all those flyweight checks, Mark McCormack had sounded me out as to whether I'd like to go to England in the spring and play in the 72-hole Piccadilly tournament that the Carreras tobacco people were putting on. (This was the forerunner, in a way, of the Piccadilly World Match-Play Championship, established in 1964, which is held annually in October.) When Mark had broached the idea of playing in a British tournament, I was all for it: I figured I could use a couple of hundred bucks.

At any rate, I flew over two days before the tournament, which was set up so that the first two rounds were split between Southport & Ainsdale and Hillside and the last two were held on Hillside. These are two of the many links clustered along the Irish Sea just north of Liverpool. (Birkdale, which is right next to them, was used for parking cars.) It was a dismal expedition. The weather was bitter cold and damp. I never adjusted to the time change—London is five hours ahead of New York—and was yawning during the daytime and wide awake at midnight. Forget about that. I simply played rotten golf: 79, 71, 70, 78. I learned a couple of things the hard way. First, a golfer can't pop over to Britain just before a tournament, switch to the small ball, and expect to produce anything like his best game. (Tony Lema managed this successfully in winning the 1964 British Open, but I think of Tony's victory as the exception that proves the rule.) Second, the field of British pros, augmented by pros from Ireland, continental Europe, South Africa, and Australia, was much more formidable than I had imagined it would be. I realized that spring how narrow the gulf between the American pros and the foreign pros had become.

I returned home in a discouraged mood. The Open, at Oakmont, was only three weeks off, and unless I got my game straightened out, I probably wouldn't finish even in the first thirty. I decided not to play in the Memphis Open and devote a week solely to practice. It went well. I decided also to familiarize myself with Oakmont. In the middle of that week I flew to Pittsburgh and played Oakmont twice. On those rounds I stepped off every fairway on the par 4s and 5s, measuring the distance from the tee to each fairway trap, then the distance from those traps (or some other permanent feature) to the front and back edges of the greens. On the par 3s I took some permanent feature near the tee, such as a tree or simply the front bank of the tee, and measured the distances to the front and back edges of the green. In the 1961 Amateur at Pebble Beach, to help me in my club selection, I had started this practice of charting the yardages and marking them down on a scorecard I carried throughout the tournament. Deane Beman, who had been doing this for a number of years, had suggested I try it. I found it to be an invaluable aid, so after that, knowing its worth, the chore of pacing off a course was never tedious for me. During my reconnaissance of Oakmont, two things stood out. First, good driving would be imperative, since the rough was thick and several new fairway-flanking traps had been added to the course's record number — something in the vicinity of 250. Second, a very high standard of putting would be required on the large, weaving greens.

My mind, I think, was still half on Oakmont and the Open when I started my first round the next week in the Thunderbird Classic at the Upper Montclair Club, in New Jersey, even though a record purse of $100,000 was at stake. I was out to get a good slice of the cake, of course, but a corner of my concentration was devoted to checking my putting to make sure that my ball had the proper rotation, and to checking my driving to make sure the ball was moving properly from left to right. From time to time, sometimes because injuries made it difficult for me to play left-to-right, I have had periods when I have played the ball for a draw instead of for a fade. When I draw the ball, I am a very ordinary player. Moreover, it is beyond my abilities, evidently, to play right-to-left for as short a period as three weeks before the draw becomes an outright hook.

At Upper Montclair, a good course with a number of exacting holes, I started with a 69 and

a 73, and was close to the leaders. On the third round, I three-putted the first three greens, and on the fourth hole I pulled my drive under a shrub. After hacking it out left-handed, I hit the green with my approach and got down a fair-sized putt for my par. This gave me such a lift that I couldn't do anything wrong the rest of the round. I birdied ten of the last fourteen holes for a 65 and a share of the lead with Dow Finsterwald. On the last round I was paired with Gene Littler, who was a shot behind us. All Gene did was birdie the 1st, 2nd, 3rd, 5th, 7th, 9th, and 11th. (A pity about that birdie on the 2nd — it ruined the pattern.) Gene made a few mistakes coming in, so when we arrived at the last hole, a 600-yard par 5, his lead was down to three strokes. I reached the home green in two with two well-hit 3-woods. Gene, bunkered off the tee, was bunkered again on his third, before the green. He played a fairly good explosion and lay four, 12 feet from the flag. I still had a chance, though a small one. If I could hole the 20-footer I had for my eagle 3 and if Gene missed his putt, I'd pick up three shots and we'd be tied. I made a good run at that 20-footer but when it slid by, that was that. Gene then finished his superb pressure round in style by holing for his par. His prize money was $25,000 and mine was $10,000.

This was by far my largest haul — it boosted me to seventh place, I think, among the money-winners — but I meant every word I said when I told some friends that night that I would rather have won the Thunderbird and received only $500. I had now played sixteen pro tournaments and still hadn't won a single one. I was beginning to wonder if I ever would.

The 1962 Open marked the fourth time that Oakmont had been the venue of the national championship. (I had picked up *venue* on my trip to England — about the only thing I did pick up.) Situated about twenty miles from downtown Pittsburgh, Oakmont is routed over strong, hilly countryside — the foothills of the Alleghenies. Today the Pennsylvania Turnpike cuts through the course. Eleven holes are on the clubhouse side, and a footbridge over the turnpike takes you to the other seven holes, the second through the eighth.

Oakmont has always been respected as one

of the most fearsome of the regular Open courses. Along with its rugged terrain and its ample length, it is pocked, as I mentioned earlier, with over 200 bunkers. As if this weren't enough, the bunkers are given a special treatment: they are furrowed with a deep-toothed wooden rake. For the 1962 Open the furrows in the bunkers were not very deep but even the light furrowing worried the field. If your ball came to rest between two ridges of sand, a conventional recovery was out of the question; all you could do was splash the ball out as best you could. Furrowing the bunkers had begun years before at Oakmont. Since the course had a clayey soil, it wasn't feasible to dig deep bunkers, for this would have presented a drainage problem. William Fornes, Jr., who for many years was the club's one-man green committee, thereupon decreed that the bunkers be furrowed to compensate for their comparative shallowness.

Oakmont's greens are also celebrated. They can be fast as lightning. At the start of the 1962 Open, they had a nice pace to them, but one knew that by Saturday's double round they were bound to be pretty slick, which indeed they were. It should be stated that the greens were hardly as severe as they had been for earlier championships. During the 1935 Open, they had been like glass — a main reason why Sam Parks, the unexpected winner, had been the only man in the field to break 300 for his four rounds. Eight years before that, when Oakmont had held its first Open — the one in which Tommy Armour beat Harry Cooper in a playoff — *no one* had broken 300. Finally, in the 1953 Open, Oakmont had been tamed: Ben Hogan's winning total was 283. Oakmont, however, had still dominated the rest of the field. Sam Snead, the runner-up, was six shots back of Hogan at 289, and Lloyd Mangrum, the third man, another three shots back at 292. As a matter of fact, on the final two rounds that year, the par of 72 was broken only six times, and there wasn't a single round below 70. For the 1962 Open, par was 71; the first hole, previously a short par 5 down a hillside, had been converted into a long par 4. There were some other minor changes, but none of them affected the course's fundamental character. In Oakmont

we were up against a real test that called for superior driving to hit and hold the sweeping fairways, for first-class iron play to the well-protected greens, and for excellent approach putting across fast, dipping contours. If you weren't right at the top of your game — forget it.

I was paired with Arnold the first two rounds. We drew enormous galleries. Latrobe, Arnold's hometown, is only thirty-five miles outside Pittsburgh, and his local admirers were in full force — and full throat — to root him on to victory, which seemed like a reasonable probability. From tee to green Arnold's game was sharp. If his putting on those first two rounds had been up to his usual standard, he could have been out in front at the halfway mark by two or three strokes. As it was, his 139 (71—68) placed him in a tie for the lead at that point with Bob Rosburg. Billy Maxwell was at 141, with Nichols, Player, and me at 142. Littler was at 143, and Rodgers at 144 despite an 8 on the first round on the seventeenth, a short uphill par 4, where his drive had lodged itself in a small evergreen.

I hadn't played quite as well as Arnold those first two rounds but I hadn't played badly. From the moment I had gotten back to Oakmont after the Thunderbird, I had been in an almost ideal frame of mind, burning with energy and low-register assurance. On my tune-up round on the Monday, I had a 71 and then had practiced till nine. Tuesday I played with Burke, Finsterwald, and Dickinson. We all played pretty well, one or two over. Following that round, I practiced driving for an hour, and after chipping and putting for another hour, I went out to play the handy three-hole loop — the twelfth, thirteenth, and fourteenth. I was hitting my shots so well I went on and played the last four holes, finishing four under par. I don't know what possessed me that day, but I still wasn't ready to quit. A little before nine, I was out practicing my putting, oblivious of the darkness and a light drizzle, when a member strolled onto the practice green and offered me his flashlight.

At the start of my opening round on Thursday, I was in this same go-at-'em mood. I birdied the first three holes, the first and the second with relatively short putts, and the third by sinking a 50-foot wedge chip. You can't ride roughshod over Oakmont like that, and by the ninth (where I took two to get out of a fairway bunker and also visited a drainage ditch) I had given those three strokes back to par and one more to boot. Then I settled down and played the in-nine in par. On Friday, I was one under going out, and again came back in par. I was doing the two most important things right: I was staying out of the rough off the tee, and I was handling the greens well. A half-dozen times I had mis-read the speed of a green on a lengthy approach putt and left myself a five- or six-footer, but I'd made them all. In fact, I hadn't three-putted a green. If I continued to play like that, maybe I could still win the Open.

On Saturday, a warm and cloudless day, I was paired for the final 36 with Billy Maxwell, al-ways a congenial partner. Arnold, paired with Bob Rosburg, was playing just behind us. A 72 in the morning enabled me to gain a stroke on Arnold and move within two shots of him. After 54 holes, Arnold was tied for the lead with Nich-ols at 212, Rodgers was at 213, and I was at 214. Arnold, I gathered, had played better than his score, a 73. His putting was still letting him down. He had taken 38 putts and had missed three 2-footers. One had come on the home green after Arnold had eagled the 292-yard sev-enteenth by driving the green and dropping a 12-footer. Otherwise he would have been the undisputed leader with a round to go.

With ten holes to go, Palmer *was* the undis-puted leader, well on his way to winning his second Open. In retrospect, the pivotal hole was the ninth. A par 5 only 480 yards long, it is uphill all the way from tee to green. There's a sizable bunker directly in front of the green, so getting home in two requires two big blows. Coming to the ninth, Arnold, one under par for the round, led me by three strokes. Though I am not abso-lutely sure of my arithmetic, I believe he led the other two remaining contenders, Rodgers and Nichols, by either two or three strokes. Rodgers was on about the fourteenth, Nichols on about the twelfth, and I was coming off the tenth when Arnold·was driving on the ninth. He hit a long tee-shot and then a strong second that cleared the trap in front. It was pushed a little, though, and the ball finished not on the green but in the

tangle of rough along the right edge. Still, Arnold was only 50 feet from the flag, so there was a good chance he would be able to get down in two for a birdie 4 and widen his lead. He fluffed his wedge chip, however, advancing the ball only a few yards and leaving it in the rough. His fourth was a wedge chip about seven feet from the cup, but when he failed to hole the putt, that was a 6. Instead of bolstering his lead by a shot, he had lost a shot. Now he led me by only two. A moment later, when I got down an eight-footer for a birdie on the eleventh, he led me by only one. Now I had a darn good chance. I matched par on the next three holes. Arnold did the same, but when he bogeyed the short thirteenth (his tee-shot found the bunker to the right of the green), he had lost the last shot of his lead. Up ahead Phil Rodgers had fallen off the pace with bogeys on the fifteenth and sixteenth, and Bobby Nichols' bid was over when he missed his par on the fifteenth and later on the eighteenth. Down the stretch it was to be a two-man fight.

Playing as carefully as I could, I completed my round with an unbroken string of pars. So did Arnold. Accordingly, we finished tied at 283 — 72, 70, 72, 69 for me, 71, 68, 73, 71 for Arnold — and a playoff was necessary.

My pars on the closing holes had not come as easily as Arnold's. On the sixteenth I had to hole a hard three-footer up a slope, and on the next green I had as worrisome a four-footer as I have ever faced. I had tried to drive the green on that mongrel par 4 — 292 yards up the side of a hill to a green closed in by bunkers, save for a narrow gap on the left. I had aimed for the opening, naturally, but I pushed the shot and put it into the right side of the large front bunker, a deep one. Considering that the ball was wedged in the groove between two ridges of sand, I came within inches of playing a super recovery. Had my explosion shot carried a foot farther, it would have landed on the trimmed fringe of the green, and since it had little or no backspin on it be-cause of the lie I had played from, it might possibly have rolled within birdie distance of the pin, positioned at the right center of the green. As it was, my ball died just where it landed in the rough, and from there I ran my chip four feet past. (Thanks to a lesson from Art Wall on the eve of the tournament on how to chip from the rough bordering the greens, I chipped well throughout the Open.)

I get goose pimples just thinking of that short putt. Overall, there was a faint break to the left to take into account, but the cup itself was sitting on a little left-to-right slope. I didn't dare play a touch putt off the double roll at that stage of the championship—I couldn't count on having the nerve or the delicacy. The wisest course, I decided, was to aim for the left-center of the cup and hit the ball firmly so that neither break would really affect its line. I blasted it into the middle of the cup. (This was the putt of which Bob Jones, who had watched it on television, wrote me, "I almost jumped right out of my chair.") Arnold, on the other hand, had a crack at a 12-footer for a birdie on the seventeenth. I had been very lucky, for that was exactly the kind of clutch putt he had been making in tournament after tournament that spring. On the last green, where I had missed a birdie putt of approximately 15 feet, Arnold had another crack at a birdie putt, a 12-footer slightly uphill, that would have won for him. This was a much more difficult putt to make, for the cup was cut at the top of a tiny knob. As I watched Arnold from the scorers' tent, I was a trifle less relaxed than Don Knotts, but having had just about the same putt myself, I thought there was a fair chance that Arnold might be fooled by the line, as I had been. I had played my putt straight for the cup, and as it crept up the knob, it had veered off to the right. Arnold must have played his same way. It veered off just the way mine had.

On Saturday I had worn what I thought was a very snazzy outfit, a white T-shirt and a pair of iridescent olive pants. Few of my friends shared my enthusiasm for those trousers. Barbara hated them—my "army refugee pants," she called them. Nevertheless, I wore them again for the playoff. Like many athletes, I am superstitious when it comes to that sort of stuff. If things are going right, I don't want to disturb them. I'll wear the same outfit, order the same breakfast, collect a Coke at the same stand on the course, eat at the same restaurant at night. When I'm playing a tournament, anyway, I love to set up a routine. When I'm home, just the opposite.

It was an exciting playoff. To begin with, the gallery—a Palmer gallery, of course—was really up for it. Some years later, Tom Fitzgerald of the Boston *Globe* told me that he couldn't recall a rougher gang of spectators at a golf tournament. "At one green, when you were lining up your putt," Tom said, "I was standing in front of a couple of bruisers and I couldn't believe my ears. 'Walk around, Arnie baby,' one of them was yelling. 'That'll shake him up.' Things like that. I thought I was at a wrestling match." But I didn't find Arnie's Army disconcerting that day. I don't think any golfer does if he's playing well, and I was fortunate enough to be at my best. I was never behind during the playoff.

On the first, which I parred, Arnold went one over when he missed his second. (The afternoon before, at the start of the fourth round, I had three-putted the first—my first three-putt green of the tournament and, as it turned out, my only one.) After six holes I was out in front by four shots. I'd birdied the fourth, and on the short sixth, which I birdied, Arnold had three-putted for a bogey. A four-stroke margin is no margin, though, when you're up against a competitor like Palmer who believes in his star. I kept telling myself not to let up, and I don't think I did, but one by one those four strokes started to slip away. I lost one on the ninth, the par 5 up the hill. Arnold birdied it after chipping to four feet. I lost another when he birdied the eleventh by punching a great pitch a yard from the pin. I lost one more on the twelfth, a par 5 598 yards long, on which Arnold made his 4 after almost reaching the green with two big woods. Even with my lead whittled down to a single stroke, I still felt quite composed, since I had continued to play my shots well. Yet with Arnold off on one of his charges, I wondered if my best would be good enough.

I didn't stop Arnold's charge. He stopped it himself on the thirteenth, a rather undistinguished par 3 that is 161 yards long. Arnold, as you know, allows for right-to-left draw on most of his shots. On the thirteenth, going with a 6-iron, I think, his timing was a shade fast. The draw didn't take and the ball hung out on the right. It looked for a moment as if it would catch the bunker to the right of the green, but it came down inches to the left of it, and bouncing off the outside bank of the hazard, kicked sharply to the left, well onto the green. This was a terrific break for Arnold. Most uncharacteristically, he failed to exploit it. He three-putted. My lead was back to two again.

A two-stroke lead is an entirely different thing than a one-shot lead with five holes to go. Except for the seventeenth, none of those five holes was what you would call a birdie hole. I felt that if I could match par in, hole by hole, I would not be tied. I played four good pars in a row, and when we came to the eighteenth my two-stroke lead was still intact. I was almost home.

On the tee of the eighteenth, a swaybacked 462-yard par 4, I made an error. In my anxiety, I let my right hand get into my drive too quickly, and I pull-hooked it into the edge of the heavy rough. The ball ended up in a really ugly lie, lodged tight on hard ground and half-covered by coarse, bunchy grass. Arnold's drive was down the fairway. He was away, and I watched carefully as he played his second. After much deliberation, he hit what looked to me like a 3-iron. He must have caught the ball a little fat. Halfway in its flight it began to slide off to the right. I came down short of the green and rolled into rough fringing the green on the right. With a two-stroke lead and Arnold off the green, I could afford to play a cautious, conservative recovery from the rough—I felt sure a 5 could win. There was no sense trying to carry the bunker in the middle of the fairway 130 yards away and about 80 yards from the green. If I put it in the bunker, it could be disastrous. Accordingly, I played a pitching wedge from the rough and laid up safely short of the bunker. I had only a 9-iron left, and hit a good pitch 12 feet to the left of the pin. Arnold needed a miracle shot now. He took a wedge. The ball jumped out of the rough fast, bounded for the hole, nearly hit the pin, and ran past it on the right—well past. It was all over. Arnold missed his tap-in when we putted out, but this had no bearing on anything except our final scores, a 71 and a 74.

I walked off the green in a slight daze. I knew that I had won the Open Championship, but when you have thought about something for years and it finally happens, your emotion blurs the whole scene and makes it unreal. Gradually I settled down and merely walked on air.

A good many things happened after that. I made the cover of *Time*. I was in great demand for exhibition appearances. Back in Columbus a Jack Nicklaus Day was organized by my friend Bob Barton. There was a parade to the State House with confetti, ticker tape, and all the rest. I rode in one car with Barbara, my folks rode in another, Jack Grout and a delegation of local professionals in a third, and so on. That was the best thing about it—all my old friends were in the act, including Stanley Crooks, the first man who had looked on me as a golfer who might develop into a champion and follow in the footsteps of Bobby Jones. Later that summer Arnold and I played an exhibition at Scioto, one of the several we played.

My own reaction after winning the championship was to try to perform like a true champion and play better golf than I had done before. I think I did, for the most part. Most of the problems that had cropped up during the winter when I was adjusting to the professional tour— my erratic driving, my troubles with my putting, my unorthodox elbow position, my inability to weed out bad rounds and to finish strongly, the difficulties of getting used to the playing conditions of tour courses, the constant travel, and all the rest—had resolved themselves, temporarily at least. With the exception of the British Open, at Troon, where my golf was as dismal as Arnold's was remarkable, I didn't play a bad tournament the rest of the year. In the Western, at Medinah, a tie for eighth; in the PGA, at Aronomink, a tie for third; in the Canadian Open, at Laval-sur-le-Lac, a tie for fifth; in the American Golf Classic, at Firestone in Akron, a tie for third. In early September I won the first World Series of Golf, a television event in which, as the U. S. Open champion, I met Arnold, the Masters and the British Open champion, and Gary, the PGA champion. Later that month I won two tour tournaments, the Seattle World's Fair Open and the Portland Open. Financially, too, it had turned out to be a tremendous year for me. Palmer led the money-winners with $82,456.23, Littler was second with $67,969.01, and I came third with $62,933.59.

Inevitably, there were a few sour notes, and I should mention them. In the second round of the Portland Open, I was penalized two strokes for slow play by the PGA tournament supervisor, Joe Black. No one was more aware than I that I had become a slow player — far slower than I wanted to be or meant to be. I don't know how it was I fell into the habit, but I suppose it came from trying to check too many things before each shot and from a conscious resolve not to hurry things. Joe's explanation for assessing the penalty was that I had failed to heed a warning at the ninth hole to speed up. That wasn't quite right. I had tried to speed up. Our threesome — Bill Casper and Bruce Crampton — played the back nine in 1 hour and 48 minutes and we completed our round in 3 hours and 50 minutes, ten minutes faster than we had the day before. Besides, I wasn't the only slow player on the tour by a long shot, and I felt I was being singled out unfairly.

The slow-play habit, let me say, is like the cigarette habit — it is so hard to break that a man is wisest not to begin it. Some weeks now I play at a good quick pace but, all in all, I haven't entirely licked my tendency to play too slow.

Having mentioned cigarettes, I am reminded that I gave up smoking on the golf course that summer. One of the scenes in the movie the USGA made of the Open showed me on the thirteenth green during the playoff picking up my cigarette after my approach putt and then put-ting out with the cigarette hanging from my mouth. I had never realized before how disgusting a golfer looks when he does that. Then and there I decided to smoke only socially, away from the tournaments.

The other sour note was struck by the dean of the College of Commerce at Ohio State. Following the Portland Open, I had returned to Ohio State for the fall quarter — I needed to make up three quarters I'd missed in order to graduate. When it came to the dean's attention that I planned to leave college for two weeks that autumn to play in two tournaments in Australia — this was a part of my contract with the Slazenger company — he asked me to withdraw from college. I thought that I could meet my golf commitments and still keep up academically — I was doing all right — but the dean was adamant and I had to withdraw.

Everything considered, though, 1962, the longest year of my life, was a very happy one. The complicated transition to professional golf had gone all right, finally. The first tournament I had won turned out to be the Open, which had been way beyond my dreams. Six months later, I was still getting used to it.

(1969)

Placing Jack Nicklaus in History
Robert Sommers

Since his first full year as a golf professional, when he defeated Arnold Palmer in a playoff for the United States Open title at Oakmont, Jack Nicklaus has been the most dominant figure in golf. And to the two Amateur Championships he won before turning pro, he has since added seventeen major professional titles, far more than his predecessor greats in golf.

But has he dominated the game more than Harry Vardon did, or Bob Jones or Ben Hogan? Bob Jones gave me the right answer many years ago when he observed, "You can only hope to be the best of your time."

There is no question that Jack is the best of his time, but how does he stack up against the aforementioned Vardon, Jones and Hogan? The question also obviously intrigued Robert Sommers when he did an in-depth comparison with particular emphasis on Nicklaus's accomplishments.

Bob Sommers was unusually well-qualified for the job. As editor and publisher of the Golf Journal, *which is published by the United States Golf Association, he has access to the most extensive library of golf literature in the world, including the observations and analyses of the writers who were witnesses to those before Nicklaus.*

Sommers has been a serious and perceptive observer of golf for more than a quarter-century, first as a writer for the Evening Sun *of Baltimore and, since 1965, in his present capacity with the* Journal. *His latter assignment has been anything but provincial and, as a result, he has been able to impart to his writing a worldwide perspective which has proved to be invaluable in this article dealing with the accomplishments of Nicklaus. Besides the evaluation, Sommers traces the day-to-day play of the 1980 Open at Baltusrol and the manner in which Jack rose to the challenge to reassert his pinnacle position.*

Quite frankly, I can find no fault with Sommers's ultimate conclusion, but I also would not contradict what Bob Jones said so many years ago.

IN THE AFTERGLOW of Jack Nicklaus's victory in the 80th United States Open Championship, in June, which he won with a record score of 272 for 72 holes over the Lower Course of the Baltusrol Golf Club, in Springfield, New Jersey, it seems appropriate that we address ourselves to the question of his place in history; whether he is the game's consummate player, or whether he is something less than that; whether he belongs in the same company with Harry Vardon, Bob Jones, and Ben Hogan, the three primary players of the last century, or whether he is a notch below them in rank.

Debates of this sort, of course, are never wholly satisfactory—no one is ever entirely convinced one way or another because so much rests on subjective analysis—but it seems worthwhile to examine some of the evidence.

To begin with, no one questions that Nicklaus is the best golfer of his time. He has been the dominant player on the PGA Tour almost from the time he became a professional late in 1961, when Arnold Palmer was at his peak. Since then he has won 67 tournaments in the United States and Great Britain, and who knows how many others in Australia, South Africa, New Zealand, Europe—wherever the game is played. Confining ourselves strictly to the PGA Tour, only Sam Snead, with 84, has won more. Whether his record entitles him to equal status with Vardon, Jones, and Hogan is another matter, and not everyone will agree that it does.

Their arguments, however, were at least weakened if not destroyed by what Nicklaus accomplished at Baltusrol. Consider this: His victory was his fourth in the Open, something that had been done only by Jones, Hogan, and Willie Anderson, a mysterious figure from the early years of the century who won four times within five years. Nicklaus won his first in 1962, and so his four Open Championships span 18 years. No one else has ever won our Open over so long a period. Julius Boros won his two 11 years apart, and Gene Sarazen won twice over 10 years. Nicklaus's score of 272 at Baltusrol was three strokes under the previous record 275 that he himself set in 1967 over the same course (matched a year later by Lee Trevino at the Oak Hill Country Club, in Rochester, New York). In a remarkable four-day period, Nicklaus also equalled the 18-hole record by shooting 63 in the first round, set the 36-hole record at 134 and the 54-hole record at 204 (also matched by Isao Aoki of Japan, who finished second, with 274). Nicklaus was never out of the lead, although he was tied at the end of 18 holes and 54 holes, and he did all this at the age of 40, when only the rare golfer still has his competitive edge. As a matter of fact, since the Open began in 1895, only Boros, Hogan and Ted Ray, an English contemporary of Vardon, won the Open after they passed 40.

This was also his 18th victory in what is popularly called the "major" competitions—U. S. and British Opens, the Masters Tournament and the PGA Championship, and, in Nicklaus's case, the U. S. Amateur. In addition to winning the Open four times, he has also won the Masters five times, the British Open three, the PGA four and the Amateur twice.

How, then, do we measure his standing in the game? By the number of tournaments he has won, by the scores he shot, by the number of "majors" he's won, or by a combination of them all, never forgetting our personal prejudices?

To use the number of major tournament victories as a gauge would be fatuous. Vardon, for example, would be out of the running. He won the British Open six times and the United States Open only once. In his time, however, a period that began in the late 19th century and extended into the 20th, the British Open was the *only* tournament for professionals that mattered. The U. S. Open was hardly worth the effort for a British golfer, and, we must remember, in that period the British were the best. When Vardon won the U. S. Open in 1900, he played only because he was here on an exhibition tour.

Hogan, too, falls short by that standard. His major accomplishments, in addition to his four U. S. Open victories, are made up of two PGA Championships, two Masters Tournaments, and one British Open. The career of Jones was built around four competitions, the Open and Amateur Championships of the United States and Great Britain. He won 13 of those, and for a period of eight consecutive years, he was never without one of those Championships.

We must also remember that the Masters is relatively new. Of those four players, only Hogan and Nicklaus competed in it seriously; Vardon didn't play at all, and Jones did only after he had been retired four years. We must also remember that, while it began in 1934, it did not become the important competition it is today until after World War II. Remember, too, that in the 'teens and 1920s, the Western Open was every bit as important as the Masters is today. Walter Hagen won the Western five times. Combine this with his two U. S. Open Championships, his four British Opens, and five PGA Championships (four of them in succession) and he has 16 victories, as many as Nicklaus since Jack became a professional.

What, then, about scoring? Nicklaus currently holds the 72-hole record for the Open and shares with Ray Floyd the Masters 72-hole record (271), but how can his scores be compared to those of Vardon's day? Obviously they can't. Equipment is different—clubs are made better and the ball is more reliable—and courses are tended differently. Putting is ever so more important today than it was in the Vardon era, and even the Jones era. Greens are so well cared for today, the player knows that if he reads the putt correctly and strokes it properly, it can do nothing else but go into the hole. Watering systems, too, have had their effect. Greens are basically softer, although the USGA tries to assure that they are firm and fast for an Open Championship. They certainly are not as hard as they were in 1950 at the Merion Golf Club, in Ardmore, Pennsylvania, where only the crisply hit ball would stay near where it landed once it hit the green. Golf is an easier game to play today.

We have to accept, also, that each generation sets its own scoring records. Hogan held the 72-hole records in both the Open (276 in 1948) and the Masters (274 in 1953), and Vardon set the British Open record at 300, in 1903. Strangely enough, Jones did not hold the scoring record for either the United States or the British Opens, but he did equal the low score for the Amateur qualifying round with 142 for 36 holes in both 1927 and 1930. What he did best of all was win.

When Nicklaus won at Baltusrol in June, it had been eight years since his previous Open

Championship, at Pebble Beach, in California, in 1972. Twice before that he had gone five years between Open victories. Although he was always a man to be dealt with in any tournament, he didn't seem to dominate the Open as both Jones and Hogan did in their best years. Jones, as we all know, won—in 1923, 1926, 1929, and 1930—four of eight Opens and he also finished second three times during that period. Hogan won four of six—1948, 1950, 1951, and 1953. Consider also that while Nicklaus clearly has the edge over both Jones and Hogan in longevity, Vardon, too, won over a period of 18 years, and also won four of eight British Opens early in his career.

Nicklaus has a few years to go to match a different kind of longevity. While Jones retired from championship golf at 28, both Vardon and Hogan were very serious contenders in the U. S. Open when they were much older than Nicklaus is today. Vardon was 50 years old in 1920 when he very nearly won the Open at Inverness Club, in Toledo, Ohio. He was leading by five strokes with seven holes to play when a gale blew in from Lake Erie, and he lost seven strokes on those last few holes. Remember, too, that in 1960, when Nicklaus, as a 20-year-old college boy, was making his first serious bid for the Open, Hogan was 47, and he very nearly won. After holing a 20-foot birdie putt on the 15th hole of the Cherry Hills Country Club, in Denver, Colorado, Hogan was tied for the lead with just three holes to play. His tee-to-green golf that day was magnificent. This was the era of the double round, and Hogan hit 34 consecutive greens. He missed on the 17th, and that cost him the Championship.

The point is that the methods of both Vardon and Hogan were so sound that even at their relatively advanced ages, from tee to green they could still play the game better than anybody. They failed on the greens in their later competitive years. Nicklaus today plays the game from tee to green better than anybody. He hit 59 greens at Baltusrol, only two fewer than he did when he won there in 1967, and, with that, he had the best percentage of greens hit of those who play the PGA Tour. Of 684 holes he played in 38 rounds through the Open, he hit 497 greens for a percentage of .727. And, for a few days in June, anyway, he once again became a great holer of putts.

For a time, when he was at the peak of his game, Hogan was a great 10-foot putter. The suspicion lingers, however, that Nicklaus is better. He is perhaps the best clutch putter we've seen since Jones. Jones always seemed to hole the putt he had to hole; Nicklaus always seems to drop the crucial putt, too.

Whenever we think of Jones and Hogan, we tend to remember that each had that one overpowering season when he simply could not be beaten (Vardon must be excused from this argument since he had only the British Open). Jones had his great year in 1930 when he entered entered seven tournaments and won six, including the Open and Amateur Championships of both the United States and Great Britain, the Grand Slam. For Hogan it was 1953, when he entered six tournaments and won five, including the United States and British Opens and the Masters Tournament. No one else has ever won those three in the same year. For those who wonder about the PGA, he had not played in it since his automobile accident, in 1949, and even if he had chosen to play in 1953, he could not have won both the PGA and the British Open because they conflicted in dates. The final match of the PGA was played the same day as the first qualifying round of the British Open, and Hogan had to qualify. (The conditions are different now; the U. S. Open Champion is exempt from qualifying for the British Open.)

Sometimes we forget that in 1972 Nicklaus was very good, indeed. In addition to winning five tournaments on the PGA Tour, he won both the Open and the Masters, finished 13th in the PGA, and finished second in the British Open by one stroke when Lee Trevino chipped into the hole on the 17th at Muirfield, in Scotland. Still, second is not first, and Nicklaus has not yet won three in a single year.

One further point of comparison. These four men—Vardon, Jones, Hagen, and Nicklaus—seem to fit neatly into two categories. In method and style, Vardon and Hogan seem to be of a kind, and Jones and Nicklaus appear to be of a pattern. It was often said of Vardon that he could not play the same course twice in one day because in the second round he'd be playing from his divot holes of the first. That was fantasy, of course, but we do know that both he and Hogan could place their tee shots probably more precisely, both for length and for direction, than anyone who ever played the game. During the last day of the 1953 British Open, for example, we do know that for those 36 holes Hogan always seemed to be playing his second shots from level lies while Hector Thompson, his playing companion that day, always seemed to have one foot above the other. Hogan and Vardon reduced the game to mathematical certainty.

Jones and Nicklaus, on the other hand, appeared to be a bit more unpredictable. While Jones and Nicklaus both hit a lot of greens, Jones often won when he seemed to have thrown away his best chance, and Nicklaus hit a lot of those greens from the rough. It is, moreover, one of Jack's great strengths that he can reach greens from the rough. That is not to say that he spends most of his time there, or that he manufactures birdies from sows' ears, but he is not the precision player that Hogan was or that Vardon was. Still, it is difficult to believe that anyone could have played nine holes better than Nicklaus's final nine at Baltusrol. It was as close to perfection as we are likely to see in this life.

To sum up, in Nicklaus we have a man whose career as a serious threat in the U. S. Open spanned 20 years, from 1960, when he finished second to Arnold Palmer by two strokes; who is the longest straight driver the game has known; as good a holer of crucial putts as ever lived, possibly the best putter of all the great players; and a man who holds the 72-hole scoring record for the Open and is co-holder of the 72- and the 18-hole (64) records for the Masters.

With credentials like this, does he deserve to be included among the four best the game has known? Yes, he does. Does he stand above the others? No, he doesn't. While his record surpasses those others, it is also true that Vardon, Jones, and Hogan raised the game to new levels. Watching Hogan, for example, we were almost convinced that if he hit a shot into a bunker, well, that's the way the hole should be played.

We were also left with the memories of Bobby Cruickshank placing a sizable bet on Jones to win the Grand Slam even before he sailed for Britain in 1930, and of that hazy morning in 1970 when Hogan played the first round of the Houston Open followed by a gallery that included, among other players of prominence, Hale Irwin and R. H. Sikes (after the round, Sikes spent 10 minutes studying a shot-by-shot account).

We are probably too close to him to determine how or if Nicklaus has elevated the game, and he is too close to the other players to expect them to follow along in his gallery just to see him play, but his game is certainly the most admired by the rest of the players, and we may yet see them gawking at him as he drills a 1-iron at the heart of a distant green.

As the Open approached, Nicklaus was not given much consideration as a potential winner. He had been in what for him amounted to a dreadful slump, and he had given no indication that he was about to break out of it. He had not won a tournament since the Philadelphia Tour event, in July of 1978, and he had finished the 1979 season ranked 71st on the PGA Tour money-winning list after never before having been lower than fourth. Things looked no brighter in 1980. Until the Open, he had played in nine tournaments, and aside from a second place in the Doral-Eastern Open, in March, had finished in such unglamorous positions as 33d, 43d, and 53d. The week before the Open, he missed the 36-hole cut in Atlanta.

It was, therefore, a surprise when he went out on a sunny, windless Thursday and shot 63 over the Lower Course at Baltusrol. Now a man who shoots 63 in the first round of the Open figures to be in front by a few strokes. Not this year; Tom Weiskopf had 63, too. These were the lowest scores in the Open since John Miller shot 63 at the Oakmont Country Club, in Oakmont, Pennsylvania, near Pittsburgh, in the final round in 1973. They were only the beginning. Three others shot 66, three more 67, and altogether, 19 players broke par 70, the most ever in the first round. When the Championship was over, 49 rounds were played under par, the most ever, and

both Nicklaus and Isao Aoki broke the previous 72-hole record of 275. Tom Watson was stunned. "I just shot the third lowest score in the history of the Open," he said, "and lost by four strokes." Watson shot 276, the same as Keith Fergus and Lon Hinkle.

The scoring was surprising because Baltusrol is generally considered among our very best golf courses. While being good doesn't necessarily mean a course is brutally hard, scoring like this is extraordinary. If it proved anything, it demonstrated that when the greens are soft, today's breed of player might shoot any score. All day long they were throwing their shots right at the flagstick, and the ball was hitting and stopping. The reason why was easy to explain. New Jersey had had about 24 inches of rainfall since January 1, but the winter had been quite dry, and most of that rain had fallen in the spring. The bases of the greens, therefore, were soft. Then, rainstorms had struck on the Monday and Tuesday nights preceding the first round, on Thursday. Otherwise, the course was just about what had been expected. The fairways were fine, cut to about a half inch, and the rough was ample, although in places the grass had gown so tall it lay flat. Aside from their being soft, the greens were true and very fast, giving a reading of over 10 feet on the Stimpmeter scale, a device used for measuring green speed. (For the sake of comparison, the average American green will give a Stimpmeter reading of 6 feet 6 inches; a green that is considered fast by a club player will read about 8 feet 6 inches.)

The first indication that we were in for some unexpected scoring came from Raymond Floyd, one of the early starters in the first round. Par at Baltusrol is a bit uneven — 34 out and 36 in. After eight holes, Floyd was four under par, and he made the turn for home in 30 strokes, matching an Open record shared by five others. To give an indication of how the greens were holding, on his four birdies on the first nine, Floyd hit his approaches to 15 feet on the first hole, five inches on the fourth, eight feet on the sixth, and five feet on the eighth. He had no such luck coming back, shot 37, and finished with Jay Haas and Calvin Peete at 67.

Weiskopf began later in the day, playing just

a few holes ahead of Nicklaus, and was off to an uncertain start. He lost a stroke to par on the first, where he was bunkered, but then made four birdies for an out-going 31. He had two sizable putts on that nine, holing from 35 feet on the sixth, a very long par 4 of 470 yards, and from 18 feet on the eighth, shorter at 374 yards. Coming back he had four more birdies, his longest from 25 feet on the 15th, a very strong par 4 of 430 yards. He played the second nine in 32 for his 63.

Nicklaus, meanwhile, was out in 32 with three birdies and a bogey on the first nine. He lost a stroke on the second, an uphill par 4 of 377 yards, where he played a 1-iron from the tee and hit the ball under a pine tree. His longest birdie putt was from 35 feet on the fifth, and he also holed from three feet on the third and from 11 feet on the seventh, another 470-yard par 4.

Nicklaus effectively shifted into high gear coming back. He began firing his approach shots at the hole and birdied three straight, beginning with the 11th. He added another birdie on the 15th and still another on the 17th, at 630 yards, the longest hole in Open history.

He was then seven under par with a chance to break the record with 62 if he could birdie the 18th. Baltusrol is unusual in that it ends with two par-5 holes. The 18th is 542 yards in length, and in 1967, Nicklaus birdied it in the last round to shoot 65 and set the record. Here, with the single-round record in sight, he played two fine shots short of the green and the bunker that guards the opening, and then a lovely little pitch to three feet. His putt, however, never once looked as if it might fall. It was right of the hole all the way and he took his 63.

Hale Irwin, the 1979 Champion, couldn't get anything going and shot 70, and Lee Trevino, who had first come to prominence at Baltusrol in 1967, shot 68.

The second round began under unfortunate circumstances. Severiano Ballesteros, of Spain, who had won the 1979 British Open and the 1980 Masters, had played an indifferent round on Thursday, often driving into the rough and finding no way to reach the greens from there. He shot 75 and, truthfully, did rather well to score that low. On Friday morning he was late for his starting time of 9:45 and was disqualified. He said he was under the impression that he was to start an hour later, and he was delayed in traffic on the way from his hotel, about two miles away, and took approximately 25 minutes to make the trip.

Weiskopf was among the early starters, teeing off before 8 o'clock, and when he hit a 5-iron shot 30 feet from the hole on the first and holed it for a birdie 3, he looked as if he would keep up his amazing pace of the previous day. At that stage he was eight under par for 19 holes, and he seemed to be loose and relaxed. Weiskopf has looked this way before, though, and still not won. He gave that stroke back on the second, where he three-putted, and then ran into serious trouble on the sixth. He drove into the rough and needed four more shots to reach the green, where he holed from one foot for 6 on the par-4 hole. He followed that by three-putting from 12 feet on the seventh, and now instead of being eight under par he was four under. After a birdie on the 13th, he closed out by making three straight bogeys on the last three holes and shot 75, giving him a 36-hole score of 138, only two under par. Weiskopf was finished. He shot 76 and 75 in the last two rounds, 289 for the 72 holes, and was in 36th place.

Nicklaus, too, had a good start, and even though he lost strokes in mid-round, he held on for 71 and a 36-hole score of 134, a record low, and a two-stroke lead. Nicklaus birdied both the first and third holes, lost one stroke at the sixth, where he three-putted from 45 feet, and then dropped three more strokes at the 11th and 12th. The 11th is a 428-yard par 4 that doglegs sharply left around some tall evergreens. A bunker also guards the bend on the left, and that is precisely where Nicklaus hit his tee shot. He came out to mid-fairway, pitched on and took two putts for 5.

Worse was coming. The 12th is a 193-yard par 3, a very good hole with a cross bunker cutting in front of the green. Nicklaus played a 4-iron from the tee, but he hit it fat, and the ball plugged in the face of the bunker. He dug at it with his sand wedge and managed to pop it into the rough, still short of the green. From there he deliberately bladed a wedge, a shot he often uses when his ball is in rough just off the edge of a green. The ball shot out of the grass much faster than he anticipated, and if it had not hit the hole and jumped a few inches off the ground, it might have gone off the back of the green. Never mind: it stopped, and Nicklaus needed two putts, giving him 5 on a par 3. He was then two over par for the day, but he made up one stroke by holing from five feet on the 17th for a birdie, and then saved par on the 18th with a marvelous little pop shot over a bank and down to the hole after he overshot the green with his third. Bob Rosburg, the former PGA Champion who is now a broadcaster for ABC, was watching and said to Nicklaus, "People don't know how good that shot was." Nicklaus, grinning, answered, "But I do."

It was on this day that many spectators began to believe that Aoki is as good a putter as he looked in the first round. On the second nine of the second round, Aoki had only one two-putt green, the 12th. He one-putted all the others — 10 putts for nine holes. He also had but 13 on the first nine, giving him 23 for the day. In the first round he had but 27, and so for two rounds he had 50 putts. Weiskopf had 71. Aoki had two rounds of 68, giving him 136 for the 36 holes, and at this point he was tied for second place with Keith Fergus, Lon Hinkle, and Mike Reid. Mark Hayes was next at 137, followed by Weiskopf and Pat McGowan, at 138. Irwin had another par 70, but he was never really a factor in this Open.

Not much had been heard of Aoki before the Open, although he has played in many of the principal tournaments and is, of course, very well known in Japan. He played in the 1979 Open at Inverness, has been in the World Series of Golf three times, and has played in the Masters six times. He has won 32 tournaments, most of them in Japan, and in 1980 played in six tournaments in Japan and won two.

The next day Aoki's putting slipped somewhat. He used 31, but his tee-to-green golf was noticeably better and he shot still another 68. Nicklaus could have run away with the Open that day, but at the end he had to struggle to hold onto a tie with Aoki. Nicklaus shot 70, even par, but after seven holes he was two under par for the round and eight under for the 43 holes. He

was out in 32, but he lost control slightly on the home nine and lost strokes on both the 14th, where he drove into the right rough and then hit into the right greenside bunker, and the 15th, where he putted poorly, leaving a 20-footer six or seven feet short, and missing from there. After a par 3 at the 16th, Nicklaus topped his second shot on the 17th, a fairway wood. He had to play a 4-iron for his third shot, hit the ball beautifully, and saved his par. He had a chance for a birdie on the 18th when he reached the green with his second shot, but once again he three-putted.

Tom Watson, meanwhile, was making progress. Watson had come into the Open as one of the favorites, but he had a dull 71 in the opening round and lost much of his following. A 68 in the second round moved him closer to the lead, and then on Saturday he shot 67, and when the day ended he was two strokes behind the leaders, at 206, a stroke behind Hinkle, at 205, and tied with Hayes and Fergus.

In this same round, Hubert Green, the 1977 Open Champion, although well out of contention, shot 65, a round that included eight consecutive 3s, from the ninth hole through the 16th. He also had two more 3s earlier in the round, 10 for the day.

In the end, the Open settled into a duel between Nicklaus and Aoki, although several others were on the fringe of the action. Hayes dropped out early and finished with 74 for the day, but Fergus hung on and could have been a more serious threat if some putts had fallen. Watson was in trouble from the beginning, pushing his tee shot on the first hole into the trees and losing a stroke to par right away, and while Hinkle once came within a stroke of Nicklaus and actually into second place, passing Aoki, he soon fell back and finished the round with 71.

Nicklaus and Aoki played what amounted to match-play golf in the last round. Nicklaus went ahead by a stroke when Aoki bogeyed the second, and went two strokes ahead with a birdie from five feet on the third. Both men lost strokes on the fourth, the lovely par 3 with the pond in front, and after they played the fifth beautifully, Nicklaus lost control of his driver. He drove into the left rough on the sixth and the right rough on the seventh and eighth. He missed the sixth green but salvaged a par, missed the seventh green and dropped a stroke, but from the rough on the eighth he lofted a high pitch, onto the green and two-putted from 30 feet. Aoki birdied there to cut his deficit to one stroke, but he bogeyed the ninth while Nicklaus made his par, and never again was he closer than two strokes behind.

For one thing, Nicklaus wouldn't allow it. The tee shot on the eighth was his last error, the result of a technical flaw he corrected right then. After that his golf was of another world. He hit every fairway in just the right spot, and he hit every green. Not only was his direction flawless, but what was more, he gauged the distance of his shots perfectly. When the hole was on the back of the green, he hit the back of the green; when the hole was on the front, he hit the front. On the 10th, for example, the hole was well to the back. Nicklaus hit a driver to a level area right of center-fairway and then played a 7-iron hole-high three feet to the right. On the 11th, a hole that doglegs left, his tee shot found the perfect spot, beyond the bend of the dogleg and safely away from the bunkers on both right and left.

One flawless shot followed another. On the 15th, he hit the only shot that looked as if it was well off line, perhaps 25 or 30 feet left of the hole, but there is hardly any doubt that he aimed left of the hole and missed his target by no more than 10 or 15 feet, for the hole was cut to the rear right, and no one leading the Open by two strokes would have gone for the hole there.

Still, he could not shake Aoki, and when they stood on the 17th tee they remained just two strokes apart. Here Nicklaus hit a thunderous tee shot that arched high, as his shots usually do, and drifted very slightly right, coming to rest no less than 275 yards from the tee. An iron followed, over the cross bunkers and short of the rise before the green, with its scraggly rough and nests of bunkers. From there he pitched 20 feet

from the hole, but there was Aoki no more than five feet away, and Nicklaus knew with certainty that Aoki would not miss that putt. Nicklaus also knew that, to avoid a playoff, if not an outright loss of the Open, he would have to birdie either the 17th or the 18th.

His face was drawn as he stood over his putt, showing the strain he had been under these last four days, but he stroked the ball perfectly, and when it tumbled into the hole, the enormous crowd that had followed him around Baltusrol roared wildly, and Nicklaus grinned a grin we have not seen before. It was the grin of fulfillment and of immense satisfaction. The Open was his, barring an eagle-3 by Aoki on the 18th.

Aoki very nearly made that eagle. His third shot, a short little pitch, just missed the hole and stopped about three feet away. Nicklaus played a 3-wood from the tee, a 3-iron short of the green and pitched 10 feet from the hole. He said later that he was not trying to hole that putt, only roll it close, but it fell into the hole for another birdie. The crowd had broken through the restraining ropes and encircled the green, and now it began to charge toward him. Nicklaus held up his hand, palm toward the gallery, much as a traffic policeman halts onrushing cars, and the crowd stopped long enough for Aoki, predictably, to hole his putt.

As Aoki's putt dropped, New Jersey State Troopers grouped themselves around Nicklaus and led him through the cheering throng, into a corridor separating sections of the grandstand to the big Tudor-style clubhouse. Fans, grinning almost as happily as Nicklaus, reached toward him hoping for a brief handclasp or simply to touch him.

Off to the side, attendants on the big scoreboard spelled out a message: Jack Is Back.

Time compressed itself: it hardly seemed that he had been away.

(August 1980)

In Search of the Perfect Swing
Larry Dorman

J. H. Taylor, one of golf's "great triumvirate" with Harry Vardon and James Braid, once described playing golf thusly: "No matter how well you play the game, you never can master it." Tom Watson could well take heed of what Taylor said. That is because Watson appears to be seeking just such an unattainable accomplishment, as this article by Larry Dorman from The Miami Herald *would seem to indicate.*

Despite his unfulfilled ultimate objective, Watson has achieved great heights as one of the game's most effective strikers of a golf ball. Since 1977 Tom has dominated week-to-week play on the pro golf tour as a four-time leading money winner and a three-time recipient of the Vardon Trophy, an even truer indication of the soundness of his swing. He has, as of this writing, twenty-six tour victories, including two Masters and three British Opens to his credit, but I am unable to accord him golf's No. 1 designation, not as long as Jack Nicklaus is a consideration, especially in the major championships. But Tom is almost ten years younger than Jack and I am not adamant in my thinking.

Like Ben Hogan and Gary Player before him, Watson is one of the hardest workers engaged in playing the game, and is not averse to pounding practice balls by the hour. He also is one of the most intelligent, a fact readily discernible to anyone fortunate enough to be able to spend time with him. If a golf swing were strictly a product of mind over muscle, I am sure Watson would be able to achieve what he is seeking.

Regardless, Tom has been golf's most successful player in recent years, and has become golf's second all-time leading money winner.

Frankly, I doubt if he ever will realize his quest for a perfect swing, but as long as he continues to play as well as he does, that is a "failure" with which he can live.

To CALL HIM COMPLEX would be to call Rubik's Cube slightly taxing. Try inscrutable, indecipherable. He seeks the unseekable, reaches what had seemed unreachable and then looks higher. He is Tom Watson, 32, the uncommon individual who merely wants to subdue golf, the most humbling game, by eradicating error.

And to know almost everything there is to know about one man's obsession with perfection is to know this: Of 1981, the year Tom Watson won his second Masters title and $347,660, he said, "I didn't do anything particularly well."

Let that sink in. This was the first time since 1976 that Watson was not the pro tour's leading money winner. It was the first time in four years he was not named PGA Player of the Year. People are calling it an off year. And Watson, who is Watson's biggest critic, is leading the chorus.

"I couldn't rely on my golf swing," he said as he stood in front of the Ram Golf exhibit at the recent PGA Merchandise Show in Miami Beach, Fla. "I couldn't think out and play a shot. I always had to think about my golf swing rather than think about the shot. Start doing that and you're fighting with yourself."

"If one word describes last year it's FIGHT," said Watson, a Stanford graduate in psychology. "I fought myself and my swing, and it wasn't a whole lot of fun."

He said he is looking forward to making it fun this year. "I'm really ready to go; I'm chomping at the bit," said Watson, who sat out the season's first tournament (Tucson) and began the new year with the Bob Hope Desert Classic where he finished five under par but considerably off the pace of Ed Fiori and Tom Kite.

For a number of reasons, golf never has been quite as much fun for Tom Watson as it should have been. Sure, he has career earnings of over $2,500,000, five major championships and 25 tour victories. Even last year, in his "off year," he had three victories.

But, from the beginning of his emergence in the early 1970s there have been the odious comparisons with Jack Nicklaus; there have been the accusations that he lacks charisma ("Charisma is winning major championships," says Watson); and there has been the albatross of the U. S. Open, the tournament he has pointed toward every year since his childhood when he would play a game called "Name The Open Champion" with his father Ray. Dad would name the year and Tom would name the winner.

He still hasn't added his own name to the list. "I don't have a fetish or a phobia about winning it; it's something I want to win," said Watson who will get another chance the third week of June at Pebble Beach.

Watson has been called distant, cold, mechanical. He certainly looked mechanical for a stretch in 1980, winning three straight tournaments and leading them all from start to finish.

Distant? Cold? The line in front of the table at the Merchandise Show in Miami Beach was 15 feet long. People were clutching posters and pictures of the man seated behind the table, stepping on the backs of each other's shoes, jostling, craning their necks.

This was not one of Tom Watson's favorite things. Everybody wanting a piece of him— *"Stand over here please Tommy, right between these two gentlemen from Ireland. That's it. OK, honey, take the picture"* — strangers shoving their hands out — *"I met you once at the Open, remember, at Inverness?"* — accepting his picture, each one signed the same, "To (blank), best wishes, Tom Watson."

He handled it all with aplomb, asking people their names, making eye contact, never letting his smile fade. You would have thought he had nothing better to do.

Watson guards his privacy, and that of his wife Linda and their two-year-old daughter Meg. But the few who know him well, such as fellow pro Bob Murphy, know him as a person with no small amount of warmth and, yes, even humor.

"It's dry, but he's a funny guy," said Murphy. "Tom never tries to be funny, I don't think he wants to come across that way. A lot of times he'll come out with a really good line, but everybody who's around completely misses it because that's not supposed to come out of his mouth.

"It's a matter of being yourself, and Tom usually comes off as a serious person because that's what he is. Serious about his game and serious about his image. I think he's concerned that he hasn't gotten the kind of press that he would like as far as making him a friendly guy. His main concern, though, is being a good golfer, and he has certainly done that, and good press should follow."

To those who would make him king, and there have been many, he always has said the same thing. Not yet. Not now. "I must win the U. S. Open to be considered one of the great players," he has said. "Right now, I certainly don't have the career of golfers like Nicklaus, Hogan and Jones."

His quest for that stature, for perfection, goes on, but the road has diverged. The search now is for golf's Holy Grail. The Perfect Swing. "To satisfy myself, I have to satisfy my desire to perfect the golf swing," he says. "This is unattainable, probably, but I still have that desire."

But the man from Kansas City realizes that "the outside world" will judge him not by his swing but by his victories, his major victories. "To the press, to the fans, to your peers, I guess it's major championships," he said. "How many of those do you win? That would be the outside world's view of Tom Watson's goal.

"Inside, it's beyond that. Well, not beyond that, just a different thought. It's perfecting the golf swing. If I do that, it will make me a better player and I'll win more."

The perfect swing. If anyone can find it, it may be this man, this perfectionist's perfectionist of whom Lanny Wadkins once said: "Tom would never tolerate a weakness. He'd go to the practice tee and beat at it till the darn thing went away."

For Tom Watson, it was no simple gift of talent that made him the game's best player from 1977 through 1980. It was a slow, upward battle, an interior fight fueled by intense desire. Watson himself has a telling observation on this score: "Sam Snead once said, 'Give me a player with a little bit of talent and a great amount of desire and I'll pick him every time over a guy with a great amount of talent and a little desire.'"

Said Stan Thirsk, Watson's instructor for 21 years: "People don't realize what kind of competitor Tommy is. Inside he burns to win. He hates to lose. You may beat him, and he'll smile and shake your hand, but inside he's thinking, 'Next time.'"

Next time. Watson has been known to hit so many practice balls that he loses feeling in his forearms. Four years ago, fellow pro Jim Simons saw Watson hit balls on the practice range at Colonial in Ft. Worth until his hands were bloody and blistered. He clawed his way from Monday qualifier in 1971–72 to leading money winner and Player of the Year.

Suddenly, there he was, standing astride the game, wearing the crown uncertainly, suffering the comparisons and remembering the wounds inflicted by people who once called him a choker. There may be no crueler label in sports and there are few people less deserving of it than Watson.

"Dumb, ignorant people said that," says 1981 U. S. Open champion David Graham.

By now, it's common knowledge how the choker business began. In the 1974 U. S. Open at Winged Foot, Watson had a one-shot lead going into the last round and blew to 79. Afterward, he was a victim of his own candor. "My swing deserted me under pressure," he said.

Ignorant people made their own interpretations. The next year at Medinah, he tied the 36-hole Open record with 135 and then shot 78–77. The next year he stumbled at the Tournament Players Championship at Sawgrass, and again the next week in the Sea Pines-Heritage Classic at Harbour Town.

No one who knows anything about golf and the difficulties of shooting oneself into contention to win in the first place could believe that Tom Watson was a choker. Certainly not Watson. "To learn how to win major championships," he says, "you have to lose major championships."

Watson showed he had learned how to win in 1977. First it was the Masters, holding off a last-round Jack Nicklaus charge and then making birdie at 17 to cause Nicklaus to falter. And then the British Open at Turnberry. Nicklaus blinked. Mostly in disbelief. It may have been the greatest golf match ever. Tied after 36 holes and paired with Watson each of the last two rounds, Nicklaus scored 65–66. And lost. Watson did

65–65. "I gave you my best shot," Jack said to Watson, "and it wasn't good enough. I couldn't shake you."

Tom Watson has always said that "the biggest person I have to overcome is myself." He gets help in that regard from Byron Nelson, who refines the swing Watson has been given by Thirsk and soothes the psyche that often becomes cluttered.

"A smart fella once told me that a fine golfer has only one fine thing, and that's his fine golf, and that if he ever forgets it, he's a fool," Nelson once said. "Tom Watson never forgets."

In 1981, it wasn't so much that Watson forgot. He became victim of his own brilliance. Too much information in there. Too much knowledge of what makes the swing perfect.

"The times I watched him last year, he was taking so many practice swings before hitting a shot that he looked like he was practicing while he was playing," said Thirsk. "You just can't do that. It's nice to have the kind of goal that Tom has, but you simply can't make the body do what you want it to do every time. Tom has to realize that.

"It's like Walter Hagen used to say: 'I know I'm going to miss at least six shots a round. When I do, it's one down and five to go. Let's go from here.'"

Watson may or may not heed that advice. What is certain is that he is ready to go from here. He tore holes in the back of Thirsk's indoor net while beating balls at Kansas City Country Club. While the freezing winds of winter howled outside, the burning desire inside began again for Watson.

"I can tell you that he'll be back," said Thirsk. "And I can tell you another thing. He'll win the U. S. Open."

(1982)

A Braw Brawl for Tom and Jack
Dan Jenkins

I don't know how many British Opens I have witnessed, but I do know I was on hand for the one hundred and sixth, which was played in 1977 on the west coast of Scotland at the Turnberry Golf Club in Ayrshire. It was the first ever for the course, which no less an authority than Gary Player has described as "the finest links in the world," and it may have been the best British Open ever. Certainly it was the most exciting."

That is because winner Tom Watson and runner-up Jack Nicklaus turned it into strictly a two-man contest with the most sustained display of golf ever to grace the venerable championship. I never have seen two great champions simultaneously rise to such a challenge. In their four trips over the course neither was over par and when they finally shook hands at the conclusion, Tom was twelve under and Jack eleven — both records — while the rest of the field, with one exception, had left the standard inviolate.

"The Open," as the British refer to the championship, is contested at stroke-play, but Tom and Jack turned it into a suspenseful match-play confrontation as they withered par and battled head-to-head on successive days before the issue was resolved in favour of Watson.

It was the kind of golf that leaves me exhausted by its sustained drama, but I was exhilarated for having been witness to it.

The "Shootout at Turnberry," as it since has come to be known, also was witnessed by Dan Jenkins of Sports Illustrated who, obviously, relished being there as much as I did. Dan, in his inimitable free and easy style, caught the import of the incomparable engagement. His account, interspersed with his humorous asides, incidental information concerning the locale and his sharp insights into the personalities involved, is Jenkins at his very best. It is the kind of treatment such an epoch-making event in golf richly deserved.

GO AHEAD AND MARK it as the end of an era in professional golf if you're absolutely sure that Jack Nicklaus has been yipped into the sunset years of his career by the steel and nerve and immense talent of Tom Watson.

You could argue that way now, in these hours after Tom Watson has become the new king of the sport in a kingly land; when Watson has already become the Player of the Year, not to mention the future; when he has done it in the most memorable way in the annals of golf; and when he has done it for the second time in this season to the greatest player who ever wore a slipover shirt — Jack Nicklaus.

You could also say it very simply with numbers. In the last two rounds of last week's British Open, Tom Watson shot 65 and 65 to beat Nicklaus by one stroke. Oh, by the way, they were playing together. Oh yes, and another thing: Watson's 72-hole total was 268, which was a new record by only eight shots. And, incidentally, the victory gave Watson his second major title of the year (and the third of his fresh and exciting career); he had taken the Masters, of course, standing up to Nicklaus in a slightly different type of pressurized situation. And, let's see, the British Open gave the handsome young Watson his sixth win of the year and some $300,000 in tour earnings.

But all of that doesn't even begin to examine what the stakes were on the gorgeous links of Turnberry on Scotland's west coast in the most atmospheric, ancient and some would argue, most treasured of golf's four major tournaments. Actually, what took place was the most colossal head-to-head shotmaking and low scoring in the history of golf.

Tom Watson and Jack Nicklaus started to lap the field on Friday, when their identical rounds of 68–70–65 had given them a three-stroke bulge on the nearest pursuers. But just when everyone was ready to concede that Friday's duel had outspectaculared anything ever witnessed from the days of the gutta-percha ball to those of the Apex shaft, Tom and Jack went out and did it all over again in Saturday's final round, spinning out the overwhelming and unbelievable drama and suspense to the very last delicate rap of Watson's putter on a two-foot birdie putt, which gave him a second consecutive 65 to Nicklaus' shabby, horrid and humiliating 66.

On each of the last two days, Watson came back from what looked to be certain doom to catch Nicklaus and finally do him in. Watson just would not go away, not in the face of Nicklaus' birdies, or his icy stare or his mighty reputation. When Watson was two strokes behind in the third round, he fought back to tie Jack, and in so doing broke the Nicklaus rhythm and the tempo of his short putts. Then on Saturday Watson came back again twice, once from three strokes down to tie, and again from two back, finishing the round with four blazing birdies over the last six holes.

Watson was in fact two shots behind the premier player of the game with those six holes left. Who can give Nicklaus two shots over six holes and beat him by one? Who could even contemplate it? Only Tom Watson in this day and time, a Tom Watson who has the best complete game in golf and has been showing that he has it all year. A Tom Watson who has the most reliable, solid swing around, who has the well-educated patience to hold himself in control, the strength and vigor of youth, and now the confidence and determination to make himself worthy of the No. 1 role he has seized.

Here's how it was at the most torturous time of all, out there at the par-3 15th hole in the last round after Watson had just stabbed Nicklaus through the front of his yellow sweater with a 60-foot birdie putt from the hardpan 10 feet off the green. That astonishing shot hit the flagstick and dived into the cup and brought Watson into a tie once more.

They went to the 16th tee and Jack and Tom looked at each other. The blond and the redhead. Yesterday and today. Then and now. Dominguin and Ordóñez.

And Tom smiled at Jack. "This is what it's all about, isn't it?"

And Jack smiled back and said, "You bet it is."

They parred the 16th, and so it came down to the last two holes, as most knowledgeable people had been thinking it would. The 500-yard 17th was a pushover par-5, an "eagle hole," surely a birdie hole. The 18th was a bothersome par-4. Anything could happen.

But now it was time for the grand final shot out of Watson's bag that would unglue Jack and make him commit the tiny but killing error that would be the difference. Tom absolutely stung a perfect three-iron right over the flag and onto the green at the 17th, where he would be putting for an eagle from only 20 feet—a sure birdie, in other words.

This had long since been match play, and the pressure was now on Nicklaus. What Watson's shot did, coming in the wake of so many others that had been hounding Jack, was bother Nicklaus just enough to make him press a sloppy four-iron that not only missed the green but also left him with an evil chip shot. Maybe only a fighter like Jack could have got that chip as close as he did, within four feet of the hole. But the mortal damage had been done.

Watson had a cinch birdie and Nicklaus had just a working chance at one. Only the day before, shots by Watson had forced Jack to miss a couple of short putts of the kind that he has never blown before but will now find himself fearing more frequently. Nicklaus missed that four-foot putt and for the first time all week Watson was alone in the lead.

When they went to the 18th, Watson struck a crisp one-iron off the tee into perfect position and then nailed a seven-iron that stuck into the flat like an arrow in the ribs of the bear. A sure birdie.

It was marvelous show biz that Nicklaus recovered from a desperate and awkward drive to reach the green in two and then sink a 40-foot birdie of his own. Fine curtain call and all that, but the putt was pure luck, the kind that only drops when you need it the least on the final hole of a major championship. Jack knew Tom had already won it, just as he probably had a deeper feeling of impending tragedy on all those earlier holes when he was unable to lose Tom. And Watson ended the drama by tapping in from two feet out.

After Watson said all of the nice things about how hard it is to keep concentrating and trying not to make any mistakes against a Jack Nicklaus, it was time for a more telling reaction. In a certain amount of privacy, Jack shook his head and said, "I just couldn't shake him."

With that, Nicklaus looked off in thought with something of the expression of an aging gunfighter. He did not say he had been expecting *someone* to come along one of these years. But the look seemed to indicate that he had finally met him.

It might be well to speak of where this all took place. For years, golfing enthusiasts from various continents had wondered if the British Open could be played at Turnberry, certainly the most scenic of Britain's links courses, and they had wished the Royal and Ancient would attempt it. Many an official within the R and A itself had wished it. But Turnberry presented serious problems as a championship site. No town, no roads, no hotels, among other things.

Turnberry, when it was not functioning as an air base during world wars, consisted of one massive hotel up on the hill overlooking the RAF runways, the Firth of Clyde, in which fishermen still hook onto crashed Hudson bombers, the island bird sanctuary known as Ailsa Craig, and the gleaming lighthouse out on the point, which had long since become the Turnberry club's logo.

All the objections to Turnberry as a site might have been valid before the British Open had regained its reputation as one of the Big Four in golf, before the Arnold Palmers and Jack Nicklauses had turned it into something other than a rickety event in which Peter Thomson beat half a dozen guys from Stoke Poges. The people would come streaming in to see it nowadays, no matter what the R and A figured. And how right it was.

Each day the great grandstands scattered over the dunes were filled by 10 A.M. and thousands more were tromping through the whin and heather as if a Mark Hayes wearing his Amana hat or a John Schroeder were real people. They stormed the tented village, as it is called, that hodgepodge of commercial exhibitions featuring everything from shooting sticks to pork pies to cashmeres at discount. Only in this championship among the Grand Slam tournaments can the spectator see players from as many as 27 different countries. Leap over a burn in the British Open and you can go from a Severiano Ballesteros waist-deep in non-Spanish flora to a

Baldovino Dassu neck-deep in non-Italian fauna.

To the British, the charm of Turnberry's links lay in the fact that its holes are closer to the sea than those of any of their Open courses. At a Carnoustie, Muirfield, Birkdale, or Lytham, for example, you can't even catch a glimpse of the water from a tee or green. You can see it at St. Andrews, but there is no way to strike a ball into watery oblivion without a hydroplane. Ah, but Turnberry. The water is always there, furnishing a series of backdrops, washing up against a competitor's concentration.

The best of Turnberry is bound up in its golf, and, delightedly, the rest of the world learned about that last week. Although it got caught in a warm calm that produced the lowest scoring in the 106-year-old championship's elegant history, Turnberry earned its way into the R and A's Open rota both with the record crowds it drew and the breathtaking action it provided, and not just from Tom and Jack.

It has never been any secret that if you could catch one of the famous old courses in England or Scotland in a dead calm, you could scorch it. Unlike American layouts, wind is 50% of the danger, as much a part of linksland golf as a pot bunker or gnarled heather. The necessity of wind to British golf is why the Open has always been staged on courses by the sea—to ensure the sternest test. But throughout the four rounds there was no wind at Turnberry.

And so with hundreds of spectators wearing no shirts at all instead of the customary Open garb of topcoats and rain gear, and with the course looking more like a Farrah Fawcett-Majors than a Lotte Lenya, the players leaped at it with glee and daring. The result was a raft of scores that would have sent old Tom Morris staggering dizzily toward a barrel of ale. It was so easy that a couple of American tour regulars, John Schroeder and then Roger Maltbie, led the first and second rounds. Schroeder with a 66 on Wednesday and then Maltbie with 71—66—137. These were Americans who would have looked more at home at the Quad Cities tournament. It was their first time over, even though Maltbie's mother is Scottish and his dad had been a flyer stationed in Scotland during the big one. The British considered them unknowns, unaware of

Maltbie's three victories on the U. S. tour.

It was in Thursday's second round that Turnberry began to take some real lumps. Hubert Green came very close to going around in a figure as weird as a California license plate. He went seven under par through the first 13 holes. Then mistakes got him when, as he later admitted, "a 59 crossed my mind." He settled for 66. At more or less the same time, however, Mark Hayes was out there shoving Turnberry inside an Amana refrigerator. Hayes plays golf in hiding, pulling a brimmed hat down over his shy, almost terrifyingly modest, expressions, and although he is a superb golfer who makes his own clubs in Edmond, Okla., and is one of the new wave of young stars, words flow from his lips every other eon. With a cross-handed putting style he was trying out for only the second time in competition, he flattened Turnberry with a 63.

It was the lowest single round—by two strokes—ever shot in the world's oldest major championship. Back in 1934 a golf ball had been hurried into production after Henry Cotton's 65 at Sandwich—the Dunlop 65, of course. And now Hayes had shot 63 and everyone was goofy over it. Except Mark Hayes. He was another American in the British Open for the first time and he didn't know about the record, which would have been even lower if he hadn't started thinking cross-handed and chosen the wrong clubs on the 18th hole and finished with a bogey. Surrounded by a mere 900 million members of the press, then, Mark Hayes was asked what his reaction was to his monumental feat. He sat there. He looked down. He thought. Finally, he said, "I have a lot of trouble figuring out the distances over here."

That was it. The *Eagle* has landed. If I have but one life to give. Give me liberty or give me. Lafayette, we are somewhere. And so forth. Mark Hayes had shattered Britain with a 63 and Amana had not sent a poet with him to Turnberry.

All of this ushered the Open into Friday and Saturday and what were to become two of the grandest, most thrilling and astonishing days that the sport has ever known. As single days in competitive golf went, Friday, July 8 and Saturday, July 9, 1977 had to rate right up there with such other landmarks as the last round of the 1975 Masters, when Nicklaus outlasted Tom Weiskopf and Johnny Miller; with the final day of the British Open in 1972, when Lee Trevino cut the heart out of Nicklaus. Nicklaus' shot at the Slam, and Tony Jacklin; and certainly with the last 18 holes of the 1960 U. S. Open at Cherry Hills when Arnold Palmer left wounded soldiers all around Denver.

History will most likely see it as better than any of those. Better than any golf — ever. The display that Tom Watson and Jack Nicklaus put on at Turnberry over those last excruciating, compelling, agonizing and interminable 36 holes can only be summed up by quoting from that old RAF monument sitting out there on Turnberry's back nine.

Somewhere on the granite it says: "Their name liveth forever more." Well, if theirs doesn't, there's not a kidney left in a pie in Ayrshire.

(July 1977)

'Best Shot Of My Life'
Dave Anderson

The title of this selection tells the whole story: a dramatic save from the deep rough alongside the green when Tom Watson chipped into the cup on the 71st hole to win his first United States Open Golf Championship and, in doing so, to thwart the bid of Jack Nicklaus for an unprecedented fifth Open crown.

Pulitzer Prize-winning columnist Dave Anderson of The New York Times *was there and, as he does so well, Dave caught the drama and the significance of the shot and the mien and character of the great golfer who made it.*

Giving an insight to the great moments in sports and to the athletes responsible for them has been traditional with Anderson for the last fifteen years in his "Sports of the Times" column. His beat is the Super Bowl, the World Series, the Olympics, boxing title fights, the Masters, the Open, the PGA and all of the other events which claim the No. 1 spot on the sport pages of the world. His light, fluid style of incisive commentary, in 1981, brought him the coveted Pulitzer Prize.

Dave is an expert on all of the games played by man, but his personal favourite is golf, which he plays with a zest and a fervour befitting a medium-handicap player.

"Have clubs, will travel," is Dave's motto and wherever an assignment might take him, his golf clubs are included with his luggage. As a result, he has become a golf course "collector." After playing four Monterey Peninsula courses while covering Watson's 1982 victory at Pebble Beach, he proudly boasted he had increased to 234 the number of courses he had played.

Dave Anderson, purely and simply, loves golf and the men who play it. This piece clearly reflects that continuing love affair.

I N SPORTS, the burden of excellence for the best athletes is that they're expected to win the best championships. If they don't, their skill is suspect. So is their nerve. So is their place in history. And in golf, the United States Open is the best championship, the most difficult to win, the most prestigious.

"If you don't win the Open," says 80-year-old Gene Sarazen, who won it twice, "there's a gap in your record."

Tom Watson has been aware of that gap in his record during his reign as the world's best golfer over the last six years. He has won three British Opens, two Masters and nearly $3 million in prize money on the PGA Tour, but that merely made the Open more important to him than it is to perhaps any other current golfer.

"To be a complete golfer," Tom Watson once said, "you have to win the Open, you just have to."

But now that burden and that gap no longer exist; now he's a "complete golfer." Tom Watson won the Open yesterday over the treacherous Pebble Beach Golf Links with a two-under-par 70 for a 72-hole total of 282 that included one of golf's most memorable shots. From the rough to the left of the green at the 209-yard 17th hole that borders the jagged rocks of the Pacific Ocean shoreline, he chipped his ball 16 feet into the cup for a birdie 2 only moments after Jack Nicklaus had finished at 284 with a 69.

"That was the best shot of my life," the new Open champion said later. "And winning the Open makes me feel my career is one plateau higher."

Tom Watson now is up there on a plateau with the best golfers in the history of the game. At age 32, he has won six major championships—three British Opens, two Masters and now one United States Open. And in four of those triumphs (the 1977 and 1981 Masters, the 1977 British Open and yesterday's classic confrontation), he conquered Jack Nicklaus, whom most golf historians consider to be the best of this or any time.

"When it got down to Jack and me, I called upon old memories," Tom Watson said later. "And they were pleasant memories. In a small

way and a large way, that helped me to win the tournament."

Just as Jack Nicklaus had to suffer as the villain who dethroned Arnold Palmer two decades ago, so Tom Watson has had to struggle for popular acceptance in the shadow of the Golden Bear's record. And yet, in their mano à mano duels in major tournaments, Tom Watson has won on all four occasions. When the new Open champion walked off the 18th green yesterday, the four-time Open champion greeted him with a smile.

"You're something else," the Golden Bear said. "That was nice going. I'm proud of you. I'm pleased for you."

In the interview tent, Jack Nicklaus was told that Bill Rogers, who had been paired with the new champion, had suggested that if Tom Watson were to chip 100 balls from that spot in the rough off the 17th green, he would not hole even one ball.

"Try about 1,000 balls," Jack Nicklaus said.

But when Tom Watson was informed of what Bill Rogers had said, the new Open champion smiled.

"Bill didn't see the lie," he said. "I had a good lie."

And when Tom Watson was informed that Jack Nicklaus had mentioned that he couldn't duplicate that shot with 1,000 balls, the new Open champion smiled again.

"Let's go out and do it," he said. "I might make a little more money."

When that chip with a sandwedge rolled into the cup for a one-stroke lead on Jack Nicklaus that he increased to two strokes with a birdie 4 at the 18th hole, Tom Watson had produced one of the most memorable shots in golf history. That chip shot will be talked about along with Gene Sarazen's double eagle in the 1935 Masters, with Jack Nicklaus's 1-iron that clanked off the flagstick on the 17th at Pebble Beach in the 1972 Open, with Jerry Pate's 5-iron to the 18th green at the Atlanta Athletic Club in the 1976 Open.

"That shot," Tom Watson said later, "had more meaning to me than any other shot of my career."

That shot meant that Tom Watson no longer

had to answer questions about why he hasn't been able to win the Open, the same questions that the now 70-year-old Sam Snead is still asked. Just as Sam Snead is the best golfer never to win the Open championship, Tom Watson had been the best current golfer not to have won it. But when Tom Watson arrived in the interview tent last night, he had a new question to answer.

"Why," he was asked jokingly, "haven't you ever won the PGA championship?"

"Now it's Arnold Palmer," he replied, laughing, referring to Palmer's inability to win the PGA throughout his illustrious career. "Before it was Sam Snead, now it's Arnold Palmer. But tonight you can ask me all the questions you want about the PGA."

When he shared the 54-hole lead with Bill Rogers Saturday night, Tom Watson had been asked how he would spend the time until he teed off yesterday in the final round. He talked about how he would watch the "Sesame Street" television show with his 2½-year-old daughter Meg.

"We'll count," he said. "but not up to 7 or 8."

In golf a 7 or 8 is disastrous. Through four rounds here, he never had a 7 or an 8; he shot as high as 6 on a hole only twice. And yesterday when he returned to the interview tent, he was asked what he had done in the hours before the final round.

"I watched 'Sesame Street' with Meg," he said, grinning. "They only counted up to two."

He was alluding to his 2 at the 17th hole, the 2 that was created by the "best shot" of his life, the 2 that put him "one plateau higher" among all the famous golfers, the 2 that won the Open for him, the 2 that will be remembered as long as golf is played.

Tom Watson had produced a memorable shot in a moment of crisis in a dramatic duel with the best other golfer of his time in the world's most important golf tournament. That's winning the way a champion is supposed to win, a champion now without a burden, a champion now without a gap in his record.

(June 1982)

Ten Shots That Rocked the World
Will Grimsley

Of all the living writers who have contributed to this book, Will Grimsley may be the most prolific and the most versatile. As sports columnist for the Associated Press, his annual output of columns, features and sidebar stories must run to nearly a million words. Whether the subject is the Super Bowl, the World Series, the Olympics, Wimbledon, a major fight or the Kentucky Derby, you can be sure that Will's coverage will be interesting, informative and expert.

Golf is no exception. Will always can be found at the scenes of major championships both in the U. S. and abroad. He and I have been good friends since he came to New York in 1947 to work at the headquarters of the wire service. Will is a native of Nashville, Tennessee, where, among other things, he was a high school classmate of Dinah Shore and where he got his start with the Nashville Tennessean. *A soft-spoken, courtly gentleman of the press, his unhurried demeanour belies one of the quickest, most acute minds ever to survey and report the golf scene. Over the years he has constantly amazed me by his ability to spend only a few minutes in conversation with me and produce a column, based on our meeting, which I would read but a few hours later. You can bet it would be clear, concise, complete and absolutely accurate. Will's pre-eminence in his field was recognized in 1976 when he was elected president of the Golf Writers' Association of America.*

Despite the daily demands of his schedule, Will, in the early sixties, found time to write a major work on the game: Golf: Its History, People and Events. *It was very well received in the U. S. at $19.95 a copy, but even more so in Japan despite the $300 the Japanese edition cost. "Ten Shots That Rocked the World" is from that book.*

As a personal aside regarding one of the ten golfers, Lew Worsham has worked for me as professional at the Coral Ridge Country Club in Florida since 1956, and I have been a guest in his home many times. Lew has a club mounted over the mantel of the fireplace and under it a plaque inscribed: "This is the house the wedge built."

The Shot that Awakened American Golf

THE BALL TRAVELED only 20 feet. It was just a putt, one of hundreds of such putts made at a critical time in an important golf championship. Yet this turned out to be one of the most important putts in the history of the game. It was responsible for the great awakening of golf in America.

"If I had not made that putt, I would never have tied Vardon and Ray for the championship," said Francis Ouimet. "Things certainly would have been different."

Ouimet was a scrawny caddy of 20 when he teed off in the 1913 U. S. Open Championship over the swank The (capital "T") Country Club of Brookline, Massachusetts. Golf was just gaining a foothold in the United States but it was a stuffy game confined largely to the rich. British players dominated the American tournaments.

The 1913 Open shifted from its usual June dates to September to permit the entrance of the famed British professionals Harry Vardon and Ted Ray, as well as other notables from overseas. No one doubted that the competition would be a duel between Vardon, the stylist, who had won five of his six British Open Crowns, and Ray, a massive figure towering over 6 feet and weighing more than 200 pounds, counting a flowing mustache.

Ray led the 36-hole qualifying with 148. Vardon was at 151. Ouimet, in cap and knickers and looking like a boy playing hooky from school, registered a creditable 152, but drew scant attention. The championship was to be contested over two days — 36 holes Thursday and 36 Friday.

High excitement swept the stodgy old club on Friday when the end of the morning round showed Vardon, Ray, and Ouimet tied after 54 holes at 225. Ouimet was a hometown boy, born in Wellesley Hills, but still an inexperienced amateur hardly expected to stand up to two of the world's foremost professionals.

It was a gray, rainy, miserable day as the tournament moved to its climax. Ray finished first with a 79, giving him 304. This hardly seemed adequate. Yet out on the course the others also were fading one by one — Wilfred Reid, MacDonald Smith, Johnny McDermott, Walter Hagen, Jim Barnes, and France's Louis Tellier.

Vardon, his putting touch shaken on the water-soaked greens, also had to settle for a 79, which left him tied with Ray. Then the roof fell on Ouimet, playing well back of the other two leaders. The young Boston caddy took a 43 on the outgoing nine and blew to a 5 on the short tenth. Spirits of the hometown gallery sagged. To tie for the lead, Francis had to play the last eight holes in 31 — a seemingly hopeless task.

Only Ouimet did not despair. He parred the eleventh with four, took a bogey five at the twelfth, and now needed two birdies on the last six holes. He chipped in from the edge of the green on the thirteenth for a birdie, parred the fourteenth, fifteenth, and sixteenth. Now he needed another birdie with two tough finishing holes to go.

The seventeenth provided the life-saver. This was a 360-yard hole, dog-leg to the right. He hit a good drive and then for his approach chose a jigger, a club between the modern five- and six-iron. The ball sailed 20 feet past the pin.

It was a tough putt, a sliding, downhill assignment. The crowd framing the green was deadly silent. Ouimet looked over the line quickly and then took his stance. There was a blare of an automobile horn on a nearby road. The crowd fidgeted nervously. Ouimet did not move. He stroked the ball crisply. It rolled easily down the slope, hit the hole dead center, banged against the back of the cup, and dropped home. It was a birdie three. Pandemonium broke loose.

Ouimet, maintaining a tremendous calm, hit a good drive at the eighteenth, but left his second short. He chipped to within 5 feet, sank the putt for a 79 and a 3-way tie at 304.

The play-off the next day was anticlimactic. Ouimet got another three at the lucky seventeen, relieving some of the pressure from Vardon, a stroke behind going to the hole. Vardon banged into a trap at seventeen and took a five. The Massachusetts caddy won easily with a 72 to Vardon's 77 and Ray's 78.

News of the sensational victory was carried on page one of many of the nation's newspapers.

Golf received a stimulus in the United States, and Ouimet acknowledged later: "That one putt did it."

The Eagle that Won the Open for Byron Nelson

Byron Nelson was one of the all-time masters of golf. It would have been a tragedy indeed if he, as in the case of Sam Snead, had been denied the one title every player wants — the United States Open.

It was unfortunate that Lord Byron reached his peak during the years of World War II, when play in the National Championship was suspended. It was during this span that he set scoring records that lasted for decades and won 11 straight PGA tour tournaments, an achievement that never has been challenged, and probably never will be.

Nelson did get his name on the U. S. Open trophy, however. The year was 1939 and the site was the Spring Mill course of the Philadelphia Country Club.

It took the unforgettable blowup by Sam Snead — an eight on the final hole when a six would have tied — to set up a three-way play-off among Nelson, Craig Wood, and Denny Shute, and it took a single fantastic shot to win it.

That was an eagle deuce on the fourth hole of the second round of a 36-hole play-off.

When Snead took his horrendous tour of the traps on the final hole of the 1939 Open, Nelson, Wood, and Shute were left tied for first with 72-hole scores of 284.

Nelson had to sink a wicked 10-foot birdie putt on the final hole to tie Wood at 68 through the first 18 extra holes. Shute, his putting sour, was eliminated when he shot a 76.

A second 18-hole play-off followed between Nelson and Wood. Nelson dropped a birdie putt at the third hole and took a one-stroke lead. Then the pair moved to the fourth, followed by a tremendous gallery of several thousand.

The fourth at Spring Mill is a difficult 460-yarder, well-trapped and playing par 4. Nelson said later that he felt certain that this hole could well prove the turning point of the match. Both players were determined to reach the green in two and go for birdies.

Both drives were good, in the fairway, and reasonably long. Wood used a wood club and got his second onto the green about 25 feet from the cup. Nelson deliberated more than usual. He could not decide whether to use a brassie or a one-iron.

"My irons always had been pretty good and I figured that I would have a better chance of both reaching the green and controlling the shot if I used a one-iron," Byron recalled later. "I knew I couldn't make a mistake."

Nelson said he concentrated on this particular shot as much as he had ever concentrated in his life. The gallery, lining the fairway and framing the green, was deathly quiet as Nelson took his stance.

"I knew it was good when I hit it," Lord Byron said. "My swing was just right, the impact was perfect. I know I had never hit a better iron."

Nelson watched the ball fly toward the green but he lost sight of it as it fell to earth. He heard a loud roar.

"I knew then it was close," he said. "I didn't know until I walked to the green that it had rolled into the hole for an eagle two. Craig Wood had played four holes in par and was three down. I was determined to protect that lead."

Nelson did. He shot a 70, Wood a 73, and Byron had his first only National Open with what he called "the greatest shot of my life."

The Nicklaus that Awed Europe

Most of the historic shots of the great champions were made in major tournaments before swarming galleries. They were usually climactic shots. They decided titles and launched careers.

Only a handful of hardy spectators — 200 at the most, one of them a former King of England — saw Jack Nicklaus unleash one of the greatest and most important shots of his career. Although few saw it, reports of it spread like a runaway brush-fire, and to Europeans, at least, the Golden Bear became golf's miracle worker.

The date was Monday, October 28, 1963. The place was the Saint-Nom-la-Bretèche Golf Course, 12 miles from the heart of Paris. The occasion was the windup of the eleventh International Golf Championship and Canada Cup matches, played in Europe for the first time.

Nicklaus and Arnold Palmer were playing for the United States against picked teams from 32 other nations, and they found it far from a breeze. The two Americans had to sink birdies on the fifty-fourth hole to gain a tie with two amazing Spaniards, Sebastian Miguel and Ramon Sota, at the three-quarter mark, with one round to play. Nicklaus was even with South Africa's Gary Player in the individual competition.

Then an eerie, souplike fog blanketed the area, limiting visibility to less than 100 yards. The final round on Sunday, October 27, had to be postponed, and on Monday, when the fog persisted, it was decided to play in the semidarkness, limiting the final round to nine holes.

When the two American players reached the sixth tee, they learned that the Spaniards, playing beautifully, had gone ahead by one stroke. The Spaniards were playing in front of the United States team.

American hopes dropped quickly when both Palmer and Nicklaus—firing blind into the dense fog—hit bad approach shots on the sixth, a 430-yard, par 4, uphill hole. Arnold Palmer's shot landed in a bunker at the left of the green, 85 feet from the flag. Jack Nicklaus found himself in the right trap, 70 feet away.

Bogeys appeared the fate of each, and with them little chance of overtaking the Spaniards in the three holes remaining.

Palmer blasted first. The ball landed 15 feet beyond the pin, seemed momentarily to stop, and then spun back 10 feet toward the cup as if yanked by an unseen yo-yo.

The gallery gasped. The rumble of disbelief was still echoing around the hillsides when Nicklaus took his stance in the other trap. His head was barely visible from the other side of the green. Three times he walked to the top of the bunker to look at the location of the hole. Then he buried his feet in the sand, paused, and swung.

The ball came out in a beautiful arch, took one bounce, and plunked into the cup.

"Incredible," said one spectator.

"Magnifique," yelled another.

"Magic—sheer magic," repeated others.

The Duke of Windsor, watching from in front of the green, became so excited he fell off his shooting stick.

It was a birdie three for Nicklaus—his fifth three in a row and his fifth birdie in the first six holes.

Nicklaus went on to play the 9 holes in 32, 4 under par. He won the individual International Trophy with a 63-hole score of 237, 5 shots ahead of Spain's Miguel and South Africa's Player. The Americans won the team trophy with a three-stroke margin over Spain.

Nicklaus never rated the sensational trap shot in Paris as the most significant of his career, personally finding it hard to choose between an eight-iron shot that gave him a 1-up victory over Charlie Coe in the 1959 National Amateur or the bold 4-foot putt he sank on the seventeenth hole of his play-off with Arnold Palmer for the 1962 National Open title—but he could never convince the Europeans.

They never stopped talking about the young Golden Bear and his five straight three's, climaxed by the unbelievable trap shot, in the Canada Cup at Paris in 1963.

The Shot that Sealed Ben Hogan's Comeback

Tension crackled like a berserk electric charge at the Merion Golf Club, outside Philadelphia, on that hazy Saturday afternoon in June, 1950.

The fiftieth United States Open Championship was drawing to its climax and in the thick of the drama was the dour, determined Texas Hawk, Ben Hogan.

This was not just another Open for the 37-year-old iron-master from Fort Worth. It was his first National Championship since the near-fatal automobile accident on a Texas highway 18 months before that had left him a battered, broken heap.

Could Hogan come back? This was what all of the golf world was asking. No one wondered about that more than perhaps Hogan himself. Now he was face-to-face with the answer.

Merion was one of the nation's historic courses, the site where Bob Jones completed his Grand Slam by winning the National Amateur in 1930. It was also an exciting layout, one that challenged the best in men and surrendered to none.

The test was particularly grueling for Hogan. His legs, shattered in the automobile accident, had not fully healed. There were circulation problems, and each night, after his play, he was forced to return to his hotel room and put his legs in traction to restore the flow of blood.

On the course, he walked with slow, stiff-legged deliberation. Spectators looked at him and winced, but the expression on the face of the Hawk never changed. His jaw was grim, his lips tight, and his eyes sparkled with fire under his familiar white cap.

The last day of the Open, 36 holes under severest pressure, has been known to break the back and spirit of strong and healthy men. It was no wonder that the fans were watching Hogan's every labored step with deep concern.

At the club house, the big scoreboard showed George Fazio and Lloyd Mangrum in with a score of 287. On the course, challengers were dropping like leaves on an autumn day—all except Hogan. He was plodding along close to par, still within reach of the title.

Hogan faltered with bogeys at the fifteenth and seventeenth; then he came up the eighteenth, a difficult finishing hole, needing a par 4 to tie. He knew what his assignment was.

It takes a big drive and a fine iron shot to get home on this 458-yard finishing hole at Merion, and indications were that the gallant little man from Texas finally was weakening. Mustering his strength, Hogan hit a good drive—long and straight to the middle of the fairway.

He chose to play a two-iron to the green. He studied the shot a long time before he finally took a last puff on his cigarette and assumed his stance. Thousands lined the fairway and packed around the green, but they were muted by the tension of the occasion.

Hogan swung into the shot. The ball sailed low and straight toward the green, but a bit to the left. Finally, the crowd let out a tremendous roar. Hogan rolled his putt 3 feet past the hole, and then sank coming back. He had his four and his tie for the title.

The 18-hole play-off was anticlimactic. No one doubted that destiny now could deny the game bantam his prize. Hogan fired a 69, beating out Mangrum by 4 shots and Fazio by 6.

The thousands who witnessed Hogan's two-iron shot to the final green acclaimed it the greatest shot under pressure that the fabulous Hawk ever played.

Hogan, a perfectionist to the end, disagreed. "It wasn't a good shot at all," he said later. "I wanted to be 25 feet closer to the hole."

Arnold Palmer's 1960 Masters Finish

Arnold Palmer made many a dramatic and climactic golf shot. Drama was the trademark of the rugged, colorful professional from Latrobe, Pennsylvania, in his sweep to a record bag of Masters championships as well as victories in the U. S. and British Opens. It was as if Palmer purposely saved the big shot for the big occasion. It was this faculty which endeared him to millions.

As for Palmer himself, there is no doubt about the shot he considers the most important one of his career. It was the six-iron shot to the final green which won him the 1960 Masters.

It was a thunderclap finish.

Palmer was on the tee at the par-5 fifteenth when news reached him that Ken Venturi had fired a final round 70 for 283. With four of the toughest finishing holes in golf ahead of him, Palmer needed two birdies to win.

Venturi was stashed away in Cliff Roberts' inner sanctum, trying on the green champion's jacket for size, answering questions from a picked handful of newsmen and awaiting presentation ceremonies when Palmer started his charge.

Palmer missed his birdie at the fifteenth and also parred the 190-yard, par-3, sixteenth.

"You've got it," a newsman said to Venturi. "Nobody's going to play those last two holes in two under par."

Venturi smiled wanly. He was afraid to hope.

Palmer now faced the seventeenth and eighteenth holes. He had stood in the same position the year before, with victory in his grasp, only to blow it by overhitting his approach on the seventeenth and missing a 4-foot putt on the eighteenth to finish bogey-bogey.

On the 400-yard, par-4 seventeenth, Palmer determined this time to keep the ball short. After a good drive, he pitched and the ball bit. He was 35 feet away. Bill Casper, Palmer's playing companion, putted out, and then Palmer, hunched over the ball with his legs forming an "X," stroked the putt. It rolled into the hole. A birdie three. Now Arnie needed only a par on the final hole to tie.

He boomed his drive 300 yards down the middle of the fairway. The crowd—total attendance for the day was put at 35,000—lined the fairway and swarmed around the green. Venturi, pale and nervous, watched on television.

Around 120 yards short of the green, Palmer yanked out a six-iron. He took a last puff on a cigarette and dropped it on the ground. He tugged at a glove on his left hand and took a jerk at his trousers—familiar gestures when he starts to move.

The crowd began murmuring and the noise was like an ocean swell. "Quiet, please. Everyone please be quiet," bellowed Ralph Hutchinson, the lavishly dressed professional announcing at the eighteenth green.

"I knew what I had to do to win," Palmer said later. "I've got to admit the tension was terrific."

He swung crisply and the ball sailed for the green. There was a tremendous roar when it hit near the cup and rolled 6 feet away. Palmer still had a putt left, and the specter of the miss the year before came up to haunt him. He played for a break and the ball went squarely into the hole. A second birdie—and the championship.

"I don't think any single shot gave me a greater thrill, or was more important to me," Palmer said afterward.

The Putt that Triggered Bob Jones's Grand Slam

It was just a 12-foot putt, hardly worth comparing with a double eagle, a hole-in-one, or a blast into the cup from out of a sand trap. Yet Grantland Rice, the famed syndicated sportswriter, and O. B. Keeler, Bob Jones's Boswell, both called it their greatest thrill in a quarter of a century of following the game—and neither saw it.

The putt took on added significance because of the circumstances under which it was made and the history it apparently unfurled.

Bob Jones sank the putt June 29, 1929, on the seventy-second and final hole of the United States Open Golf Championship. The site was the West Course of the Winged Foot Golf Club at Mamaroneck, New York.

The putt gave Jones a tie and ultimately the championship. He had won two of them before and he was destined to win a fourth, in his Grand Slam year of 1930. Nevertheless, Jones himself said he never made a more important shot.

These were the circumstances:

It was the final round of the tournament and as Jones left the twelfth green he appeared a certain winner. He had a six-stroke lead over his nearest challenger, Al Espinosa, with only six holes to play. Nobody made up that kind of a deficit on the great Jones.

Suddenly the tournament experienced a sharp turn of fortunes.

Espinosa, with a fat eight at the twelfth, shrugged his shoulders and conceded he had blown his chance. Loose and relaxed, he proceeded to play the last six holes in 22 strokes for a closing 75—a total score of 294.

Jones, playing behind the veteran professional, relaxed. He bogied the thirteenth, took a disastrous seven at the fifteenth, and 3-putted the sixteenth from 20 feet. Now he had dissipated his 6-stroke lead and needed to finish 4 – 4 for a tie.

Excitement was electric. Spectators swarmed onto the course. Sportswriters tore up their leads of a Jones victory and rushed to the closing holes to catch the drama. Among these were Grantland Rice and O. B. Keeler.

Jones got his four at the seventeenth. On the eighteenth, he hit a good drive up the middle but his pitch caught the rim of a deep bunker and rolled down the embankment, stopping in the tall grass just short of the sand.

Jones chopped the ball out of the heavy grass. The ball rolled onto the green but stopped at 12 feet from the flag. It was a tough putt over curving terrain. He would have to play a break of at least a foot to get it into the hole.

"I couldn't look," Keeler said later. "I was afraid if I watched he would miss the putt." Rice said he also turned his head away and waited for the crowd reaction.

They heard a sharp click. Then they waited for what seemed like endless minutes. There was a gasp, then a loud roar. Jones had made it. He had tied Espinosa for the title.

Viewers said later the ball had rolled slowly over the ice-slick green, hesitated, seemed to stop, then dropped home. It was one of Bob's famous "dying ball" putts.

If he had missed, Jones would have shot an 80, his first in the Open Championship. He would have blown a six-stroke lead and the title. Many speculated that such a collapse might have wrecked his brilliant career.

Instead, Jones went out the next day and shot rounds of 72 and 69 to crush Espinosa in the play-off by the margin of 23 strokes.

"I will always believe," Rice wrote later, "that the remainder of Bobby's career hung on that putt and that from this stemmed the Grand Slam of 1930."

Walter Hagen's Miraculous Shots that Failed

For many years, when old-timers gathered around the locker rooms in Britain to discuss momentous golf shots, precedence was given to a Walter Hagen shot that failed to come off. Golf-minded Britons regarded it as more dramatic than most of the successful shots that clinched championships and changed golfing history.

It was a shot that could have hit home, but did not. Nevertheless, it served to accentuate the brashness and showmanship of this swashbuckling American professional who excited world galleries for two decades.

The occasion was the 1926 British Open Championship at the Royal Lytham and St. Anne's course. Bob Jones had finished the 72 holes in 291 for the lead. It looked secure as Hagen came to the par 4 final hole needing an eagle 2 to tie — secure, that is, to everyone except the cocky Hagen.

"It had been done before, I thought it could be done again," the Haig explained later.

Hagen's drive on the eighteenth was straight down the middle and long enough. It left him a 150-yard approach to the green.

Hagen strode a few yards toward the green to survey the assignment. Jones and the British star, J. H. Taylor, watched tensely from the club house balcony.

Jones acknowledged later that he felt fidgety and uneasy. "I didn't know what this fellow might do," Bobby said.

Hagen walked back to his ball and then turned to the official scorer, standing nearby.

"Would you please go up and hold the flag?" Hagen requested.

The scorer looked at the Haig incredulously and blinked. He thought he must have misunderstood.

"What's that again, sir?" he said.

"I'd appreciate it if you would go up and hold the flag," Hagen repeated.

Hagen said it loud enough this time for many in the gallery of 10,000 packed around the green and along the fairway to hear. A buzz went through the crowd. "Does this man really expect to sink that shot?" "Who does he think he is?"

There was some method in Hagen's seemingly mad request. By concentrating the attention of the gallery on the official holding the flag 150 yards away, he eased his own tension.

Hagen said later he could concentrate on his shot. If he should miss, the gallery would consider the official — not Hagen — a goat for holding the stick at such a distance.

The Haig set himself over the ball. There was not a move or a sound when he swung crisply through the ball.

The shot was better than Hagen dared hope under the circumstances. It flew straight at the pin, landed on the edge of the green, and rolled toward the hole. The crowd gasped.

The ball, rolling at a fast pace, skipped over the hole and dropped into a shallow scooped-out sand trap at the back of the green. The applause was deafening.

Had the flag stick been left in the hole, the ball probably would have struck it and plunked into the hole for a tying deuce. It seemed immaterial that Hagen took a bogey five and finished third at 295.

"I turned my back on you, Walter," Jones told Hagen later. "A guy with that much confidence would be fool lucky enough to make it."

Billy Joe Patton's Moment of Glory

The distinctive feature of the Masters Golf Tournament is that it never has been won by an amateur, but the big April spectacle in Augusta, Georgia, got a fright in 1954. That was the year of Billy Joe Patton's spectacular charge and his unforgettable hole-in-one.

Billy Joe was a scrambling, exciting lumber executive from Morganton, North Carolina, who left an indelible print on golf in the mid-1950s, when Ben Hogan was at his peak. A leading amateur, Patton attracted large galleries because of his flair for driving the ball a country mile, battling his way miraculously out of trouble, and all the while carrying on a running dialogue with his worshipful following.

His greatest moment of glory came in the 1954 Masters, the year after Hogan had made his triple slam of winning the Masters, U. S., and British Opens.

Billy Joe started by winning the driving contest, the day before the tournament opening, with a prodigious drive of 338 yards on his first of three drives. Told he was entitled to two more drives, he said, "No, thanks, I might miss the next one altogether."

The bespectacled, crew-cut North Carolinian, slamming and joking his way out of traps and rough, tied old E. J. (Dutch) Harrison for the opening round lead with a 70, 2 strokes better than defending champion Hogan and 4 better than Sam Snead.

The crowd flocked behind the uninhibited amateur the next day and, playing in a stiff wind, he delighted the flock with a 74 which gave him the undisputed lead at 144. Hogan had 145, Snead 147.

Newsmen had a holiday. "Hold on, boys," Billy Joe cautioned. "I may shoot an 80 tomorrow." He did not go quite that high but he did scramble to a 75 under easier playing conditions, and with 219 he fell 5 shots back of a rallying Hogan.

On the final round, the bulk of the gallery deserted Patton and flocked to the two old pros, Hogan and Snead. It stacked up as a strictly Hogan-Snead show.

Hogan was putting out on the third green when a loud roar rumbled through the trees. "It's Billy Joe," somebody yelled and there was a stampede toward the area of the ovation — the sixth hole.

There Patton had just sunk a hole-in-one to move back into contention.

The sixth at Augusta is the "Juniper Hole," 190 yards, par 3, a steep slope from tee to green. The pin was placed dangerously close to the edge of the green, and only a gambler would go for it.

Nobody ever denied Billy Joe was a gambler. He chose a five-iron, changed his stance a couple of times, and hit. The ball cleared the front edge of the green, rolled toward the cup, and finally lodged against the pin. The pin was carefully removed, and the ball dropped — a hole-in-one.

Fired by new confidence, Billy Joe took a hitch in his belt and started moving. He birdied the eighth and ninth, passed Snead, and caught Hogan. Disdaining caution, he hit out boldly on every shot and fired at the pin on every green. On the par 5 thirteenth, he went for the green and dumped his approach into the water, winding up with a double bogey seven. It was costly. Snead and Hogan tied for first at 289, Patton one stroke back at 290. Snead won the play-off.

Billy Joe never regretted it. "I didn't come to play safe," he said.

Lew Worsham's $62,000 Eagle

No single golf shot, except possibly Gene Sarazen's double eagle in the 1935 Masters, has created as much attention as Lew Worsham's $62,000 eagle in the 1953 World's Championship at Tam O'Shanter in Chicago.

The circumstances could not have been more dramatic. The tournament was the world's richest at the time. It was being shown on national television, before the eyes of millions. The shot, last of the day, produced a movie-thriller climax.

The date was Sunday, August 9, 1953, the final day of Industrialist George May's All-America and World Championship tournaments, which lured leading golfers in quest of the fabulous prize money.

Chandler Harper, playing in the next to last threesome, thrilled the viewers by lacing his second shot in the 370-yard, par 4 finishing hole to within 1 1/2 feet of the pin and sinking for a birdie three.

This gave Harper a 72-hole score of 279 and apparently the first prize of $25,000 cash plus a series of $1,000 exhibitions. Only one group remained on the course.

The big TV cameras zeroed in on the smiling Harper and he was being congratulated as the winner when the final threesome lumbered down the eighteenth fairway. In the threesome were Doug Ford, Dave Douglas, and Lew Worsham, playing in semiprivacy.

Few knew it, but Worsham needed only to duplicate Harper's birdie to tie for first place and necessitate a play-off. His drive was down the middle, nestling in a good lie in the little valley between the elevated green and elevated tee. He was 104 yards — by measurement — from home. The green was guarded on the left and right by trees. A small river ran in front of it.

While officials and well-wishers were swarming around the happy Harper at the eighteenth green, Worsham, the 1947 National Open champion from Oakmont, Pennsylvania, swung easily through the ball. The ball soared to the green, hit about 25 feet short of the pin, rolled over a small ridge and into the cup.

Pandemonium followed. The eagle deuce gave Worsham a 31 for the back 9 and a score of 278, winning by one stroke.

First prize was $25,000 and an option to play exhibitions at $1,000 each for George May. Worsham played 37 of these, making his total prize money $62,000.

The shot and its attendant victory was tasteful to the Oakmont pro for another reason. The year before, in the same tournament, Worsham had a four-stroke lead with nine holes to play but drove out of bounds on the fourteenth and fifteenth holes to blow his chances.

Observers estimated at first that the eagle was made with a wedge from 140 yards. Later, from movie film, Worsham had the distance measured and it was put exactly at 104 yards.

"I knew it wasn't 140 yards; I couldn't hit a wedge that far," Worsham said. "The club I used was a double service wedge. It was a combination of sand and pitching wedge."

George May later abandoned sponsorship of the Tam O'Shanter tournament because of constant conflicts with the Professional Golfers Association and some of the players, but not before erecting a small monument to one of the greatest — and most profitable — golf shots ever played.

Gene Sarazen's Double Eagle

In the early days of the Masters Tournament, when only a handful of sportswriters covered the event instead of the hundreds who came later, the press quarters were set up on the second floor porch of the Augusta National Club's white club house, overlooking the eighteenth green.

There, men such as Alan Gould of The Associated Press, Henry McLemore of the United Press, Bill Richardson of *The New York Times*, Grantland Rice, and O. B. Keeler pecked out stories that were read around the world.

Such was the setting on a crisp April day in 1935 with the second Masters going into its final-round climax.

Handsome Craig Wood had just holed a birdie three on the seventy-second hole for a score of 282. Green-coated officials and spectators rushed up to congratulate him. He appeared the certain winner. A few players were still on the course, none apparently with a chance for the title.

This was not an age of quick communication. No telephone wires stretched to the outlying holes. There were no walkie-talkies. Reporters depended on runners, usually unemployed Negro caddies, to get their details.

Alan Gould of the AP was preparing his night lead based on a Craig Wood victory when one of his runners came up puffing with a report from the course.

"Mistuh Sarazen had a two at fifteen," the runner said.

"A two!" blustered Gould. "Go back out there and get the score right."

No. 15 was a 485-yard, par 5 hole. Nobody made it in two.

Moments later, the runner returned, still breathless. "Yes, suh, Mister Gould, it really was a two."

Sarazen was just moving to the fifteenth when he squinted at the club house in the distance and saw the commotion raised by Wood's finish. Word drifted back on Wood's score.

"What do I need to win?" the bouncy Gene asked his Negro caddy, Stovepipe.

"Let me see," the caddy figured. "You need four three's." Par in was 5 – 3 – 4 – 4.

Walter Hagen, playing with Sarazen, hit his second short of the pond guarding the green. Sarazen, always a go-for-broke competitor, knew this would not be enough. To insure a birdie four on the hole, he had to clear the water.

His drive was about 250 yards but the lie was close. He and his caddy deliberated over whether to use a three-wood or four-wood and finally decided it would take a four to give the ball its needed loft.

Gene took out a lucky ring and rubbed it on Stovepipe's close-cropped head. Both laughed. The tension eased.

"I rode into the shot with every ounce of strength and timing I could muster," Sarazen said later. "The split-second I hit the ball, I knew it would carry the pond."

The ball flew like a rifle shot, not more than 30 feet in the air. The ball dropped on the green and rolled into the cup. The small crowd framing the green let out a thunderous roar. This brought hundreds streaming from the club house.

The shot had carried 235 yards. It was a rare double eagle two.

Now the gallery had swelled to 5,000. Sarazen got his three on the short sixteenth, missing a 10-foot putt for a birdie, then parred the seventeenth. Now Gene needed a birdie three on the final hole to win, a par to tie.

As tension mounted, the determined little battler hit a good drive and then cut a four-wood through the crosswind to the green, 30 feet from the cup.

Gene babied the putt to within 3 feet and then sank for 282 and a tie. The crowd went wild. With the momentum generated by his surging finish, Sarazen beat Wood by 5 strokes in the 36-hole play-off the next day.

And Alan Gould apologized to his runner.

(1966)

222

A Common Man with an Uncommon Touch

Curry Kirkpatrick

Little did anyone know, myself included, that when Lee Trevino burst onto the golf scene during the 1967 United States Open at Baltusrol we were seeing the beginning of a legend. His fifth place finish there earned him some space in the newspapers as the "unknown" who had brought only two pairs of pants and three sport shirts with him to play in golf's most prestigious tournament. We didn't know at the time that that was all he had to his name, but the $6000 he won changed that situation in a hurry.

Since then, Lee has never had to worry where his next buck was coming from. What a blessing that has been. Not only to him, but to the millions who have watched and who have admired this modern-day Horatio Alger story. Lee has added colour, humour and a certain spontaneous impertinence to a sport which never has been overburdened by such attributes, and he has done it in such a good-natured way as to marshal thousands to his gallery ranks as proud members of "Lee's Fleas." I am one of them.

Sports Illustrated, when it selected Trevino as its "Sportsman of the Year" in 1971, characterized him best as "a common man with an uncommon touch." Curry Kirkpatrick, that magazine's bright young writer who did this feature on Trevino, didn't pull any punches in detailing the rags-to-riches story. And despite his wretched, raucous beginning, Lee comes off a real winner, and deservedly so.

In the ensuing eleven years, Trevino has gone on successfully to defend his British Open championship in 1972 and to win sixteen of the twenty-six tour titles, including the 1974 PGA Championship at Tanglewood and the World Series of Golf at Firestone, two courses of my design. These latter victories evoked a typical Trevino comment: "Now I know I've got Trent Jones in my pocket."

IF GOLF EVER NEEDED a certain kind of man to dull the harsh scorn of its critics, he was found in 1971. Golf found Lee Trevino, a common man with an uncommon touch who has bewitched, bothered and bewildered the custodians of the game's mores. What Lee Trevino has done is take the game out of the country club boardroom and put it in the parking lot where everybody—not just doctors and lawyers but Indian chiefs, too—can get at it. Trevino's special appeal is to the poor, the minorities, the people who before his emergence as a star could never make a reality of golf the way they could of baseball, say, or football or boxing. This distinction is never more apparent than when Trevino stands against the other eminences of the game: Palmer and Nicklaus, Casper and Player.

For the most part, these men had earned and cornered what present-day big-time golf was about before Lee Trevino—big homes with swimming pools, conglomerates, armies of middle-class followers. Then he came along, exploding our myths, massaging our viscera, yapping, yapping, yapping.

Bobby Goldsboro, the singer and a close friend, has described Trevino's impact. "Every time Lee talks about winning, it is of the hard work it took to get ahead," says Goldsboro. "He is talking to those kids who are living the way he used to, telling them what they *must* do. It's nice to believe that some of them will turn out all right because of Lee."

In El Paso right now, at any ceremonial occasion where the name of Lee Trevino is invoked, that city's "Singing Policeman," Ramon Rendon, bursts into his rendition of Don Isidro A. Dovali's now classic, *Qué Viva Lee Trevino:*

Qué Viva Lee Trevino, El Super-Mexicano.
Qué Viva Lee Trevino . . .
ser un campeón completo.

Beneath the lyrics' surface lie the tales of driving ranges, Band-Aids covering tattoos, wild parties, Marine details, gag lines, Lee's Fleas, the band swing, the hustle, the popularity—in short, a total cabbages and kings scenario—but they would be nowhere without Trevino's ability to hit a golf ball and to win tournaments.

His victory in the U. S. Open at Rochester in 1968, fashioned while playing against one of the finest artisans on the tour, Bert Yancey, and while being pressured by Jack Nicklaus thundering up ahead, was considered a fluke—until he won the Hawaiian Open later in the year and finished the season with $123,127 in prize money. In 1969 he won the Tucson Open, the World Cup individual prize and more than $100,000 again. In 1970, though his only two victories came early in the year, Trevino accomplished what he likes to refer to as "the triple crown." He was the leading money-winner with $157,037, led the Exemption Point Standings and won the Vardon Trophy for lowest scoring average.

This summer Trevino's achievement of winning the Open championships of the United States, Canada and Great Britain in less than a month was the stuff of which instant legends are made. But a quick examination of the few weeks prior to his historical feat reveals just how well he was playing. In the six weeks after the tour arrived in Texas in May, he accomplished the following:

Dallas—Tied for second, one stroke back of the leader going into the last round; finished tied for fifth.

Houston—Eleven shots back after 36 holes, tied for the lead with five holes to play; missed the playoff by one shot.

Fort Worth—Tied for the lead with nine holes to play; lost by four shots in 15- to 20-mph winds on the back nine.

Memphis—Won tournament.

Atlanta—Missed playoff by one shot.

Charlotte—Lost in playoff.

And then came the hot streak when Trevino beat Nicklaus in a playoff at Merion for the U. S. title, beat Art Wall in a playoff at Montreal for the Canadian title and beat the Formosan Lu for the British championship. With luck, he might have won an astonishing six tournaments in seven weeks.

Wherever one went there was Lee Trevino. On newsstands, radio, TV. Throwing a hat. Swinging a club. Laughing. Frolicking. Transcending the game of golf. Engraving his spirit onto the pop culture of America. Shortly it became easy to forget where he had come from and how far this squat, swarthy, happy fellow with the magnificent Mexican-American face had gone in four short years.

Lee Buck Trevino was born out of wedlock on Dec. 1, 1939. He was raised by his maternal grandfather, Joe Trevino, an immigrant from Monterrey, and his mother, Juanita, in an old maintenance shack on the outskirts of Dallas. Old Joe was a gravedigger at Hillcrest cemetery and a beer drinker of astounding durability who, Lee says, "was the only man I ever knew could sit in a bar from nine in the morning to nine at night, then get up and drive away." Also, Joe Trevino was one of those rare individuals who stopped working only because it was time to die. That was two years ago, and when his grandson buried him it was where the old man had requested: alongside a goldfish pond at Hillcrest and not, as Old Joe said, "way back in some corner and forgotten."

In the old days the Trevino shack, devoid of electricity or plumbing, sat in a hayfield off the Glen Lake golf course where the skinny little Mexican boy used to scavenge for balls. For an early golf indoctrination he hit horse apples with an abandoned five-iron and played putting games with his grandfather in the yard. "It was a lonely life," Trevino says. "I was never around anybody. I was all by myself, no one to talk to. I'd just go hunt rabbits and fish."

Lee finally had to quit school in the eighth grade to help finance the simple luxury of food for his family, which included two sisters. "Starches are cheap and Mexicans are usually overweight because they eat starches," he says. "I never knew what steak was. The closest we ever came to real meat was Texas hash and baloney. We'd drink Kool-Aid."

Trevino worked at Glen Lakes for a time before taking a job at Hardy Greenwood's driving range and pitch 'n putt course in North Dallas. He played enough golf in the next two years to get his handicap down to five, but his interest in the range dwindled. When offered an ultimatum by Greenwood, Trevino quit his job to join the Marines.

"I was messed up and lost," he says. "I wasn't settled down. I didn't know what I wanted to do. Never had any dates. I'd fall in love with a fence post." As a machine gunner in the Far East, Trevino found a camaraderie that he never knew at home. He had friends, people to talk to, duties, responsibility. "It was like camping out," he says. "I volunteered for everything. These were guys my own age and we were having a ball."

He enjoyed the experience so fully that he re-upped for two. He was assigned to Special Services, where he spent the rest of his tour playing golf and teaching rifle range classes on Okinawa. "Maybe it was the best time of my life," says Trevino. "I think I learned my sense of humor in the Marines, laughing and raising hell. And, of course, there was golf. If I hadn't joined, I know I'd be in prison today." In the fall of 1960 he got out of the corps and went back to Dallas with one purpose: to play golf.

Hardy Greenwood is a tall, spare man of 56 with a voice the texture of hardpan. He demands frugality as well as loyalty (on occasion he will accost a customer who has scuffed a ball a few feet and is preparing to hit it again, with "Hold it; at Hardy's we hit 'em just once"). He was overjoyed to have Lee back. He had taken young Trevino under his wing at 14 and introduced the youngster to amenable habits—regular meals, haircuts, cleanliness. He was the first person to encourage Lee to make a living at golf. He was the closest thing to a father Trevino ever had.

"We always like to say we raised Lee," says Greenwood. "We take the credit, the wife and me. He had the great natural swing even back then. He was good at everything. He picked up balls faster than anybody I ever had here. He mowed the greens, washed balls, cleaned the range, ran the shop. I could go out of town and Lee would take better care of the place than I did. But he was a hardhead, too. He sure has learned. I told him the last time he was here, 'You sure did grow up to be the smartest Mex I ever saw.'"

While Trevino worked hard from two PM to midnight at Hardy's, he played hard, too. He began swinging into early morning golf games at Tenison Park municipal course with Arnold Salinas, one of seven children in the kind of close-knit Mexican-American family that Trevino had always longed for; to this day Salinas remains his closest friend. The two enjoyed the same pursuits—card games, bowling, drinking beer, chasing waitresses, especially golf. When they first met at Tenison it was in competition to see who was the best Mexican player in town. Trevino was. After a lengthy night of celebrating victory, Trevino picked up Salinas at six in the morning for another round.

"What?" said Salinas. "I don't throw up till noon."

For the next couple of years Trevino's days were remarkably similar. Eighteen holes at Tenison. Work all day at Hardy's. Play all night with Salinas. Trevino was not becoming so wild, though, as to lose his ambition. He hit 1,000 balls nearly every day.

Trevino has since cultivated an image as a transcendent hustler, far beyond what his friends back in Dallas remember as the truth. "A hustler he is not and a hustler he has never been," says Salinas, who is now taking a fling at pro golf himself. "To hustle is to deceive. Lee was just there with his game and everybody knew it. They came over and said, 'I want four a side.' Lee said, 'You got it.' That's no hustle. He made the games hard and forced himself to play his best."

Erwin Hardwicke, then and now the resident pro at Tenison, remembers "the little Meskin bugger coming through the door with his white T shirt and his Bermuda shorts and the worst clubs going. When we found out he was Hardy's boy, we let him play for free," says Hardwicke. "He 'bout lived over here after that. 'Boys,' he'd say. 'We're burnin' daylight. I got to get back to work. Let's play.' Man, could he play. It was uncanny how that little Meskin could play."

In 1963 Greenwood applied for playing privileges for his young friend, but possibly because Trevino had no official record, he was turned down. Two years later, just after winning the Texas State Open, Trevino wanted to apply for a PGA card. Greenwood refused to verify his employment.

Neither man will go into detail about their split, but friction had been building for some time. Trevino had been married for a couple of years, had fathered a son, Ricky, and then was divorced when his wife could not cope with his devotion to golf and his long absences from home. In the spring of 1964 Trevino went on a savage, uninhibited tear—drinking to excess, eating, in his own words, "trash" foods, sleeping irregularly and seldom in the same place. He lost 50 pounds. "My granddad said the only way you forget about a woman is to find another one and he was right," says Trevino. He found Claudia Fenley, a 17-year-old ticket-taker at the Capri Theatre downtown. They dated at the Cotton Palace bowling lanes and soon after were married.

Whether Greenwood disapproved of Trevino's erratic life-style or felt betrayed of his trust he will not say. "Lee just wasn't thinking right to go out on the tour," he explains. "Physically, he was always ready. But messin' around with that drinking.... I told my wife, 'We were right to hold Lee back.' Everything seems to have worked out. That Claudia done wonders for him."

Furious at the time, Trevino "got hot, got drunk and then made some calls." The Dallas area chapter of the PGA declined to help and Trevino is still angry. "I didn't get a fair shake, that's all," he says. "Now there's some of them even take credit for what I've done. I don't hold grudges but I won't even *look* at those people anymore."

Inevitably, Trevino's hard work on the practice range and reputation as a player of substance saved him. A wealthy cotton farmer named Martin Lettunich, who spent his off hours betting on and attempting to play golf, brought him to El Paso, introduced him as "my Mexican tractor driver" and watched with glee as Trevino ate up everyone around for respectable sums of money. The Trevinos lived for a while in a trailer on a farm before moving into a motel hard by Horizon Hills Country Club, where Lee had been hired as an assistant pro.

Although Trevino was intent on earning his card and joining the tour, he had not yet honed the rough edges of his personality, making the efforts in his behalf by Bill Eschenbrenner and Herb Wimberly, two local pros, that much more difficult. The head professional at El Paso Country Club, Eschenbrenner had worked as a boy at Rivercrest in Fort Worth watching Ben Hogan and he recognized Trevino's ability. "I had faith in him," Eschenbrenner says. "He had Hogan's action in the swing. It's that secret, or whatever it is, to take the club to the top and lock it. Just dead lock it, and keep it that way all the way through."

Eschenbrenner and Wimberly were pushing for Trevino through their own New Mexico chapter of the PGA when Lee borrowed some money to play in the U. S. Open at San Francisco in 1966. He finished 54th. The following year the PGA came through with his card, but Trevino was so discouraged by his previous showing that Claudia herself had to send in his $20 qualifying fee for the 1967 Open. Suddenly everything came together. At Odessa, Texas, Trevino shot the lowest qualifying rounds and then finished fifth in the Open proper at Baltusrol. Super Mex was on his way.

"The key to Trevino as a man is that he remembers," says Eschenbrenner. "He is devoted to the PGA. When he joined he said he'd be the best member the New Mexico chapter ever had, and he has been. Most of the big names pay lip service. This guy has played in our New Mexico pro-am in a blizzard. Every year he tells me to put him down for one of our sectional tournaments, and he's there."

Since the start of 1968 Lee Trevino has finished in the top 10 in 50 PGA tournaments, more than anyone in the game. He has won more money in that time than anyone except Jack Nicklaus. He has represented the United States on two Ryder Cup and three World Cup teams. And he has done it all with a swing that suggests a lumberjack going after the nearest redwood.

In purely technical terms Trevino's swing is all wrong. He takes the club back on an extremely flat plane from an open stance that is aiming left. To avoid the danger of duck hooking, he blocks out solidly with his left leg firm as he comes into the shot. At that moment he corrects whatever else is negative by the use of his hands. With this instinctive hand action — which along with food and white-billed caps is one of the few things Ben Hogan has ever praised — he opens the club face at impact and fades the ball left to right, dipping his right shoulder along the plane.

Always a hooker off the tee, Trevino watched Hogan one day in 1961 as he hit marvelous fade after marvelous fade. His outlook on the game changed immediately. "Before, I had always been upright — a picture," says Trevino. "Then I had got me this awful-looking sweepy swing so I could hook it. When I saw Hogan it dawned on me, left to right, left to right. I have to throw my club way out right to fade it now. I get into that low shoulder turn because of my height. I can't get power upright."

Dave Hill acknowledges the importance of Trevino's shoulder turn. "If he ever gets up high with it, he's got to go back to eating tacos," says Hill. "His right side stays so low he never has to worry about getting over the ball too much. Lee doesn't know it, but he plays with his right arm and right shoulder almost exclusively. He's the best I've ever seen at coming through with the right hand and wrist."

Frank Beard marvels at Trevino's nerves as much as the hand action. "He's a very quick player," Beard says. "He's never in a vise like some of the slower guys. He also practices more than any human being I know. The man *works*."

Jack Nicklaus says: "Only the player himself knows what his weak shots are and which ones he is scared of hitting. If there is a weak part in Lee's game, it's probably the flat swing — not being able to hook the ball when he has to. The swing isn't wrong; it just limits the things he can do. When Trevino isn't hitting it straight, he's in trouble because his flat swing can't get the ball high enough out of the rough. The thing is I've never seen him when he wasn't hitting it straight. He probably hits more solid shots than anyone out here."

The difference between the good players in golf and the best lies not in the swing but in an infinitesimal part of the brain. "There are a lot of fine strikers of the ball," says Nicklaus. "Trevino is a fine striker *and* a fine thinker. He knows what he's doing all the time. Where to hit? What to hit? Why?"

Trevino agrees that he is a planner. "I think about what I should make on a hole in every tournament," he says. "For instance, if I've got a par-3, 220-yard hole I'll hope to play the thing in one over par for four rounds. I won't go for the pin, just the green, and I almost never gamble."

"Weaknesses? There are a lot of them. I'm a terrible fairway bunker player. I used to be the world's worst putter, but playing on good greens has made the difference there. I also used to be a very bad long iron player. Up to two years ago I couldn't hit a two- or three-iron for nothin'. But I practiced."

Trevino is at his strongest on one-on-one, when he can use psychology against an opponent. His ability to manipulate emotions on the course is a regular staple of the legend. "On the greens I'll tell my caddie, 'That thing broke a ton, Neil,' when I actually pulled the putt. The other guy, he might hit his putt wrong now. Course, I only did this sort of thing before I got to the tour," Trevino adds and winks, conveniently neglecting to mention that Neil did not become his caddie until after he had joined the tour.

Undoubtedly most of Trevino's shots will be forgotten long before people stop talking about The Snake. Trevino first unveiled his rubber toy at the Colonial Invitational in Fort Worth when he did a springy number with it for the caddies there. A month later on the first tee of the Open playoff at refined, patriarchal old Merion, he whisked the snake over to Nicklaus, whereupon the golfing universe did one of two things: applauded this little Mexican proponent of antiestablishmentarianism, or looked down their noses at such an ungrateful wetback.

Most of the players were dumbfounded; some unforgiving. They did not know that on the tee Nicklaus had noticed the snake in Trevino's bag and waved for him to throw it over. "I thought it would relieve the tension," Jack says. "It relaxed *me*."

Trevino says: "No more snakes. Too many people were angry."

The incident at Merion has been one of the few times Trevino was considered to have overstepped the boundaries in his showmanship on the tour. Unlike Chi Chi Rodriguez, who infuriates many of his playing companions with his dancing, swordplay and matador tricks, Trevino's chatterboxing gagman performance seems to have made no enemies.

"There's a difference," says one player. "Some acts are a facade, a fake. Lee is sincere as he can be. He fools around and then hits the ball. For the 20 seconds it takes to select a club and make the shot, he's as much a Hogan—a concentrator—as anybody ever was."

Off the course, Trevino has become a thorough entertainer with few flaws. In short public speeches, working without notes, he is a gem—no grammatical errors, embarrassing pauses, confused "uuuuhhhhs" or overblown language. Unless the situation calls for a humorous departure from it, his English is perfect. In informal conversation, however, there are a whole lot of "don't make no difference" and "them people used to could play" constructions.

"He just doesn't concentrate unless he has to," says Claudia. "Yeah," says Trevino. "There wasn't much tellin' where I could've went if I had got education."

He talks about the future. "I could be a comedian," he says. "I mean a real comedian. I know when to raise my voice and when not to. A guy gets too loud on me on the course, I say, 'I do the jokes here, sir. It's not too often Mexes get inside the ropes.' You think I'm good in tournaments? Oh boy. Come to a clinic. I get nine thousand dollars for one of them babies, twelve thou on weekends. But I'm worth it. You get 18 holes of golf plus a comedy act."

In his nonpublic communication with the touring professionals, Trevino jabbers on in this way, but he does not tarry long in locker rooms.

"He's a hard man to get close to," says one veteran. "He has a few friends out here—Orville Moody and Cesar Sanudo maybe—but even they don't know him too well. I've never had a serious sit-down conversation with him. Every time we'd start, he'd go into that meaningless machine-gun yak. And then he'd have to leave and go somewhere. It's like he's afraid to shut up so we can find out what he's really like."

Trevino says he avoids clubhouses because "too many drunks want to grab your hand and hold onto it. I have to quote for them: 'I'm not in love with you, sir. Let go.' That usually stops them. I'm not a country-club player. I'm a municipal guy."

There was a period last year when Trevino had not won a golf tournament. Business problems were multiplying. He was drinking heavily on tour and keeping late hours. His mother was sick with cancer—she died this fall—and his marriage was falling apart. Still, his was a cheery countenance wherever he traveled the tour, and in time Claudia started showing up at several way stations along the golf trail. He toned down the night life and the alcohol and, of course, he started winning again. A fortnight ago Trevino was asked when does he ever feel depression.

"When I remember my mother being so ill," he replied. "But I stop that quick. I've visited a lot of hospitals with crippled kids and burned-up people in them. Men with car payments and kids to put through college and all those other financial burdens should go visit a hospital whenever they start feeling sorry for themselves."

Trevino's charitable donations are well known: $10,000 to the family of his former roommate, Ted Makalena, after he won the Hawaiian Open; $2,000 for a caddie scholarship fund in Singapore after the World Cup; $5,000 to the St. Jude Hospital in Memphis after he won the Memphis Open; $4,800 to the Clunder Lodge orphanage near Southport following the British Open. He spends time and money on the Christmas Seal and Easter Seal campaigns nationally and sponsors projects for the Boys Club and Shriners lodge in El Paso. But he disassociates himself from political movements, especially those with a Mexican-American complexion. Trevino will not comment on Cesar Chavez because "I don't believe in helping just one race or nationality," he says. "People ask me if I'm doing this winning and making this money for my people. It doesn't matter. I'm doing it for my wife—and she's white. A lot of Mexicans don't like that. A lot of whites don't like it, either, I suppose. I'm only concerned with the poor—black, white, yellow, red—and the youth. Promoters turn me off right away when they shill for Mexicans as a group. A Mexican-American hospital, for instance. No blacks allowed in? No Jews? I don't want to segregate. That's exactly backwards."

At home in El Paso where, one presumes, he can be genuinely himself, Trevino is a happy-go-lucky, wisecracking, loud and noisy hombre—which surely must be a tipoff to all those who seek hidden meanings and the "truth" behind the man. Claudia, a pert blonde with a Sandy Duncan cuteness about her and a good head for business, has adapted well. Alone, she picked out an attractive five-bedroom ranch-style home in the manicured neighborhood of Eastridge while the family awaits the construction of a house near Trevino's new golf course and resort complex on the New Mexico border. Trevino's first son, now 9, lives with his mother in Columbia, Mo. Lesley, 6, and Tony "Baloney," 2, live with Lee and Claudia in El Paso.

Recently, on a warm October night in the middle of a short vacation at home, Lee Trevino took his family along with a convivial retinue of friends and relatives to the circus. He ate popcorn, pulled cotton candy and held fast to his Mickey Mouse helium balloons as the tumblers, jugglers, clowns, elephants, tigers and assorted trapeze and balancing people wowed the audience. Eyes glistening, head shaking, amazed, Trevino responded with little gasps of surprise. "I'm lovin' this tonight," he said at one point. "Really I am. Someday I hope my kids will understand how lucky they are to be here." It was, of course, Lee Trevino's first circus.

(December 1971)

Persistent Player Gaining on Goal To Be Greatest
Nick Seitz

The only man I know who spends more time in an airplane than I do is Gary Player, the intense little South African with one of the most positive attitudes in golf. His unwavering desire to succeed has made him a world-class golfer mentioned in the same breath with Jack Nicklaus and Arnold Palmer as a modern-day triumvirate which television once dubbed "The Big Three."

Like millions of others, I have been an admirer of Gary since he first began his trans-oceanic flights from Johannesburg a quarter-century ago to compete on the American golf tour. I have also been privileged to count him a good friend. With the possible exception of Ben Hogan, another great achiever, no one has worked harder at the game than Gary. And the results have been worth the effort. Besides his twenty-one victories on the U. S. tour, Gary has three Masters, two British Opens, two PGAs and the 1965 United States Open to his credit, along with national titles in half a dozen countries around the world. He is a golfer who has made the most of his capabilities.

Additionally, he has been a goodwill ambassador of the game and one of mankind's great humanitarians — he gave his U. S. Open purse to junior golf and to cancer research. He also defied his country's apartheid policy by sponsoring and playing a series of exhibitions in South Africa with Lee Elder, America's premier black golfer, in 1975.

Nick Seitz, one of the most influential writers extant, as editor of Golf Digest, brings Player to life in this profile which, though dated, conveys the unmistakable drive, determination and the almost fanatical will to succeed of the most successful "invader" ever to make his presence known on the American golf scene.

PHIL RITSON, his early teacher, remembers sharing a room with a 16-year-old Gary Player and waking in the morning to find Player staring into a mirror and declaring, "I'm going to be the greatest golfer in the world! I'm going to be the greatest golfer in the world!" He must have said it 50 times, Ritson remembers, and then he went out and practiced sand shots by the dawn's early light.

Twenty-two years later, Player is one of a very few golfers who could be ranked great, and he has lost none of his zealous determination. It is easy to imagine him today in front of a mirror repeating his vows or out slapping sand shots as the rest of us slumber heedlessly through the pre-breakfast hours.

Depending on the day you ask him, he speaks with iron resolve and eyes that burn with the intensity of automobile headlights of one towering goal or another. He wants to win more tournaments than anybody else ever, he wants to complete a second cycle in the four major championships, he wants to strike the ball as purely as Ben Hogan. And he continues to compete around the world week after week in his unwavering quest for immortality.

"Of all of us," observed David Graham, the bright young touring pro from Australia, "he must deserves his success. Sometimes he carries his positive thinking too far—he's the only guy I know who can shoot 80 and say he hit the ball super—but then he's a great self-promoter. He's a credit to the sport, and his record is better than people realize. The man won a major tournament 15 years ago and he won two more majors in 1974."

I buy Graham's assessment. We have had enough lightweight debate over Player's sincerity in matters of physical fitness, race relations and international diplomacy. There is no denying that his enthusiasm can overflow the banks of thoughtfulness and spill out into ridiculous overstatement. For instance, he says with revival-tent fervor, "I know I've worked harder than any human being up to age 38, not just at golf but at developing my body, my public relations, my mind." A truly well-developed mind might not make a claim like that. A course on which Gary has just shot 67 always seems to be the toughest he has ever overcome. An almost compulsive competitor, Player has to have a test of character. If he doesn't have an obstacle to clear, he will erect one to keep up his interest, and at positive thinking he should give Norman Vincent Peale two a side.

But we should appreciate that Player is essentially a golfer and should be judged by us, as golf followers, essentially as a golfer. It is on the course, single-mindedly confronting—almost embracing—his next problem, that the real Gary Player reveals himself.

In 1974 Player was overshadowed by Johnny Miller, who almost forgot how to lose. Miller deserves the honors he got, including the PGA Player of the Year Award, but Player deserves more acclaim than *he* got. Certainly the PGA should re-evaluate its somewhat specious points system for determining a player of the year when Player finishes sixth.

Player in 1974 might have come closer to winning the Grand Slam than anyone has. In 1953 Ben Hogan won three of the four major tournaments but didn't enter the fourth, the PGA Championship. Six others have won two majors in a session since the Masters began in 1934: Craig Wood, Sam Snead, Jack Burke, Arnold Palmer, Jack Nicklaus and Lee Trevino. Did any of them come as close to the slam as Player? He won the Masters from behind and the British Open from in front (his seventh and eighth majors over-all), was tied for the lead in the U. S. Open after two rounds and was never more than five shots from the top in the PGA, matching the tournament record of 64 in the second round.

Player also won at Memphis in this country and took six titles abroad to go over 100 for his pro career. He capped the year by winning the Brazilian Open where he shot a shocking 59. "It was my best year," he says, "and maybe the best year anyone ever had." All this the year after major surgery, more serious than most of us realized, took him out of action and out of our field of attention.

As usual, Player came back from adversity with redoubled desire, in one case flying for two solid days and nights and disembarking from the plane to go straight to the course and win another tournament. He says he has traveled a total of four million miles to play golf, and that is one record that should outlive us all. Unlike the other superstars, he still practices as much as he plays, devising competitive games to make himself concentrate. He might hit chip shots, for example, until he sinks three dozen, come hell, high water or darkness.

Where does he get his dedication? How does he sustain it?

To reply, Player flashes back to his boyhood. We are eating in a New York restaurant, Player with the meticulousness he applies to everything, cutting his streak into uniformly small bites, drinking warm water laced with lemon juice to aid his digestive processes. He talks of his mother's death when he was eight and the insistence then and thereafter of his father, a good golfer who worked in the South African gold mines, that affirmative thinking is the only response to a challenge. That was his first exposure to positive thinking.

An older brother, Ian, further influenced him at an early age to try harder than the rest, Player says in his new book *Gary Player: World Golfer*. Ian, who refused to be held back by a chronically bad knee, laid out a five-mile track where the two ran together. One day the young Gary wearied and went to his knees, wheezing that he couldn't finish.

He writes, "My lungs felt as if they would burst. Without any warning Ian yanked me to my feet and cuffed me on the side of the head. 'What do you mean you can't make it, man?' he exploded, his face flushed red with anger. 'You can do anything you want to. Remember that. There's no room for *can't* in this life.' I'll never know how I did it, but even though my feet felt like they were weighted down with lead and my leg muscles were knotted with pain, I ran the rest of that five miles without stopping for anything. Believe me, I was cured of ever threatening to quit in front of Ian again."

It was Ian, Gary says, who gave him his first golf club, which he had whittled from a stick.

Soon after Player devoted himself to golf he made Ben Hogan his hero. He still reveres him, although there has been friction between the two. Hogan's example convinced Player that a small man without great natural athletic ability could construct a winning golf game.

"I promise you Hogan knows more about striking a golf ball than any man who ever lived," Player says. "If I could just ask him five questions and get his answers I'd be a lot better player than I am."

You no doubt have heard the story about Player calling Hogan at his equipment plant from overseas for help with his swing. The conversation is supposed to have gone something like this:

"Mr. Hogan, this is Gary Player. I would like to ask you a question about the swing."

"Gary, who do you work for?"

"The Dunlop company."

"Well, call Mr. Dunlop." Click.

Many experts suspect Player has always fought a pull-hook shot pattern because he wants to swing shorter and flatter like Hogan. Player periodically proclaims victory over his roundhouse hook; after winning the '74 Masters he announced he had found The Secret. *Golf Digest* instruction editor Larry Dennis pried it out of him — Player said he was holding his head more upright so he wouldn't block his natural backswing turn — but going into the 1975 season Player was still hooking dramatically at times.

The fact is, the tense-looking Player's game invariably is less imposing on the face of it than that of any other top player, what with his hooking and finishing his swing off-balance and using unorthodox strategy. He can shoot 68 and appear to be shooting 15 strokes higher. But he frequently brings off daredevil recovery shots. It doesn't hurt him to be off balance at the finish of his swing as long as he's in balance when he contacts the ball, and his strategy has a way of working out.

Says Phil Ritson, "Gary has the willpower to completely blot a bad shot out of his mind. He forgets it immediately and begins planning the next one. Every shot is a separate little game with him."

Perhaps most crucially, Player gives every shot his utmost respect and concentration whether it's a trouble shot or a tap-in putt. "The thing I admire so much about him," says Byron Nelson, "is that he just never wastes a stroke, not once in a year. He plays each shot for everything it's worth."

There is a story about Player emptying a shagbag on the practice green and making one-foot putts for an hour. A fellow pro asked him what in the name of Harry Vardon he was doing. "I'm getting used to sinking putts," was Player's answer.

At 38, we see no indication that Player's awesome dedication is flagging. He reminds us when we compare all-time greats that a player really should not be evaluated until his career is done, and implies that his is far from ended.

Says Jimmy Demaret, a peer of Hogan's, "Player is self-disciplined and physically fit, and I think he can be a super player for five more years without exhausting himself. When he gets in his 40s, his legs will get weak and then his nervous system will go. He won't be another Sam Snead, playing top golf at 62. He isn't big enough. But in my time Player and Hogan are the most dedicated golfers I've ever seen, and I've seen a few."

If the next five years are anything like 1974, Player might not have to play longer than five more years to satisfy even himself.

(February 1975)

The Game Is Her Life and Only Love
Barry McDermott

October 15, 1981, was a red-letter day for me for two reasons: it marked the unveiling of the new Crooked Oaks Golf Course on Seabrook Island, and I met Beth Daniel for the first time. We both had journeyed to the South Carolina resort with the same purpose: to participate in the formal dedication of the course, Beth as the resort's playing representative on the LPGA tour, and I as designer of the second golf course on the island.

Meeting with this young, dedicated golfer was a revelation. A quiet, soft-spoken woman, she seemed totally unaffected by having been the leading moneywinner and the LPGA's "Player of the Year" in the season previous. She obviously has set for herself even higher goals. Honest and straightforward, Beth impressed me as one who would be certain to achieve them.

By way of confirming my observation from a more practical standpoint was her golf game, which was put on display in an initial test of the new golf course. I was amazed by her power and accuracy and her uncanny ability to analyze a hole on the tee and play it the way I had intended it to be played. My initial exposure to Beth was an absolute delight, and I certainly was pleased to contemplate that her affiliation with Seabrook would indirectly reflect on me as a designer of one of its courses.

Admittedly, my meeting with Beth was casually brief and under the most favourable of circumstances. That is why I was so interested in reading Barry McDermott's feature on her in Sports Illustrated. It confirms my belief in her future greatness, but it also is a revelation in that it gives an insight into what really makes someone like Beth tick, and the kinds of demands she makes on herself in seeking to achieve her goals.

FUN? WELL, not really. True, Beth Daniel is the major figure in her game now, having unseated that smiling face, Nancy Lopez-Melton, the media heartthrob who almost single-handedly propelled the LPGA from newspaper agate to headline type. But Daniel has discovered that with stardom have come all these people looking at her, studying her, eating away at her time and privacy, challenging her to get back into the kitchen if she can't stand the heat. Her inclination is to put on a fake nose and dark sun glasses. Daniel doesn't want to be adored, only appreciated for what she is: the best woman golfer around. If she can get her putter fully straightened out and her temper cooled down, and if everyone will stay behind the gallery ropes so she can hit practice balls from dawn to dusk, she could become the finest female golfer of all time.

Naturally shy and reclusive—she and her similarly inclined roommates at Furman called themselves The Possums—Daniel is a reluctant superstar, just as the young Jack Nicklaus was some 20 years ago when he arrived, fat, rumpled and socially awkward, to challenge the charisma of Arnold Palmer. Daniel happens to be tall and thin—gawky, if you will—and she, too, is uneasy among people and happiest on a lonesome, uncrowded road, preferably one that leads to a private golf course. When she joined the tour two years ago and got her first look at the mob chasing after Lopez, as she then was, Daniel was aghast. "I'll never be another Nancy," she said at the time.

And she isn't. Last season, while winning four tournaments and a record $231,000 in prize money, becoming LPGA Player of the Year, setting standards for consistency and displaying a nearly flawless swing, Daniel almost got herself suspended for throwing clubs and digging up greens. She chewed out a photographer who aimed his camera at her at the wrong moment and sighed loudly and pointedly at any journalist who dared ask what she considered an inane question. "I'm a golfer, not a movie star," she says. "I come across on first impression like a jerk, stuck-up, really a cold fish."

But holy mackerel, this woman can play! All time great Mickey Wright took a look at Daniel

and announced, "In three years people will be saying, 'Nancy who?'" And Daniel's caddie, a 53-year-old former jet fighter jockey named Dee Darden, says he would tote her bag for free because "She hits shots that just make you tingle." Over the last half of the 1980 season, after she'd figured out to some extent how to get the ball into the hole from six feet, Daniel played the best run of golf anyone ever saw on the women's tour. Discounting a tournament in Atlanta, from which she withdrew because of a muscle spasm in her back, she dominated the tour—utterly and completely. At one point she won three straight tournaments, among them the World Series of Women's Golf. Only once did she finish worse than fifth, in the U. S. Women's Open, in which she was 10th. Week after week, from Birmingham to Japan, a span of 19 tournaments, she either won or had a chance to win.

Women's golf used to be a sideshow. As recently as 10 years ago, the tour consisted of a small band of impoverished players plying the back nines of America. Country clubs limited women's play to ladies' days and occasions when the demand from men for course time was low. But with the rise of feminism, Title IX and a new professionalism in the LPGA management, this has all changed. Daniel grew up on a course, the Country Club of Charleston, S. C., where she could get out and play as often as the boys did. She entered amateur tournaments all over the world. She even competed on the men's team at Furman. And by the time she was ready to join the tour, she didn't have to act like a lady. If she missed a shot she said something stronger than "darn." And she'd stick a club in the ground or bounce one off her caddie and roar like Tugboat Annie. In other words, if she could play like a man she could act like one, too.

Lopez joined the tour in 1977 and almost immediately was dubbed Wonder Woman. Hers is still the standard against which Daniel's performance is measured. When Johnny Miller mounted a challenge to Nicklaus a few years ago, it was noted that while he won a lot of Phoenixes and Tucsons, he couldn't win with Nicklaus in the field; in fact, he couldn't finish ahead of Nicklaus, even when neither of them won. In the last half of last season, when she finally stopped fighting herself, Daniel beat Lopez-Melton in nine of the 14 tournaments in which both were entered. And that success provided a measure of inner peace. "Inside I'm much more relaxed now," says Daniel. "It's not like a matter of life or death. I get upset still, but that's just the competitiveness in me."

Daniel has discovered one way to ensure tranquility: when the walls start closing in on her, she disappears, taking a week or two off. She also tenaciously guards her freedom by not taking on a multitude of commitments for personal appearances and endorsements—easy money to most top players. As a result, she stands to lose perhaps $200,000 a year, according to her manager, Vinny Giles. When she leaves the course she is drawn toward solitary pursuits—reading books, watching television, or listening to Willie Nelson laments on her elaborate stereo system. "I'm a very private person," she says. "I don't thrive on popularity. Everyone wants to be popular, and everyone wants to be wanted, but Lopez is in the limelight so much that she gave up something precious: her time. I treasure mine too much for that."

It has been said that Daniel plays like a man. Actually, she plays like a machine. When the gears are meshing properly, as they were last August and September, no one can touch her. Even when Daniel plays poorly she will nonetheless be somewhere on the leader board. And even scarier for her rivals, at 24, some three months older than Lopez-Melton, Daniel is still emerging from the insulated Southern environment that protected her during her childhood. She's only starting to discover just how good she can be.

The Swing. Golfers talk about Daniel's swing as the best among women players since Wright starred in the mid-'60s. It's long, slow and rhythmical, its cadence reminiscent of Sam Snead's. Because Daniel is 5'10", she generates enormous power. She's easily the longest driver on the tour. Nicklaus' competitors used to say of him, "He plays a different game." In women's golf, Daniel plays a different course, one a lot shorter than that confronting other players. At a tournament in Dallas last September, one rival told her, "Beth, I wanted to shoot my ball out of a cannon today so I could keep up with you."

It's because of this swing that most people believe Daniel will dominate the tour for seasons to come. Four years ago, Judy Rankin, who was then the LPGA's leading money-winner, watched a teen-aged Daniel shoot a back-nine 34 and told her husband, "Someday that girl is going to beat all of us. She's the closest thing to Mickey Wright I've seen." Says two-time Open champion JoAnne Garner, "She's got all the shots. There aren't many players who have the ability to shoot 65 every time they tee it up. She's one of them."

To be compared with Wright in only your second year on the tour is exhilarating stuff. Wright won 82 tournaments during her long LPGA career, grinding out the miles by automobile because she had a fear of flying. Perhaps because she feels a kinship—one legend observing the birth of another—Wright has closely watched Daniel's progress. "Obviously, she has the desire, and that's the most exciting thing you can see in a young player," says Wright. "Her record in 1980 is just a start for her, I'm sure."

Women golfers and tennis players have progressed from being discriminated against to something near equality, but for a few of the best, that apparently hasn't meant satisfaction. Chris Evert Lloyd and Lopez-Melton, having attained the top in their respective professions, seemed almost as if they couldn't wait to trade the glory for an apron and a husband. Evert Lloyd wavers between retiring and playing. And Lopez-Melton reduced her schedule following her marriage in 1979 and has said that in the near future she will leave the tour to have children.

Says Wright of the new breed, "They start earlier and burn out earlier. Plus, once you get the money sack full, the motivation fades. But Beth strikes me as one that will maintain her drive for a long time. She struck me that way three or four years ago. She really seems to want to be the best." Says Daniel, "I haven't achieved anything yet. If I were to quit golf today, I would go down in history as nothing."

The bottom line on Daniel is that while she's well on her way to mastering golf, she remains indentured to it. Life is golf. The game's history is her scorecard. And if it comes down to it, she will give up love, friends, time, money, anything it takes to mark that scorecard so that no one ever will forget who she was.

In 1979, her rookie year, full of expectation and burdened by promise, Daniel wore out the practice tee. She complained that the LPGA put too much pressure on her by proclaiming her "the next Lopez." She told a boyfriend that her life didn't have enough room for two loves. And she broke the heart of a man who gave up his job for her.

This fractured romance illustrates just how important being the best is to Daniel. She met the fellow at a tournament in the East. They went out, and she giggled like a schoolgirl. He attended a couple of tournaments in the New York area and even flew to Dallas to be with her. The, on the course, she found herself scanning the gallery for him instead of looking at her shot. She told the guy to get lost. "It probably wouldn't have worked out anyway," Daniel says now—she'd had the same problem before. "If I were to meet someone, it would be really hard for me to have a relationship because right now I give so much to golf that I couldn't give 100% to a relationship."

Tommy Bell, a former sportswriter for *The Columbia State* in South Carolina, quit his job, caddied for Daniel in her erratic rookie year and wrote a book about the tumultuous odyssey. So far it's unpublished, but Bell calls it *Mommas, Don't Let Your Babies Grow Up To Be Caddies*. The book is a log of the tour, but it's also the personal narrative of how a 29-year-old man becomes immersed in Daniel's quest for greatness; how he changes from an objective journalist, nicknamed Clark Kent by the other players, to a caddie who grows misty-eyed when Daniel hits a good shot. The year starts with Daniel lobbing a putter at Bell after missing a short putt. The two are laughing friends, not lovers; buddies who make up nicknames for things. Her putter becomes Sam Wilson, and Tommy's old Volvo is called Arnold, after Arnold Palmer. In the end, on her birthday, after he has given her a present, she fires him, an acrimonious parting from which Bell still hasn't recovered.

He now lives in Hilton Head Island, S. C., where he's an insurance executive. After his year on the tour, he and his wife divorced and he sold his house and moved into a trailer. For a time he was jobless and nearly destitute. When the women's tour visited Hilton Head last spring, Daniel told him, "Tommy, I really care about you."

"If you cared about me," said Bell, "I'd still be caddying for you."

Wrong. If she cared less about golf, he'd still be caddying for her.

Now Daniel sees the episode as a good idea that didn't work. She believes that she and Bell were too emotional, an unstable pairing, always near the flash point. Though Daniel won a tournament and $97,000 in her rookie year, she wound up looking at her caddie as if he had a buzzard on his shoulder, and she acknowledges that they parted "on real bad terms."

"There has to be a professional relationship between caddie and player," she says. "We thought we could be friends and work together, too. But it got to the point that it was hurting me more than helping. He was too emotionally involved in my golf game and in my life, even down to trying to pick my friends. I was so stifled that I couldn't be myself."

Now Daniel's caddie is the unemotional Darden, who, after a career of seeing emergency lights go on in Air Force cockpits, doesn't get upset about anything that takes place on a golf course. Darden carries the bag and leaves the driving to Daniel. "Dee just takes everything in stride," Daniel says. "I get mad and he doesn't react, and as a result I don't get mad as much. And if I yell at him, he just talks on like nothing happened. I get embarrassed and apologize."

Golf is a frustrating game; Ben Hogan called it a game of misses. And on those days when Daniel's misses pile up, when her clubs—her "babies," as she calls them—sass her, she slams them around, occasionally displacing a piece of golf course in the process. Or she berates Darden. Or lasers anyone who happens to come into her field of vision with a mean-faced glare. As a teen-ager, she almost conked a country-club mother with a helicoptered club. On another occasion, in a basketball game, she heaved the ball at a referee. Early last season, before she began winning consistently, she implored reporters not to write that she had flipped her nine-iron into the air after a bad shot. She'd already been fined twice for similar transgressions. "Now I'll be suspended," she said. Then she managed to persuade LPGA officials that she hadn't tossed the club in anger.

Daniel's occasional eruptions, described as "competitive fire" by those close to her, have for the most part disappeared. Winning has helped. Then there was the LPGA, whose gendarmes would somehow materialize whenever Daniel's temper started to sizzle. "They were after me," she says. "Every time I had a bad hole they would show up in a golf cart and start writing in their notebooks." It should be recorded that at the Women's Open—a tournament not administered by the LPGA—Daniel got hot under the collar more than once and had her worst showing of the last half of 1980.

Of course, when you are young and can hit the ball like Daniel, and when you have won two U. S. Amateurs, finished second in a pro tournament while still in college and beaten more than three-fourths of the field in a *men's* college tournament, when you come on tour and are interviewed almost daily as to why you aren't running away with all the titles and money, you tend to get a little snappish.

Daniel grew up in Charleston, the daughter of Lucia and Bob Daniel. Her father is a Coca-Cola distributor, a former cheerleader for The Citadel and a golf nut who has such a wild backswing that he has snapped a club in two by bouncing it off his shoulder. As a prosperous businessman, Bob could afford to give his daughter the best coaching and pay her way to state and national amateur tournaments. He cheered her on. Each week from the time she was 16, Beth would join her father and his friends for a small-stakes game of golf. She competed on equal terms, playing from the men's tees. "She always could hit the ball as far as any man out there," Bob says. "And practice. . .I've seen her work so much that her hands would bleed. If there was anybody overdedicated to a sport, it was she." On the infrequent occasions when Beth lost, she'd say, "The sun don't shine on the same dog's behind all the time." In her parents' home there is a trophy, a gift from one of the

participants in the weekly game, on which the same line is inscribed, except that the "don't" has been changed to "does."

The sun does shine on Daniel almost constantly now, but it seemed to take its time coming over the horizon. Al Esposito, the kindly pro at the Country Club of Charleston, a $7.50-per-half-hour instructor, first tutored Daniel when she was eight. In those days she was small for her age, so Esposito had her hold the club with all 10 fingers, a departure from the standard overlapping grip. Well-meaning people over the years have urged her to change it, but from the beginning Daniel has let advice from anyone but her teacher roll right off her back.

"If I told her to stand on her head and grip the club with her feet, well, by golly, she'd do it," says Esposito, who's now 60 and recently retired. "When I first saw her, she was so little that you would've thought she was least likely to succeed. But she was determined. She'd pull her bag over her shoulder, and off she'd go. She just played and practiced and practiced every opportunity she got. I remember an early pee-wee tournament. She beat several of the boys and one of them said to me, 'Beth can sure play golf, but I'm going to beat her tomorrow.' Beth was standing there and she said, 'We'll see.' But you should've seen the expression in her eyes. They got so cold. It reminded me of Ben Hogan. And the next day she beat the boy again."

From then on, Esposito says, he was convinced that only one thing could come between Daniel and greatness, and that was boys. "But, by golly, she didn't let me down," he says. "Boys didn't mean a thing to her. Golf was her love."

In 1972, when Daniel was 15, Esposito left the country club to take a job at Charleston's municipal course, and his star pupil came under the tutelage of Derek Hardy, a transplanted Briton with a knack for teaching junior girls. Hardy refined Daniel's swing with a drill she still uses today. It involved hitting eight-iron shots with a half swing. Daniel resolutely performed the exercise for six months. The next summer she started winning state junior tournaments.

To the surprise of everyone—including her parents, who had made room reservations for only the first couple of days of the tournament—at 18 Daniel sailed through the 1975 U. S. Amateur, beating, among others, a phenom named Lopez.

A few years earlier, after Daniel had performed poorly in a junior tournament, a headline in a Charleston newspaper had referred to her as a "local duffer." But after her triumph in the Amateur, she returned to confetti and noise-makers. A crowd of about 300 welcomed her at the airport, beginning a love affair with her hometown that continues today. Except for the Navy base, Daniel is the biggest thing around. "This town considers Beth as its daughter," says Mac Holladay, head of the local Chamber of Commerce. "She's our patron saint." After she won her second amateur title in 1977, she was honored on billboards around the city, and the Chamber threw a victory party attended by some 500 people. It was there that *She's a Winner*, a paean to her accomplishments, was first sung. That same year a large portrait of Daniel was hung inside the entrance to the clubhouse of the Country Club of Charleston. The local media began following her every move. When she turned pro in 1979 the Charleston newspapers staffed her first tournament. "They put the monkey on her back early," says Esposito. "Every shot she hit had to be perfect."

However, Beth's perception of the value of success and adulation probably was fashioned by her disastrous performance at the 1976 U. S. Amateur. Putting too much pressure on herself to prove that her victory the year before wasn't a fluke, she was eliminated in the first round. That night she got off the plane in Charleston to be greeted only by her family and Esposito.

"Have you learned anything?" Esposito asked, nodding at the empty airport.

"I certainly have," she said.

The lesson was about the fickle nature of fans; if they could ignore her when she was down, she certainly wouldn't need them when she was on top. And so she discourages the public—and the press—from getting too close. It's no wonder that she is happiest on the player's side of the gallery ropes, where no one can touch her. When she feels the need to disappear, she leaves neither a forwarding address nor a telephone number. Sometimes her family draws her home, but rather than practice at the country club while in Charleston, she drives the 30 miles to Seabrook Island, a resort she represents, where she can hit in solitude. That's the way she wants it. She still has a tape recording of the song composed for her 1977 victory party, and one can imagine her riding down the road—in her Mercedes Benz now—alone but not really lonesome, because her babies are in the trunk. She's at the top of her sport but not yet near the historic pinnacle she intends to reach. There are still years of scorecards to be marked. She listens to the song on the car's tape deck. *She's on top, ain't it fun! / Ah, now Beth, you're Number One.*

(1981)

A Judicial Precedent in a Delicate Matter — Golf

Red Smith

It generally is agreed that golf is a gentleman's game. It seldom is given to violence. Why should it be otherwise considering the kind of scenic setting in which it is played, usually under the most favourable circumstances and conditions? It is a pastoral pastime of pleasure and modest pursuit, save for the professional golf tour where the dollar is the great dominator.

Golf also is a sport that has been conspicuously absent from the courts of law. Golfers, traditionally, seem content to resolve any differences over a drink at the nineteenth hole or, in the extreme, reluctantly resort to reference to The Rules of Golf.

Infrequently, however, such forms of recourse have proved to be unsatisfactory, with the result that the purveyors of justice have been forced to intervene to settle a matter. These "landmark" occasions are such a rarity that they have tended to evoke national interest.

As a case in point, I cite an instance in which golf matters before the bar of justice elicited the attention of one of the nation's most widely-syndicated columnists: 1976 Pulitzer Prize winner Red Smith of the New York Times.

Smith set his sights on a divorce case in Oklahoma, giving it more notoriety than it deserved in a column written for the old New York Herald-Tribune *in 1963, eight years before going with the* Times. *The wind-up of the case is a "chestnut" as old as golf but, written in Smith's fluid, graceful style, it assumed new freshness.*

THERE ARE 93 PAGES of fine type in that lively bestseller, "The Rules of Golf," but not a single paragraph was any help to the judge in Tulsa, Okla. Hearing the divorce case of a golfing couple, District Court Judge Raymond W. Graham had to lay down the law for himself.

Breaking golf clubs, His Honor ruled, does not constitute legal proof that a man is a person of "vicious temperament."

"But," the court added sternly, "under no circumstances should he be permitted to strike his wife over the head with the clubs.

"That would be evidence of a vicious temperament, even if she did push him while he was making a swing."

This may be good jurisprudence but it's lousy golf, and neither the United States Golf Association nor the Royal and Ancient Club of St. Andrews is going to go along with Judge Graham.

Any broad who nudges a guy on the backswing can bloody well afford a busted skull if he's willing to risk a bent shaft. The overlapping grip is recommended, with a slightly open stance.

Perhaps the judge realized he was being unreasonable, for he tried to square it with some rules of etiquette for the distaff side.

"The fact that the wife threw her clubs at the caddie," the Okie Solomon went on, "is not necessarily evidence of vicious temperament. But she threw his clubs out the window of a moving auto, and ordinarily this would be evidence of extravagance and waste.

"However, if he spent the entire day on the golf course and neglected to remember an important anniversary dinner, she could be justified in throwing them away."

So now judicial precedent is established, to serve forever as a guide in these delicate matters.

Not for a moment too soon, either, for that globe-trotting tournament for the Canada Cup and International championship is about to start on the Saint-Nom-la-Breteche course here and the French they are an excitable race, to say nothing of the Japanese, Mexicans, Arabs and Portuguese.

If Abdel Halim Mohammed Abdel Halim of the United Arab Republic should bend a two-iron over the haircut of Sweden's Ake Bergkvist, the International Golf Association will know how to rule.

In 10 short years, the Canada Cup carnival has played more scenes and attracted wider attention than Elizabeth Taylor. Started in Montreal in 1953, the show has pitched its tent in Washington, D.C., England, Tokyo, Mexico City, Melbourne, Dublin, Puerto Rico and Buenos Aires, and next year it goes to Maui, Hawaii.

Two-man teams from 33 countries go 72 holes, with the low team score taking the cup and the low individual card getting the International championship.

Arnold Palmer and Jack Nicklaus are defending the cup which the United States has won three times in a row — Palmer and Sam Snead in 1962, then Snead and Jimmy Demaret, then Palmer and Snead again.

Roberto de Vicenzo, of Argentina, is here as the individual champion.

But back to Judge Graham and his unsympathetic attitude toward golfers who forget their wedding anniversaries. Though he may not be aware of it, the very thing he suggested as a mere hypothesis has actually happened, though this particular case never reached court.

"Now remember," this guy's wife told him as he stowed his sticks in the car, "it's our silver anniversary and I'm having the crowd for dinner. I've got to have the car by 4 o'clock, you hear? No excuses."

Naturally, the guy pledged his solemn word, and naturally it was 6 PM when he returned.

"Now wait a minute," he told his spouse, "hear me out first. You know how George is, wasn't ready when I arrived to pick him up. So we missed our starting time and had to wait at the first tee. But even so it would have been all right.

"Talk about luck, on the first green George missed from this close — never could putt, you know — and he got sore and had a stroke and dropped dead.

"Well hell, honey, the very first green! You can imagine how it was after that. Hit the ball — drag George — hit the ball — drag George — ."

What's Good for the Goose...

Art Buchwald

Washington-based Art Buchwald won his Pulitzer Prize in 1982. Nationally syndicated by the Los Angeles Times, *he is certainly the funniest man on the Potomac.*

Here Buchwald focuses on the outcome of a more violent incident than that described by Red Smith in the previous selection. His typical tongue-in-cheek treatment of the case, interspersed with humorous, irreverent asides, is the kind of satire readers of his column, including subscribers to Pravda *and* Izvestia, *have come to know and laughingly appreciate.*

A NEW CHAPTER in the annals of justice — or is it golf — was written last week when a Washington physician was charged with beating a Canada goose to death with his putter on the 17th green of the Congressional Country Club.

The charges brought by federal wildlife authorities were originally investigated by the country club's board of directors, but they came to no conclusion as to what really happened. Dr. Sherman A. Thomas, the accused golfer, said that his approach shot to the green hit the goose, one of two hanging around the 17th hole. In his medical opinion, the goose was in such agony from the blow of the ball that the doctor decided to put it out of its misery. Instead of pulling the lug on the goose, he struck it several times with his putting iron, thus performing the first mercy killing of a feathered bird on any golf course since the game was invented.

But there is another version, and this is the reason the wildlife people have preferred charges. Dr. Thomas, according to an eyewitness, was about to putt when the goose honked. This, the witness maintains, so enraged the physician that he attacked the goose with his putter and killed the bird.

The doctor is charged with "knowingly killing a goose out of season" and also with being "illegally in possession of a dead Canada goose." Even had Dr. Thomas killed the goose when the hunting season was on, he would still have been in violation of the law as the Bird Act specifies you can only go after geese with shotguns, bows and arrows, falcons and goshawks.

Putters are out of the question.

If the doctor is found guilty he could receive a maximum sentence of six months in jail and a fine of $500.

So much for killing one's goose.

The main question is how does this affect the game of golf?

Every golfer I heard out gave me a different interpretation of the rules.

One said, "I believe that Dr. Thomas should have been penalized one stroke for each time he hit the goose."

But someone else in the locker room disagreed. "No, you cannot be penalized no matter how many times you strike at the bird, providing you don't move your ball. From what I understand, Thomas approached the ball; the goose honked; he left the ball on the green, and started to swing his putter at the Canada's head. It might be considered illegal bird killing, but it certainly is not illegal golf."

"Wait a minute," another duffer said. "Thomas' story was that his ball accidentally hit the goose on his approach shot to the green. Therefore, although he had to play his ball from the spot where it fell after it struck the bird, he was still under par when he attacked the goose with his putter."

"But why the putter?" someone asked. "Wouldn't it have been more merciful if he had done it with a five iron?"

"It's all right for us to sit here, in the locker room and Monday-quarterback Thomas' choice of irons, but I believe you have to be in his golf shoes before you can say which club he should have used. I might have killed the goose with a driver. You might have killed him with a niblick, but Thomas was right there and decided a putter was all that was needed."

"I believe we need a club ruling on this. Today it's Thomas, tomorrow it could be one of us. I want to know exactly how many shots I am permitted before I get a birdie."

"As long as we're at it," another chap said, "I would like to ask the grounds committee what a Canada goose was doing there in the first place. Correct me if I'm wrong, but aren't Canadians forbidden from using the course during the hours when members are playing?"

"I believe there is a bylaw on it," someone replied.

"But let's find out the exact wording as to when you stuff a goose and when you putt it."

The Curious Game of Golf
John Kieran

One of the more amazing contributors to these pages is John Kieran who, despite spending most of his life before a typewriter, is best known for having been a panel member of "Information Please," a radio quiz show of intelligence and wit which enlivened the airwaves for fourteen years beginning in 1938. Kieran became a cerebral celebrity along with Franklin P. Adams and Oscar Levant, as they weekly defied the efforts of master of ceremonies Clifton Fadiman to stump them with questions concerning almost any subject — some extremely profound — sent in by a nation-wide audience of listeners.

Kieran was the rugged, tweedy-looking member of the group while the other three evoked the image of the dilettanti. His image was true to life in that he was a naturalist with many authoritative books to his credit and a sports expert who had written The History of the Olympics, *in addition to being a lover of poetry and font of general information gained as a long-time newspaperman.*

He also was a pioneer in the sports department of the New York Times *as the first member of the staff ever to be designated as the golf writer. In his autobiography,* Not Under Oath, *Kieran revealed he especially liked covering the sport because he regarded every golf course as a wild game refuge where he could further his study of nature.*

Kieran also originated the daily "Sports in The Times" column, which he wrote from its inception in 1927 until 1943. The selections here, which represent material that appeared originally in different versions in his columns in the newspaper, were consolidated into a book, The American Sporting Scene, *which Kieran did in collaboration with artist Joseph W. Golinkin. In the two selections taken from "The Curious Game of Golf," Kieran displays a rare, albeit humorous, insight into situations only a golfer could appreciate. He also reveals a mastery of the short story form which would do justice to an O. Henry.*

IT WAS A DISTRESSINGLY hot day, and hardly a breath of air was stirring. Flies were buzzing around the super-heated courtroom. The magistrate leaned forward and said to the prisoner at the bar, a mild-appearing gent enough:

"Why did you shoot him?"

The prisoner at the bar told a rambling tale. He was called to order a dozen times by the magistrate and four times by his own counsel; but he blundered ahead, and the whole miserable story came out. He had gone out to his golf club that day, as was his custom. He was small of stature, as any one could see. He was a peaceful man by instinct and habit. The automatic pistol? Well, he carried that because he was erratic off the tee—usually landed in the underbrush, often down some ravine—and he was afraid of snakes. There were a lot of snakes lurking in the underbrush out there. He could get plenty of players to prove that. When they sliced into the brush you could hear them hacking and whacking around in there, and when the ball bounded out on the fairway again they were "playing 3"; and the noise was due to killing a snake in there, or maybe a couple of snakes. It was a common occurrence.

Well, he was playing with this fellow Smirk in the club tournament for Class D players. He never had liked this Smirk, anyway. He referred to Mr. Smirk once as "the deceased." The magistrate looked at the police sergeant in surprise, and the police sergeant glared savagely at the mumbling prisoner. He, the prisoner, had taken three putts on the first green. It was annoying, but it was a habit with him and he bore up under it. This Smirk, "the deceased," who had taken only one putt but was still three feet from the hole, conceded himself that putt to win the hole 6-5. He asked Smirk not to do that. He thought all putts should be holed out. It was in the rules. Smirk—"the deceased"—was a big, pot-bellied man and he had a loud, overbearing laugh. He used it a lot. Too much. He laughed when the prisoner said a man ought to hole out his putts.

The prisoner reminded this Smirk of what once happened at the Winged Foot Golf Club when the late and lamented "Nibs" Nobles was the president. It was about the time that Bob Jones slaughtered Al Espinosa in the play-off for the open championship there. In 1929—that

was right, thank you, Judge. It seems that, in a club tournament, one man conceded himself a three-foot putt on the first green. His opponent thereupon conceded himself a ten-footer on the second green. The first offender then conceded himself a full brassie shot to the green at the third, whereupon the party of the second part pulled a masterly trick. After slicing into the rough off the fourth tee, he conceded himself the match by 5 up and 4 to play. The matter was carried to the club president, "Nibs" Nobles, who took proper action. He had both offenders driven off the club grounds with sticks and their names stricken from the rolls.

So the conceding of putts led to trouble, as the prisoner had told "the deceased," and he said it over again at the second green where this fellow Smirk conceded himself another annoying putt. But the real argument began at the third green. The prisoner said to Smirk:

"If you're so sure of holing it, why don't you hole it?"

"Why, it's ridiculous to waste the time," said Smirk. "Nobody could miss a putt like that."

"Not if he picked up without trying," agreed the defendant; "but I once saw Walter Hagen miss one like that—and Macdonald Smith miss one shorter."

Smirk roared with laughter and smote the defendant on the back, making him cough. When the coughing spell was over, the defendant said to Smirk:

"I warn you against conceding yourself another putt of any kind."

At the fourth green Smirk had a three-footer, and the prisoner at the bar glared at him so fiercely that he decided to hole it out. To his discomfiture, the ball rolled by the hole—but not far, because this Smirk reached out with his putter while it was still rolling and hooked it back. It's an old trick. It makes it impossible to miss the next one, there being no next one to miss. In addition to being an old trick on the links, it was the last straw in this case. The defendant, at this point, admitted drawing his automatic and dropping this Smirk in his tracks.

He didn't remember much of what happened after that. He came in and told some fellows around the club about it. The police had come. The automatic was on the table right there. Only one shot had been fired. Rules were rules. If those fellows who conceded themselves putts think they couldn't miss 'em, why do they go on for years refusing to hole 'em? He had no feeling of regret. He was not sorry for Mr. Smirk, "the deceased."

"Why do you call him the deceased?" queried the magistrate.

"What!" said the little prisoner with a wild look. "Isn't he dead?"

"No, no!" said the magistrate. "Nothing as bad as that. Just a light flesh wound. He's in the corridor, and we'll have him right in to testify. You're lucky it's for felonious assault and not first-degree murder."

The little man seemed stunned for a moment. Then he jumped up, grabbed the automatic off the table, and dashed into the corridor. Two shots were heard. The little man came back into the courtroom, tossed the automatic back on the table, and said with an air of deep satisfaction.

"Okay now. Make it murder."

And thus the case was brought to a successful conclusion and the story has a happy ending.

This could have happened only in jolly old England. The famous Hoylake course is a windswept, seaside golf terrain near Liverpool—the "Royal Liverpool" is the high-hat name for the course—and the usual weather report for the area is "Rain, followed by storms." It's a very old club, stuffed with all honorable parts and loaded down with elderly members, stiff and starchy on the outside but "decent old chaps, oh, very!" underneath it all. Golf is practically a religion with them, and the playing of the game is a rite. The rules of the game as laid down by the Royal and Ancient are as the laws of the Medes and Persians to them. That was why they were horrified when the Oxford and Cambridge golfing societies came down there of a bad day to play their annual undergraduate matches. There was so much water in the bunkers, due to recent rains, that the carefree university captains agreed to call it "casual water," even in the bunkers, an astounding and shocking violation of the rules and traditions according to the Council of the Elders at Hoylake. They stalked into the clubhouse indignantly, steaming with wrath and uttering emphatic comments. The universities were seething hotbeds of red radicalism, by Jove! The Home Secretary should take steps. In their days the university had been a school for gentlemen and not a kennel for graceless cubs.

Thus the storm raged while the Oxford team played the Cambridge team, blandly indifferent to the condemnation of the whole proceedings by the Council of the Elders at Hoylake. But it was another day and another hand that rocked the old Hoylake club to its foundation by the pocket veto of the utterly priceless putt. Among the good amateur golfers of that era in England— about ten years ago—were the two Humphries brothers. They belonged to the younger set at Hoylake and played the game in a comparatively lighthearted way, not wayward enough to upset the elders until this fateful day on which were played the finishing rounds of a rather important medal score tournament. The elders were out in force because it was an important event, and many noted players were going over the famous course, and their medal scores would go into the archives to be preserved for posterity.

A breathless courier sped in over the windswept terrain with the startling news that one of the Humphries brothers was burning up the course and the old record of 70 for amateur players was in grave danger. Just which of the Humphries brothers it was, deponent sayeth not; but on this particular day he was going great guns despite wind and weather and was on the eighteenth tee with a par for a 68. Out burst the elders from the taproom of the clubhouse to witness the conclusion of such a wonderful round and the establishment of a new amateur record for the famous old course. It would be an event that would make golf history at Hoylake. It had to be properly witnessed and certified. Chairs and benches were carried out and placed around the home green, and the elders took their seats as solemnly and as deeply moved as if they were witnessing a coronation in Westminster Abbey. Hardly had they seated and settled themselves with dignity when they saw the Humphries chap play a stiff iron for his second shot over the nasty cross-bunker on the way to the green. The ball rolled up on the green and came to a stop about twelve feet from the hole.

"What does he lie?" shouted one of the grandees to those of the galloping gallery that had come up to the green with the hero.

"He has that putt for a 67!" gasped one of the runners, his voice quivering with mingled fatigue and excitement.

"A-a-ah!" said the elders in unison, and then they looked at one another in awe. Remarkable! Historical! Absolutely astounding! Every move was important now. This would be something to discuss for years to come. The smallest detail would figure in the great chronicle of golf at Hoylake.

Humphries came along with a group of reverent attendants. Even the carefree young player seemed to be sobered by the solemnity of the epoch-making occasion, the importance of that moment in golfing history. His lips were set in a grim line, and he was carrying his iron club as though it were a shining sword and he were St. George advancing to smite the dastardly dragon. He moved up on the green, and the crowd closed behind him, making the circle complete around the green. His companion's caddie went to the flagstick. Humphries glanced at his ball and called to his own caddie for a putter. The great moment was at hand!

Mind you, he was lying 66, and the hallowed amateur record that had stood for years was 70. From twelve feet away he could take three putts and still earn a great place in Hoylake history. Two putts—two very ordinary putts—would give him a 68, which would be a regular "double-oxer" by way of record-smashing on the old course. One putt for a 67. Well, it would be an act of God or at least a minor miracle and maybe too much for human hearts to ask for and human eyes to see—but the old record was doomed, a new one was in the making, and that was the great thing to see. Take it far and easy, laddie!

Humphries knelt down behind his ball and studied the line to the hole. The silent watchers held their breaths. The whine of the wind coming in off the sea was the only audible sound, a proper orchestral accompaniment to a great golfing feat at Hoylake. Having surveyed the line from the ball to the hole, Humphries arose and walked to the far side of the green. He knelt down and sighted the line from that direction. More tension in the gallery that ringed the green. One of the elders, while this was going on, put his hand over his heart. It was pumping furiously and the dashed heart specialist had warned him against undue excitement. But—harrumph!—he couldn't miss this! The Hoylake amateur record being smashed to smithereens and he to walk away from the sight like a lily-livered coward! He would stick it, by Jove! Oh, rather!

Having surveyed the line of putt fore and aft, Humphries went to the west and east and took beam sights on the target, all very carefully. Ten minutes had passed. Perspiration was breaking out on the foreheads of the elders. The veins in their faces were beginning to stand out like whipcords. Finally Humphries went up to the ball, putter in hand, and bent over and took his stance. Everybody in the gallery leaned breathlessly forward, all eyes fixed on the little white ball. Humphries stood there with his club resting behind the ball for a full minute. Then he suddenly straightened up, called to his caddie, and changed to another putter.

By George! this was nerve-racking in the extreme! Why didn't the confounded chap get on with it? Flesh and blood around the green couldn't stand up under it much longer. The elders would be toppling out of their seats and sprawling lifeless on the green. Again Humphries took his stance, and again breathing was suspended all around. Back stepped Humphries a second time. He called his caddie and changed back to his first putter.

By this time almost everybody in the gallery was a shattered nervous wreck. Strong men felt like screaming to let off tension. The elders were staring with popping eyes and parted lips. Humphries knelt down behind his ball to take one final look at the line of putt. Then, looking around at the assembled multitude, he said in a tone of decided annoyance:

"Oh, this is far too difficult—I'll never hole it!"

And, with that, he picked up his ball, put it into his pocket, and stalked off through the horrified gallery. The Council of Elders, of course, collapsed in a dignified body. It was the worst thing that ever happened at Hoylake.

How Bobby Jones and I Blew the British Open
Charles Price

Of all the golf writers with whom I have spent innumerable enjoyable hours, I would have to say that Charles Price has been closer to more great players than has anyone else endowed with the ability to relate his experiences via the written word. Besides his close association with Bob Jones, Charley spent a winter on the pro golf tour as an amateur playing companion with the likes of Ben Hogan, Sam Snead, Lloyd Mangrum, Jimmy Demaret, Lew Worsham and dozens of other legendary names. Those associations alone set him apart.

Charley was the first editor of Golf Magazine *and now contributes to that publication as a columnist, in addition to writing occasionally for* Esquire, Holiday, *in-flight magazines and other publications relating to travel. For two years he was an Associate Producer of* Shell's Wonderful World of Golf, *a made-for-TV competitive series of taste and class which, incidentally, Charley has in abundance. For many years he was golf promotion director for Sea Pines Plantation on Hilton Head Island, South Carolina, and in that capacity almost single-handedly put the Harbour Town Golf Links and the Heritage Classic tournament on the map.*

Price writes with a style and wit that is both pointed and provocative. He also writes with authority as a dyed-in-the-wool devotee of golf. This is readily apparent in The World of Golf, *a history of the game which is less of a documentary and more of an insight into the players and their performances than are most books devoted to the subject. Charley also was responsible for compiling an anthology of articles from* The American Golfer. *It is a remarkable collection which focuses upon joyous periods of the initial madness over the game in the U. S. before the descent of the Great Depression stifled it and, unfortunately, publication of the magazine.*

In "How Bobby Jones and I Blew the British Open," Price typically puts down his ability as a golfer. But, as one who has suffered at his hands on a golf course, I can say his talents are considerable and second only to his magnificent gifts as a writer.

IN 1964, BOB JONES and I did a book together. I say "did" because actually Bob had done all the writing years before in a series of newspaper columns distributed internationally by the McNaught Syndicate between 1927 and 1932 and in a series of pearl-like essays for *The American Golfer*, the old Condé-Nast monthly magazine published until the Depression killed it off in 1935. Together, they added up to some 600,000 words, or about the length of six average novels. It was my job to cut them down to a publishable 90,000.

That job was not only the most pleasant I have ever had but the easiest. For one thing, Bob could write better than I ever could. For another, I could have thrown the entire collection down a flight of stairs and still have had enough pages left at the bottom to make as good a book on golf as I have ever read. Altogether, it was the most perceptive, most artful, most eloquent collection of thoughts on this maddeningly mysterious game I have ever assimilated, and I guess I have studied or at least perused almost everything in the whole, considerable library of golf. It was powerful prose, some of it pure poetry. Edited down, it was published in 1965 by Doubleday & Company under a title that was simplicity itself: *Bobby Jones on Golf*. If it is not in *your* library, let me tell you something. You don't have a library.

I worked on the book all winter in my Manhattan apartment, sifting and cutting and dovetailing until my mind boggled and my soul ached, at which time I would hop a plane to Atlanta for a conference with Bob at his law office. After all, this was Bob Jones, the likes of which golf had never seen before and never would again. This book had to be right. He had not wanted to do it in the first place because of his flagging energies. But Doubleday and I had talked him into it, if for no other reason than to get it into libraries, where it would be read long after all other golf books—most of which had been unwittingly plagiarized or downright pirated from Bob's writings anyway—had been given to the Salvation Army. So far as my puny efforts were concerned, I was chiseling Bob's words on marble.

One morning in his office after a long discussion over the manuscript, we broke for our favorite lunch: two martinis and a hamburger, which were phoned out for by his secretary, Jean Marshall, from a local bar and deli. Bob hated to eat in public. He was then so crippled from that hellish disease, which doesn't strike down one person in ten million—syringomyelia—that he could barely handle a knife and fork. Just turning over the pages of the manuscript was a chore for him. He had always been a chain-smoker, but now merely stuffing a cigarette into the holder, which he used to keep from burning his fingers, had become a task that sometimes made him swear. "Damn!" he would mutter and then keep on trying. One thing he didn't want was help. But I would use these frustrating moments to light up a cigarette of my own whether I wanted it or not, and then use the lighter on his desk so I could also light his cigarette in a gesture of common courtesy he couldn't refuse, all the while trying to act lackadaisical and hoping he wouldn't see my eyes water. It was a simple enough lighter, encased in leather, which he could trigger by pressing a button. But sometimes he lacked even the strength to do that, this by a man who could once hit a golf ball effortlessly an eighth of a mile. That lighter today sits on my desk, and the Chinese Army couldn't take it away from me.

We puffed on our cigarettes and sipped our martinis. "You know?" he said, admiring his drink. "I shouldn't drink these. They interfere with my medicine."

"I know," I replied. "I shouldn't drink them, either. They make me drunk."

Bob chuckled. Nobody I have ever met chuckled as warmly as Bob Jones. It came clear up from his shoelaces.

We were now into our second martini. I used the aura of alcohol to spring on him an almost irreverent thought I had been harboring for years. I wanted his reaction. "You know something, Bob?" I said. "As golfers, you and I have something in common."

"What's that?" he said suspiciously.

"We both retired from competition at twenty-eight. You because you had beaten everybody and I because I had never beaten anybody."

It hurt his sides, but Bob decided to laugh

anyhow. The line turned out to be a private joke between us that we shared for the rest of his days.

"What's your handicap?" he asked.

"It's still one," I said. "But I can't play to it anymore. Never could, as a matter of fact."

"Neither could I," said the amateur who had finished either first or second in ten of the last eleven American and British Open championships he had played in. He paused for a moment, obviously gathering some thoughts. "Why don't you go to the British Open this year? It's at St. Andrews."

"What the hell am I going to do there? Sell balloons?"

"No, play," he said. "I'm serious. You told me once you had never been to St. Andrews. This would be a good time to go. It would help you to better understand some of the things I've been talking about."

The whole idea was so absurd, so farfetched, so ridiculous, so fantastic, so preposterous that I almost laughed out loud. Here was the greatest championship player in the history of a 600-year-old game asking *me* to travel clear across the Atlantic to compete in the oldest athletic contest in the world over the most sacrosanct ground in golf. I felt like a pimp being asked by the Pope to visit the Vatican.

So I went.

But I did not go unarmed. I hit 7,000 practice balls and played ten rounds of golf in one week. I showed up at JFK Airport with a cracking leather golf bag the size of a steamer trunk, both black and brown brogues, six tweed sweaters, an array of argyles, four mouse-colored slacks, a leather cap, two rainsuits and a hip flask. If I couldn't play like a Scotsman, at least I was going to look like one.

I also carried with me a copy of a letter of introduction Bob had sent to the secretary of the Royal and Ancient Golf Club, of which he was a member and, at his own insistence, a dues-paying one, this despite the fact he had not long before been made, during a tear-jerking ceremony at the local town hall, what amounts to an honorary citizen of St. Andrews, the first American to have been so honored since Benjamin Franklin. For added insurance, I also had a letter

from Joe Dey, who was then Executive Director of the USGA. If I couldn't get into the R&A clubhouse, I wasn't going. I was damned if I was going to have to eat in a refectory tent with the likes of Arnold Palmer, Jack Nicklaus, Gary Player and Tony Lema. Gawd! I was an amateur! A *gentleman* golfer! Besides, the bar was in the clubhouse.

One of the first things you learn at St. Andrews during the British Open is that almost anybody can get into the R&A's clubhouse. All you need is one of four different badges. One is marked "Member," of which the R&A has almost as many as the YMCA. Another is marked "Guest," which includes all the members' relatives, all their relatives' friends, and all their friends' relatives. A third is marked "Contestant," which means you are one of more than 300 hopeless optimists who have entered the championship but haven't yet qualified. The fourth is marked simply "Player," which means you are exempt from qualifying by virtue of having won something somewhere, such as the U. S. Open. Now I know what the pros mean when they point to a guy and say, "He's a player." You better damned sight be one when you play in the British Open at St. Andrews. The Old Course has a way of making you wish you had stuck to horseshoes.

The first thing you ask your caddie about the Old Course when you step to the first tee is, "Where is it?" In front of you is nothing even remotely resembling a golf course, just a sea of rolling gray mounds leading nowhere, a metaphysical morass of emptiness devoid of challenge or even direction. I've seen empty parking lots that were more beautiful.

But you learn. Lord, how you learn! I mean the hard way, even with a caddie like mine, Carnegie, who kept pointing me in the right direction and choosing all my clubs. Once when I wanted to hit a five-iron, Carnegie shook his head and tapped my three-wood. "You nay wan' no mashie here," he said. "Use you' spoon." Another time when I wanted to use my three-wood, Carnegie tapped my five-iron. "I know," I said, "I nay wan' no spoon here. Use my mashie." He was right, too. Every time. Carnegie, I was to discover, was something else again, a goddamn genius in my estimation. He was 102 years old and hadn't had a haircut since he had been ninety. Although it was July, he wore a gray, herringbone Chesterfield that came clear to his ankles and that had been given to him by Lloyd George just after the Versailles Conference. The coat, I was to learn, also served as his pajamas. With the natural stoop from age, he looked to me at first like Albert Einstein. After he had caddied for me all week, I thought he *was* Albert Einstein. And could he drink! He consumed more Scotch on a golf course than Hagen spilled off one. One morning he showed up with a particularly vicious hangover. The veins in his nose looked as though they had turned varicose and he was hobbling. What happened, I asked, staring at his game leg. It seems he had come home so drunk the night before that his own dog had bitten him.

There are two ways to play in the British Open at St. Andrews if your game is rusty, your nerves are shot and you have no talent to begin with. One is to try and win it, in which case you won't have to go home. You will be *taken* there. In a straightjacket. The saner way is to try not to win it, in which case you are offered three alternatives. One is to score a ten on the final hole if you are leading—which can be a bit embarrassing. The second is to purposely fail to make the cut which is not as easy as it may sound. If the wind comes up, you can score two nineties and still find yourself obliged to play the last two rounds. The third and surest alternative is not to qualify in the first place. This is the tack I decided to take. I wasn't going to travel clear across the Atlantic to make an ass of myself. I'd post a couple of seventy-sixes or such, and go home bloodied but unbowed.

The two qualifying rounds were to be played over two other courses while the Old was left to the "players" for practice rounds. We "contestants" were assigned either to the New Course, which dates back to Queen Victoria, or to the Eden Course, which for all I knew dates back to King Canute. I was assigned to the Eden. But it made no difference. I hadn't played either one and didn't intend to. I was too busy getting in my licks over the Old while I still had the chance.

I was paired with a local amateur who I shall call Angus because I can't remember his name and because I am sure he has tried very hard to forget mine. Carnegie and I dutifully reported to the first tee ten minutes ahead of my starting time. Had it not been that Carnegie knew Angus, we might never have met each other. I saw Angus in the crowd, but I thought he was a hustler from Miami Shores. He had on white plastic shoes, canary yellow pants, a loosely knit purple cardigan and a tennis visor. Everything had either an alligator or a penguin on it. By contrast, everything I was wearing had a belt in the back: my black brogues, my gray tweed slacks, my leather cap, even—in what I thought would be smashing fashion—my Norfolk jacket. If I had had a beard, you would have thought I was old Tom Morris. "Tell me," said Angus after we had shaken hands, "do all Americans dress like you for golf?"

"Only when we want to keep warm," I replied, bowing my head and scraping my shoe against the ground.

"I see," said Angus, doubtfully. It was high noon. There wasn't a cloud in the sky or a breath of air. And the sun was hot as a boil.

I won't go into all the birdies I had in the first round because there weren't any. I scored a seventy-six, just as I had predicted, which left me a very comfortable twelve-stroke margin for failure over Cobie Legrange, a professional from South Africa, who had had a nifty sixty-four, thank God. Angus and I shook hands as we walked off the eighteenth green. "Joyed it," said Angus crisply. "Crashing," I replied.

The next day—which, if everything went well, would be my last—I decided to do my Sherlock Holmes bit. You know. Deerstalker cap, meerschaum pipe and a greatcoat, which I tossed cavalierly over my shoulders without bothering to put my arms through the sleeves, continental fashion. It was 82° in the shade. Eyeing me for a full minute on the first tee, Angus finally pulled some words together. "You must know Bing Crosby," he said.

"No," I said. "Why do you ask?"

"No particular reason," he replied. "I just presumed everybody in show business knew Bing Crosby."

The round started off with a new catastrophe. I birdied the first hole. On the advice of Carnegie, I used my niblick for my second shot and hit it three inches from the hole. Well, what's done is done, I reminded myself, and went on to the second, where I made a nondescript par four by holing a wedge. To get to the third hole at the Eden Course you cross a bridge over the railroad tracks which lead from Edinburgh to nearby Leukers. Had I known what was ahead of me, I would have thrown myself across them and waited for a high-speed express. The third hole is a medium length par three with an immense green shaped like a caved-in fedora. I hit what I thought was a perfect shot, a cold top that rolled more than 100 meters onto the putting surface. The putt I had left would have to dip into a valley, roll up a hill, and then break sixteen feet to the right to get anywhere near the hole. I could four-putt and still not lose face. As luck would have it, the first putt stopped on the lip of the cup.

The fourth hole was built to fit my game: a wide-open dogleg to the right, which I couldn't have bogeyed if I tried. So I didn't and ended up making a birdie. I can't remember the very short fifth — a par four — but I do recall parring it after two woods. Then came the horrendous sixth — a 186-yard par three to a highly elevated green, the wind at my back from off the Estuary at about thirty-five knots. I cannot remember what club I used — it was something Carnegie tapped with his forefinger — but I distinctly remember taking a backswing. I'm positive of that. I must have, for the ball went into the hole! Carnegie told me it was the first hole-in-one made at St. Andrews during a British Open since the war; the last war, that is. Strictly speaking, though, it was not the British Open but only the qualifying rounds. And it was not the Old Course but the Eden. But it was still a hole-in-one. Carnegie would have told me anything to get that bottle of Scotch he knew he was going to get.

So there I stood — four under par after six holes while quietly trying not to qualify 3,000 miles from home for a championship I did not want to play in in the first place. Suddenly, newspaper reporters and photographers came from everywhere. Arnold Palmer had failed to file an entry and Tony Lema, who would eventually win the championship, had not yet shown up. So the story for the day was that an unknown Yank, and an amateur at that, was burning up the Eden Course. Class, someone once said, is the ability to undergo pressure with grace. So what did I do? I just did what comes naturally. I vomited.

The press bombarded me with questions. "Where do you live?" they asked.

"New York City," I answered.

"What is your occupation?"

"I'm a steamfitter."

"What's your home course?"

"Central Park."

"We didn't know there was a course there."

"Neither do the police."

"Did you ever win anything?"

"Yeah. The sixth at Aqueduct."

By the time I had made the turn, the gentlemen of the press acted true to their nature. They left me. Alone once again, things started going my way. I had an unplayable lie, lost two balls and hit three more out-of-bounds. To guarantee that no more miracles might happen on the eighteenth, I picked up. Now, at last, I was back where I belonged — in the gallery.

The day after the British Open I was back in New York, and three days after that I was back in Atlanta to see Bob Jones for our final conference on the book. "What happened at St. Andrews?" said Bob as I settled into a chair.

"I lost," I said.

"Well-l-l-l," said the greatest golfer in the world to the worst, "we can't win them all, can we?"

The American Golfer
Charles Price

Of all the writers whose works are included in this book, my good friend Charles Price is one of the best I have read at putting a time and place into its proper perspective. Charley is a master at creating the mood and feel of a particular period. No better examples are needed than these selections chronicling two successive eras in the history of the game. I knew both eras well: the "Roaring Twenties," when I played most of my competitive golf while I was attending college, and the Great Depression, when I embarked upon my career as a golf course architect.

What halcyon days the twenties were! Millionaires were made almost overnight and golf courses sprang up almost as rapidly. I am sure the prosperity which prevailed then was instrumental, in part, in my choosing the career I did. The mood and character of the time, which Price has captured so well, were that there was nothing that could not be accomplished and money was no object.

The dark days that followed revealed the other side of the coin — which was totally lacking in lustre. What a time to start a career! More golf courses were being ploughed under than there were sites being selected for a game which could only be regarded as an extravagance, considering the state of the nation's economy.

Despite the unrelenting pall which hung over every aspect of daily life, the game managed to survive. Ironically, it was a time that produced a breed of players of such quality and in such numbers that the perceptive Price was prompted to term it "the Vintage Era."

In recognition of this, nearly fifty years later, this productive era inspired a tournament in the American desert called The Vintage International. Fittingly, it was limited to senior players.

"The Birth of Golf's Vintage Era," which follows "The American Golfer," was especially written by Price for the tournament's program book. As such it was read by only a few thousand. But I found it to be of such insight and interest that I felt it deserved a wider distribution.

THE AMERICAN GOLFER is supposed to have been not so much a real person as an outrageous state of mind, like the era he lived in — the Roaring Twenties. It is typical of the distortion with which this period is often looked back upon by golfers that the Roaring Twenties sometimes include the first half of the Thirties. It is an almost pardonable error. After all, people have been playing golf for three hundred years longer than they have been playing the piano.

The American golfer is supposed to have always dressed in knickers baggy enough to have concealed a dozen oranges at each knee and in argyles whose screams could be heard six fairways off. He smoked Melachrino cigarettes and drank instant gin. His wife was a flat-chested, gum-chewing nincompoop who spent half her nights dancing the Charleston to saxophones and snare drums. Together, they tooled their way in a roadster to the country club, their clubs tossed into the rumble seat. He spent a casual day intentionally losing a match to his tyranical boss (probably his father-in-law) and she spent a day taking lessons from some tweedy Scottish professional with a theatrical burr in his voice and a habit of discussing in painful detail how he had won the Caledonia Open somewhere back around the Boer War.

The husband shot consistently in the 90's over a course no more hazardous than a pool table. He sported approximately twenty-six hickory-shafted clubs, only four of which he actually used: a brassie, a mashie, a niblick and a putter that he took home to bed with him because his wife at the time was secretly in love with Rudolph Valentino. She — well, she couldn't shoot 110 in the shade, mainly because she spent most of her time on the course flirting, applying lipstick, or deciding which end of the caddie to hit the ball with.

That's what the American golfer is supposed to have been.

For a reason that altogether misses its mark with the golfer of that period, this version of the American golfer is always painted by Americans who never hit their first golf shot until after the last World War. It's worth noting that *they* play golf in short pants instead of knickers, colored sweat socks instead of argyles, smoke Salems instead of Melachrinos, and drink instant vodka instead of gin. Their wives, to continue, are flat-chested without trying to be, chew tranquilizers instead of gum, and spend half the night dancing some form of the Twist rather than the Charleston. But let's not go into all that here. The point is that each of us has a pompous tendency to regard the youthful ways of our antecedents as slightly ridiculous.

The American golfer may have been peculiar, even humorous, but he was never ridiculous. He just seems that way today because he had as marvelous a capacity for laughing at himself as we sickly do today at others. He did this through H. T. Webster and Rube Goldberg and Gluyas Williams and Clare Briggs and Fontaine Fox, using pen and ink, and through George Ade and Irvin S. Cobb and Don Marquis and Ring Lardner, using the typewriter. (If you can't laugh at Lardner, you really are sick.)

In many respects, the American golfer as he is portrayed here could only have prevailed during those uninhibited years which invariably follow a major war. Until 1920 golf was played almost exclusively at golf clubs, as distinct from country clubs. Clubhouses were built on the scale of bungalows then, not motels. Golf shops had not yet become haberdasheries but, rather, were little more than shacks, redolent with the intoxicating odors of shellac, pitch and old leather and dirty from lampblack, hickory shavings, and bits of twine, "Whipping" it was called.

Then, in the space of the dozen years during which the American golfer came into his own, golf clubs became country clubs in every sense of the word, with clubhouses built on the order of Grand Central Terminal. No, come to think of it, Grand Central must have been built on the order of them. Once, Olympia Fields, near Chicago, had four eighteen-hole courses, a hundred houses, a hospital, a fire department, two thousand caddies, dining halls that could feed fourteen hundred people simultaneously, a dancing pavilion large enough to have accommodated a Democratic Convention, and a veranda that wasn't quite as long as the back stretch at Arlington Park. You weren't a "member" at Olympia Fields; you were a citizen.

At the beginning of those twelve years, there probably were no more than 500,000 golfers in America. At the end, there were easily ten times that number. And the country clubs that were built to handle them reached a figure that was not surpassed until 1963, many of the originals having gone bankrupt during the depression or having been used as the sites for housing projects soon thereafter.

The American golfer was also peculiar in that he bought gold-plated putters, elbow girdles, practice nets, and lessons that were given by phonograph records. There was nothing ridiculous about this extravagance. It only seems ridiculous when you see golfers buying them forty years later, now that we know how worthless they are.

But make no mistake! The American golfer knew how to play golf, his extravagant ways notwithstanding. Indeed, with his wooden shafts, his mismatched irons, his slick grips, his balloon ball, his lofted putters for skimming the ball over peanut-brittle greens—and no "sand wedge" mind you, but using instead a delicate pitch out of a bunker with a niblick—he played an introspective brand of golf that we might never see again, developing an individualistic style that flew in the face of almost everything academic we had known about playing the game, and winning championships with a competitive spirit that sometimes bordered on genius.

In the space of nine years Walter Hagen, who had already won two National Opens, won nine more major national championships here and in Great Britain, successfully defending one of his titles an unprecedented three successive times. In eight years Bobby Jones played in twenty-one major championships and finished either first or no worse than second in seventeen of them. During that period he won more than sixty per cent of the championships he entered. After he had won them all—each of the four big ones in a single cataclysmic season—he quit because he was twenty-eight and civilized enough to realize that there should be a limit to any man's share.

The scores they won by? Well, there are dozens and dozens of courses all over the world where Hagen set unofficial records, often on his first and only tour of the layout, which have yet to be broken. And Jones set course records that often didn't last more than twenty-four hours because he broke *those* records the day afterwards.

But they were Jones and Hagen, whose molds somebody threw away. Of the others, there was, well, Glenna Collett, for one. In 1925 she played against Joyce Wethered in the wind at Troon in the third round for the title of the Ladies Golfing Union, which comprises the women's amateur championship of Great Britain. The match lasted fifteen holes. Glenna was one over par, but she lost. Miss Wethered had played a stretch of ten holes in four pars and six birdies. They met again four years later for the same title at St. Andrews, this time in the final, at thirty-six holes. Glenna went out in 34 during the first round but eventually lost again—three and one—because Miss Wethered played the next eighteen holes in 73. I don't know whether you have ever played St. Andrews in the wind, but it has been known to make scratch players switch to tennis.

Then there was old Mac Smith, a tweedy Scottish-American pro who won sixty-odd tournaments—not one of them, incredibly, a major championship—and who never once stooped to bragging about how he had won any of them. Mac Smith had a swing that was as graceful as the leap of a cat. He had a peculiarity of never taking divots. He just sort of brushed the ball off the turf, treating it, in the words of Tommy Armour, "as though it were on altar cloth."

Back in 1910 Mac tied for first in the National Open, but lost the play-off to his brother Alex. Twenty-three years later he won the Western Open at Olympic Fields—coincidentally while using steel shafts for one of the first times. He missed only one green in regulation figures and was off the fairway only once in the entire seventy-two holes. One thing you can say for those American golfers, they were durable.

Oddly enough, the American golfer was almost as much British as he was American. Nearly half his ranks on the professional tournament scene were born either in England or Scotland, and no American golfer, professional or amateur, was considered a bona fide competitor unless he played at least part of his golf on the British Isles. He did this almost as a gesture of courtesy toward Harry Vardon, J. H. Taylor, Harold Hilton, Ted Ray and the others for having come over here an era before to show us how the game ought to be played. As things turned out, it was an odd way of thanking them. For during those years, Americans won twelve of the sixteen British Opens played, becoming thereby the unquestioned leaders of the game throughout the world. Not even the most ardent Anglophile tried to make an argument of that.

The Birth of Golf's Vintage Era
Charles Price

IN SEPTEMBER OF 1930, ten months after the stock market collapsed, Bobby Jones won the National Amateur at Merion, thereby completing the Grand Slam — winning the Open and Amateur Championships of both the United States and Great Britain in a single cataclysmic season. The Grand Slam has remained not only unique in golf for the past half century but may prove when the century is over to have been its supreme athletic achievement. It is a record that cannot be broken and can only be tied, as writer Herbert Warren Wind has put it, "about the time women are running the four-minute mile."

Jones, who was privately and publicly the most beloved figure in the entire, considerable history of the game, unwittingly did golf a disservice. The Grand Slam precipitated a mood of anti-climax from which it seemed the game could not recover. How could you follow that act?

Jones had been an immensely heroic sports figure in an age that had more than its share of them: Jack Dempsey, Gene Tunney, Babe Ruth, Ty Cobb, Red Grange, Bill Tilden, to name just a few whom the most casual sports reader would recognize even today. Among them, Jones had been looked upon as singular — more accomplished at his game than the others were at theirs. What's more, he had been an amateur in a decade that deified the dollar and he had been able to beat the professionals at their own sport, finishing no worse than second in ten of his last eleven open championships. Winning four in the United States and all of the three in Great Britain he had entered. To this immense competitive nature, Jones added a public image of flashing good looks, an apple-pie personality, and the articulated wisdom of a man twice his age. Then, only weeks after he had completed the Grand Slam, he unceremoniously announced his retirement from formal competition. He was then twenty-eight, an almost laughable age to retire from anything, let alone golf, a game at which men have often won major championships into their forties and major tournaments into their fifties.

On the note of this uncommon grace, Jones quit the sports scene at the peak of a career that could not be improved upon, leaving an afterimage of such perfection that his name has continued to be used ever since as a synonym for golf at its most impeccable.

Not unexpectedly, the year 1931 turned out to be perhaps the most lacklustre in the seventy years people had been keeping records of important competitions and certainly in the fifty they have been keeping them since. The United States Open was won by a former puddler in a Connecticut steel mill who had lost a finger on the job and whose unlikely name was William Burkauskus, which for golf purposes he anglicized to Billy Burke. To nobody's surprise, Burke never managed to win anything else more important than the Great Falls Open, in New York, where he became something of a barroom hero by winning it twice.

To the public's bewilderment, the United States Amateur was won by Francis Ouimet, who had not won a major event since the National Amateur seventeen years before. Many golf fans outside New England had thought Ouimet had either retired or had died without their somehow having heard about it. Ouimet was a clerk in a Boston brokerage, and was the first golfer since old Walter J. Travis at the turn of the century to wear glasses.

In Great Britain the 1931 championships had been even less dramatic. Tommy Armour won the Open Championship over the links of Carnoustie, in Scotland, an hour after he had thought he had finished third. After Armour had posted his score, the tournament was still being led by an Argentinian named Jose Jurado, who could not speak English. On the last hole Jurado intentionally took a safe 5 when he did not understand that he needed a gambling 4. Soon afterwards, Macdonald Smith, the hometown favorite who was now playing in America, came to the final three holes needing a 3 – 4 – 5 finish, or three American pars, to tie Armour. Instead, he finished with a 6 and two 5's. Armour became

the Open Champion while working on his third highball.

At the British Amateur a recent Cambridge graduate named E. Martin Smith had been practically pushed by friends into the championship at Westward Ho!, in England, just for laughs, like a schoolboy being pushed onto a dance floor at his first party. To everyone's astonishment, including his own, he won it. And to nobody's astonishment, he never won anything else.

So there you have the golf scene as the public saw it one year after Bobby Jones left it. So far as the public was concerned, the American championships had been won by a nine-fingered Lithuanian and a four-eyed clerk, while one of the British titles had been taken by a man who didn't know he had won it until after it was over and the other by a man who found it hard to believe after he had. To compound the gloom, the implausibly cavalier Walter Hagen, pushing a fattening forty, had won the last of his eleven titles three years before, and Gene Sarazen, who had been born two weeks before Jones, and had actually won the United States Open the year before Jones had won his first, had somehow only been able to capture one other title while Jones had rung up thirteen.

Golf, it seemed, could not fall any lower—which may account for the astounding bounce it then took. In the short space of those ten Depression years, the game would undergo a revolution unlike any it had known before, which had been quite a while when you stop to think that people have been playing golf three hundred years longer than they have been playing the piano. Indeed, in proper historical perspective, that decade may even prove to have surpassed in importance the post-World War II boom or the television renaissance started in 1960 with Arnold Palmer as its star.

To start things off in the Thirties, Sarazen fulfilled his great expectations by winning a British Open, another United States Open, another Championship of the Professional Golfers Association to add to the one he had captured back in 1923, and by winning the second playing of Bobby Jones's new Masters Tournament. (Sarazen had missed the inaugural event because of a prior commitment.) Almost entirely on the strength of Jones's public and personal magnetism, the Masters Tournament was soon destined to rank, along with the American and British Opens and the American PGA, as one of the titles heralded in golf as the Big Four. Since duplication of Jones's Grand Slam now seemed so improbable as to be beyond belief, winning the Big Four came to be regarded as the professional, or Jones-less, Grand Slam.

But what really set the decade apart was that it produced, from what would have to be regarded as nowhere for a game that had traditionally always been terribly tweedy and patently plutocratic, some of the most simply stupendous talent the game had, or has, ever known. Steel shafts had now superseded those of hickory quicker than the internal combustion engine had replaced the horse and buggy. Using them, men such as Sam Snead, from the Allegheny hills of western Virginia, and Byron Nelson and Ben Hogan, from the cattle and oil flatlands in central Texas, began playing a brand of golf so new, so streamlined that even Jones stated it was one "with which I am not familiar."

Abroad, the revolution was not quite so sweeping. But its impact was felt nevertheless. With a career that was slashed in half by World War Two, a London professional with an aristocratic air named Henry Cotton won three British Opens between 1934 and 1948, this in an age when no other Briton was able to win the title more than once.

By some curious case of historical myopia, the Depression Thirties have constantly been put out of focus as being nothing more than an interim period between the Age of Jones and the post-war boom when, in historical fact, they may have been the most advanced ten years in the game as we now know it: a game with four-mile courses over which superpowered professionals humiliate par for a breed of amateurs who watch their golf from Barco-loungers and play it from E – Z – Go's. The Thirties were the vintage years for the tender grapes golf now bears. Indeed, every contestant in the first Vintage Invitational Tournament first started playing golf, tournament golf, or his best tournament golf in that unlikely, anticlimactic decade following Bobby Jones's Grand Slam —

the years when nothing in golf was supposed to happen.

Close behind Sarazen, Cotton, Snead, Nelson, and Hogan were such titleholders-to-be as Jimmy Demaret, Paul Runyan, Ralph Guldahl, Henry Picard, and Johnny Revolta, all backed up by such consistent tournament winners as George Fazio and Dutch Harrison. Playing junior golf or about to were Al Balding, George Bayer, Jack Burke, Jack Fleck, Doug Ford, Jay Hebert, Arnold Palmer, Bob .Rosburg, Mike Souchak, Bob Toski, Art Wall, Harvie Ward, and Cary Middlecoff. In South Africa a young amateur named Bobby Locke was winning everything in sight, open as well as amateur, and in far-off Buenos Aires young Roberto De Vicenzo was getting ready to graduate from the caddie ranks. Britain's Great Triumvirate—Harry Vardon, J. H. Taylor, and James Braid—were still playing golf on a non-championship level in the September of their careers, having racked up no less than sixteen British Opens among them.

If in 1931 you had been, say, nineteen—as Snead, Nelson and Hogan then were—you would be hard put to think of a profession with less promise than that as a golfer. Lion tamer would have made sense, and riding a barrel over Niagara Falls might have got your mother's blessing. But not golf.

In the decade that led to the Depression, the Roaring Twenties, not everybody was lighting cigars with dollar bills, contrary to the astigmatism with which we look back on it. In 1926, for instance, the median income in this country was $2,000, and only two per cent of the population made more than $10,000. By 1931, of course, those figures had dropped even more dismally. In the entertainment and leisure fields, of which golf was looked upon as particularly frivolous, this economic pinch was painful. When the stock market crashed in 1929, the nation had 6,000 golf courses supported by two million players, almost all of whom came from that $10,000-and-up segment of the population. After the crash, a third of these golfers had to give up the game, meaning that no more than one per cent of the country played the game at all, and golf and country clubs were going bankrupt by the week. It wasn't that the dollar wasn't worth anything. In point of fact, it had never been worth more. Most daily newspapers, as good a thumbnail index as there is to an economy, cost three cents, and New York's *Daily Mirror* sold for only two. A good suit of clothes sold for $30, a pair of fashionable shoes for less than $10. Hamburger was eight cents a pound, bread four cents a loaf. Ralph Guldahl, who was then twenty and already a full-fledged professional, recalls buying Pet Milk for his infant son, in 1935, at four cents a can. (It's .43 today.) No, the dollar would buy plenty. The trouble was, nobody had one.

In 1929 Horton Smith, at the age of twenty-one, won fifteen tournaments and the then unheard of sum of $15,500. Two years later, Billy Burke, who was a consistent money-winner if not title-winner, became leading money-winner with a third that amount, $1,000 of which he got alone for winning the National Open. In 1934 Paul Runyan topped the money list with $6,767. At the end of the year, an accountant told him that, after expenses, he had earned precisely $10. Even Byron Nelson, who had been winning money as early as 1934, when he was only twenty-two, and who won the Masters Tournament in 1937, did not earn enough money to file an income ax return until 1939, the year he won the National Open.

So this was the world of golf the young men of 1931 decided to enter as a profession. Had they decided to sell bubble gum in a nursing home, their futures could not have looked more bleak. Yet it was one of the miracles of that golfing age that out of it grew the professional tournament circuit, or simply The Tour, as it is called by the PGA today, which this year offers $13,000,000 in prize money. "Until then," recalls Jimmy Demaret of the Thirties, when he was in his twenties, "what passed for a tour was nothing but a bunch of strung-out conventions during which the manufacturers tried to teach club pros on vacation how to sell their merchandise. As a bribe for bringing the convention to whatever town it was in, they got the local businessmen to put up $3,000 or so in prize money as a come-on. But, hell, nobody fooled himself into thinking he could make a living out there. I forget what year it was George Jacobus, who was then president of the PGA, announced the total prize

money would be $100,000. Maybe 1936. Anyway, Runyan, I think it was, figured out that the bunch of us who played more or less steady would have to spend half a million winning it. Even in 1940, when I won seven tournaments, ending with The Masters, I couldn't go on to the next tournament because I had to get back to my club, Brae Burn, in Houston. I was afraid I might lose my job."

That next tournament, the one Demaret had to pass up, was the old North-South Open in Pinehurst, North Carolina, which was the first individual tournament won by Ben Hogan. (He had won the Hershey Four-ball with Vic Ghezzi in 1938.) The week afterwards, Hogan won the Land of the Sky Open in Asheville, and the week after that the Charlotte Open, eventually finishing the year leading money-winner. That purses did not escalate overnight during the Thirties is evidenced by Hogan's total winnings, which were $10,656, or almost $5,000 less than Horton Smith had won back in 1929.

"Strange as it may seem," Nelson recalls, "we didn't play those tournaments for money. None of us even gave a passing thought to becoming rich or even well-off. We just loved to play golf and just had it in us to have to compete. I don't remember anybody seriously talking about money."

Adds Demaret: "Why should we have played just for money? There wasn't any. We'd have played if first prize had been a Hoover button."

Bobby Jones had made the Grand Slam using hickory shafts, as did virtually all of his competition. Until steel shafts became popular, the fragile hickories continued to be replaced in golf shops by club professionals, who sanded them down and brought out the grain with lampblack and shellac. To help them with these and other duties, such as club cleaning, they hired teen-age caddies with good manners and promising golf games. In a thought process that can now only be viewed as a hangover from the Victorian days of child labor, the United States Golf Association declared each of these youngsters, whatever their age and however briefly they may have worked, non-amateurs. Since regaining your amateur status then required a wait of years, during which you were not permitted to compete in anything, many of these youngsters drifted into professional golf by circumstance rather than by choice.

Consequently, every professional of that period, until Lawson Little turned professional after winning both the U. S. and British Amateurs back-to-back in 1934 and '35, had started his golf career first as a caddie and then as a shop boy. They were "professionals" by the time they had finished high school, some of them before they had even started it. Those few who were not professionally classified soon stopped playing amateur golf because they couldn't afford to and still play the brand of golf they were capable of. In 1928 Guldahl, who was then seventeen, turned professional in the middle of a tournament; at the end of the third round, to be precise. This was during the Texas Open, in San Antonio, and was a permissible practice if not a common one. Guldahl was tied for fourth going into the final round and saw no reason why he shouldn't grab some of the prize money. Apparently, neither did anyone else, for nobody objected. Guldahl snapped one of his hickory shafts in that last round, however, and finished out of the money. Still, it was a very wise move. He went on to win two National Opens in a row — and almost a third — plus a gang of other events, including the 1939 Masters, breaking a number of scoring records in the process. Some knowledgeable golfers of that period say he was the first of the machine-like players, even before Snead, Nelson, and Hogan.

Not all of the golf being played, however, was machine-like or even very good. In 1935 the National Open was played at Oakmont, the notoriously tough course just outside Pittsburgh. It was won by Sam Parks, who was just turning twenty-six. A graduate of the University of Pittsburgh, where he had been captain of the golf team, Parks had supplemented his income as a junior executive for a local steel company by turning professional and playing on the winter tournament circuit. He was the only man in the field at Oakmont capable of breaking 300. He might have been tied by Jimmy Thomson, a handsome young pro from North Berwick, Scotland, but wasn't because Thomson had ignominiously *four*-putted the next to last green. Asked

once how he could possibly take four putts even for something as exalted as the National Open, Thomson replied it had been easy. "You see," he said, "I don't know how to play golf and I never have. The game mystifies me. I am a pro because I come from North Berwick, there not having been a caddie is a little like coming from Rome and never having been an altar boy. I was *expected* to become a pro. After Parks won the Open and I finished second, some promoter signed us up for a series of exhibitions all through western Pennsylvania. We played one coal town after another, sixteen exhibitions in all, and lost fourteen of them. In Erie, two bartenders took us on and beat our brains out."

Having been born in 1910, Jimmy Demaret was the perfect age for that most imperfect of golf ages. "I can't remember when I wasn't a golf pro," he recalls today. "I never considered myself anything else and never wanted to be anything else. I was a carpenter's helper for a while, but that was only because my father had been a carpenter. I played semi-pro baseball, as a shortstop, and was good enough to get a major-league try-out. But I never followed it up. In the late Thirties I used to sing a little professionally. I was a guest singer with bands like Ben Bernie, Lawrence Welk, George Hamilton, and Bernie Cummings. The William Morris Agency offered me $1,500 a week for six weeks in a New York theatre. That was unbelievable money for those days. But I stuck to golf. And it wasn't because I thought I could make more money. Hell, I just loved to play, that's all."

Wild stories of how the pros of the Thirties survived have been kicked around locker-rooms and nineteenth holes for two generations. By now they have been so steeped in arnica and scotch that hardly anybody believes them, particularly the pros on The Tour today, to whom the Great Depression seems as hazy as the Johnstown Flood did to the pros forty years ago. They find it hard to believe that somebody as majestic as Ben Hogan once survived on hamburgers and chocolate bars. But he did.

Much was made of a story that amateur Johnny Goodman, who in 1933 became the last amateur to win the National Open, had traveled from his home town of Omaha to Pebble Beach,

California, on a cattle car to play in the 1929 National Amateur, where he defeated Bobby Jones in the first round. That was then news because it was *before* the market crashed, and it hurt the story not at all that Goodman had put out Jones, particularly in the first round. But, after the crash, Demaret for one (and probably others) rode freight trains to tournaments often. In 1934, feeling more affluent, Demaret rode to the Texas PGA Championship from Houston to Waco with his clubs and a caddie-friend in the "blinds," the vestibule which separates the rear of a day coach from the front of the car behind it. On the way back, he was able to afford seats because he had won the title. His prize money had been $25.

But for ingenuity, not to mention gall, none of them ever matched professional Joe Ezar. Stranded in England in 1938, Ezar got back to the United States by stowing away aboard the *Queen Mary* on her maiden voyage. When he was discovered, Ezar paid for his passage by giving trick-shot exhibitions off the end of the fantail.

Nobody of that era, probably, had times tougher than the late Lloyd Mangrum, who played all through it only to end up as a GI in the European Theatre, where he was twice wounded. He came out of the Army to win the National Open in 1946 and establish a reputation for winning more money with less potential than any pro in the decade that followed. He was a hardbitten man with cobalt eyes, a gambler's instincts, and the touch of a pickpocket. In his latter years, sipping Chivas Regal and playing gin rummy far into the night at his club in California, he never mellowed. He admired the golf of the pros who superseded him, but regarded their lives as not much more fulfilled than those of bank clerks.

"Nobody really knows what it is like to play golf for money until you haven't got any," he once said. "I wouldn't change those early days for anything. Sometimes we had to win money to get out of town, to pay the hotel bill. When we couldn't win enough, we'd sneak down the fire escapes. Later, when we won some, we'd send the hotel a money order. Nowadays all the pros got sponsors. Sponsors, for chrissake! You know who my sponsors were? Them ladders! That's who! Them lousy ladders!"

From the Thirties—the Vintage Years—it would be difficult to think of a professional who has had a more fruitful, or varied, career in golf than George Fazio. He started as a caddie, became a shop boy, then a clubmaker's assistant, an assistant pro, a teaching pro, a head pro, a tournament player, a club owner, and a highly respected architect. Now living in Florida, where he is ensconced at the Jupiter Hills Golf Club, of which he is one of the owners and where he now instructs Tour professionals, Fazio looks back at the Thirties with the unfashionable patriotism that only the son of an immigrant Italian tenant farmer could. "Corny as it may sound, the golf that happened in the Thirties could only have happened in America. We lived on dreams, and they came true.

"After World War II, I offered to send my mother and father back to the old country for a visit. They looked at each other. Then they began to look all around them. Finally, they looked back at me, 'Why?' they said. 'Why?' And that's all they said. Did they have to say anything more?"

The Old Man
Grantland Rice

Despite his departure in 1954 from "this veil of tears," a phrase he might have originated, Grantland Rice left an indelible imprint on the American sporting scene as a writer of unlimited scope, staggering production and monumental achievements during the fifty-odd years his by-line was in conspicuous evidence.

A courtly, diffident gentleman, Granny was the antithesis of the shoving, shouting, sensation-seeking reporters who seem to have taken over today's journalistic world. Admittedly, he was of less hectic times, but his quiet dignity and warm, paternal personality earned him the respect and admiration of his press room contemporaries and of the athletes he immortalized. Rice wrote of all sports in his nationally-syndicated column, "The Sportlight," in hundreds of magazine articles and in the scripts for a series of movie short subjects which also bore the title of his column. He loved the games men play, especially golf. It was a diversion which gave him temporary relief from his daily deadlines and afforded him the companionship of many of his friends.

Granny and I shared many a moment together and they are a fond remembrance. This was especially so during the early Masters when we were able to roam the fairways unhampered by restraining ropes and the throngs which now make such movement impossible. It was Granny, incidentally, who was responsible for changing the name of the Augusta National Invitation Tournament to the Masters. Through his writings he gave it an initial impetus toward its eventual acknowledgement as one of golf's four major championships.

I have selected "The Old Man" because Walter J. Travis was one of golf's most remarkable pioneers and because Rice knew him better than anyone, as Rice had worked with him as editor of the old American Golfer, *which Travis founded.*

"Little Sees It Through" also warrants perpetuation as Rice was witness to the final victory of Lawson Little in achieving golf's unprecedented "Little Slam," when he won both the British and United States Amateur championships, back-to-back, in successive years.

IN MANY RESPECTS Walter J. Travis will stand as the most remarkable golfer that ever lived. Just consider, as a starter, these two facts. He won the first tournament he ever entered at the age of thirty-five, a month or so after he had hit his first golf ball. He won the last tournament he ever entered, the Metropolitan Championship, at the age of fifty-four, in 1915, and on his way through he beat Jerry Travers, the United States Open champion of the same year.

Here was a man who started golf at middle age, or well beyond the competitive prime of life. He began a difficult game, a game demanding the imitative power of youth, at the age where most men leave off as champions. He was of slight physique, with rather slight hands and slender wrists. He weighed no more than one hundred and forty pounds. Yet against all these handicaps he wrested four national championships from the best golfers of America and Great Britain.

Few learn golf in a lifetime. Championship golf is usually a matter of many years of struggle from a young start. Travis picked up his first golf in October, 1896, when he was nearly thirty-five years old. Two years later he had reached the semi-final round of the Amateur Championship. Within four years of his golfing debut he was the amateur champion of his country — and for four years — 1900, 1901, 1903 and 1904 he was champion of either America or Great Britain.

He was forty-four years old when he invaded Great Britain and brought back the famous cup from Sandwich. After that invasion such American stars as Chick Evans, Jerry Travers, Francis Ouimet, Fred Herreshoff, Bob Gardner, Bobby Jones, Bill Fownes and many others were to try for the same height in vain for the next twenty-two years. It was not until 1926 that Jess Sweetser duplicated the Travis achievement, and Sweetser at the time was twenty years younger than his famous predecessor had been.

Many years ago, when Walter J. was in his prime, the late George W. Adair, who played with him often, made this comment on his game: "Travis can beat any golfer that ever lived on a golf course only ten yards wide with a keen wind blowing."

Some of his forgotten achievements are remarkable. In one match at the old Westchester course he hit the flagstick three times and missed it only by inches on other occasions.

In a thirty-six hole match with "Snake" Ames at Garden City he had 36 – 36 — 72 in the forenoon and 36 – 36 — 72 in the afternoon. He had exactly par on thirty-four of the thirty-six holes played. On one of the most testing of all golf courses this must stand a record for deadly consistency.

On another occasion at Garden City he had six consecutive 2's in one week on the difficult and elusive second hole. At the age of sixty he had 66 and a 68 in one of the Florida championships and at the age of sixty-four he played Garden City in 73, even par, and just two strokes above the record of the course.

It must be remembered that such great golfers as Bobby Jones, Jess Sweetser, Walter Hagen, Johnny Farrell, Tommy Armour and Gene Sarazen started golf when they were seven, eight or ten years old, under good instruction, when it was possible to develop a fine swing instinctively. They also had surpassing physical powers.

But consider the case of a rather slight, slender middle-aged man who started at thirty-five to build up his own game without any outside help, and who, within a short while, stood as the amateur champion of the two greatest golfing nations in the world.

Walter J. Travis could do more with a putter than any golfer in history. He was probably no better than Jerry Travers upon the green itself. But he could also use the putter effectively off the green and from bunkers where the ball was lying well.

He devised the scheme of smaller holes on the practice course at Garden City, holes only a trifle larger than the ball. He practiced here for hours. When you can drop them steadily in a two-inch cup, one double the size looks like a keg.

One of his main angles in regard to putting was to imagine you were driving a tack into the back of the ball and let the putting blade go on through. He considered putting largely a right-handed affair and the right hand predominated in his grip. The left was merely a steadying aid.

But he was something more than a magnificent putter. He was straight down the course from the tee and almost every type of iron usually left the ball fairly close to the cup. He had a peculiar grip, no overlapping or interlocking, with the right hand well under, but he understood the value of flexible wrists that were firm but never tight or tense.

One of Travis' great contributions to American golf was a detail which frequently made him enemies. This was an insistence on playing the game in the letter and spirit of the rules. He would tolerate no deviation from the correct path, even in a friendly round. In the early days of the game, when there was an even greater laxity in playing by the rules than anyone can know today, he set a standard which gradually took effect.

There was still another feature to his play — he never played a careless, indifferent shot. No matter how unimportant the match, he played every stroke as if he were in a championship test. He made careful, accurate golf a habit. He thought too much of the game to desecrate it with any indifferent effort. Every shot was a problem to be worked out and worked out in the right way. His rank as a course architect was high, for he knew the value of holes and how they should be arranged to call for skill and to keep up sustained interest.

He was fifty-four years old when he faced Jerry Travers, his leading rival for many years, for the last time, at Apawamis in 1915. Travers had been his hardest barricade. He had checked Travis out of many championships. In this last meeting they came to the final hole all square with the Metropolitan Championship at stake, and for old time's sake, Travis sank a thirty-foot putt to win, one-up. He knew this was his last chance to beat a victorious opponent from many years gone by and yet no one ever swung the blade of a putter with a smoother, steadier stroke as he sent the ball spinning across the green into the cup.

It was always a treat to play with the Old Man. Even though his conversation was scarce, one could learn more from him in a few words than from almost anyone else in a long day's talk.

He had the courage of an unbroken will and an unbreakable determination. There was no faltering in any crisis, where he was usually at his best.

There has been only one Bobby Jones in golf. And there, also, has been only one Walter J. Travis.

Little Sees It Through
Grantland Rice

IT HAS REMAINED for Lawson Little of Stanford University to kill off the roulette feature of golf. In his last four Amateur Championships, British and American, there have been twelve different survivors for the four semi-final rounds, but it was Lawson Little who came marching on to his thirty-first match-play victory.

When anyone can pick up thirty-one consecutive championship matches, twenty-five of these at eighteen holes, the killing route, there is little to be said about the part that luck can play.

There was something more important than the mere record of these thirty-one victories from Prestwick to Cleveland. There were the manner and method of his two finishing thrusts against his two hottest challengers, Johnny Goodman of Omaha and Walter Emery of Oklahoma City.

Here were two rivals who fought him tooth, nail and scalp. They nailed him at the time when the long strain must have been at its tautest point. Yet the answer is this: in the face of high class challenging golf, Little played the last eleven holes of these two rounds eight strokes under par. He played these last eleven holes in nine under even 4's — or just two over even 3's — through a stretch that included three par-5 holes.

And with the faraway goal at last in sight, where he might have been expected to waver a bit or start slipping, he finished off the big job with a birdie and an eagle. His closing salute against Emery at the 520-yard sixteenth hole was a long drive into the face of a head wind, and then a 240-yard spoon shot through a cross wind that dropped the ball just twelve feet from the cup. To polish up every closing detail, he then rolled this putt in for an eagle 3 as Emery lay stone dead for his birdie 4.

Seven times in this Amateur Championship test at Cleveland, Lawson Little found himself struggling in the rear, facing quick starters who got the jump. Young Rufus King jumped him three holes the first day by opening up with

4 – 4 – 3 – 3 – 2. These quick starters can be deadly poison over an eighteen-hole route, but in each case the long-hitting Californian soon hammered his way to the lead again, and he kept on hammering until the match was over.

What feature of golf gave Lawson Little his fourth consecutive championship? The peculiar part is that no single feature, but a blend of several essentials, left him master of the field.

One. Long, straight hitting, despite several narrow fairways guarded by trees and ravines. His length from the tee was amazing enough, but not as amazing as his uncanny accuracy.

Two. His fine iron play, from an eight-iron pitch to a two-iron, where the ball usually landed almost directly on the line, and rarely missed the green.

Three. His consistent putting that reached a brilliant peak the last day with a smooth, even stroke under perfect control.

Four. His cool, unruffled, determined match-play temperament that considered nothing except the next shot to be played; that allowed no discouragement to wander in; that permitted no break in his all-week concentration.

No amateur living has guns enough to blow away this quadruple fortress that embraces power, skill and all that is needed on the mental side to complete the picture.

The recent championship at Cleveland was replete with thrills. There was the showing of Chandler Egan and Ellis Knowles, the two veteran entries who were on golf's firing line thirty years ago. Both won extra-hole matches against stout competition and both were around par when they finally slipped out.

There was the early downfall of Francis Ouimet and Chick Evans, who were caught on somewhat struggling rounds.

There was the high class of Charley Yates of Atlanta, Western Champion Maurice McCarthy of Cleveland, Reynolds Smith of Dallas, George Voigt of New York, and Ross Somerville of Canada. Somerville, as usual, stuck grimly to the finish where a birdie 3 from Emery caught him on the nineteenth green.

But it was the shadow of Lawson Little that dominated the scene from start to finish. It was soon evident that the Californian was riding the crest of his best game, and that he was getting better day by day. With Scotty Campbell eliminated in a sub-par war, it was also evident that if the field ever let Little loose into the thirty-six hole pasture there was small hope left of turning him back.

No two better men in the tournament could have been chosen for the job than Johnny Goodman and Walter Emery, not only fine golfers, but also game, cool, seasoned competitors, who had no intention of beating themselves. In this semifinal group, Joe Lynch of Boston and Georgetown was the only stranger, but Lynch had earned his place by some heavy hitting and hard fighting in the tougher spots.

It was felt as the week's play moved along that, if anyone could take Little's measure, it would have to be Goodman or Emery. Goodman held his match all square at twenty-seven holes by turning in a 32 to start the afternoon round — just 4 under par. But down the stretch Goodman suddenly ran into a heavy blast that included five birdies in the last seven holes, a pace too fast for anyone to meet.

It was a pace where pars might as well have been 7's or 8's. "Can Little keep this up?" was the prevailing question. Emery, after winning the first three holes, was still all square at the eighteenth. Three down at the twenty-eighth, and apparently on his way out, the Oklahoma law student suddenly turned, won the next two holes, and forced Little once more into a hot corner. How would Little meet this new challenge? His answer was 4 – 3 – 3 – 3, with a birdie and an eagle on the finishing two holes.

There were two hundred and four matches fought out through the week, so you can imagine the picture. For the first three days it was like being in the middle of four beehives. But the galleries were enthusiastic and well-mannered all the way, and there were enough thrills to last a season. For example, Walter Emery handed the crowd no less than eleven 2's, a record for any championship count.

All in all, the four-time champion within two years had too much in the way of power, control, timing, touch and concentrative determination to be stopped. He kept on hitting the ball too consistently with every club, he made too few mistakes, to be caught and held.

He was nineteen under par for the week in spite of several stymies that blocked out other birdies, and he was ten under par the last two days when the pressure was greatest. These are figures that tell the story far more eloquently than any set of words could ever hope to do.

(1964)

266

Tee Time
Ring Lardner

Generally, I am one to skim hurriedly over any articles relating to golf instruction. I have found it is nigh impossible to relate the printed word to the performance of the muscles. Also, with the exception of the books devoted to a particular technique, I have come to the conclusion that the various tips, capsulated corrections and short cuts to scoring promulgated in the various golf magazines only tend to sow the seeds of confusion in my mind. Correction of golf problems generally can be found only in consultation with a pro. He is the best qualified to analyze any aberration and to ascertain the best way to eliminate it or to adjust to it. That is why, when I run into any trouble with my game, I entrust myself to the capable hands of Lew Worsham, the former United States Open Champion who also is pro at the Coral Ridge Country Club in Fort Lauderdale, Florida, where I play most of my golf.

My announced aversion to passive instruction, however, does not go so deep as to cause me to ignore it completely, especially when an absolutely unique approach to it is presented in the inimitable style of the great Ring Lardner. Ring, one of America's best-loved humorists and author of some of baseball's funniest stories, including You Know Me Al, *also was able to make golf a less serious game. There is no better example than "Tee Time," which appeared in* Colliers *in 1929.*

THE FEW DEVOTEES of golf who are not entirely unhinged realize that lessons, regular or occasional, from a competent instructor will improve their game. Even Bobby Jones, I am told, seeks advice and comfort from his old teacher when trouble with one or two clubs is making it impossible for him to get below 66 on an ordinary championship course. And the lesser lights are dissatisfied with themselves often enough to keep all our professionals busy from dawn till dark, from March till December and beyond.

Unfortunately, the trouble with the majority of golfers is not confined to one club or two but is limited only by the number of clubs they have in their bag. The average pro pays no attention to this and insists on attempting to correct your mid–iron faults or your driving eccentricities, to the exclusion of everything else. And more unfortunately still, the average pro fancies himself as a raconteur and when you pay ten dollars presumably for a half-hour golf lesson, what you get is a five-minute golf lesson and twenty-five minutes of funny things MacGregor and Mac-Pherson did at St. Andrews.

In this lecture, which costs you five cents, I will try to cover as many phases of the ancient "sport" as my space allotment will allow, promising to lay off of any reference to twa Scotchmen till I can no longer resist. Let it be understood that I do not claim to have originated all the bits of advice and hints herein set down; some of them I have picked up from other experts and used with slight changes for the better.

As a game of golf usually begins on the first tee and as the first hole at most courses is at least a par four, I will start out with a few words about the drive. In a recent issue of *The American Golfer*, Miss Collett had an article titled How Far Can a Woman Drive? I could only skim it through while sorting the laundry, but the gist seemed to be that there was no limit if she would remember to stop once in a while at the filling station. I have suggested to The American Golfer's editor, a southern boy, that a still more interesting article could be written not by a member of Miss Collett's sex on How Far Can a Woman Drive a Man? However that is apart from our topic.

The initial tee shot is made with a driver provided the people ahead of you are fifty yards or more away from the tee. If they are less than fifty yards, it is better to use a mashie or niblick and attempt to shoot over their heads instead of between them.

A mashie isn't a bad bet anyway, especially if your ball remains on the tee after you have driven. If you hit a ball with a mashie it will sometimes go farther than if you miss it with a driver.

The All-Important Balance

The essential of good driving is balance, and when the word balance is employed in reference to golf, it is obvious that physical balance is meant. Your weight should be evenly distributed and that often takes years because the average person with a fat stomach usually has narrow legs and the matter of transferring part of the tonnage from one side to another can only be accomplished by studying evenings. Balance is important in other sports as well; in baseball for example. Babe Ruth has a whopping torso and ankles like a flea's. But for this uneven apportionment of weight he might develop a balance that would enable him to meet a ball squarely instead of half topping it.

Assuming that the reader is not a novice and can get off the tee in two strokes, I will take up the third shot which is generally puzzling on account of the ball being in a field of timothy or a moat or lolling against the foot of a tree.

If you haven't time to wait for the harvest or a drought or the felling of the tree, remember there is no rule forbidding the use of two clubs at once and a little practice will enable you to handle a driving iron and a putting cleek as if they were a pair of tongs. In this manner the ball may be placed in a more favorable lie or filliped onto the fairway, and from there you ought to reach the trap nearest the green with two brassies and a jigger.

Quoting again from *The American Golfer*, Chick Evans says the real shot to learn (for getting out of a trap) is the explosion shot, but "sand, because of rain and dew, has different weights, and the weight of the sand has much to do with the distance," meaning the distance you should hit behind the ball.

It is almost impossible these days to find a

caddy who will carry a set of scales besides your clubs, umbrella, books, picnic lunch, spare tire and overnight bag, but most modern locker-rooms are equipped with steelyards; if yours is not, a penny or nickel weighing machine will usually be found in the nearest railroad or subway station and enough sand may be carted there in a wheelbarrow to give you an idea how much length and strength to put into your stroke. Personally I have made a majority of my explosion shots on the fairway and with not very good results, owing, no doubt, to an unwillingness to hold up the game while the grass was being weighed.

How often we hear it said of an otherwise fine golfer that he is lamentably weak on short putts! I have never had one and so am hardly competent to instruct others how to overcome the weakness, but it seems logical to me that the player thus afflicted can get round the difficulty by not sending his approaches so near the hole.

Putting on a smooth, level green is comparatively simple and almost anybody ought to be able in three putts to get close enough so that the opponent will concede.

A different problem is presented on an uneven, rolling, tricky green, but I believe that our best golfers employ wrong methods in dealing with same. I have observed Bobby Jones, Walter Hagen and other so-called stars waste precious moments walking around, behind the ball and in front of it, to different positions from which to study the contour of the ground, thinking their eyes can be trusted to tell them how much to allow for this mound or that depression.

Resorting to Strategy

The practical way is to let the ball decide matters for itself; in other words, putt two or three times to see what happens before you go for the hole. If your first or second putt drops into the cup so much the better; if not, you at least know what the trouble was.

The golfer who finds himself in a battle with an opponent who is mechanically his superior may often win a match by the use of strategy.

For example, suppose it is your shot and the other guy's ball is ahead of yours, on the green, in the rough, or on fairway. You say to him, "Please move your ball," being careful to kind of mumble your words.

The instant he complies, you can claim the hole if it is a match play or have him disqualified if it is a medal play. If he attempts to defend himself by asserting he only committed the foul because you asked him to, you can pretend he misunderstood, that what you actually said was, "We move this fall."

Legitimate Methods

Three or four years ago I inadvertently got into a match with the late Walter Travis at Belleair, Fla. I was on the edge of the eighth green, about forty feet from the hole, in so many strokes. Mr. Travis was fifty yards behind me in one. "Please move your ball," he said. I did so in a spirit of levity. Mr. Travis then played a roundup shot which would have struck my ball if I hadn't moved it. As it was the ball stopped four inches from the cup. This was not an attempt at fraud on Mr. Travis' part but it gave him the match, as I picked up and went back to the club-house, conceding him the next eleven holes.

Another thing to remember is that while the ethics of golf forbid coughing, talking, sneezing, snoring, or making any other sort of noise while the opponent addresses the ball, it is not illegal to use mustard gas or throw flares or tickle his ears with a wisp of straw.

Mr. Alex J. Morrison (*The American golfer* once more) writes that a man is most successful in negotiating golf shots when he is tired and therefore relaxed. It would seem, then, that a golfer facing an important match should first tire himself out. The individual probably knows best how to accomplish this is his own case. Personally I have found the following methods almost equally effective: Crawling on hands and knees from your office or home to the golf club; dancing all night with Aunt Jemima; moving the piano into the bathroom and the bathtub into the garage; arguing with a football coach.

Which reminds me of the story of the countless Scotchmen, most of them named Sandy. They were playing at St. Andrews for the first time.

"Weel," said Sandy, "gin ye swing mair hooly, Sandy, ye'll nae rax the sheugh."

"Weel," was Sandy's reply, "gin ye hae ane bittle, ye mecht misken yon clatch."

How to Make a Hole in One
H. I. Phillips

"How to Make a Hole in One" appeared in Colliers *in 1930. Phillips, of course, was renowned as a humorist who served to brighten hundreds of newspapers with a daily column of irreverent observations of the national scene and anything else which struck his funny bone which, obviously, was not very far from his typewriter.*

IN MAKING A HOLE in one I stand with the feet fairly wide apart and the weight evenly distributed on both heels. I use the interlocking grip, a three-quarters swing, a thirty-five cent ball and the regulation prayer.

I generally wear light underwear, as there is nothing that will upset a stroke more than the itch that comes from a woolen or hair-lined undershirt at the moment of the upswing, and prefer golf socks that are smart without being vulgar.

It is remarkable how many inquiries for help come to a man every time it leaks out, as such things will, that he has made a hole in one. Since I made my last one (I refer to it as my last purely because all my golfing friends insist it will be my last) I have had letters, phone calls and telegrams (collect) from all over the country pleading for suggestions and advice. I had no idea so many golfers were having trouble with this most satisfying stroke in golf. It seems to me there must be hundreds who don't quite get the hang of the hole in one.

The following is typical of the many letters I have received:

Dear Sir:

I am an American business man living with my folks and quite contented but for one great disappointment in life. For years I have wanted to make a hole in one, and while I have from time to time come close to it I have never realized my ambition. This feeling of a frustrated desire has preyed upon my mind until I am a shadow of the man I used to be before I put on short pants and let golf come into my scheme of things.

Yesterday I spoke to a friend who told me about your success in this respect and suggested that I write you and ask what I should do to succeed.

Any help from you will be greatly appreciated, and if it works I will be a new man.

Sincerely yours,
Caspar Steukle,
Bisbee, Arizona.

Here's How It's Done

Mr. Steukle's voice is but one of thousands crying in the rough. It seems to me to be no less than a stern duty to give the great army of disappointed golfers the benefit of my experience and success.

My hole in one was made on September 21, 1929, on the number two hole at the Race Brook Country Club, Orange, Connecticut, at seven minutes after two, daylight saving.

[The editors of Collier's have investigated and found that the author is not lying. Mr. Ralph Walker, a fellow member of the Race Brook club and not related to the author by marriage or otherwise, was his partner on the day in question and gave an affidavit that Mr. Phillips made his hole in one as claimed. Mr. Bobby Pryde, father of Connecticut golfing, certifies that Mr. Walker is a gentleman of veracity.]

Most of the people in seeking advice on making a hole in one ask five questions:

First: Is it really difficult to accomplish?

Second: How long should a man keep trying for a hole in one before giving up and resigning himself to more than one stroke per hole?

Third: Is it a gift or an acquired instinct?

Fourth: Why make a hole in one?

Fifth: What's the secret?

The answers in the order named are:

1. Massachusetts.

2. Daniel Boone, August 2, 1712.

3. Appomattox Court House.

4. There are two reasons for making a hole in one. The first is that it is immensely labor saving. When you get the ball directly from the tee into the cup, it eliminates that most intricate and annoying feature of golf known as putting. Anything that will cut down the time used up in putting is helpful, and anything that will eliminate it entirely is like a bequest from a rich uncle in Calcutta. If you get the ball into the cup from the driving tee you are all washed up on that particular hole and do not even have to visit the green unless you want the ball back. If you do not get a hole in one and the ball lands, say, nine or ten inches from the hole you have to go to the green and take four or five putts. This is not only annoying but positively silly.

The other reason for making a hole in one is that it brings you a lot of free merchandise, gets your name in the papers and gives you some justification in trying to outtalk the other locker-room nuisances.

There may have been a time when a golfer got nothing but his name in the local paper and a few drinks of gin, but that era is no more. Today he is the recipient of enough stuff to furnish a flat. Before my feat had been announced in the papers more than a week, mail and express men began arriving at my home and office with awards from various big advertisers.

A golf ball company took the ball and mounted it in a glass case, suitably inscribed. A certificate of membership came from the Hole-in-One Club and with it a case of ginger ale. Then came two safety razor sets, a cigarette case, a humidor, a dozen golf balls, a load of wooden tees, a subscription to a golf magazine, an offer of a thirty per cent discount on a sweater, a fountain pen, two dozen razor blades, and an offer of marriage from a widow in Wyoming.

5. The secret of a hole in one is perseverance. As to stance, form, grip, etc., these are all matters of individual preference. If I were to emphasize one point to aspirants to membership in the Hole-in-One Club of America I should stress the advantage of short courses over long courses and the use, whenever possible, of courses where the greens have a tendency to slope from all sides toward the middle. Loose clothing is a distinct advantage. (I knew a man who missed a hole in one once through playing in a tight shirt that ripped as he went into his back-swing.)

Now, personally, I have a hole-in-one style that is not orthodox. I depend a good deal on psychology. I have to feel in the mood. It has been my experience that unless a golfer feels like a hole in one he cannot get the desired results.

In making my "ace" I always stand at right angles to the ball, bring the club back slowly and whip the clubhead through smartly, from left to right, using plenty of wrist action and not losing my balance until just before hitting the ball.

A good many golfers believe the open grip is better for hole-in-one purposes than the interlocking, but I use the interlocking because after making my "ace" I find I am less apt to drop my club in the excitement and run off without it.

I also prefer a wooden shaft over steel for this particular play and believe, too, from my experience that a hole in one is more easily accomplished in Nile green stockings of a medium weight and in roomy plus fours with no buckles missing.

It is my conviction also that the player should be relaxed physically and mentally, and not at the moment of the backswing engaged in any argument with his partner over the score at the previous hole.

I make these statements for the benefit of the many golfers who have never made a hole in one and who do not seem to be making much progress in that direction. I, too, had difficulty attaining this goal. It did not come naturally to me. For years I struggled unsuccessfully to get the ball from the tee into the cup in one stroke. (As a matter of fact I was pretty lucky for many years to get a ball off the tee in one stroke.)

To master the secrets of making a hole in one was, however, always my ambition and suddenly I got the knack of it out of a clear sky.

It was so easy, in fact, that I did not at first believe it myself, a state of mind which seemed to be pretty general among fellow golfers to whom I proclaimed the feat later. A somewhat hysterical dash from the tee to the green by all concerned, including caddies, revealed the ball nestled comfortably in the cup, however. I had gauged everything perfectly. It was very simple. I don't expect any serious trouble in the future, barring the return of an old tendency to press, lift my head and swing with my eyes shut.

No golfer ever knows how wonderful life is until he has made a hole in one, and it is to help others to feel this thrill and experience this happiness that I am writing this article. What is the use of a man making a hole in one if he is not willing to help others?

Don't Concentrate

First of all, the reason so many golfers do not make holes in one is that they think too much about it. It is all right for a golfer to say to himself, "It would be nice to make a hole in one here," just before addressing the ball, but he should then let the matter drop. It is no good standing over the ball and thinking, "This has got to go into the cup." "If this isn't an ace, what a bum I'll be," etc. This destroys confidence, upsets the mental balance and in many cases induces the heebie-jeebies.

The day I made the hole in one I scarcely had given it a serious thought. It was on the number two hole, a drive of about 137 yards across a lake full of lost balls, and generally half full of thrifty New Englanders looking for them. I had teamed up with a Mr. Ralph Walker, a New Haven undertaker, who had no cases that afternoon but who nearly had a couple the moment after my ball plopped into the cup. I have since realized that in view of what happened I was under a big disadvantage in playing a twosome, as it is impossible to play golf with less than one partner and if anything had happened to Mr. Walker I should have been without a witness, which would have been about the greatest tragedy that could come into a golfer's life.

It was a mild clear September day, one of those days when conditions for a hole in one are more favorable than at any time in the year except possibly early June and the last ten days of October.

We had done fairly well on the first hole, a par five (Mr. Walker getting an eight and I a seven), and neither of us questioning the other as the game was young and no suspicions had developed.

The number two hole is all water carry, the drive being from a little peninsula running out into the lake like a sore thumb. Two swans and a flock of ducks dart about the waters. These were a mental hazard to visitors, but members who play the course right along get so accustomed to them that they can't play any water holes without waterfowl on them and have been even known to express a yen for alligators and sea lions.

"There's a rather fresh breeze," said Walker, "coming across the lake. You'd better allow for it."

He is quite a flatterer.

"What would you use?" I asked.

"I'm taking a Number 6," said my undertaker friend.

"What do you think?" I asked my caddy, who seemed strangely disinterested.

"I think a Number 5," he said.

So I took a Number 4, not wanting to offend either, fidgeted around a bit, struck my stance (which is that of a street foreman straddling a manhole), looked at the flag a few times, waggled the club for a moment or two and then took a sock at the ball. It sailed high in the air.

"In the water!" I exclaimed as I watched its flight.

"Too high, I guess," said Mr. Walker.

"I should've used a Number 3," I said, getting my alibi ready.

And then it happened. . . .

The ball cleared the water by a foot and rolled slowly onto the green, just reaching the cup and plunking into it.

"It's in!" cried Mr. Walker, dancing around and slapping me on the back.

Well, you could have knocked me over with a niblick, and it might have been a good thing if you had.

I stood quite limply for a moment. Then my astonishment gave way to emotions not even approached on the morning I saw my first Christmas tree. The earth shook, the near-by hills seemed to shimmy, the birds burst into song and, if I am not mistaken, one of the ducks gave a queer gurgle and sank out of sight. The exact details are not clear in my memory, but I know I danced with Mr. Walker, kissed the caddy and was on the verge of throwing money at a swan.

Then Mr. Walker escorted me around the pond to the green, where we gazed at the ball in the cup.

"Some golfer!" said Mr. Walker.

"Don't I know it?" said I.

And that, boys and girls, is how I made a hole in one. I attribute my success to clean living, the fact that I never touched tobacco until I was eleven years old, and have always made it a habit to go to bed early in midwinter, particularly if anybody seemed about to suggest a rubber of bridge.

Note from Collier's Editor:

[Your account of the hole in one is interesting

but you do not say anything about the other subsequent sixteen holes that day. What, for instance, did you get on the third hole, and what was your score for the day?]

A Sorry Sequel

Well, it is pretty mean to go into things like that. The truth is I didn't do so well there. The third tee is seventy-five yards from the second green and faces another direction, yet my first drive went cock-eyed and into the water hole across which I had made my "ace," believe it or not!

"You wouldn't think it could be done," I remarked to Mr. Walker at the time.

"It never has been before," nodded my partner.

This smote my morale and I dubbed my second drive, too. From that point on it was pretty terrible and, if you must know, my score for that five par hole was TEN (10). It must have been something I ate. The other fifteen holes are nothing I like to think about either, and when we got back to the club house and totaled up the cards my score for eighteen holes was 103, despite the hole in one.

But what of it? No golfer, however good, can be perfect!

(1930)

Twilight Hour
Ben Wright

Several years ago I had the distinct pleasure of working on a movie short subject, From St. Andrews to St. Basil's, which dealt with golf course architecture and in which Ben Wright interviewed me regarding my thoughts on the subject. I had known Ben several years prior to that and had found him to be a most enjoyable person, glib, gregarious and the possessor of an unusual ability for mimicry, especially of those dialects peculiar to his native England.

During our extended time on camera, I also was impressed by his great knowledge of the often misunderstood subject under discussion and by his appreciation and knowledge of the history and tradition of the "Old Course."

Ben, obviously, was as well qualified to conduct the interview as I was to offer my opinions on a work with which I had been involved long before he was born. Ben, who now resides in New York, cut his journalistic eyeteeth as a sportswriter in Manchester before branching out to do free-lance work, specializing in golf, for the London Observer *and the* Sunday Times. *For many years he was the first—and only—golf correspondent for the* Financial Times, *which carried his by-line from some of the world's most far-reaching outposts of the game.*

As an unusually articulate and fluent observer of golf, it was inevitable that television should discover Ben. It was through his work on the BBC and Britain's commercial network (ITV), in addition to his later affiliation with television in Australia, where his globe-circling assignments took him occasionally, the he was signed by CBS in 1972 to add a "British touch" to its televised golf tournaments. His obvious accent and his unbridled honesty have more than filled that requirement.

"Twilight Hour" is a fictional account of a great champion's fall from the heights. It confirms Ben's great knowledge of golf and his insight into how such a situation could come about. In reading it, I wondered whom Ben had in mind.

THE PALE SPRING sunlight was surprisingly warm on the back of my neck as I swung the Jaguar on to the road for London Airport, and Wentworth.

"I find that if I have the hood down on my way to an early morning start the catarrh clears quicker," I said jokingly to Rod Dixon, who was huddled up in the passenger seat. Rod was a lean, wiry fellow, very tall, who hated draughts. He looked at me, not needing to say anything to express his feelings. He knew as well as I did that I had been on the bottle again the night before.

The grass verges sparkled with the heavy dew. The air had a sharp, invigorating quality that not even the fumes of the rush hour could poison. I felt good, better than I had done for months. I was forty-three, but knew, as did the women, that I looked a lot younger. This was my twentieth season in big-time golf. The Press boys had expressed their hopes that the nineteenth would be my last. Ed Sawley, in the *Clarion*, had written a piece the previous August, asking why I went on, when I had won every honour available, had made a fortune from the game, and didn't know how to win any more. He didn't say it in so many words, but I — and his several million readers — didn't have much difficulty in grasping the message.

Damn him! It had been a poor season compared with some of the earlier great years, perhaps. There had been three occasions when I had led the mob going into the back nine of the last round, and each time I hadn't quite pulled it off. But didn't that happen to everyone? I hadn't had the breaks, that was all. I couldn't remember hitting a bad shot, but there had been a few bad kicks, and a bad lie or two. It was easy for that bastard Sawley to talk, but he couldn't play to eighteen if he tried, and he tried almost every morning of every tournament. I'd met him countless times when I had sneaked away for a quiet round with a popsy on a nearby track, and he always looked smug when he spotted me. It was all right for him to knock back the hard stuff every night, with a girl on each arm, while his wife sat at home watching the television, but the great Peter Durward to take a girl for a run out was a crime. Sawley had never forgiven me for

not inviting him to the swinging party we had after my last Open win.

Suddenly the headache was back with me, and I was feeling as I expected to feel after last night's shindig.

"What does Sawley have to say about me in the *Clarion*?" I asked Rod, and pushed the pile of papers at him. He shuffled them, cursing quietly and competently as I accelerated hard to pull round a lorry, and the back page was whipped into his face.

"Burly Peter Durward, five times Open Champion, but now reckoned to be in the twilight of his career, last night led the big field in the Ensign tournament on Wentworth's Burma Road by no fewer than eight shots after two rounds. His second round of 67 for a 141 total threatened to leave his rivals so far behind that a boxing referee might have called it no contest. But Durward's frailty in a tight finish has been thoroughly exposed in recent years, and there will be a big crowd at Wentworth today to see if Durward can hold off the challenge of the tough Australian Ron Yates."

"That's enough," I interrupted angrily, and braked hard to pull up at traffic lights I had almost failed to notice. I picked up the *Bugle*, and read: "One question will be answered at Wentworth today. Can Peter Durward, whose performances last season particularly have led one to believe that his nerves are getting the better of him, hold on to an eight stroke lead in the Ensign tournament, and win the first prize of ß5,000?

"Three times a lead of first six, then five and then seven shots, was insufficient last year. It seems incredible that a man who won five Open Championships in the 'sixties should be considered a doubtful winner."

I got no further. A horn was blasting behind me. I let in the clutch with a bang, and we left the offending idiot groping his way through a screen of exhaust fumes and the acrid smoke from burning rubber.

How dare that Sawley write that I was a rich man? The divorce had cost me a small fortune. Audrey had never been the type to take a back seat while I travelled all over the world. She had cost me a fortune when we were married, and almost as much now we were divorced. And how had she been stupid enough to expect me not to take advantage now and again, when women were falling over each other to fall upon me? I suppose it wouldn't have been so bad if the kid she'd caught me with at Hoylake hadn't been so young and apparently innocent. It was this very youth that she couldn't stand, the freshness that she had lost so many years before. There wouldn't have been such a lot of trouble if only Audrey had stayed at home where she belonged—and not insisted on traveling everywhere with me. And the scandal hadn't helped to further my public image. It was about that time that people stopped asking me to play exhibition matches every week-end. Peasants!

At Wentworth Old Harry was waiting for me—faithful Old Harry—whose legs had seemed to grow more bowed as he had humped my bag around most of the great golf courses of the world. Old Harry still had a smile for me, even though he had drunk himself into a coma the previous evening, as he always did when he had sufficient money to reach the oblivion he sought.

"Tailor-made for the boss today," he said to Rod as my thin companion lifted his own gear out of the boot. Rod hadn't qualified for the last two rounds of this one. He seldom did. But he sought out my company like a loving dog. A studious type, he was off to practise, as diligently as ever. There was something rather pathetic about him. He just wasn't equipped for our rat race, either physically or mentally. He was a dead ringer for ulcers—far too nice for the game. But, my God, how he tried.

"I'll do a bit with the wedge, Harry," I said, and he smiled knowingly as we walked past the deserted tennis courts. He knew that I wouldn't try anything more strenuous when I was nursing a hangover. The dry feeling in my mouth was beginning to get worse, as it had done so often in recent years, as did the tightening of the stomach muscles, as the time for the long walk to the first tee drew near. Oh for the long gone days when golf was easy, and I managed to enjoy a friendly game, not regard the whole damned business as a torture.

Ron Yates, a small, powerful-looking Australian, was working out on the practice ground. I would bet that he had been there for hours.

We were due out last together, as we had been more than once in the past three seasons. Yates was a dour, up-and-coming young man, one of the game's really hard workers. He had to work hard to keep a wife and six children, and their big house on the outskirts of Sydney. The thick, pale hair on forearms as thick as tree trunks glinted in the morning sunshine. It was getting warmer now. But as far as I was concerned Yates was a dull little man. He despised me for having enjoyed myself, something he had never experienced.

"Fancy you can hold me off today, old fella?" Yates didn't even look up. He just went on hitting number seven iron shots like bullets. My stomach took another twist. "You've no chance with a swing like that, Aussie." I replied, and started to hit my shots at Old Harry. Yates stopped, and watched with a thin smile on his lined, tanned face. I hooked one a little, and he said nothing, but whistled quietly through his teeth, as he chewed gum monotonously.

By now the usual small crowd had gathered, and I hated them for enjoying the needle in the situation. The sweat started to gather in little beads that I could feel on my forehead. I heard a small man in a cloth cap say in north-country tones, exaggerated for my benefit: "Yon fat one's not half t'man he used to be." I gritted my teeth, and went on hitting my shots with furious intent.

Yates had finished, and while he waited for his caddie, Blondie Newman, to gather up the horde of practice balls, he strolled over, picked my driver out of the bag, swung it two or three times, and pulled a face. I hated the arrogance of the little upstart, his insolent air of self-confidence. It had always annoyed me that he believed he was going to hole every putt. I had known that feeling ten years ago, but now I know I had to get the ball as near the hole as possible with the iron shots to feel I had any chance of holing the first putt, and sometimes the second.

"I'm surprised you can get the ball off the

ground with this thing." It was Yates speaking of my favourite driver, the heavy club I'd used for my last two Open wins. I had made it myself.

I didn't want to get involved in an argument with such an ignorant little man, especially with so many people about, but I was angry now. "You wouldn't know a good club if you fell over one. You're not old enough to have seen a home-made club, laddie. All the clubs you've handled were mass-produced—a load of rubbish—and I don't suppose you'd know how to change a grip, anyhow." The words came rushing out, and I felt better momentarily. A few people sniggered embarrassedly. Yates said nothing, but I knew by the two spots of high colour on his cheekbones that I had hit home.

He muttered something, and walked away. I motioned to Old Harry, who had been waiting patiently a hundred yards away, to collect the balls, and signed autographs as I waited for him. There was a crowd of several hundred people round the first tee, and it seemed like thousands on each side of that wide first fairway. Cars were coming up the hill in a steady stream. I felt sick. My hands felt fat and meaty. I could feel the sweat in the small of my back, tickling me as it ran down the back of my vest.

I don't remember much about that morning round, in view of what was to come. We played shot for shot to the turn, were both out in 33 and by then had pulled even further away from the rest of the pack. I do remember feeling really tired on the back nine. But I hung on until the last three holes. I took three putts on the six-teenth and Yates, damn him, got wonderful fours at the last two against my fives to be round in 68 and 71. He hadn't spoken all morning, but as we walked up the hill, jostled by the horde, he grinned: "I'm after you. I'm right on your tail, old man. And you don't look so good."

I didn't feel well. My legs were leaden. My mouth was so dry, my tongue felt so swollen that I was almost choking. But I wasn't going to let Yates know how poorly I felt. "I've had a touch of headache this morning, but even then you could only beat me by three shots. You'll not get near me this afternoon."

My heart was beating a little too often for comfort, and my thighs were like jelly as I flopped on to a bench in the dressing room. Jenkins offered me a massage, but I knew that would only shake me up and make me feel worse. I opted for a couple of Alka Seltzers, a quick wash, and sneaked into the Golfers' Bar. No one was about, so I ordered two large Scotches, and felt better when I had downed them quickly. I strolled down to the front door, and sure enough the crowd gathered around the first tee seemed larger than any I had ever seen at Wentworth.

All eyes were on me as I entered the dining-room. Or if they weren't, I felt what seemed like hundreds burning into me. Yates was sitting alone at a table for four in the far corner, eating healthily as usual. I sat down as far away from him as I could, even if it meant suffering the conversation of the elderly couple already sitting at the table. Thankfully, they were eating their dessert course.

"Getting darned windy out there," the man said loudly, when we had got over the tiresome preliminaries. "You chaps really earn your money on days like this," chirruped his wife. I wanted to tell her that we chaps earned our money every day, and deserved every penny of it, but instead I got on with the ham salad that might have been sand, for all I could taste of it.

Thankfully, the elderly couple soon left, wishing me luck so profusely that I knew they couldn't have cared less if I dropped dead on the first tee. Come to think of it, it wouldn't have been a bad way to go. I ordered black coffee in the hope that it might do something for me. The dining-room was emptying fast. I hadn't seen Yates go, but if I knew him as well as I thought he would be on the practice ground again by now. I couldn't delay my appearance on the first tee much longer.

The wind had risen considerably, and was blowing in great gusts against the front door of the clubhouse. Old Harry was waiting for me on the first tee, when I managed to thread my way through the huge crowd that surrounded it. Yates was there already, too. There was a great buzz of expectancy. I looked at the faces of all these people, most of whom were smartly, expensively dressed. I hated them all. They were poised like vultures, waiting to feed off the ample Durward flesh should he make one tiny slip, and fail to hold off this damned Australian. The British sports-watching public, with their love of masochistic post-mortems, would be asking themselves what was wrong with our golfers—and supplying a hundred different answers—if Yates beat me. They'd been saying rude things about idle British professionals for fifteen years before I had won my first Open, and they were looking forward to being able to say it again.

The great British sporting public. They didn't know what it was like to be out there all alone, looking at a four-foot putt, and knowing that if you holed it you might be ß20,000 better off before the year was out. They didn't know or care what it was like to miss it, and never forgive yourself. They didn't know what it was like to look at that putt and see the hole growing smaller and the ball getting bigger until there was no way of getting the one into the other. I remembered the time when I had been faced with such a putt to win my sixth Open in succession. The last green at Royal Lytham on a beautiful Friday evening in July, and just four feet between me and a record that would probably stand forever. I had stood there physically incapable of making the shot. The club had felt like a monstrous lump of lead in my twitching, sweat-drenched fingers. I had made the excuse that people were talking in that vast crowd, and I couldn't concentrate. There was bound to be someone talking somewhere. And sure enough I had only to walk from the ball and glare, and there they were turning on two innocents, whispering to each other under the stand. When I started the routine of lining up the putt all over again, I had convinced myself I had no chance of holing it. The ball never even touched the hole, and I had never been the same again.

Now this huge crowd had gathered, hoping to see the great Peter Durward fail again. They wanted to see me crack up, so they could turn to each other and ask why these fellows didn't get out when they were still at the top of the tree. It was the same with boxers. The crowds would flock to see an old champion get a real hiding,

long after he should have retired from the ring. They had seen him hand it out so many times. Now they yelled for the champion's blood to be spilled. I felt that although there was only an excited buzz of conversation, this crowd was really yelling for mine.

I'll show them, I thought, but it was only a tiny gesture of defiance. I knew it was going to be a desperate struggle to hold off this Australian.

The starter burbled his usual, useless pieces of information and Yates took up his stance, feet wide apart, and flailed into the ball with all the brutish strength at his command. The wind got under it, took it high, and stopped it short. The little Australian banged his club on the ground in anger. I teed the ball so low that a tee was hardly necessary, shortened my swing, and hit a screamer that never rose more than ten yards from the turf, scything through the breeze like a swallow, and rolling on and on. The crowd liked it. I felt good and whispered to Yates: "That's how it should be done, you ignorant ape."

Yates hit a fine iron shot just short of the green. My ball finished six yards past the hole. The Australian chipped up dead. And as soon as I hit my putt I knew I was too strong, but never realised the ball would roll five feet past the hole down the hill. The sick feeling came back into my stomach. My mouth dried up within seconds. I knew I was going to miss that putt.

"Just inside the right lip." It was Old Harry whispering softly in my ear.

"It looks dead straight to me," I replied, but I compensated by aiming just right of centre. The ball hit the left lip of the hole and kicked away round the back of it to the right. I was in a fury as the crowd gasped. I was about to knock the thing in with the back of my putter when Old Harry whispered, "No, sir." He was right. I holed the tiny putt, but one of those precious five shots had gone. "It's terrible to see you old fellas with the yips," Yates said as we walked to the second tee.

I was still sick with anger when I hit my tee shot—too strong. My ball caught in the lush grass at the back edge of the green as it rolled back down the slope. I couldn't make up my mind whether to chip or putt. I chose the putter, and squeezed the ball out right and short. Yates rammed in his putt from five yards, and as the crowd let out a deafening roar he flung his putter away and turned to me, his mouth full of chewing gum, and winked. It seemed an age before that crowd of Australians was quiet again. The roar had brought a fresh crop of idiots scampering through the undergrowth. One couple were being told to keep quiet noisily when I hit my next putt just wide of the left lip—and another two shots had disappeared.

I told myself I must hang on now, if only to frustrate this enormous flock of vultures.

We both made good fours at the third, where I chipped dead from just off the front edge, but the wind got hold of my second shot to the fourth green, and whisked it wide of the bunker on the left. I couldn't get near the hole from this spot, because it had been cut so close to the trap. I could do no better than settle for a five to Yates' four, and the lead had been slashed to only one shot.

I was up against it, and felt terribly tired all of a sudden. I could hardly stop yawning. But I matched Yates' threes at the next two holes, and although my second shot went through the seventh green, I laid a masterly putt stone dead down the hill for my four. Two more fours apiece at the eighth and ninth lost me no more ground, and so to the short tenth. A huge crowd had gathered at the back of the green, just visible through the pine trees. Yates just made the front edge of the green. But those spectators were so close to the pin I decided to hit the ball straight at them. I was convinced they wouldn't see the ball coming over the trees in time to get right out of the way. I'd done this kind of things hundreds of times before, and had never seriously injured anyone.

But to my amazement and dismay I watched the crowd melt away like magic as the ball sped at them. I could see it bounce on and on. I was furious, and glared at their grinning faces as I walked past them. But I could do no better than pitch up strong to make sure of reaching the putting surface. Yates' putt from fully 18 yards never looked likely to finish anywhere but in the centre of the hole. I missed mine, and the Australian was in front.

Suddenly I could hardly control my laughter. It was all so bloody silly and pointless. How stupid I must look—hitting that silly little white ball with a lump of metal or wood on the end of a rod, and not even hitting it straight. But what made me decide on a new plan of action was the arrival of Sawley, and Jim Mapson of the *Bugle*, and the rest of the Press mob, who had driven out across the course when they smelled sensation—on looking at the hole-by-hole scoreboard close to the clubhouse after a large lunch and larger quota of free booze. I would give them, and that flock of vultures something to write and shout about. So Durward couldn't win any more? All right, then, I would live up to the bad name they had given me. I decided to make a deliberate blunder at every possible opportunity from now on.

Yates hit an enormous drive down the eleventh fairway, which even kicked left round the corner towards the green. I kidded the crowd I was going for a big one too, but just hooked it enough to catch the trees. The crowd scampered off in a ferment. Now all my worries had gone. I was going to enjoy myself immensely making fools of these swine. And that little runt Yates. I would make it such a hollow victory for him he wouldn't get any enjoyment out of winning. He was hoping to grind my nose into the turf. But I would do the work for him. The British love an underdog. I would get them so much on my side they would probably lynch Yates before the round was over.

Old Harry was desperately upset when he found the ball tangled in the roots of a beech tree. I tried to back the ball out sideways, taking good care to hit another tree. And to my delight I required another shot to force the ball clear, and on to the fairway. Poor Old Harry. I suppose he saw the source of supply of his booze drying up with frightening rapidity.

To have missed the green would have been too obvious, but I managed to take three putts from eight yards with no trouble at all. Seven, to Yates' four.

As I walked to the twelfth tee I noticed that Yates had a rather bewildered frown on his forehead, and some of the people around me were close to tears. Others, of course, were fairly slobbering with glee.

A thin line of tall trees a hundred or so yards in front of the tee was tailor made for my purpose. Yates sent a superb four wood shot fractionally over the top. I took the three wood, and just caught the uppermost branches with what looked like a perfect shot. The ball dropped like a winged bird. The crowd gasped audibly. I was completely stymied. It was all such lovely fun.

I would tell you more, but after that my memory of it all gets a little vague. And besides, I can hear that rather unpleasant nurse coming down the corridor. At least with feet as big and clumsy as his he can't catch me unawares. I'm not supposed to have pencil and paper, you see.

(1965)

The Day Joe Ezar Called His Shots for a Remarkable 64

Peter Dobereiner

The demands of my chosen field require that I am constantly on the move. Most of my traveling for many years has been by airplane. This means that I spend considerable time in airline terminals waiting for connecting flights, often to places where only one plane a day is the norm. Because of these delays, I always carry one or two current golf magazines in my briefcase so that time I spend waiting is not a complete waste.

As a result, I have had the opportunity to read hundreds of short articles on various aspects of the game of golf. Many articles have been of lasting interest, while others were forgotten almost as soon as I had finished them. I have made a point to clip and save those which have amused me for one reason or another. The remaining pieces in this book are among them.

Peter Dobereiner has a more comprehensive contribution elsewhere in these pages. This next story recalls what can only be described as the most incredible round ever played by a character even more incredible.

THE LAST TIME I heard of Joe Ezar he was working on the roads down in Florida. He was a nobody. And yet if Joe had been a different kind of person, a fraction more stable and just a touch less fond of the bottle, he might today be enshrined in golf's Hall of Fame. Maybe not. For perhaps it was just that maverick streak in Joe which made possible the most extraordinary round of golf ever played.

The hands which today embrace a shovel were gifted with a golfing talent of rare quality. This is an appropriate moment to recall Joe's finest hour, which took place 40 years ago — in July 1936 — during one of his trips to Europe. And if it does not qualify him for the Hall of Fame it does at least deserve a footnote in the history of golf.

Joe, a swarthy Armenian – American, was a colorful character in those days. He won a lot of money, not in prizes so much as in fanciful side-bets. He needed cash because he was a man with a very expensive thirst indeed.

Europe in 1936 was boiling up for the war and Joe fitted in perfectly with the mood of those who wanted to squeeze the last drop of carefree enjoyment out of a life which could not last. In Germany he won some cash and when he found that he could not take it out of the country, Joe invested the lot in the current status symbol of wealth, a flashy camel's hair coat. Joe loved that coat and lived in it. He refused even to leave it in the locker room when he played golf and draped it over his shoulders on the course, like a cape.

The precious camel's hair was never out of his sight and he had it with him for the Italian Open of 1936 at Sestriere, up in the mountains near Turin. Henry Cotton, who had won the British Open in 1934 and was to win it again in 1937 and 1948, was the king of European golf and on this occasion he had turned the Italian Open into a procession with two hot rounds, including a course-record 68.

That evening he and Ezar were entertaining the crowd with an exhibition of golfing virtuosity, Cotton hitting the orthodox shots and Ezar producing an impressive repertoire of trick shots. Joe's final stunt was to drop three balls on the green 35 feet from the hole and invite bets that he could not hole one of them. Considering the rough state of the green, it was a fair bet and several people accepted the challenge. Joe holed the first two balls and laughingly collected his winnings.

The prime objective of the exercise had succeeded, to sort out those in the gallery with a taste for some action. One of them happened to be the president of the Fiat motor company. "What do you bet I can't equal the course record tomorrow?" asked Joe. The sporting tycoon smiled: "I'll tell you what I'll do. I will give you 5,000 lira for a 66, and 10,000 for a 65."

"What about a 64?" asked Joe.

"In that case," said the president expansively, "I'll make it 40,000."

"Very generous of you," said Joe. "Now I will tell you what I will do. I will put down the score I will make on each of the 18 holes for my 64."

He took a card and wrote down his target figures for every hole, finishing with a birdie 3 at the last. Cotton looked at the card and remarked: "You're mad." Joe headed for the bar.

In the morning Joe was in no mood for golf. His caddie pulled him out of bed and propped him under a cold shower. Joe protested that he was too drunk to play. "Oh no you're not," said the caddie, who also had a wager going on the round.

Joe made it to the first tee and wanted to play in his camel's hair, to keep out the bitter morning air of the mountains. His caddie persuaded him to compromise; he could wear the coat between shots.

Cotton, his playing partner, advised him to forget the whole thing. "Nobody could do it. You're asking for 18 successive miracles." Joe proceeded to rip off eight successive miracles. "You could call that round the biggest fluke of all time," recalls Cotton, "but the fact is that he did it. He had all the luck in the world, chipping in and holing impossible putts, but the figures came out just as Joe had predicted. Right up to the ninth. He had marked it down for a 3 but a poor tee shot cost him a 4."

However, he made the unlikeliest of 3s at the next hole where he had predicted a 4. And for the rest of the round Joe's luck stayed with him. Through the bedlam of the crowd Joe reeled off his predicted figures, all the while complaining to Cotton that he was too sick and nervous to hold a club. Still, he did it. He had his 64.

Like all golfers who specialize in trick shots, Ezar had a style which exaggerated hand-and-arm action and rather reduced leg-and-body movement. He played from a wide, flat-footed style and delivered a tremendous lash at the ball with those powerful arms. Cotton described his method as being composed of good points taken to excess. Ezar's right shoulder looked to be too much under his chin at impact; his head too far behind the ball; his eyes fixed too firmly on his divot scrape long after the ball had departed; his clubface held square to the shot for too long after impact.

Yet Joe made it work, and never better than on the final drive across the chasm of the dogleg—not unlike the layout of the famous 16th at Cypress Point—to hit the flagstick all of 290 yards away.

If he was almost sober by this time, he did not remain that way for long. Within weeks Joe was broke again, and he faced the problem of getting back to America. Here was a real challenge for the man who had once bet he could get his entry accepted for the British Open after the closing date, and, what's more, that he would lead after two rounds. He did exactly that, collected his $2,000 winnings and did not even turn up for the third round.

Joe had been present when Trevor Wignall, a columnist for the London Daily Express, was interviewing Cotton. Wignall mentioned that he was to sail on the maiden voyage of the Queen Mary to New York. Here was Joe's chance to get safely home. At Cherbourg he tagged his golf bag "Trevor Wignall" and saw it taken aboard. Joe followed, along with all the other well-wishers making their *bon voyages*, and hid in a cupboard in Wignall's stateroom. Twelve hours later, after the liner had safely cleared Southampton water, Joe emerged and told Wignall what he had done.

The writer asked Joe what he had done with the rest of his baggage. "This is all I've got," said Joe, indicating his precious camel's hair coat. Joe wanted to remain a stowaway but Wignall fixed it with the purser for Joe to work for his passage by giving exhibitions of golf on deck. So Joe came home in style.

If you happen to be driving through Florida and come across an old man in a threadbare camel's hair coat shoveling gravel by the roadside, stop and shake his hand. And if you should have a spare fifth in the car he would certainly appreciate it. But do not, whatever you do, take him up on any bets.

It's Like Catching Lightning in a Bottle
Art Spander

This piece was written by the sports columnist for the San Francisco Examiner, Art Spander, *whose credentials include several golf-writing awards. Art gives a new slant to the old Scottish axiom, "Golf is a humbling game."*

THE ONLY SIGNIFICANT thing to understand about golf is that it's impossible to play. Once this salient point is grasped—and a Vardon grip is not required in this situation—then everything else is secondary.

Then you no longer have to walk off a course looking like you've just lost your home in a fire. Then you don't have to wonder how a pro can miss a six-inch putt. Then you realize why next to fishermen golfers are the biggest storytellers in sport.

I remember a phrase Arnold Palmer used in one of his books, that golf was simple enough to be played by children and so difficult it could never be mastered by anyone—including Arnold Palmer. George Archer, among many, said it was like catching lightning in a bottle. Just about the time you thought you had it, you came to the frightening realization you don't.

Sure the pros, those guys with swings so beautiful they must have been painted by Renoir, achieve a measure of success. Some win millions of dollars and dozens of tournaments. But even the most successful have days, sometimes months, when they wish they were stocking shelves or maybe selling stocks. It's that type of game. Infuriating.

That's why there's a monument to Arnold Palmer at Rancho Muni in Los Angeles for taking a 12 on a par-five hole. That's why the most famous legend at the Bing Crosby National Pro-Am is about Porky Oliver taking a 16 on the par-three 16th hole at Cypress Point. That's why a Japanese pro who took a 13 on the 13th hole at Augusta National two years ago got as much ink as the tournament leader.

Talk to anyone who's ever taken a swing in anger—and the way most of us chop around, that's the only way we make a swing—and you'll hear tales of disappointment, of frustration. Of Tommy Bolt hurling clubs the way Ron Guidry does baseballs. Of Ivan Gantz slugging himself after missing a short putt. Of Ky Laffoon cursing in both English and Indian. And of Lefty Stackhouse grabbing a thorny bush to punish his right hand for jerking the putter.

You'll hear of the time Jack Nicklaus walked to the tee at Columbine Country Club in Denver for a practice round before the 1967 PGA Championship and hit a drive 50 yards. And the time Danny Edwards six-putted the 14th green at Pebble Beach. And the time Bob Rosburg got so angry talking about the holes he didn't like at a certain course that he withdrew even before hitting a shot.

The problem with golf is that you have no one to blame for your ineffectiveness—except yourself. Your left fielder can drop a fly in baseball, your forward can dribble out of bounds in basketball. But when there's a screwup in golf, friend, the fault lies in ourselves.

No wonder golfers are more adept at creating excuses than they are at perfecting the one-piece swing. The wind was blowing, the sun was shining, the fairway grass was too long, the grass on the greens was too short. One character in a P. G. Wodehouse novel complained bitterly about the uproar of butterflies in an adjoining meadow. Those careless insects.

No wonder there's a small poster hanging in many pro shops—and taverns—which shows a Japanese man saying: "I just came from America where I go to golf course and learn about a game called, 'Ah S---.'"

No wonder the late curmudgeon H. L. Mencken once made this proposal: "If I had my way, a man guilty of golf would be ineligible for any public office in the United States, and the families of the breed would be shipped off to the white slave corrals of the Argentine."

No wonder a cartoon in one of the monthly golf magazines depicted a skeleton in heavy rough, one boney hand clutching a golf club, and a guy coming upon him yelling out to his caddy: "You can't get out of this stuff with an eight iron. Give me a wedge."

It's not that I enjoy failure, or that I'm irreverent enough to want people to pull their drives or shank their putts. It's just that I watch them trying to get some recreation or maybe some recognition by chasing a little white ball — and then listen to them asking why they didn't take up tennis. Chinese Water Torture must be more fun.

That's why when you do catch that lightning, when you do hit a five-iron stiff or hole a 25-footer or win anything from a handicap flight championship to the U. S. Open, it means so much. It's the relief you get when you stop beating your head against the wall.

Alistair Cooke, the historian and television celebrity, didn't come upon the game until he was well into his career and had moved from England to America. He knew life without golf. He now knows life with it. He described the sport (the torture?) in this manner: ". . . an open exhibition of overweighing ambition, courage deflated by stupidity, still scoured by a whiff of arrogance."

In other words, it's impossible to play. And don't tell me that Al Geiberger once shot a 59. I won't be swayed by facts.

Slamming
Suki Sukiyuki
Lawrence Theodore, Jr.

Lawrence Theodore, Jr. is a pseudonym for a literary figure whose passion is golf. His story of an imaginary Japanese golfer, which first appeared in Golf Digest *in 1952, was one of the first pieces of fiction published by that magazine. It was included in* The Best of Golf Digest, *a book published to commemorate the magazine's first twenty-five years.*

THERE WAS A JAPANESE golf professional at the swank Hamilton Country Club in Bombay, India, who caused more of a furor in international golfing circles, until his untimely death in 1924, than any Bobby Jones or Walter Hagen.

Suki Sukiyuki Jr., known to his fans as "Slamming Suki," was probably the only golfer in history to win a major golf championship right-handed one year, and left-handed the next. He accomplished this remarkable feat in capturing the British Open in 1919 and 1920.

The bright star of Suki's fame faded, however, when his unparalleled triumphs were disallowed by the sacrosanct Royal and Ancient Golf Club on the grounds that he had employed to his own advantage a type of follow-through not sanctioned in British play. This follow-through, not uncommon among Asiatic golfers, consisted of striking the ball twice in a single swing, but with such great speed that to the unaided eye it appeared to be but a single stroke. Slow-motion movies brought the fact to light, however, and this Suki's record-smashing 275 in 1920, his left-handed year, was actually 550.

Born the son of well-to-do peasants in the Honshu province of Japan, Suki spent his early childhood in the Honshu tradition—breeding goldfish and skiing the slopes of Mt. Fujiyama. Suki Sr., however, soon realized that his young son was in need of schooling of a more formal nature than was then available in Honshu, and sent him post-haste to a private school in Tokyo. One day a group of boys from the school went out to the Imperial Links to see a golfing exhibition by the famous Duncan MacPhee, who was then on a worldwide barnstorming tour. From that day forward Suki was a slave to gutta percha and hickory. His wealthy parents had him outfitted and arranged to have him take instruction from Tama Shanti, the dour Japanese champion. This was unfortunate in that Shanti was an exponent of the aforementioned illegal follow-through. Suki, for his part, was an apt pupil and within nine months had officially taken Shanti to the cleaners, becoming the new champion of all Japan—a title he never relinquished.

Seeking new fields to conquer, Suki entered the Chinese Closed, at Hong Kong, in 1910. It was there that he inadvertently discovered his amazing ambidexterity. On the 18th hole of the final round and needing but a triple bogey to win, Suki was in trouble. He had hooked his drive into a rice paddy, blasted out and into a small forest of yew trees, and, on his third shot, rolled up tight against the right side of a small ornamental pagoda. His cushion was fast deflating. The hot Chinese sun was pouring down. Suki took off his pith helmet and mopped his sloping brow. What to do?

He assayed the impossible lie, his grinning opponent, and the green some 290 yards away. Smiling thoughtfully, he drew from his bag an adjustable club which some admirer had given him after the Japanese Open the year before, as a kind of good luck piece. Now was certainly the time for it! Setting it for a left-handed driving-iron position, he wound up and struck. The shot was one of those low screamers, straight as a chopstick, that begins to rise slowly and then almost ascends to the heavens. The direction was true, the distance was perfect, and Suki had holed out, left-handed, from almost 300 yards away. This became the famous "Pagoda Shot" and heralded a new era for "Slamming Suki" Sukiyuki.

After Hong Kong, Suki dropped out of competition for six weeks, bought himself a set of left-handed clubs and practiced intently. He found that left-handed he was just as proficient as right-handed, if not more so. He decided to enter the Shanghai Open and play strictly left-handed. He won, going away.

After garnering every conceivable Far Eastern trophy, Slamming Suki made plans to sail for England where competition was stiffer. This project was, however, postponed by World War I.

With the close of the War, Slamming Suki made good on his plan for a tour of the British Isles. He arrived in England early in 1919, just in time for the Ulster Open. Suki immediately became the darling of the galleries. He was physically unprepossessing, but his toothy grin, owl eyes behind thick, black horn-rimmed glasses, and of course his booming shots with either hand, captivated the golfing public.

1919 was the year that will not soon be forgotten by those who know golf. It was, of course, the year of Suki's "Big Sweep" of British golf. He won the British Open right-handed, the Irish Sweepstakes left-handed, the Scotch Low-ball right-handed, and, to cap everything, the Welsh PGA Championship alternating left- and right-handed strokes.

Suki's fame was unparalleled. He was feted in all of the golfing capitals of the British Isles.

Soon after the 1920 Open, however, the shocking truth of the "double hit" technique which had led to Slamming Suki's amazing successes was bared to the world via the slow-motion camera. After returning his many laurels to assorted second place winners, Suki packed his bag, took his two sets of clubs, and set sail for Bombay, India, and the Hamilton Country Club. He was disillusioned and vowed never again to set foot in the Western World.

Suki remained at Hamilton, as professional in residence, until one said day in 1925. He was in the Bombay station waiting for a train to Karachi, where he was to defend his Indian Invitational title. Becoming impatient, he stepped on the track to see if the train was coming. He was instantly struck on the left side by the incoming express and hurled to the next track where he was struck on the right side by an outgoing local. Thus Slamming Suki Sukiyuki died as he had lived—ambidextrously.

Where Is Golf Going?
Charles Price

*"Where is golf going?" was a question
posed by Charles Price in one of his
columns in* Golf *magazine. His other
works in this book are less controversial
than this, which is Charley at his most
provocative — standing on an editorial
soapbox lecturing about the lexicon,
decrying the length of golf courses and
pointing a finger at the paradox of par.*

BEYOND LEARNING things for their own sake,
the only satisfaction in reading deeply,
really deeply, into the subject of golf — its
lore, its famous figures, its historical development, anything beyond curing your slice — is a
certain smugness in knowing something about
the game that somebody else doesn't, or would
be expected to, an advantage that comes in
handy at the 19th hole after you have had your
brains beaten out on the previous 18. Let's say
you casually mention at the clubhouse bar that
nobody has ever sunk a putt longer than three
feet on the last green to win the U. S. Open. (And
nobody ever has.) "Really?" the other person
says. "I never knew that!"

Now people begin to look at you in a different light. You may have just played the course in
a score resembling an area code, but suddenly
the others in your foursome know your real
game must be much better, or should be, and
they blame today's miserable performance on an
attack of sciatica or something else you just
didn't bother complaining about. You have become a truer golfer, somebody who has felt
obliged to become knowledgeable about things
the rest of us take for granted.

In digging up golf lore, however, sometimes
you learn things other people don't know but
should be expected to. For example, many of us
play golf all our lives using words every time we
do so — such as tee, rough, fairway — without

any notion of what they really mean. The next
time some grille-room architect starts criticizing
the course because the tees were set too far back
or the rough was too long or a fairway too narrow
ask him just what he means by the words tee,
rough, or fairway. He'll look at you as though
there were no answers.

Both fairway and rough were originally
terms used by ship pilots in Scotland, the game,
as we know, having originally been played there
hard by the sea, on linksland. A pilot took over
from a ship's captain as it entered the harbor
because he was familiar with the "fair way," the
safest passage through the "rough," meaning the
rocks and shoals that lay beneath the water.

The derivation of the word tee is a bit cloud-
ier, but it seems reasonable to assume by most
etymologists that it is derived generally from the
word that describes the letter T, or specifically
the sign T (a T without the serifs) that is often
used to mark an exact place. But that's not very
precise for golf purposes, particularly since in
some old games, such as curling, it is something
you aim *at*, not from. Looking deeper, though,
we find that the sign T is an ancient architectural symbol dating back to the Egyptians and
the pyramids, meaning that something which is
to be built, such as a wall, should begin wherever
the T is marked. It is still in limited use, although seldom if ever by architects. Some direct
mail firms use it on the first bit of literature they
send you. Thus, if they get back a reply with the
symbol on it, they know not to send you any
more queries. They hooked you in the beginning.

Those derivations have been mentioned casually in this column before. They are brought
up again because perhaps, in these times of five-
hour rounds, we ought to ask ourselves where
our courses are going or, to be more explicit,
where our architects are taking them. Tees — the
starting places — cannot be stretched back much
farther than the 7,000-plus yards they have already gone merely to satisfy those professionals
and strong-armed amateurs, constituting less
than one half of one per cent of the golf population, who insist the game should be played with
a driver off 14 tees; the par fives and all the par
fours. (Off a par three, paradoxically, the driver is

deemed unfair.) The logic seems all the stranger when you stop to think that, in point of historical fact, the driver was the last club to be added to the normal complement until the wedge came along. Dismiss the word. Forget you ever heard the term "driver." Without it, we would be playing our shots off the tees on those holes where we cannot reach the greens with a brassie, as golfers did up until this century. If that thinking seems too stagnant, stop to think that Sam Snead, who is the greatest tournament player in history and once one of the longest off the tee, has never used a driver. What he does use may have the numeral one written on its soleplate, but in truth the club is closer to a brassie, the number 2-wood.

When you are speaking of 400 or 500 yards added to a golf course's length, you must also think in terms of the breadth that goes with that length and the land around it that is out of play, not to mention the land between the holes you are adding it to. Now you are speaking in terms of acres, suburban acres, expensive acres — times 300 new golf courses a year — and this country is already losing tens of thousands of acres of arable land a year to industry. Putting the situation in not too farfetched a way, if you know anything at all about the growth of the game in America, we may some day be playing golf through smokestacks by continuing to let distance for distance's sake dictate the game to us. All this would be because a minuscule minority thinks golf isn't golf unless you are required to use a one-wood off the tee of a par-four hole instead of a lesser wood, even, God forbid, an iron.

Length plus money plus headlines — which has become the natural order of things on the Tour — does not equal leadership. Babe Ruth may have been the greatest ballplayer who ever lived, but it is ludicrous to think what kind of manager he would have made. As newer, younger, and longer pros join the Tour, the older and wiser ones begin to see the folly of the whole, muscle-bound situation whereby courses should be built to accommodate them. Hubert Green is now one of the older and wiser, if we swallow the fact that 35 is old, and he has gone on record as saying length for length's sake is missing the point of golf, even professional golf, the real point being "to keep the ball under control." Only by shortening courses, not lengthening them, can we separate the players from the ball-hitters. Some evidence in favor of this argument may be found in Jack Nicklaus today. Now that he is no longer among the longest hitters, he easily leads almost everybody else out there in hitting greens in regulation figures. It may be that he always has, for the Tour has not kept such statistics for long. Regardless, it seems safe to predict that whatever winning he does in the future will be over shorter courses than he has in the past. Now that he has passed 40, he'll simply "think" the ball into the hole better than the others. It happened to Snead. It happened to Ben Hogan. And it'll happen to you.

Length should be a premium in golf, not the be-all-and-end-all of the game. There is nothing new about that thought. But as the years go by, then the decades, we find that we are doing nothing about the thought beyond paying it lip service, just as we try to stop slow play and poor etiquette on our courses by tacking educational posters in our locker rooms. But the powers that be in golf can do something, which is not to say they ever will. Those powers are the USGA and the TPA Tour, but no longer the PGA, which has become so self-serving and materialistic it might just as well call itself a lobby, rather than a professional organization, and open up an office on K Street in Washington with all the opportunistic others.

The influence of the USGA and the Tour, subtle as it may seem to the weekend golfer, is enormous. The USGA standardizes the ball we use, including its velocity, which is in effect telling us how far it can be hit. It also regulates the clubs we hit that ball with. And it dictates the severity of the courses we play our championships over, including the rules they are played under, a power that eventually trickles down to the Scotch Foursomes and Blind Bogeys we casually play on Sunday afternoons. For all this we should be forever grateful, because the USGA has saved a Byzantine game from degenerating into a pop culture, like jogging.

The Tour is just as influential in its theatrical way. With its weekly events for thousands of spectators, all marvelously encapsulated on TV for millions of chairbound others, it established our standards of excellence and dramatizes what our behavior ought to be. For a $5 match most otherwise mature amateurs would do themselves a favor by emulating the restrained behavior those young pros exhibit for $50,000.

Would it be asking too much, then, for the USGA to limit the tee markers at their championships and the Tour at their tournaments to, say, 6,800 yards? It probably would be too much. But in 10 years, or 3,000 golf courses from now, there would be no point in architects designing one any more than that length. If 10 years seems a long time, keep in mind that you are speaking of a game that is almost 600 years old.

And what of our rough, the rocks and shoals we are supposed to find a fair way through? In USGA championships it has become unconscionably tall, four and a half inches now being about standard, almost three times the diameter of the ball. If you can find the ball at all, recovering from it means you ought to practice pumping iron, not finessing golf shots. And why do we find nine out of 10 trees in the rough, not to mention practically every bunker, sometimes both, one behind the other? If a tree or a bunker in the rough becomes a double negative—and what else can you call it?—what do you call a bunker behind a tree in the rough? Whatever it is, there are any number of pros trying to find the fairway who think it ain't no good, never.

While rough on both sides of the fairway may be taken for granted by those who have played golf for less than 20 years and all of it in America, it actually is an architectural hangover from those days when courses were crammed into 100 acres or so of farmland. Parallel fairways were then the rule, not the exception they have become—all this to protect the players going in one direction from those going the opposite. With virtually every course now designed being part and parcel of a real estate development, parallel fairways have become as obsolete as the par-six hole.

And what of par itself, that USGA pipedream that gets reinterpreted every 15 years or so? To the USGA's horror, it gets bettered now and then. So what? It's not supposed to be perfection but, more accurately, the score that an expert would be expected to make. Still, the USGA treats it as something sacred like the Ten Commandments (which nobody can live up to, either). After all, it wasn't until 1906 that anybody broke 300, or four times 75, in a championship. It wasn't until 30 years later than anybody broke 284, or four times 71. And both those courses in their day—Onwentsia and the Upper at Baltusrol—had pars that today would be considered Mickey Mouse by anybody's standards.

So let par be broken. Much as it might horrify this generation, it won't upset that undergraduate at Yale or Stanford who is going to be the USGA's president 30 years from now. Even Hogan, among astute others, has said it is only a matter of time until professionals start scoring in the 50s. What will today's version of par then become? Forty-eight? If par is realistically 71, which is the USGA's current *idée fixe* of it, why is it that the only expert in history who has been able to equal it throughout his career has been Nicklaus? Since hardly anybody today knows what tee, rough, and fairway mean then maybe our children's children will some day ask what par means. Indeed, some of us already are asking.

Acknowledgements

Compilation of an anthology of the extent and scope of this book would not have been possible without the invaluable aid and advice of numerous people. The help of the following was greatly appreciated: Ken Giniger, who conceived the idea for the book and who edited its contents. Sol Zatt, who handled the 1001 details vital to the preparation and production. Arthur "Red" Hoffman, whose encyclopedic knowledge was invaluable in the selection of content material and for providing background on many of the author-contributors. Rick Remmert, who was responsible for much of the research and the initial effort of compiling it. Judith A. Posner, who also did considerable research. Eilleen M. Vennell, who provided the much needed liaison between me and others involved. Elizabeth M. McGehee, who prepared the manuscript. Mel Hurtig, a golf addict, as I am, who was responsible for the publication of the book. And to my many friends in golf and mostly to the author-contributors who made this book possible.

Robert Trent Jones
Montclair
New Jersey
July 8, 1982

Every effort has been made to obtain permission from copyright owners to use material included. Where material has not been properly acknowledged the editor would appreciate being informed so that corrections can be made in future editions.

"The Lure of Golf" by Herbert Warren Wind from *Herbert Warren Wind's Golf Book*, published by Simon & Schuster. Copyright © 1971 Herbert Warren Wind. Reprinted by permission of the author.

"The Birth of the Linksland Courses" by Sir Guy Campbell from *A History of Golf in Great Britain*, 1952.

"What Makes It Great?" by Robert Trent Jones, published by Winthrop Laboratories, July 1969. Reprinted by permission of the author.

"The Rise and Fall of Penal Architecture" by Arthur "Red" Hoffman from *Golf Journal*, April 1974. Reprinted by permission of the author.

"Nature's Masterpiece" from *The Crosby: The Greatest Show in Golf* by Dwayne Netland. Doubleday and Co., Garden City, N.Y. Copyright © 1975 by Golf Digest/Tennis, Inc.

"Pine Valley: Monumental Challenge to Accuracy" by Cal Brown, from *Golf Digest*, October 1969, and *The Best of Golf Digest: The First 25 Years*. Copyright © October 1969 by Golf Digest/Tennis, Inc.

"Workers, Arise! Shout Fore" from *The Americans* by Alistair Cooke. Copyright © 1979 by Alistair Cooke. Reprinted by permission of Alfred A. Knopf, Inc.

"The Masters Is Made in Japan" by Richard W. Johnston, *Sports Illustrated*, October 16, 1972. © 1972 Time, Inc. Reprinted courtesy of *Sports Illustrated*.

"Ingenuity at Akron" from *The Curious History of the Golf Ball: Mankind's Most Fascinating Sphere* by John Stuart Martin. Copyright 1968. Reprinted by permission of the publisher, Horizon Press, New York.